THE ART OF WATCHING FILMS

THE ART OF WATCHING FILMS

JOSEPH M. BOGGS
Western Kentucky University

SECOND EDITION

Mayfield Publishing Company
Palo Alto, California

Second edition

Library of Congress Catalog Card Number: 84–061921
International Standard Book Number: 0–87484–712–5

Manufactured in the United States of America
10 9 8 7 6 5 4 3 2

Mayfield Publishing Company
285 Hamilton Avenue
Palo Alto, California 94301

Sponsoring editor: C. Lansing Hays
Manuscript editor: David Andrews
Managing editor: Pat Herbst
Art director: Nancy Sears
Designer (interior and cover): Janet Bollow
Cover art: Christa Kieffer
Production coordinator: Ron Newcomer & Associates, San Francisco
Production manager: Cathy Willkie
Compositor: Allservice Phototypesetting Co.
Printer and binder: R. R. Donnelley & Sons

Photographer: Ernest C. Raymer

TO RAYMOND AND VIRGINIA BOGGS

My first adventure in the art of watching films was at the age of three. I weathered the newsreel and cartoon with maturity and poise, but when the M-G-M lion gave out his trademark roar, I was terrified and ran screaming up the aisle. My parents caught me, calmed my fears, and returned me to my seat. This book is dedicated to them . . . with love, respect, and gratitude for their constant support from that day to this.

CONTENTS

PREFACE xiii

CHAPTER 1

FILM ANALYSIS 1

The Uniqueness of Film 2
Difficulties of Film Analysis 4
Why Analyze Films? 6

CHAPTER 2

THEME AND FOCUS 11

Determining the Theme 12
Basic Types of Film Themes 12
Evaluating the Theme 24

CHAPTER 3

FICTIONAL AND DRAMATIC ELEMENTS 29

Film Analysis and Literary Analysis 30
The Elements of a Good Story 31
Dramatic Structure 40
Symbolism 44
Characterization 54
Conflict 66
Setting 70
The Title's Significance 76
Irony 77

CHAPTER 4

VISUAL ELEMENTS 83

The Importance of the Image 84
The Cinematic Film 85
Elements of Cinematic Composition 86
Production Design/Art Direction 106
Editing 110
Cinematic Point of View 127
Techniques for Special Visual Effects 133
Lighting 145
Other Important Factors 150
Movie Magic: Special Effects in the Modern Film 159

CHAPTER 5

SOUND EFFECTS AND DIALOGUE 165

Sound and the Modern Film 166
Dialogue 167
Three Dimensionality in Sound 168
Visible and Invisible Sound 170
Points of View in Sound 172
Special Uses of Sound Effects and Dialogue 175
Sound as a Transitional Element 182
Voice-Over Narration 183
Silence as a "Sound" Effect 186
Rhythmic Qualities of Dialogue and Sound Effects 187

CHAPTER 6

THE MUSICAL SCORE 189

The Remarkable Affinity of Music and Film 190
The Importance of the Musical Score 191
General Functions of the Musical Score 192
Special Functions of Film Music 194
Economy in Film Music 202
Synthesizer Scoring 202

CHAPTER 7

ACTING 205

The Importance of Acting 206
The Goal of the Actor 207
Differences between Film Acting and Stage Acting 208
Types of Actors 215
The Star System 217
Casting 218
Actors as Creative Contributors 233
Subjective Responses to Actors 235

CHAPTER 8

THE DIRECTOR'S STYLE 239

The Concept of Style 240
Subject Matter 241
Cinematography 243
Editing 244
Choice of Setting and Set Design 245
Sound and Score 245
Casting and Acting Performances 246
Narrative Structure 247
Evolving Styles and Flexibility 249

CHAPTER 9

ANALYSIS OF THE WHOLE FILM 263

Overcoming Viewer-Centered Problems 264
Preconceptions: Reviews and Other Sources 271
The Basic Approach: Watching, Analyzing, and Evaluating the Film 275
Other Approaches to Analysis, Evaluation, and Discussion 280
Rereading the Reviews 286
Evaluating the Reviewer 287
Developing Personal Criteria 288

CHAPTER 10

ADAPTATIONS 293

The Problems of Adaptation 294
Adaptations of Novels 298
Adaptations of Plays 314

CHAPTER 11

GENRE, REMAKES, AND SEQUELS 325

The Genre Film 326
Remakes and Sequels 337

CHAPTER 12

OTHER SPECIAL FILM EXPERIENCES 347

The Foreign-Language Film 348
The Silent Film 357
The Historically Important Film 362
The Social Problem Film 364

CHAPTER 13

CENSORSHIP AND OTHER FORCES THAT SHAPE THE AMERICAN FILM 365

Does Film Shape or Reflect American Values? 366
The Hays Office: 1922–1934 367
The Motion Picture Production Code: 1930–1960 368
Understanding the Code 370
Censorship in Transition: 1948–1968 375
The MPAA Rating System 378
Understanding the Rating System 379
Changing Formulas for the Treatment of Sex, Violence, and Language 385
Film: An Industry and an Art Form 388

CHAPTER 14

THE ART OF WATCHING MOVIES ON TV 393

Sound 395
The TV Viewing Environment 395
Conventions and Habits of Watching Television Movies 396
Commercial Breaks 397
Missing Segments 399
Network versus Local Stations 399
Censorship 400
The Made-for-Television Film 402
Changing TV Watching Habits 404
State-of-the-Art Video Equipment 408

Comprehensive List of Questions for Analysis 415
Glossary 443
Index 447

PREFACE

The underlying assumption of this book is that there *is* an art to watching films, and that special skills and techniques can sharpen and enhance the film experience. *The Art of Watching Films* is designed to encourage students to practice and develop this art. It is *not* designed to transform ordinary filmgoers into expert movie critics. But by suggesting what to look for and how to look for it, this text *will* help them to become more aware of the complexity of the film art, more sensitive to its subtle nuances, rich textures, and varied rhythms, and more perceptive in "reading" its multilayered blend of image, sound, and motion.

This approach—the analytical approach—is by no means the only valid one. A great many other approaches to film study are used successfully and beneficially. But the analytical approach has one distinct advantage: It is teachable. The emotional and intuitive approaches are so highly subjective and vary so greatly from one individual to another that they are difficult to share in the classroom. The analytical approach, on the other hand, can be structured to suit the classroom situation. It provides a thorough, systematized, rational, and orderly framework for the study of film.

So *The Art of Watching Films* is designed not as a typical textbook, but as a flexible framework that can be applied to a wide variety of films. And unlike most film texts, *The Art of Watching Films* makes no presumptions of prior cinematic knowledge on the student's part. A concerted effort has also been made to focus on *essential* information and to present it clearly and directly, avoiding peripheral material not applicable to a large number of films. Cinematic jargon is held to a minimum and, where possible, simplified to help the student grasp the meanings quickly. I have also tried to avoid the pedantic tone that often flaws film texts, and to choose material that is both insightful *and* interesting, in an effort to achieve the proper blend of information and entertainment that is essential for any introductory film text.

Regarding the formal organization and intent, the book is designed to provide an essential understanding of film techniques, current practices, and basic principles of film art. The questions at the end of each section point the students toward direct application of that knowledge to the film under study. *The Art of Watching Films* is thus intended to complement each film studied. It is a kind of treasure map to help students discover complex aspects of film art they might otherwise overlook and lead them to a deeper understanding and appreciation of the filmmaker's art, developing skills and habits of perceptive watching in the process.

The questions are integral to this intent. They direct students to the very heart of the most important text, the film being analyzed. The questions help students organize and focus their analytical thinking as they prepare for class discussion or written assignments. But the questions serve another extremely important function: They increase student involvement in the film experience, encouraging them to participate *actively* in an exciting quest, instead of passively contenting themselves with surface details.

Although the chapters can be read in sequence, *The Art of Watching Films* has also been designed to be used as a handbook. The streamlined handbook format, with clearly titled topics divided into small, easily digestible chunks, makes the information easily and quickly accessible. Pictures closely integrated with the text serve to whet the students' curiosity, encouraging them to dip in at random to sample sections of special interest. In this way the format reinforces the book's basic purpose of stimulating the student's interest in film.

Changes in the Second Edition

Although the general purpose and structure of the second and first editions are similar, some very important changes have been made. In the first edition, I attempted to explain common practices and techniques in general terms, without providing detailed examples from classic and current films. At the time, I believed that withholding examples would challenge the student to discover his or her own examples in the films under study, sharpening awareness and powers of observation in the process. Five years of experience with the book in my own classes has shown me the error of my ways. My students needed lots of examples to fully comprehend most of the basic concepts or techniques. The second edition, therefore, is as rich in examples as I can possibly make it.

A great deal of effort has also gone into collecting photographs that truly illustrate rather than simply embellish or decorate the text, and the second edition has almost tripled the number of illustrations in the first edition. Clear, concise captions relate each picture to the text, often serving as capsule summaries of sections of the text.

The questions, a feature key to the first edition's success, have been refined and enlarged. A comprehensive list of questions again appears at the back of the book, so the instructor can quickly locate questions appropriate to the film under study. A glossary and a full index have also been included.

A "cleaner" organizational structure has been achieved, with the first eight chapters focusing on the basic elements of film art in preparation for Chapter 9, which provides a framework for integrating knowledge of all these elements into an analysis of the whole film. Chapters 10 through 14 deal with special kinds of film experience and concerns.

Almost every chapter of the first edition has been expanded and updated with examples from recent films, and important new sections on film as industry/art form, special effects, production design/art direction, remakes, sequels, and the genre film have been added. Two new chapters have been added: "Censorship and Other Forces that Shape the American Film" and "The Art of Watching Movies on TV," including a brief section on the use of VCRs and videodisc players in film analysis.

But the underlying purpose of this book remains that of providing students with enough guidance so that they may discover new insights themselves and, in the process, stimulate, challenge, and sharpen their powers of observation. In a sense, this text can only function as a map to aid in finding the treasures embodied in the real "text" of any film course—the films themselves.

Acknowledgments

If the second edition of *The Art of Watching Films* is a significantly better book than the first, the improvement is largely a result of the input and the generous assistance provided by many people.

For their help with collecting studio stills, I am indebted to Jim Ausenbaugh, Irene Nolan, Barbara Doussard, Bill Hance, and Bob Longino.

For making their large collection of feature film videotapes available for my research, I am grateful to Jim R. Jones and Jeff Boswell of Video Station.

Sincere thanks are also in order for my long-time friend, Thomas M. Hayes, whose sound advice on a number of matters has greatly facilitated my work, and for Patience Nave, who always manages to help me bring order out of chaos at the last minute, in ways too numerous to detail here.

A special "thanks for the use of the hall" goes to Chuck and Carolyn Spivey, owners of Mr. D.'s Pizza, for allowing us to photograph an editing sequence in their hospitable and cozy restaurant.

I am also grateful for the hours spent and the extraordinary patience shown by our models, Patricia Minton-Taylor, Craig Taylor, Denise Medich, Harriett Akins, Jan Witherspoon, Dean Nason, Jerry Sharer, Tom Deller, Robert Allen, Paul Wedge, Mike Adams, Kenny Stewart, Paul Trout, Randy Dillard, Mike Buser, and Scott Boggs, and those who assisted with the photography, John Dowell and Harriett Akins.

For reading parts of the manuscript and making valuable suggestions, I am indebted to David VanHooser, Ernest C. Raymer, Tom Wallace, Mike Boggs, Dennis Petrie, Lowell Harrison, Helen Crocker, James Heldman, Frank Steele, and especially to Jennifer Bussey, who read the whole manuscript.

The text has also benefited from the criticism and suggestions of Greg Beal, Syracuse University; Ralph Berets, University of Missouri; Charles Chess, San Jose State University; Eric Fielding, Brigham Young University; Mark Hall, Butte College; Arthur Knight, University of Southern California; Robert Lee, San Diego State University; James A. Pearse, Baylor University, David J. Powpowski, Mankato State University; and Gary J. Prebula, California State University at Long Beach.

Like the creation of the medium it describes, producing a film textbook can also be a collaborative art. Special thanks are hereby extended to my collaborators: Christopher Allen, film student *par excellence,* who assisted with research and writing; Holly Gloar, wizardess of the word processor, whose dedication and nimble fingers enabled us to meet crucial deadlines; Ernest C. Raymer, photographer and friend, whose camera, lighting, and darkroom skills produced the excellent original photographs in Chapter 4; and David B. Andrews, copy editor and personal cheerleader. This book is better in every respect as a result of David's cheerful and enthusiastic support, sound advice, organizational genius, and competent copy editing.

THE ART OF WATCHING FILMS

CHAPTER 1

FILM ANALYSIS

THE UNIQUENESS OF FILM

Throughout its brief history, film has struggled to achieve its proper place as a reputable art form, on a par with painting, sculpture, music, literature, and drama. Even today, the tremendous expense involved in producing motion pictures continually reminds us that film is an industry as well as an art form. Each "work of art" is the child of a turbulent, difficult, but necessary marriage between businessmen and artists. Despite this ongoing battle between aesthetic and commercial considerations, film has established itself as a unique and powerful art.

As a form of expression, the motion picture is similar to other artistic media, for the basic properties of these other media are woven into its own rich fabric. Film employs the compositional elements of all the visual arts: line, form, mass, volume, and texture. Like painting and photography, film exploits the subtle interplay of light and shadow. Like sculpture, film manipulates three-dimensional space. But, like pantomime, film focuses on *moving* images, and like the dance, these moving images have rhythm. The complex rhythms of film resemble those of music and poetry, and like poetry in particular, film communicates through imagery, metaphor, and symbol. Like the drama, film communicates visually *and* verbally: visually, through action and gesture; verbally, through dialogue. Finally, like the novel, film expands or compresses time and space, traveling back and forth freely within their wide borders.

Despite these similarities, film is unique, set apart from all other media by its quality of free and constant motion. The continuous interplay of sight, sound, and motion allows film to transcend the static limitations of painting and sculpture—in complexity of its sensual appeal as well as in its ability to communicate simultaneously on several levels. Film even surpasses drama in its unique capacity for varied points of view, action, manipulation of time, and boundless sense of space. Unlike the stage play, film can provide a continuous, unbroken flow, which blurs and minimizes transitions without compromising the story's unity. Unlike the novel and the poem, film communicates directly—not through abstract symbols like words on a page that require the brain to translate—but through concrete images and sounds.

What's more, film can treat an almost infinite array of subjects:

> It is impossible to conceive of anything which the eye might behold or the ear hear, in actuality or imagination, which could not be represented in the

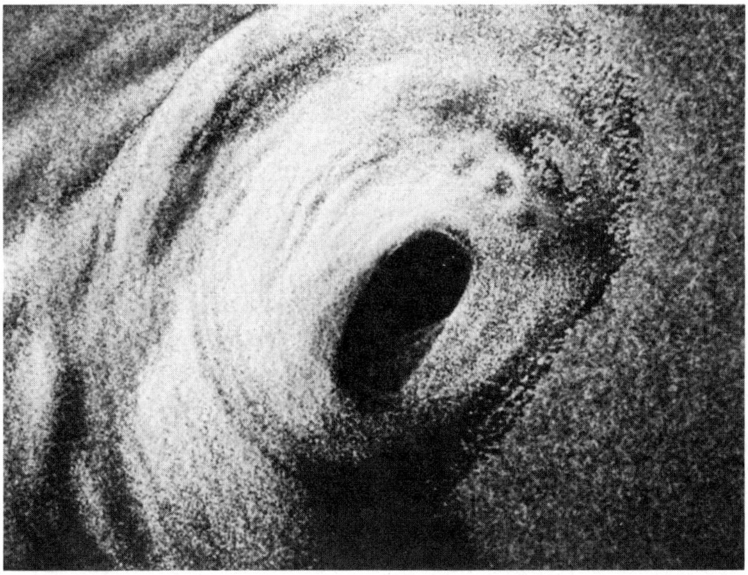

| 1.1 | Unlimited Potential of Film: William Hurt regresses into a more primitive state in a scene from *Altered States.*

Roget - Persistence of vision
1889 - invention of motion picture camera by Dickson
George Eastman - strip film
1894 - Kinetoscope "peepshow" Edison Co.
1895 - first movies
Thomas Edison owned 1st movie studio Black Mariah
narrative story (first films)
George Melies (french) invented early technical techniques (masking) (dissolve, multiple exposure fast & slow motion)
1902 - The Trip to the Moon (Melies)
Edwin S. Porter Parallel editing or cross cutting The Great Train Robbery
D. W. Griffith

> medium of film. From the poles to the equator, from the Grand Canyon to the minutest flaw in a piece of steel, from the whistling flight of a bullet to the slow growth of a flower, from the flicker of thought across an almost impassive face to the frenzied ravings of a madman, there is no point in space, no degree of magnitude or speed of movement within the apprehension of man which is not within reach of the film.[1]

Film is unlimited not only in its choice of subject matter but also in the scope of its approach to that material. A film's mood and treatment can range anywhere between the lyric and the epic; in point of view, it can cover the full spectrum from the purely objective to the intensely subjective; in depth, it can focus on the surface realities and the purely sensual, or delve into the intellectual and philosophical. A film can look to the remote past, or probe the distant future; it can make a few seconds seem like hours, or compress a century into minutes. Finally, film can run the gamut of feeling from the most fragile, tender, and beautiful to the most brutal, violent, and repulsive (Fig. 1.1).

Of even greater importance than film's unlimited range in subject matter and treatment, however, is the overwhelming sense of reality it can convey, regardless of subject. The continuous stream

1. Ernest Lindgrin, *The Art of the Film.* New York: The Macmillan Co., 1963, pp. 204–205.

of sight, sound, and motion creates a "here and now" excitement that completely immerses the viewer in the cinematic experience. Thus, through film, the most complete and utter fantasy assumes the shape and emotional impact of the starkest reality.

The technological history of film can in fact be viewed as an ongoing evolution toward greater realism, toward erasing the border between art and nature. The motion picture has progressed step by step from drawings, to photographs, to projected images, to sound, to color, to wide screen, to 3-D. Experiments have even been conducted attempting to add the sense of smell to the film experience by releasing fragrances throughout the theater. Aldous Huxley's novel *Brave New World* depicted a theater of the future where a complex electrical apparatus at each seat provided tactile "images" to match the visuals:

> Going to the Feelies this evening, Henry? . . . I hear the new one at the Alhambra is first-rate. There's a love scene on a bearskin rug; they say it's marvellous. Every hair of the bear reproduced. The most amazing tactual effects.[2]

Although Huxley's "Feelies" have not yet become reality, the motion picture has succeeded, through Cinerama and other wide- or curved-screen projection techniques, in intensifying our experience to a remarkable degree. In fact, by creating images that are larger than life, films have sometimes been made to seem more real than reality. A cartoon published shortly after the first Cinerama film (*This Is Cinerama*, 1952) was released clearly illustrates the effectiveness of this device. The cartoon pictures a man groping for a seat during the famous roller-coaster sequence. As he moves across a row of seats, a seated spectator, in a panic, grabs his arm and screams hysterically, "Sit down, you fool! You'll have us all killed!" Anyone who has seen this film knows the cartoon is no exaggeration.

DIFFICULTIES OF FILM ANALYSIS

The very same properties that make film the most powerful and realistic of all the arts also make analysis difficult. To begin with, film in its natural state is continuous; its flow cannot be frozen in time and space. Once frozen, a film is no longer a "motion"

2. Aldous Huxley, *Brave New World*. New York: Harper and Bros., 1946, p. 23.

picture, for the unique property of the medium is gone. Therefore, we must direct most of our attention toward responding sensitively to the simultaneous and continuous interplay of image, sound, and motion on the screen. This necessity creates the most difficult part of our task: We must somehow manage to remain almost totally immersed in the "real" experience of a film while at the same time maintaining a fairly high degree of objectivity and critical detachment. Difficult though it may seem, this skill can be developed, and we must consciously cultivate it if we desire to become truly "cineliterate." Recent innovations in video cassette recorders (VCRs) and videodisc players can be of great value in developing analytical skills and habits.

The technical nature of the medium also creates difficulties in film analysis. It would be ideal if we all could have at least some limited experience in cinematography and film editing. Since this is impossible, we should become familiar with the basic techniques of film production so that we can recognize them and evaluate their effectiveness. Since a certain amount of technical language or jargon is necessary for the analysis and intelligent discussion of any art form, we must also add a number of important technical terms to our vocabularies. Although many difficulties face us in our early attempts at film analysis, none of them will be insurmountable if we are willing to develop the proper attitudes, skills, and habits essential to perceptive analysis.

The most difficult part of our task has already been stated: We must somehow manage to become almost totally immersed in the "real" experience of a film and at the same time maintain a fairly high degree of objectivity and critical detachment. The complex nature of the medium also makes it difficult to consider all the elements of a film in a single viewing; too many things happen too quickly on too many levels to allow for a complete analysis. Therefore, if we wish to develop the proper habits of analytical viewing, we should see a film twice whenever possible. In the first viewing we can watch the film in the usual manner, concerning ourselves primarily with plot elements, the total emotional effect, and the central idea or theme. Then, in a second viewing, since we are no longer caught up in the suspense of "what happens," we can focus our full attention on the hows and whys of the filmmaker's art. Constant practice of the double-viewing technique should make it possible for us to gradually combine the functions of both viewings into one.

We must also remember that film analysis does not end the minute the film is over. In a sense, it really begins then, for most of

1920 Broken Blossoms
Lillian Gish (ice floe)
Mary Pickford (America's sweetheart)

United Artist (1919) formed by M. Pickford, D.W. Griffith, C. Chaplin, D. Fairbanks)

Pearl White (serials)
cliff hangers

Cecil B. DeMille
used women in film in extreme sexual situations (popularized the bathroom scene)

The Law of Compensating Value
vamp (ire) (bad girl)

"It" girl Clara Bow
Theda Bara (bad girl)
vamp

Swashbuckler Douglas Fairbanks Sr.
The Thief of Bagdad

Rudolph Valentino
sex appeal
Sheik
Son of Sheik
Valentino "look"

Comic —
Mac Sennett (producer)
Keystone Studios (owned)
discovered:
 C. Chaplin
 Mabel Normand (female director)
 Stan Laurel
 Fatty Arbuckle

Charlie Chaplin
 The Little Fellow
 (The Tramp)
 Making a Living
 88 films
 6 features

Buster Keaton
 physical comedy
 Stone Face

Harold Lloyd physical
 comedy

Harry Langdon — baby
 face Comedian

Laurel & Hardy — first
 did silent films

the questions posed in this guide require the reader to reflect on the film after leaving the theater, and a mental replay of some parts of the film will be necessary for any complete analysis.

WHY ANALYZE FILMS?

Before turning to the actual process of film analysis, it may be worthwhile to look into certain fundamental questions that have been raised about the value of analysis in general. Perhaps the most vocal reactions against analysis come from those who see it as a destroyer of beauty, claiming that it kills our love for the object under study. According to this view, it is better to accept all art intuitively, emotionally, and subjectively, so that our response is full, warm, and vibrant, uncluttered by the intellect. This kind of thinking is expressed in Walt Whitman's poem "When I Heard the Learn'd Astronomer":

> When I heard the learn'd astronomer;
> When the proofs, the figures, were ranged in
> columns before me;
> When I was shown the charts and the diagrams, to add,
> divide, and measure them,
> When I, sitting, heard the astronomer, where he lectured
> with much applause in the lecture-room,
> How soon, unaccountable, I became tired and sick;
> Till rising and gliding out, I wander'd off by myself,
> In the mystical moist night-air, and from time to time,
> Look'd up in perfect silence at the stars.

If we were to agree with Whitman, we would certainly throw analysis out the window completely as a cold, intellectual, bloodless, and unfeeling process that destroys the magical, emotional, and mystical aspects of experience. But if this is so, why should we bother to analyze films at all?

The flaw lies in the either/or, black and white extremism of Whitman's view, in the polarization of poet and astronomer. It denies the possibility of some middle ground, a synthesis that retains the best qualities of both approaches, embracing as equally valid both the emotional/intuitive and the intellectual/analytical approaches. This book is built on that middle ground. It assumes that the soul of the poet and the intellect of the astronomer can live as one within all of us, that the two can actually work together, without cancelling each other out, to enrich and enhance the film experience. If this is true, beauty, joy, and mystery can be experienced intellectually as well as intuitively. With the astronomer's telescope, we can experience the poetic beauty of Saturn's rings, the moons of Jupiter, and the Milky Way—mysteries of the universe invisible to the naked eye. Likewise with the tools of analysis, we can discover the deeper reaches of understanding that only the poet within us can fully appreciate.

So analysis need not murder our love of the movies. By creating new avenues of awareness, analysis can make our love for movies stronger, more real, more enduring.

Analysis also suffers from the misconception that we not only destroy our love for the object, but destroy the object as well. As Wordsworth states in "The Tables Turned":

> Sweet is the lore which Nature brings;
> Our meddling intellect
> Misshapes the beauteous forms of things
> We murder to dissect.

Here, Wordsworth conjures up an image of the medical student working on a cadaver, or the physician performing an autopsy. This is another false conception. To assume that analysis destroys the beautiful is to assume that physicians, because they have carefully studied the human body, its bone and muscle structure, its circulatory and nervous systems and all its many organs, are no longer awed by this miracle of life in all its complexity—warm, vibrant, and pulsing with energy. Film analysis does not work with parts that are dead, nor does it kill. Film analysis takes place only in the mind. Each part being studied still pulses with life, since analysis still sees each part as connected to the lifeline of the whole. And that's the point. The analytical approach enables us to see and understand how each part functions to contribute its vital energy to the pulsing, dynamic whole.

The following quote from Richard Dyer McCann's introduction to *Film: A Montage of Theories* might well serve as the basic assumption of this book:

> Arnold Hauser contended, and I think rightly, that "all art is a game with and a fight against chaos." The film that simply says life is chaos is a film which has not undertaken the battle of art.[3]

If we accept McCann's judgment, the analytical approach is essential to the art of watching films. Analysis means breaking up

3. Richard Dyer McCann, ed., *Film: A Montage of Theories*. New York: E. P. Dutton and Co., Inc., 1966, p. 56.

the whole to discover the nature, proportion, function, and interrelationships of the parts. Film analysis, then, presupposes the existence of a unified and rationally structured artistic whole. Therefore, the usefulness of this book is restricted to the structured film, the film developed with a definite underlying purpose and unified around a central theme.

Limiting our approach to the structured film does not necessarily deny the artistic value of the unstructured film. A great many of the films being produced by experimental or underground filmmakers do communicate effectively on a purely subjective, intuitive, or sensual plane, and are meaningful to some degree as "experiences." But many of these films are not structured or unified around a central purpose or theme, and therefore cannot be successfully approached through analysis.

It would be foolish to suggest that the structured film cannot be appreciated or understood at all without analysis. If the film is effective, we should possess an intuitive grasp of its overall meaning. The problem is that this intuitive grasp is generally weak and vague, and limits our critical response to hazy generalizations and half-formed opinions. The analytical approach makes it possible for us to raise this intuitive grasp to a conscious level, bring it into sharp focus, and thereby reach more valid and definite conclusions on the film's meaning and value.

The analytical approach will help us reach more valid and definite conclusions on the film's meaning and its value, but this in no way implies that it can reduce the film art to rational and manageable proportions. Analysis neither claims nor attempts to explain everything about an art form. Film will always retain its special magic and its mystical qualities—none of which can ever be reduced to a simple matter of $2 + 2 = 4$. The elusive, flowing stream of images will always escape complete analysis and complete understanding. In fact, no final answers exist about any work of art. A film, like anything else of true aesthetic value, can never be completely captured by analysis.

But the fact that there are no final answers should not prevent us from pursuing some important questions. Our hope is that, through analysis, we can reach a higher level of confusion about films, a level where we are reaching for the higher, more significant aspects of the film art as opposed to the mundane, the practical, and the technical. If we can understand some things through analysis so we learn to "see" them habitually, our minds will be free to concentrate on the more significant questions.

Analysis has the further advantage of helping us to lock the experience in our minds so that we may savor it longer in our memory. By looking at a film analytically, we engage ourselves with it both intellectually and creatively, and thus make it more truly our own. Furthermore, because our critical judgments enter into the process, analysis should also make us more discriminating in our tastes and more selective in the films we really admire. A great film or a very good one will stand up under analysis; our admiration for it will increase the more deeply we look into it. But a mediocre film can impress us more than it should at first, and we might like it less after analyzing it.

Therefore, analysis can be seen to have several clear benefits. It allows us to reach more valid and definite conclusions on the film's meaning and value, it helps us to "lock" the experience of a film into our minds, and it sharpens our critical judgments. But the ultimate purpose of analysis, and its greatest benefit, is that it opens up new avenues of awareness and new depths of understanding. It seems logical to assume that the more understanding we have, the more completely we appreciate art. If the love we have for an art form is built on rational understanding, it will be more solid, more enduring, and of greater value than love based solely on irrational and totally subjective reactions. This is not to claim that analysis will create a love of films where none exists. The love of film does not come from a book or from any special critical approach. It comes only from that secret, personal union, the intimate meeting of film and viewer in a darkened room. If that love does not already exist for the viewer, this book and its analytical approach can do little to create it.

But if we truly love films, we will find that analysis is worth the effort, for the understanding it brings will deepen our appreciation. Instead of cancelling out the emotional experience of watching the film, analysis will enhance and enrich that experience, for as we become more perceptive and look more deeply into the film, new levels of emotional experience will emerge.

CHAPTER 2

THEME AND FOCUS

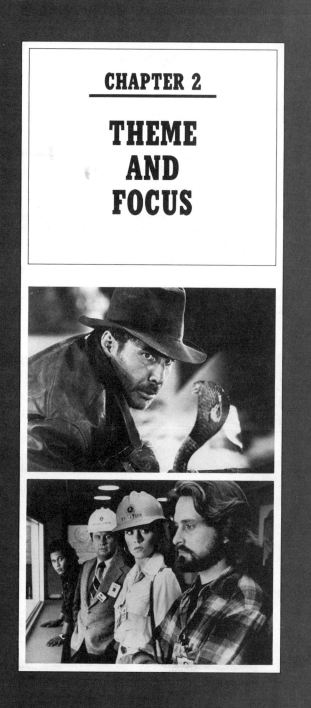

|2.1|

|2.2|

|2.3|
Plot as Theme: *Raiders of the Lost Ark* [2.1], *The Road Warrior* [2.2], and *Moonraker* [2.3] are fast-paced action films focused on "what happens."

DETERMINING THE THEME

As the sum total of all elements, the theme serves as the basic unifying factor in the film. Therefore, each element within the film must contribute in some manner and to some degree to the development of the theme, and must be analyzed in terms of this relationship. It is essential, then, that the viewer make some attempt to determine, as accurately as possible, the nature of that theme.

Unfortunately, determining the theme is often a very difficult process. We cannot expect the theme to be revealed in a blinding flash of light midway through the film. Although we can easily acquire a vague, intuitive grasp of the film's basic meaning from simply watching it, accurately determining and stating the theme is quite another matter. Often we will not accomplish this until we leave the theater and begin thinking about or discussing the film in abstract terms. Sometimes, just telling someone who hasn't seen the movie about it will provide an important clue to the theme, because it is natural to first describe the things that made the strongest impression on us.

Determining the theme can, in fact, be considered both the beginning and end of the analytical approach. After seeing the film, we should tentatively identify its theme, to provide a starting point for our analysis. Of course, the analysis itself will clarify our vision of the film and help us see how all its elements function together as a unique whole. Ultimately, our analysis might not support our original conception of the film's theme. If it doesn't, we should be prepared to reconsider the theme in light of the new direction our analysis has taken.

BASIC TYPES OF FILM THEMES

The traditional use of the word *theme* as it applies to fiction, drama, and poetry always connotes a central idea, variously referred to as the point, the message, or the statement. This interpretation of theme is much too confining for practical film analysis, which must consider a wide spectrum of approaches to filmmaking, from *Smokey and the Bandit* to *Reds,* from *Days of Heaven* to *Pink Floyd: The Wall.* To assume that all the films along this spectrum are structured around a central "message" can only distort or confuse our analysis. Therefore, we must expand the concept of theme to mean the central concern around which a film is structured, the focus that unifies a film.

In film, this central concern, or focus, can be broken down into five more or less distinct categories: plot, emotion, character, style or texture, and idea. These five ingredients are of course present in *all* films. But four of the five are usually subordinate to the primary focus.

Plot as Theme

In many types of films, such as the adventure story or the detective story, the primary emphasis is on the chain of events, on what happens. These films are generally aimed at providing us with a temporary escape from the boredom and the drabness of everyday living. So the action must be exciting and fast-paced. The characters, the ideas, and the emotional effects in these films are all subordinate to the plot, and the final outcome is all important. However, the events and their final outcome are important only within the context of the story; out of context, little if any real significance in a general or abstract sense can be attached to them. The essence or theme of such a film can best be captured, therefore, in a concise summary of the central action (Figs. 2.1, 2.2, and 2.3).

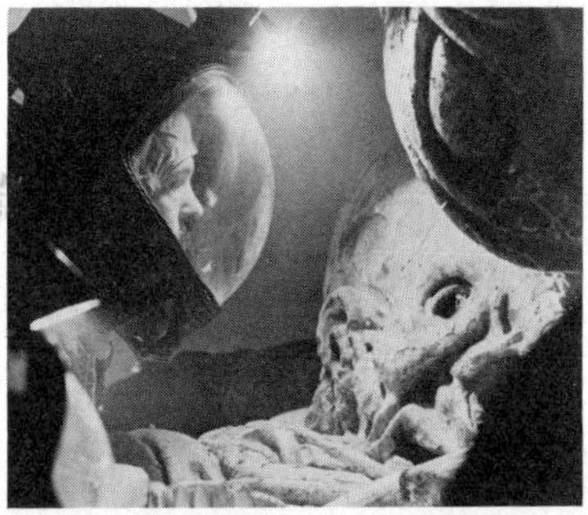

| 2.4 | Emotional Effect or Mood as Theme: A wide variety of emotional effects or moods can serve as a thematic concern in modern films. There are movies to scare us, like *Alien* . . .

Emotional Effect or Mood as Theme

A highly specialized mood or emotional effect serves as the focus for a relatively large number of films. In such films, a single primary mood or emotion prevails throughout the film, and each segment of the film acts as a stairstep leading to a single powerful emotional effect. Although plot may play a very important role in such a movie, the chain of events itself is subordinate to the emotional response caused by those events. Most horror films, the Alfred Hitchcock suspense thrillers, and romantic tone poems such as *A Man and a Woman* can be interpreted as having a mood or emotional effect as their primary focus and unifying element. The theme of such films can best be stated by simply naming the primary mood or emotional effect created: horror, suspense, romance, and so on (Figs. 2.4, 2.5, 2.6, and 2.7).

| 2.5 | There are movies to make us laugh, like *Arthur* . . .

Some films, of course, may be a balanced combination of two emotions, a fairly even mix that makes it difficult to tell which

| 2.6 | And movies to make us cry, like *Love Story* . . .

| 2.7 | And even movies to make us feel romantic, like *Somewhere in Time.*

| 2.8 | Mixed Emotions: Some films do not really focus on building a single emotional effect but are actually able to blend two different effects into the same story, as is the case in *Silver Streak,* which we might classify as a comedy/suspense film.

emotion dominates. *Silver Streak's* theme, for example, might be classified as comedy/suspense; the theme of *An American Werewolf in London* might be classified as comedy/horror. An analysis of such films would have to consider the elements that contribute to each effect, and also the way the two thematic emotions play off each other (Fig. 2.8).

Character as Theme

Some films, through both action and dialogue, focus on delineating a unique character. Although plot is important in such films, what happens is important primarily in how it helps us understand the character being developed. The major appeal of such characters lies in their uniqueness, in those qualities that set them apart from ordinary people. The theme of such films can be best expressed by a brief description of the central character, with emphasis on the unusual aspects of the individual's personality (Figs. 2.9, 2.10, and 2.11).

|2.9|

|2.10|

|2.11|

Character as Theme: Some films, such as *Sergeant York* [2.9], *The Great Santini* [2.10], and *Raging Bull* [2.11], focus on the unusual aspects of unique people.

|2.12| |2.13|

Style or Texture as Theme: *Days of Heaven* [2.12] and *Three Women* [2.13] both leave us with the feeling that we have experienced a "one of a kind" movie with a unique style or flavor.

Style or Texture as Theme

In a relatively small number of films, the filmmaker tells the story in such a unique way that the film's style or texture becomes its dominant and most memorable aspect. Such films have a very special quality that distinguishes them from others, a unique "look," "feel," rhythm, atmosphere, or tone that echoes in our memory long after we've left the theater. This unique style or texture permeates the entire film, not just isolated segments, with all the cinematic elements woven into one rich tapestry. Such films are often not commercially successful because the mass audience may not be prepared for or comfortable with the unique viewing experience such films provide (Figs. 2.12 and 2.13).

Idea as Theme

In most films that are of serious intent, the action and characters have a significance beyond the context of the film itself, a significance that helps us more clearly understand some aspect of life, experience, or the human condition. Such a theme can, of course, be stated directly through some particular incident or character. But most often the theme is arrived at indirectly, and we are challenged to seek our own interpretation. This less direct approach increases the possibility that the film will be interpreted in different ways by different viewers. But different interpretations are not always contradictory. They may be equally valid—even complementary—saying essentially the same thing in a different way, or approaching the same theme from a different angle.

Perhaps the first step in determining an idea theme is to abstract the subject of the film in a single word or phrase—for example, jealousy, hypocrisy, or prejudice. Of course, some themes can be stated this explicitly while others cannot, so we shouldn't despair if we can't always characterize the theme with a single word or phrase. At any rate, the identification of the true subject of the film is a valuable first step in film analysis.

If possible, however, we should attempt to carry the determination of theme beyond merely identifying the subject, and see if we can formulate a statement that accurately summarizes the theme as dramatized by the whole film and underscored by all its elements. If it is possible to summarize the theme in a specific statement, it might fall into one of the following categories.

Theme as a Moral Statement Films of this nature are intended primarily to convince us of the wisdom or practicality of a certain moral principle and thereby persuade us to apply the principle to our own behavior. Such themes often take the form of a maxim or proverbial formula, such as, "The love of money is the root of all evil." Although many modern films have important moral implications, very few are structured around a single moral statement, and we must be careful not to mistake a moral *implication* for a moral *statement* (Fig. 2.14).

| 2.14 | Moral Statement Theme: It is very doubtful that any young person who has seen *Midnight Express* will ever attempt to smuggle drugs out of Turkey, or any other foreign country, for that matter.

Human Nature Theme: Films like *Lord of the Flies* [2.15] and *Deliverance* [2.16] take a penetrating look at the nature of humankind with the thin veneer of civilization removed.

|2.15|

|2.16|

Theme as a Statement About Human Nature Quite different from those films that focus on a unique character are those that focus on universal or representative characters. Such films move beyond the mere character study into the realm of "idea as theme," since such characters take on significance beyond themselves and the context of the particular film in which they appear. These characters represent mankind in general, so they serve as cinematic vehicles to illustrate some truth about human nature that is widely or universally acceptable (Figs. 2.15 and 2.16).

Theme as a Social Comment Modern filmmakers are very concerned with social problems, and show their concern in films that focus on exposing the vices and follies of people as social beings or criticizing the social institutions they have established. Although the underlying purpose of such films is to encourage social change, they rarely spell out specific methods of reform; usually they concentrate on clarifying the problem and emphasizing its importance, thus convincing us of the necessity for reform. A social-problem film can make its point in a variety of ways: It may treat its subject in a light, satirical, or comic manner, or savagely and brutally attack it.

Obviously, the social-comment theme has much in common with the human-nature theme. But there is a primary difference. The social-comment theme concerns itself not with criticizing universal aspects of human nature, but only with the special functions of human beings as social animals and with the social institutions and traditions they have created (Figs. 2.17 and 2.18).

The Struggle for Human Dignity as Theme In many serious films there is a basic conflict or tension between two opposing sides of human nature. On one side is the temptation to succumb to the animal instincts, to wallow in weakness, selfishness, cowardice, brutality, stupidity, and sensuality. On the other side is the struggle to stand erect, to display courage, compassion, sensitivity, intelligence, a spiritual and moral sense, and strong individualism. This conflict is best shown when the central characters are

Social Comment as Theme: Films like *Guess Who's Coming to Dinner?* [2.17] (interracial marriage) and *The China Syndrome* [2.18] (dangers of nuclear reactors) are continually forcing us to examine current social problems.

|2.17|

|2.18|

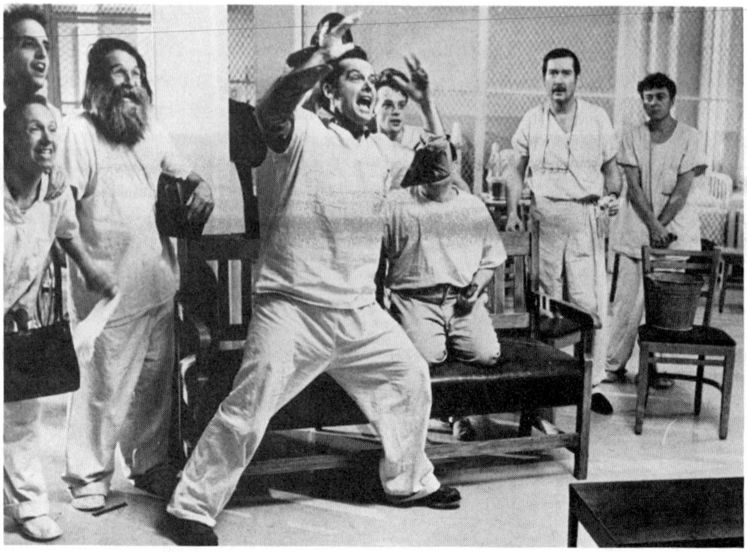

| 2.19 | Struggle for Human Dignity as Theme: In *One Flew Over the Cuckoo's Nest* Jack Nicholson, as McMurphy, helps his fellow inmates "enjoy" the World Series on a dark and silent TV set.

placed in a position of tremendous disadvantage, having been "dealt a bad hand" in some way, so that they must play against tremendous odds. The conflict may be external, with the character struggling against some dehumanizing force, system, institution or attitude, or internal, with the character struggling for dignity against the human weaknesses present in his or her own personality.

Although the character may triumph in the end, that is certainly not always the case—the struggle itself gives us some respect for the character, win or lose. Boxers have often been treated in films with this "dignity" theme. In *On the Waterfront,* Terry Malloy (Marlon Brando) achieves dignity by leading the dock workers to rebel against a corrupt union, but Malloy's failed career as a boxer clearly echoes in his personal struggle: "I coulda had class . . . I coulda been a contender . . . I coulda been *somebody*! . . . Instead of just a bum, which is what I am." In the *Rocky* series, Sylvester Stallone bases the title character on that of Terry Malloy, and gives Rocky Balboa the chance to "be somebody" in each film. *Requiem for a Heavyweight* is another example: Over-the-hill fighter Mountain Rivera (Anthony Quinn) fails to preserve his dignity, but succeeds in winning our respect (Fig. 2.19).

Complexity of Human Relationships as Theme Films of this type focus on the many and varied problems, frustrations, pleasures, and joys involved in the spectrum of human relationships: love, friendship, marriage, divorce, family interactions, sexuality, and

| 2.20 | Complexity of Human Relationships as Theme: Albert Finney and Diane Keaton, in this scene from *Shoot the Moon,* show that "breaking up is hard to do."

| 2.21 | And *Starting Over* isn't always easy either, as Jill Clayburgh and Burt Reynolds show.

| 2.22 | Ties That Bind: Even family ties can be difficult, as Shirley MacLaine and Debra Winger show in *Terms of Endearment.*

so on. Some of these films show a gradual working out of the problems, others simply help us gain insight into the problem without providing any clear resolution. Although a great many films of this sort deal with universal problems in the continuing battle of the sexes, we must also be on the lookout for unusual treatments such as *Midnight Cowboy*—a "love" story about two men—and *The Odd Couple*—a "marriage" treatment (Figs. 2.20, 2.21, and 2.22).

| 2.23 |

| 2.24 |

| 2.25 |

Gaining Maturity as Theme: In movies like *American Graffiti* [2.23], *My Bodyguard* [2.24], and *Summer of '42* [2.25] young people go through experiences that cause them to become more aware or more mature.

Coming of Age/Loss of Innocence/Growing Awareness as Theme The major character or characters in such films are usually (but not always) young people whose experiences force them to become more mature or to gain some new awareness of themselves in relation to the world around them. Such themes can be treated in a variety of ways: comically, seriously, tragically, or satirically. The central characters of these films always differ in some way at the end of the film from how they were at the beginning. The changes may be subtle and internal, or they may be drastic, significantly altering the outward behavior or life-style of the characters (Figs. 2.23, 2.24, 2.25, and 2.26).

Theme as a Moral or Philosophical Riddle In some cases a filmmaker purposely strives to evoke a variety of subjective interpretations by developing a film around a riddling or puzzling quality. The filmmaker might suggest or mystify instead of communicate clearly, and pose moral or philosophical questions rather than provide pat answers. The typical reaction to such films is, "What's it all about?" Since this type of film communicates primarily through symbols or images, a thorough analysis of these elements will be required for interpretation, and a degree of uncertainty will remain after even the most perceptive analysis. Such films are, of course, wide open to subjective interpretation. The fact that subjective interpretation is required, however, does not mean that the analysis of all film elements can be ignored: The theme should still be the sum total of all these elements, and individual interpretation should be supported by an examination of them (Figs. 2.27 and 2.28).

| 2.26 | Adult Education: The maturing process doesn't necessarily end at age 21, as Michael Caine and Julie Walters learn in *Educating Rita.*

The thematic categories just described are intended to give the student some help in pinpointing the themes of most films. Certainly many exceptions will arise—films that do not seem to fit clearly into any one category as well as those that seem equally suited to more than one category. In our efforts to determine theme, we must also be aware that certain films may possess, in addition to the single unifying central concern defined as theme, other less important areas of emphasis called *subthemes* or *motifs*. These are images, patterns, or ideas that repeat throughout the film, and are variations or aspects of the major theme. Above all, we should remember that the statement of theme does not equal the full impact of the film itself; it merely clarifies our vision of it as a unified work and leads us to a greater appreciation of how the elements contribute to the artistic whole.

Theme as Moral or Philosophical Riddle: In *2001: A Space Odyssey* [2.27] and *Persona* [2.28] directors Stanley Kubrick and Ingmar Bergman suggest multiple meanings that mystify us.

| 2.27 |

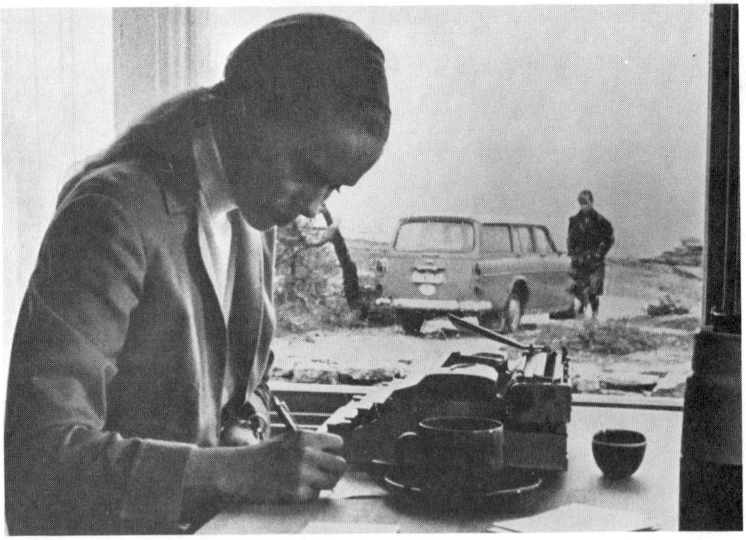

| 2.28 |

EVALUATING THE THEME

Once the theme has been determined, it is important to make some kind of evaluation of it, especially in the serious film that attempts to do more than simply entertain. Evaluating the theme is, for the most part, a subjective process, and any attempt to provide systematic guidelines would be prejudicial. A few generalizations, however, are permissible.

| 2.29 | **| 2.30 |**

Themes Limited in Time and Place: *Wild in the Streets* [2.29] and *Billy Jack* [2.30] dealt with problems and issues that seemed very relevant in the late '60s and early '70s, but many of their concerns seem ridiculous today.

In evaluating the theme, one standard commonly applied is universality. A universal theme is lasting, meaningful not just to people here and now, but to all people in all ages. Therefore, a theme with universal appeal may be considered superior to one with appeal strictly limited in time and place. Four social-problem films can be used to illustrate this point. *Wild in the Streets* (the generation gap of the 1960s) and *Billy Jack* (a grab bag of '60s problems) made a powerful impact on young film audiences when they were released, but seem ludicrous today (Figs. 2.29 and 2.30). On the other hand, *On the Waterfront* (union corruption in the 1950s) and *The Grapes of Wrath* (the plight of migrant farm workers in the 1930s) still speak to us in loud, clear voices, in spite of their age. Of course, migrant farm workers still have their problems, and some unions are still corrupt, but those films endure because of their artistry, because of their real and powerful characters heroically struggling for human dignity. Their universal appeal has made these films classics.

| 2.31 | Universal Themes: Although the problems of the migrant farm workers forced out of the Dust Bowl in the '30s have disappeared, many people still have similar problems; thus, the strong, universal themes of *The Grapes of Wrath* resist the passage of time.

Of course, there is no formula for the classic, the film we never tire of (Fig. 2.31). But the classic film has a sense of "rightness" to it, time and time again. Its power does not diminish with the passing years, but actually increases because of the film's timeless themes and motifs. *The Grapes of Wrath* is not a simple story of

|2.32|

|2.33|

What Makes a Classic? *Patton* and *MacArthur* both treat famous generals who have won their place in history. *Patton* [2.32] seems destined to become a film classic; *MacArthur* [2.33] is already gathering dust as a footnote in film history.

migrant workers forced to leave the Oklahoma Dust Bowl in the 1930s. It is about the common man, the downtrodden, the underdog, about courageous men and women, about the people who endure and their constant struggle for human dignity. And *Casablanca* is more than a story of two people losing each other and finding each other again in a world too chaotic for romantic dreams. It is about a beautiful woman and a mysterious man, about war, about responsibility, about courage, duty, and most of all, about doing "the right thing." Such classics endure because these strong, universal themes are important to everyone regardless of time and place (Figs. 2.32 and 2.33).

This does not mean that we place no value on themes that lack universality. Even if a theme's appeal is strictly limited to a specific time and place, it should have some relevance to our own experience. We will naturally consider a theme that says something significant to us superior to one that doesn't, regardless of its universality or lack of it.

We also have the right to expect that an idea theme be intellectually or philosophically interesting. In other words, if a film attempts to make some kind of a significant statement, that statement should be neither boring nor self-evident but should interest or even challenge our minds.

QUESTIONS

On Theme and Focus

1. What is the film's primary concern or focus: plot, emotional effect, character, style or texture, or idea? On the basis of your decision, answer one of the questions below.

a. If the film's primary concern is plot, summarize the action abstractly in a single sentence or a short paragraph.

b. If the film is structured around a mood or emotional effect, what is the mood or feeling it attempts to convey?

c. If the film focuses on a single unique character, describe the unusual aspects of his or her personality.

d. If the film seems to be structured around a unique style or texture, describe the qualities that contribute to the special look or feel of the film.

e. If the film's primary focus is an idea, answer the following questions:

(1) What is the true subject of the film? What is it really about in abstract terms? Identify the abstract subject in a single word or phrase.

(2) What comment or statement does the film make about the subject? If possible, formulate a sentence that accurately summarizes the idea dramatized by the film.

2. Although a filmmaker can attempt to do several things with a film, one goal usually stands out as more important than the others. Decide which of the following was the filmmaker's *primary* aim and give reasons for your choice.

a. Providing pure entertainment, that is, temporary escape from the real world.

b. Developing a pervasive mood or creating a single, specialized emotional effect.

c. Providing a character sketch of a unique, fascinating personality.

d. Creating a consistent, unique feel or texture by weaving all of the complex elements of film together in a one-of-a-kind film experience.

e. Criticizing humankind and human institutions, and increasing the viewer's awareness of a social problem and the necessity for reforms.

f. Providing insights into human nature (demonstrating that human beings *in general* are like that).

g. Creating a moral or philosophical riddle for the viewer to ponder.

h. Making a moral statement to influence the viewer's values and/or behavior.
i. Dramatizing the struggle for human dignity against tremendous odds.
j. Exploring the complex problems and pleasures of human relationships.
k. Providing insight into a "growing" experience, the special kinds of situations or conflicts that cause important changes in the character or characters involved.

3. Which of the above seem important enough to qualify as secondary aims?

4. Is the film's basic appeal to the intellect, to the funnybone, to the moral sense, or to the aesthetic sense? Is it aimed primarily at the groin (the erotic sense), the viscera (blood and guts), the heart, the yellow streak down the back, or simply the eyeballs? Support your choice with specific examples from the film.

5. How well does your statement of the film's theme and purpose stand up after you have thoroughly analyzed all the film elements?

6. To what degree is the film's theme universal? Is the theme relevant to your own experience? How?

7. If you think the film makes a significant statement, why is it significant?

8. Decide whether the film's theme is intellectually or philosophically interesting, or self-evident and boring, and defend your decision.

9. Does the film have the potential to become a classic? Will people still be watching it twenty years in the future? Why?

CHAPTER 3

FICTIONAL AND DRAMATIC ELEMENTS

FILM ANALYSIS AND LITERARY ANALYSIS

Film is a unique medium, with properties that set it apart from other art forms such as painting, sculpture, fiction, and drama. It is also, in its most popular and powerful form, a storytelling medium that shares many elements with the short story and the novel. And since film presents its stories completely in dramatic form, it has even more in common with the stage play: Both forms act out or dramatize, show rather than tell, what happens.

The greatest distinction between film and the novel, short story, or play is that film is not as handy to study; it cannot be effectively frozen on the printed page. Since their medium is print, both novel and short story are relatively easy to study. They are written to be read. The stage play is slightly more difficult to study because it is written to be performed, not read. But plays are printed, and because they rely heavily on the spoken word, imaginative readers can conjure up at least a pale imitation of the experience they might have watching it performed. This cannot be said of the screenplay, for a film depends greatly on visual and other nonverbal elements that cannot easily be expressed in written form. The screenplay requires so much "filling in" by our imagination that we cannot really approximate the experience of the film by simply reading it, and reading the screenplay will be worthwhile only if we have already seen the film. Thus, most screenplays are not really published to be read, but rather to be remembered.

Still, film should not be ignored simply because it is less handy to study. And the fact that we do not generally "read" films does not mean we should ignore the principles of literary or dramatic analysis when we see a film. Literature and films do share many elements, and though they are different mediums, they communicate many things in similar ways. Perceptive film analysis is built on the same principles used in literary analysis, and if we apply what we have learned in the study of literature to our analysis of films, we will be far ahead of those who do not. Therefore, before we turn to the unique elements of film, we need to look into those elements that film shares with fiction and drama.

Dividing film into its various elements for analysis is a somewhat artificial process, for the elements of any art form never exist in isolation. It is impossible, for example, to isolate plot from character: Events influence people, and people influence events; the two are always closely interwoven in any fictional, dramatic, or cinematic work. Though it is somewhat artificial to consider these elements separately, the analytical method uses such a fragmenting technique for ease and convenience. But it does so with the assumption that we can study these elements in isolation without losing sight of their interdependence or their relationship to the whole.

THE ELEMENTS OF A GOOD STORY

What makes a good story? Any answer to this question is bound to be subjective; however, some general observations might be made that will apply to a large variety of film narratives.

A Good Story Is Unified in Plot

As mentioned before, the structured film is one that has some broad underlying purpose or is unified around a central theme. Regardless of the nature of its theme, whether its focus is on plot, emotional effect, character, style or texture, or idea, the fictional film generally has a plot or story line that contributes to the development of that theme. Therefore the plot and the events, conflicts, and characters that constitute it must be carefully selected and arranged in terms of their relationship to the theme.

A unified plot or story line focuses on a single thread of continuous action, where one event leads to another naturally and logically. Usually a strong cause and effect relationship exists between these events, and the outcome is made to seem, if not inevitable, at least probable. In a tightly unified plot, nothing can be transposed or removed without significantly affecting or altering the whole.

Thus, every event grows naturally out of the plot, and the conflict must be resolved by elements or agents present in and prepared for in the plot itself. A unified plot does not introduce out of thin air some kind of chance, coincidental, or miraculous happening, or some powerful superhuman force that swoops down out of nowhere to save the day. Consider, for example, this hypothetical scene from a western. A wagon train is attacked by a horde of Indians. Doom seems certain. Suddenly, out of nowhere, appears a battalion of U.S. Cavalry troops—who just happened to be passing by on maneuvers, a hundred miles from the fort. Although such accidental, chance occurrences happen in real life, we reject them in fiction. The arrival of the cavalry to save the settlers would

|3.1|

|3.2|

|3.3|

The Way Things Really Are: *High Noon* [3.1], *Urban Cowboy* [3.2], and *Silkwood* [3.3] are believable because they conform to our own experiences.

be acceptable if a reason for it were established earlier in the plot (if, for example, a rider had been sent to bring them).

Although plot unity as described above is a general requirement, exceptions do exist. In the film whose focus is the clear delineation of a single unique character, unity of action and cause and effect relationships between events are not so important. In fact, such plots may even be episodic (that is, composed of events that bear no direct relationship to each other), for the unity in such films comes from how well each event contributes to our understanding of the character being developed, rather than from the interrelationships of the events themselves.

A Good Story Is Believable

To really become involved in a story, we must be convinced that it is true. But "truth" is a relative term, and the filmmaker can create truth in a variety of ways.

1. Externally observable truths—"the way things really are." The most obvious and common kind of truth in a film story is the approximation of life "as it is." To borrow Aristotle's phrase, these are such stories as "might occur and have the capability of occurring in accordance with the laws of probability or necessity." This kind of truth is based on overwhelming evidence in the world around us, and it may not always be a pleasant truth. Human beings are flawed creatures; married couples don't always live happily ever after and tragic accidents, serious illnesses, and great misfortunes often befall people who don't seem to deserve them. But we accept such truths because they conform to our own experience with the way life really is (Figs. 3.1, 3.2, and 3.3).

2. Internal truths of human nature—"the way things are supposed to be." Another set of truths seems true to us because we want to or need to believe in them. Some of the greatest film classics do not even pretend to represent the actualities of real life; instead they offer a fairy-tale or happily-ever-after ending. The good guy always wins, and true love conquers all. But in a very special way, these stories are also believable, or at least can be made to seem so, because they contain what might be called "internal truths," beliefs in things that aren't really observable, but that seem true to us because we want or need them to be. Indeed, the concept of poetic justice (the idea that virtue will be rewarded and evil punished) serves as an example of such an internal truth. We seldom question poetic justice in a story simply because it is "the way things are supposed to be." Thus many film stories are convincing because they conform to an inner truth, and satisfy a human need to believe. Of course, such truths can ring very false to those who do not want or need to believe them (Figs. 3.4, 3.5, and 3.6).

3. Artistic semblance of truth—"the way things never were and never will be." Filmmakers are also capable of creating a special kind of truth. With their artistry, technical skills, and special effects, they can create an incredible imaginary world on the screen that, for the duration of the film, seems totally believable. In such films, truth depends on the early and thoroughly convincing establishment of a strange or fantastic environment, sense of another time, or unusual characters, so that we are caught up in the film's overall spirit, mood, and atmosphere. If the filmmaker is skillful at creating this "semblance of truth," we make an agreement to willingly suspend our disbelief, and leave our skepticism and our rational faculties behind as we enter the film's imaginary world. If the fictional reality is successfully established, we may think to ourselves, "Yes, in such a situation almost anything can happen." By communicating this pervasive and real sense of an unusual situation or environment, filmmakers in effect create a new set of ground rules by which we judge reality. And for the brief period of an hour or two, we can believe thoroughly in the "truth" of *Rosemary's Baby, The Day the Earth Stood Still, King Kong, Mary Poppins, The Wizard of Oz,* or *E.T.* (Figs. 3.7, 3.8, and 3.9).

Thus the plausibility of a story depends on at least three separate factors: the objective, external, and observable laws of probability and necessity; the subjective, irrational, and emotional inner truths of human nature; and the semblance of truth created by the filmmaker's convincing art. Although all these kinds of truths may be present in the same film, usually one kind of truth will be central to the film's overall structure. The other truths may contribute, but will play supporting roles only.

|3.4|

|3.5|

|3.6|
The Way Things Are Supposed to Be: We also "believe" in movies that present images of the world as we might like it to be, such as *Flashdance* [3.4], *Rocky III* [3.5], and *The Black Stallion* [3.6].

A Good Story Is Interesting

An extremely important requirement of a good story is that it capture and hold our interest. Of course, a story can be interesting in many ways, and few if any stories will have equal appeal to all filmgoers, for whether a story is interesting or boring is, to a great extent, a subjective matter dependent on the eye of the

|3.7|

The Way Things Never Were and Never Will Be: By using their special brand of artistry, filmmakers can create an imaginary world on the screen that makes us willingly accept incredible settings, characters, and events in such films as *Battle for the Planet of the Apes* [3.7], *Poltergeist* [3.8], and *Nosferatu the Vampire* [3.9].

|3.8|

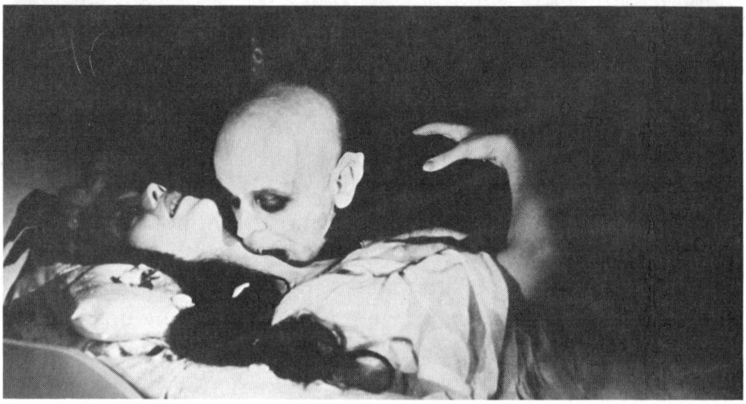

|3.9|

beholder. Some of us may be interested only in a fast-paced action-adventure film, others may be bored by anything without a romantic love interest at its center. Still others may be indifferent to any story that lacks deep philosophical significance.

But regardless of what we expect from a motion picture, whether it be the relaxation gained from simply being entertained or a clue to understanding the universe, we never go to the movies to be bored. Our tolerance for boredom seems very limited: A film may shock us, frustrate us, puzzle us, or even offend us, but it must *never* bore us. Thus we fully expect the filmmaker to heighten the film's reality by doing away with all the irrelevant and distracting details. Why should we pay to watch the dull, the monotonous, or the routine when life provides them absolutely free of charge?

Even the Italian neorealist directors, who stress everyday reality in their films and deny the validity of "invented" stories, argue that their particular brand of everyday reality is not boring because of

3.10 Suspense: Suspense is not always a matter of life and death. There may be a very exciting kind of suspense involved in wondering how two very different characters are going to work out what seem to be irreconcilable differences, as is the case with the characters played by Walter Matthau and Jill Clayburgh in *First Monday in October.*

its complex echoes and implications. As Cesare Zavattini puts it, "Give us whatever 'fact' you like, and we will disembowel it, make it something worth watching."[1] To most of us, the terms "worth watching" and "interesting" are synonymous.

SUSPENSE

To capture and maintain our interest, the filmmaker employs a multitude of devices and techniques, most of which are in some way related to what we call *suspense*. These elements create a state of heightened interest by exciting our curiosity, usually by foreshadowing or hinting at the outcome. By withholding bits of information that would answer the dramatic questions raised by the story, and by floating some unanswered question just beyond our reach like a carrot dangling before a donkey, the filmmaker provides a motive force to keep us constantly moving with the story's flow (Fig. 3.10).

ACTION

If a story is to be interesting at all, it must contain some elements of action. Stories are never static; some sort of action or change is essential if the story is to be worth telling. Action, of course, is not limited to physical activities such as fights, chases, duels, or great

1. "Some Ideas on the Cinema." *Sight and Sound,* October 1953, p. 64.

|3.11| External Action: The exciting action in *Blue Thunder* requires little thought to appreciate. We are kept on the edge of our chairs throughout and, by the film's end, totally exhausted with the constant fast-paced tension.

|3.12| Internal Action: Although there is little real physical action in *Manhattan*, the internal action occurring within the mind of Isaac Davis (Woody Allen) is extremely interesting and exciting.

battles. It may also be internal, psychological, or emotional. In films such as *Star Wars* and *The Road Warrior*, the action is external and physical; in *Diner* and *Manhattan*, on the other hand, the action occurs within the mind and the emotions of the characters. Both sorts of films have movement and change; neither is static. The interest created by the exciting action in *The Road Warrior* is obvious, and needs no explanation. But the action within a human being is not so obvious. Nothing very extraordinary *happens* in *Diner*, but what takes place in the hearts and minds of its characters is extremely interesting and exciting.

Internal action stories naturally require more concentration from the viewer, and they are more difficult to treat cinematically. But they are worthwhile subjects for film and can be as interesting and exciting as those films that stress external and physical action (Figs. 3.11 and 3.12).

A Good Story Is Both Simple and Complex

A good film story must be simple enough so that it can be expressed and unified cinematically. Poe's idea that a short story should be capable of being read in a single sitting also applies to the film. Experiencing a film is less tiring than reading a book, and our "single sitting" for the film may be a maximum of, say, two hours. Beyond that time limit, only the greatest films can prevent us from becoming restless or inattentive. Thus the story's action or theme must usually be compressed into a unified dramatic structure that requires about two hours to unfold. In most cases, a limited, simple theme, such as that in *Manhattan*, which focuses on a small slice of one person's life, is better suited for the cinema than a story that spans the ages in search of a timeless theme, as D. W. Griffith attempted in *Intolerance*. Generally, a story should be simple enough to be told in the time period allotted for its telling.

However, within these limits, a good story must also have some complexity, at least enough to sustain our interest. And although a good story may hint at the eventual outcome, it must also provide some surprises, or at least be subtle enough to prevent the viewer from predicting the outcome midway through the film. Thus, a good story usually withholds something about its conclusion or significance until the very end.

But new elements introduced into the plot at the very end may make us question the legitimacy of the surprise ending, especially if such elements bring about an almost miraculous conclusion to the story or make too much use of coincidence or chance. On the other hand, a surprise ending can be powerful and legitimate when it is prepared for by the plot, even when the plot elements and the chain of cause and effect leading up to it escape our conscious attention. The important thing is that the viewer never feel hoodwinked, fooled, or cheated by a surprise ending (as happens in the surprise endings of DePalma's *Carrie* and *Dressed to Kill*). Instead the viewer should gain insight by means of the ending, which occurs only when the surprise ending carries out tendencies established earlier in the story. A good plot is complex enough to keep us in doubt, but simple enough so that the seeds of the outcome can all be planted.

The filmmaker's communication techniques must also be a proper blend of simplicity and complexity. Filmmakers must communicate some things simply, clearly, and directly, so that they are clear to all viewers. But to challenge the minds and eyes of the most perceptive viewers, they must also communicate through implication and suggestion, leaving some things open to interpretation. Some viewers, of course, will be bored by films that are too complex, that make too much use of implication or suggestion. Other viewers—those who prefer an intellectual challenge—will not be interested in films that are too direct and simple. Thus the filmmaker must please both those who don't

| 3.13 | Complexity: The levels of confusion created by the constant jumping back and forth between illusion and reality in *The Stunt Man* may stimulate some viewers, but may be too complex to provide the relaxing entertainment expected by others.

| 3.14 | Simplicity: The broad slapstick comedy and the frantic car and truck chases in *Smokey and the Bandit II* may entertain viewers looking for escapist entertainment, but bore others who demand more depth and complexity.

appreciate films they cannot easily understand and those who reject films they understand all too easily (Figs. 3.13 and 3.14).

Filmgoers' views of life will also greatly influence their attitudes toward a film's complexity or simplicity. If they see life itself as complex and ambiguous, they will demand that kind of complexity and ambiguity in the films they see. Thus, viewers may reject the escapist film because it falsifies the nature of existence by making it seem too easy, too neat, too pat. Other viewers may reject the complex view of life presented in realistic or naturalistic films for the opposite reason—because it is too full of ambiguities, too complex, or because it does not conform to the inner subjective "truth" of life—life as we would like it to be.

A Good Story Uses Restraint in Handling Emotional Material

A strong emotional element or effect is present in almost any story, and film is capable of manipulating our emotions. But this manipulation must be honest and appropriate to the story. Usually we reject as "sentimental" films that overuse emotional material. In such films, we might even laugh when we're supposed to cry. So the filmmaker must exercise great restraint.

Reactions to emotional material, of course, depend on the individual viewer. One viewer may consider the film *Love Story* a beautifully touching and poignant experience, while another may scoff and call it "sentimental trash." The difference often lies in the viewers themselves. The first viewer probably responded fully to the film, allowing himself to be manipulated by its emotional effects without considering the filmmaker dishonest. The second viewer, though, probably felt that the film unfairly attempted to manipulate her emotions and responded by rejecting the whole film.

When the emotional material in a film is understated, however, there is little danger of offending. In understatement the filmmaker consciously downplays the emotional material by giving it less emphasis than the situation would seem to call for. In *To Kill a Mockingbird,* Atticus Finch (Gregory Peck) uses a simple phrase to thank the boogeyman, Arthur "Boo" Radley (Robert Duvall), for saving the lives of Scout and Jem: "Thank you, Arthur . . . for my children." The effect of understatement is demonstrated here by the tremendous emotional weight carried by the simple phrase "thank you," which we often use for the most trivial favors. The normally insignificant phrase takes on great significance, and we are moved by what is *not* said. The voice-over narration from the same film offers another example of understatement:

> Neighbors bring food with death and flowers with sickness and little things in between. Boo was our neighbor. He gave us two soap dolls, a broken watch and chain, a pair of good luck pennies, and our lives.

A wide variety of elements and techniques influence our overall emotional response to a film. Both understatement and the overuse of emotional material are reflected in the way the plot is structured, in the dialogue and the acting, and in the visual effects. But the filmmaker's approach to presenting emotional material is perhaps most evident in the musical score, which can communicate on a purely emotional level and thus reflects accurately the peaks and valleys of emotional emphasis and understatement.

QUESTIONS

On Story Elements

How does the film stack up against the five characteristics of a good story?

1. How well is it unified in plot or story line?

2. What makes the story believable? Pick out specific scenes to illustrate what kinds of truth are stressed by film: (a) objective truth, which follows the observable laws of probability and necessity, (b) subjective, irrational, and emotional inner truths of human nature, or (c) the semblance of truth created by the filmmaker?

3. What makes the film interesting? Where are its high points, its dead spots? What causes you to be bored by the film as a whole or by certain parts?

4. Is the film a proper blend of simplicity and complexity?
   a. How well is the story suited in length to the limits of the medium?
   b. Is the film a simple "formula" that allows you to predict the outcome at the halfway point, or does it effectively maintain suspense until the very end? If the ending is shocking or surprising, how does it carry out the tendencies of the earlier parts of the story?
   c. Where in the film are implication and suggestion effectively employed? Where is the film simple and direct?
   d. Is the view of life reflected by the story simple or complex? What factors influenced your answer?

5. How honest and sincere is the film in its handling of emotional material? Where are the emotional effects overdone? Where is understatement used?

DRAMATIC STRUCTURE

The art of storytelling, as practiced in the short story, novel, drama, or film, has always depended on a strong dramatic structure—that is, the arrangement of parts aesthetically and logically in order to achieve the maximum emotional, intellectual, or dramatic impact. Two structural patterns are followed by so many fictional films that they deserve brief treatment here. Both patterns contain the same elements: *exposition, complication, climax,* and *resolution* or *denouement.* These two types of dramatic structures differ only in the arrangement of these elements, and can be differentiated by the way they begin.

1. Expository or chronological beginning. The first part of the story, which is called the *exposition,* introduces the characters, shows some of their interrelationships, and places them within a believable time and place. The next section, in which a conflict begins and grows in clarity, intensity, and importance, is called the *complication*. Since dramatic tension and suspense are created and maintained during the complication, this section is usually longer than the others. When the complication has reached its point of maximum tension, the two forces in opposition confront each other at a high point of physical or emotional action called the *climax*. At the climax, the conflict is resolved and there follows a brief period of calm called a *denouement,* in which a state of relative equilibrium returns (Fig. 3.15).

2. In medias res beginning. *In medias res* is a Latin phrase meaning "in the midst of the action," and refers to a method of beginning a story that has enjoyed immense popularity since the time of Homer. (Both his *Iliad* and *Odyssey* begin in this fashion.) Since capturing the audience's interest at an early stage is always critical, many films are structured to begin *in medias res;* that is, opening with an exciting incident that actually happens *after* the complication has developed. Thus a state of dramatic tension exists and interest is assured from the beginning. The necessary expository information is filled in later as the situation permits, through such means as dialogue (characters talking about the situation or events that led to the complication) or flashbacks (actual filmed sequences that go back in time to provide expository material). In this manner exposition can be built up gradually and

| 3.15 | Expository Beginning: In *Greystoke: The Legend of Tarzan,* the story begins in England with preparations for the ill-fated ocean voyage of Tarzan's parents, before Tarzan is even born. It then continues in true chronological order until the film's end. Pictured is the boy Tarzan (Daniel Potts) with his friend Droopy Ears.

|3.16| *In Medias Res* Beginning: *Ordinary People* begins after the event that causes all the tension and conflict (the death of Bucky) has already occurred, and that major event is revealed later in fragmentary bits as dreams and memory flashbacks.

spread throughout the film instead of being carefully and completely established at the beginning, before dramatic interest starts to build (Fig. 3.16).

The following two passages from John Steinbeck's short story "Flight"[2] are used to illustrate the difference between the expository or chronological beginning and the *in medias res* beginning when visualized in cinematic form.

First, consider how an expository or chronological beginning might be developed from this passage:

> About fifteen miles below Monterey, on the wild coast, the Torres family had their farm, a few sloping acres above a cliff that dropped to the brown reefs and to the hissing white waters of the ocean. Behind the farm the stone mountains stood up against the sky. The farm buildings huddled like little clinging aphids on the mountain skirts, crouched low to the ground as though the wind might blow them into the sea. The little shack, the rattling, rotting barn were gray-bitten with sea salt, beaten by the damp wind until they had taken on the color of the granite hills. Two horses, a red cow and a red calf, half a dozen pigs and a flock of lean, multi-colored chickens stocked the place. A little corn was raised on the sterile slope, and it grew short and thick under the wind, and all the cobs formed on the landward sides of the stalks.
>
> Mama Torres, a lean dry woman with ancient eyes, had ruled the farm for ten years, ever since her husband tripped over a stone in the field one day and fell full length on a rattlesnake. When one is bitten on the chest there is not much that can be done.
>
> Mama Torres and three children, two undersized black ones of twelve and fourteen, Emilio and Rosy, whom Mama kept fishing on the rocks below the farm when the sea was kind and when the truant officer was in some distant part of Monterey County. And there was Pepé, the tall, smiling son of nineteen, a gentle, affectionate boy, but very lazy. Pepé had a tall head, pointed on the top, and from its peak, coarse black hair grew down like a thatch all around. Over his smiling little eyes Mama cut a straight bang so he could see. Pepé had sharp Indian cheek bones and an eagle nose, but his mouth was as sweet and shapely as a girl's mouth, and his chin was fragile and chiseled. He was loose and gangling, all legs and feet and wrists, and he was very lazy. Mama thought him fine and brave, but she never told him so. She said, "Some lazy cow must have got into thy father's family, else how could I have a son like thee." And she said, "When I carried thee, a sneaking lazy coyote came out of the brush and looked at me one day. That must have made thee so."

2. From "Flight" in *The Long Valley* by John Steinbeck. Copyright 1938 by John Steinbeck. Copyright © renewed 1966 by John Steinbeck. All excerpts are reprinted by permission of Viking Penguin, Inc.

In the film version of this expository or chronological beginning, the camera would first show the Torres family farm from a distance, then move gradually closer to show us the children playing near the house, with Mama Torres perhaps standing in the doorway, talking to herself as she looks out toward Pepé and the other children. A beginning of this sort would have no dramatic tension but would effectively establish the setting, introduce the major characters, and show something of their interrelationships.

In the *in medias res* beginning, the filmmaker might choose the scene described in the following paragraph, in which the dramatic tension is already clearly established and the major action of the plot is already under way.

> Pepé started up, listening. His horse had whinnied. The moon was just slipping behind the western ridge, leaving the valley in darkness behind it. Pepé sat tensely gripping his rifle. From far up the trail he heard an answering whinny and the crash of shod hooves on the broken rock. He jumped to his feet, ran to his horse and led it under the trees. He threw on the saddle and cinched it tight for the steep trail, caught the unwilling head and forced the bit into the mouth. He felt the saddle to make sure the water bag and the sack of jerky were there. Then he mounted and turned up the hill.

If the film started in this way, the relationship between Pepé and his mother would have to be established later through a flashback. But providing exposition is not the only function of flashback. Few stories are structured in a pure, straight chronological sequence, and divergence from strict chronological order is very common in film, where the visual flashback gives it great structural flexibility. Through use of the flashback, the filmmaker can bring us information as he or she desires, when it is most dramatically appropriate and powerful, or when it will most effectively illuminate the theme. (*Flash-forwards*, where the scene jumps from the present into the future, has been tried in such films as *Easy Rider* and *They Shoot Horses, Don't They?*, although it is doubtful whether this device will ever gain widespread acceptance.) As long as coherence is maintained so that a clear sense of the relationships between one scene and another is established, the director can violate strict chronological order at will.

Sometimes, however, a director may purposely try to confuse the time sequence. In the haunting and mystifying *Last Year at Marienbad*, Resnais seemed determined to keep us wondering whether the scene we are watching is taking place in the present (this year), past (last year) or, in fact, whether it really took place at all.

QUESTIONS

On Dramatic Structure

1. Does the film use the expository (chronological) or the *in medias res* beginning? If it begins with expository material, does it capture your interest quickly enough, or would a beginning "in the midst of the action" be better? At what point in the story could an *in medias res* beginning start?
2. If flashbacks are used, what is their purpose and how effective are they?

SYMBOLISM

In most general terms, whether in a work of art or in everyday communications of the most ordinary sort, a symbol is something that stands for something else. It communicates that "something else" by triggering, stimulating, or arousing previously associated ideas in the mind of the person perceiving the symbol.[3] All forms of human communication involve the use of symbols, and we clearly understand their meaning if we already possess the ideas or concepts associated with or built into the symbol. For example, a traffic light communicates its message to us symbolically. When the light turns green or red, we do more than observe with interest the change from one color to another; we respond to the symbolic message it gives us. To a cavewoman who had never seen a traffic light, however, the change in color would have no symbolic meaning, for she would lack the built-in associations with those colors that our experience in modern society has provided us. It would, therefore, be very dangerous for the cavewoman to walk around in the heart of a busy city without some awareness of the symbolic importance of traffic signals.

It is equally dangerous for a student to approach a work of art without some understanding of the nature, function, and importance of its symbols. The things that take on symbolic meaning in a film are almost unlimited in range. In many stories, the setting

3. To avoid complex distinctions between terms, the words *symbol* and *simile* are sometimes used in this book when the term *metaphor* may be more technically correct.

takes on strong symbolic overtones. Characters are often used symbolically, and once characters become symbolic, the conflicts in which they take part become symbolic also. Therefore, it is essential that we become consciously aware of the special nature of symbolic communication in film.

In any story form, a symbol is something concrete (a particular object, image, person, sound, event, or place) that stands for, suggests, or triggers a complex of ideas, attitudes, or feelings and thus acquires significance beyond itself. A symbol therefore is a special kind of energized communication unit, which functions somewhat like a storage battery. Once a symbol is "charged" with a set of associations (ideas, attitudes, or feelings), it is capable of storing those associations and communicating them any time it is used.

Universal and Natural Symbols

Universal symbols are "precharged"—ready-made symbols that are already infused with values and associations understood by most of the people in a given culture. By using objects, images, or persons that automatically evoke many complex associations, filmmakers save themselves the job of creating each of the associated attitudes and feelings within the context of their films. They need only to use these symbols appropriately to make full use of their communication potential. Thus such symbols as the American flag (triggering the complex set of feelings and values that we associate with America), or the cross (evoking a variety of values and feelings associated with Christianity), can be used effectively as symbols for a broad audience. Reactions would vary according to the viewer's attitudes toward the ideas represented, but all people from the same culture would get the general symbolic message.

Many universal symbols are charged with their meanings externally—through past associations with people, events, places, or ideas—rather than through their own inherent characteristics. For example, there is nothing inherent in the shape of a cross to suggest Christianity; rather the religious values and ideas attached to the crucifixion of Christ over the ages have given the cross its symbolic meaning. On the other hand, some objects have natural or inherent qualities that make them particularly well-fitted as symbols. A buzzard, for example, may be used as a symbol of death, without the need to establish its symbolic value. This, of course, is partly due to its appearance. Buzzards are black, a color associated with death, but the habits of the buzzard are also important. A buzzard is a scavenger, a creature that feeds only on dead flesh, and will not even come near a living creature. Probably of even greater significance is a buzzard's *visibility* as a symbol: By soaring in long, lazy circles over an area where something is dead or dying, the buzzard signals the presence of death. Thus, buzzards communicate the idea of death indirectly but clearly, so an observer need not see the dead object itself to know that death is present. The habits or life-styles of hawks and doves are equally significant in determining their symbolic meanings.

Creating Symbolic Meanings

In many cases, however, filmmakers cannot depend on precharged or ready-made symbols, but must create symbols by charging them with meaning derived from the context of the film itself. This is done by first loading a concrete object or image with an electrical charge of associations, feelings, and attitudes, and then employing the now charged symbol to evoke these associations. Consider how John Steinbeck develops the symbolic value of a knife in his story "Flight":

> Pepé smiled sheepishly and stabbed at the ground with his knife to keep the blade sharp and free from rust. It was his inheritance, that knife, his father's knife. The long heavy blade folded back into the block handle. There was a button on the handle. When Pepé pressed the button, the blade leaped out ready for use. The knife was with Pepé always, for it had been his father's knife.

In charging an object with symbolic value, storytellers have a dual purpose. First, they want to expand the meaning of the symbolic object in order to communicate meanings, feelings, and ideas, and second, they want to make it clear that the object is being treated symbolically. Thus many of the methods used to charge an object symbolically also serve as clues that the object is taking on symbolic value (Figs. 3.17 and 3.18). There are four primary methods of charging symbols to which we must pay special attention:

1. Through repetition. Perhaps the most obvious means of charging an object is by drawing attention to it more often than a simple surface object might seem to deserve. Through such repetition, the object gains in significance and symbolic power with each appearance (Fig. 3.19).

|3.17| **|3.18|**

Charging the Symbol: Two symbolic representations of death use completely different qualities to build the symbolic meaning. In *The Seventh Seal* [3.17], Ingmar Bergman uses a traditional image for portraying death: a grim reaper carrying a scythe, a pale-faced, mysterious man in a black cloak and hood. In *All That Jazz* [3.18], however, Bob Fosse uses a beautiful, seductive woman (Jessica Lange) dressed in white to express the same idea.

|3.19| Repeated Images of Symbolic Separation: In this scene from *Shane,* Jean Arthur, as the farmer's wife Marion, stands inside the house while Alan Ladd, as Shane, the ex-gunfighter who is now the farmer's hired hand, stands outside looking in the window. This symbolic separation is repeated visually throughout the film—Shane is always an outsider, present with, but not part of, the warm family circle or the close-knit group of farmers. On several occasions, Shane is framed through an open doorway, looking in on a warm family scene inside, or sitting off to the side by himself in a meeting of the farmers. The scene shown here has additional levels of meaning: Shane and Marion have a strong but unspoken mutual attraction, but keep a "wall" up between themselves out of basic human decency and their mutual love and respect for the farmer (Van Heflin).

2. Through value placed on an object by a character. An object is also charged symbolically when a particular character places value and importance on it. By showing extraordinary concern for an object (as in Pepé's treatment of the knife, or in the Captain's concern for his palm tree in *Mister Roberts*), or by repeatedly mentioning it in the dialogue, the character indicates that an object or idea has more than ordinary significance. Symbols charged in this way may be of relatively minor importance, functioning only to offer us symbolic insight into the character. Or they may have major significance to the overall dramatic structure, as illustrated by the famous "Rosebud" symbol in *Citizen Kane*.

3. Through context in which the object or image appears. Sometimes an object or image takes on symbolic power simply through its placement in the film, and its symbolic charge is built up through associations created (1) by its relationship to other visual objects in the same frame, (2) by a relationship established by the editorial juxtaposition of one shot with another, or (3) when it occupies an important place in the film's structure.

One particular symbolic image in the film version of Tennessee Williams' play *Suddenly Last Summer*—the Venus flytrap—illustrates all three methods of charging an image by context. The Venus flytrap is a large, white flowered plant whose leaves have two hinged blades. When an insect enters the space between them, the blades close like a mouth on it, trapping the insect inside. The plant then "feeds" on the insect. Once the nature of the plant and its feeding habits are made clear, the Venus flytrap is used to suggest or represent a major idea in the play—the carnivorousness or cannibalism of its characters. The plant's nature is explained by Mrs. Venable (played by Katherine Hepburn), and it is seen to occupy a position near her chair so they share the same visual frame. As Mrs. Venable talks about her dead son Sebastian, we begin to see the relationship between the woman and the plant, for her conversation reveals her to be a "cannibal," savagely feeding on and deriving her nourishment from the memory of her dead son.

The same effect could be achieved through editorial juxtaposition by cutting immediately from a close-up of Mrs. Venable's mouth as she drones on about her son to a close-up of the "jaws" of her Venus flytrap snapping shut on an unsuspecting insect.

Even if it were not further charged within the context of the film, this image could still function effectively as a symbol if its symbolic function were made clear by the importance of its position within the film's overall structure. Consider, for example, how the image might be used only at the beginning and the end of the film. As the film begins, a close-up of the Venus flytrap serves as a background to the titles. Then, as the titles draw to a close, an insect lands on the flower and is trapped as the jaws close suddenly around it. The object is not seen again until the film's closing shot, where it appears again, seducing another insect into its folds. In this case we would be forced, by the sheer weight of its structural position, to consider the plant's symbolic function and its meaning to the film as a whole.

4. Through special visual, aural, or musical emphasis. Film has its own unique ways of charging and underscoring symbols and providing clues to the audience that an object is to be seen symbolically. For example, visual emphasis may be achieved through lingering close-ups, unusual camera angles, changes from sharp to soft focus, freeze frames, or lighting effects. Similar emphasis can be achieved through sound effects or use of the musical score. Individual natural sounds or musical refrains can become symbolic in their own right if complex associations are built into them by any of the three methods above.

Symbolic Patterns and Progressions

Although symbols may function singly without a clear relationship to other symbols, they often interact with other symbols in what might be called symbolic patterns. In such a case, the filmmaker will express the same idea through several symbols instead of relying on only one. The resulting symbolic pattern may even have a certain progression, so that the symbols grow in value or power as the film progresses.

An excellent example is the complex pattern of symbols that gradually builds up to the climax of *Suddenly Last Summer.*[4] The idea of a savage universe, inhabited by creatures who devour each other, is established by the symbol already described, the Venus flytrap, and its association with Mrs. Venable. From this point on, other symbolic images are used with the same meaning in a pattern of ever-increasing dramatic power. The next symbolic image in this pattern appears in Mrs. Venable's description of a sight she and Sebastian witnessed on the Encantadas:

4. Tennessee Williams, *Suddenly Last Summer.* Copyright © 1958 by Tennessee Williams. All rights reserved. Reprinted by permission of New Directions Publishing Corporation.

> Over a narrow black beach of the Encantadas as the just-hatched seaturtles scrambled out of the sandpits and started their race to the sea . . . To escape the flesh-eating birds that made the sky almost as black as the beach! . . . And the sand was all alive, all alive, as the hatched seaturtles made their dash for the sea, while the birds hovered and swooped to attack and hovered and—swooped to attack! They were diving down on the hatched seaturtles, turning them over to expose their soft undersides, tearing the undersides open and rending and eating their flesh. . . .

Having set up three symbols of the same idea (the flytrap, Mrs. Venable, and the birds) the playwright gives us a suggestion of their significance as Mrs. Venable continues her story:

> He spent the whole blazing equatorial day in the crow's nest of the schooner watching this thing on the beach until it was too dark to see it, and when he came down from the rigging he said, "Well, now I've seen Him," and he meant God . . . He meant that God shows a savage face to people and shouts some fierce things at them, it's all we see or hear of Him. . . .

The next image in the pattern occurs in Catherine's (Elizabeth Taylor) description of Sebastian himself, which adds strong overtones of homosexuality to the already shocking image:

> We were going to blonds, blonds were next on the menu . . . Cousin Sebastian said he was famished for blonds, he was fed up with the dark ones and was famished for blonds . . . that's how he talked about people, as if they were—items on a menu—"That one's delicious-looking, that one is appetizing," or "That one is not appetizing"—I think because he was nearly half-starved from living on pills and salads. . . .

As the next image in the pattern begins to develop, there is an effort to link the children that constitute this image with the earlier image of the carnivorous birds.

> There were naked children along the beach, a band of frightfully thin and dark naked children that looked like a flock of plucked birds, and they would come darting up to the barbed wire fence as if blown there by the wind, the hot white wind from the sea, all crying out "Pan, pan, pan!" . . . The word for bread, and they made gobbling voices with their little black mouths, stuffing their little black fists to their mouths and making those gobbling noises with frightful grins!

At the film's climax, the image of the carnivorous birds is repeated, but this time on a completely human level, which makes it even more shocking:

> Sebastian started to run and they all screamed at once and seemed to fly in the air, they outran him so quickly. I screamed. I heard Sebastian scream,

> he screamed just once before this flock of black plucked little birds that pursued him and overtook him halfway up the hill.
>
> I ran down . . . screaming out "Help" all the way, till— . . . Waiters, police, and others—ran out of the buildings and rushed back up the hill with me. When we got back to where my Cousin Sebastian had disappeared in the flock of featherless little black sparrows, he—he was lying naked as they had been naked against a white wall, and this you won't believe, nobody has believed it, nobody would believe it, nobody, nobody on earth could possibly believe it, and I don't blame them!—they had devoured parts of him.
>
> Torn or cut parts of him away with their hands or knives or maybe those jagged tin cans they made music with, they had torn bits of him away and stuffed them into those gobbling fierce little empty mouths of theirs. . . .

This incident takes place in a village whose name is also symbolic: Cabeza de Lobo, which means "Head of the Wolf," another savage and carnivorous image.

Thus by means of a complex pattern of symbols, the film makes a statement about the human condition. The idea of the earth as a savage jungle where creatures devour each other is made clear by a series of symbols: the Venus flytrap, the turtle-devouring birds, Sebastian's own "hungers," and the little human "cannibals" of Cabeza de Lobo. And Williams has arranged these symbols in order so that they become increasingly vivid, powerful, and shocking as the story unfolds.

Allegory

When an entire story is structured so that every object, event, and person has a corresponding symbolic meaning, the story is known as an *allegory*. In allegory, each symbolic meaning and abstraction is part of an interdependent system that tells a separate and complete story on a purely allegorical or figurative level.

A major problem with allegory is the difficulty of making both levels of meaning equally interesting. Often, so much importance is placed on the "symbolic story" that we lose interest in the "concrete story." The difficulty arises primarily from the fact that allegorical characters, to be effective as symbols, cannot have many unique and particular characteristics, for the more unique and particular the characters are, the less representative they can be. But these difficulties do not necessarily prevent allegory from being effective in cinematic form, as is evidenced by such excellent films as *Woman in the Dunes, Swept Away, Lord of the Flies,* and *The Seventh Seal* (Fig. 3.20).

| 3.20 | Allegory . . . Life as a Dance Marathon: Michael Sarrazin and Jane Fonda participate in an endless dance marathon representing the continuous struggle of life in *They Shoot Horses, Don't They?*

Complex or Ambiguous Symbols

Although filmmakers want to express their ideas clearly, they may not always want to express them too simply or too clearly. Thus, although some symbols may be very simple and clear, others may be complex and ambiguous. Such symbols can seldom be interpreted with one clear and certain meaning; there may be no single "right answer" to what a given symbol means, but several equally valid but different interpretations. This is not to say that a filmmaker using ambiguous symbols is deliberately trying to confuse us. The intention is usually to enrich or enhance the work through complexities.

Similes

Closely related to symbolism is the filmmaker's use of what might be called visual similes. Whereas a symbol stands for or represents something else, a film simile is a brief comparison that helps us understand or perceive one image better because of its similarity to another image. This is usually achieved through the editorial juxtaposition of two images in two successive shots. If, for example, the filmmaker wants us to react in a certain way to a group of old ladies in the midst of a gossip session, he or she may cut from a shot of the gossips talking together to a close-up of the heads of several frantically clucking chickens. Thus, in purely visual terms, the filmmaker has told us that the old ladies gossiping are like a bunch of old hens. On a more serious plane is an example of a simile taken from Eisenstein's *Strike,* where shots of workers being pursued and killed are alternated with simile shots of a butcher slaughtering a bull.

In both of the above examples, the secondary images are extrinsic, meaning that they have no place within the context of the scene itself but are imposed artificially into the scene by the filmmaker. In the realistic or naturalistic film, such extrinsic similes may seem forced, heavy-handed, or even ludicrous, destroying a sense of reality that may be very important to the film. On the other hand, comedy or fantasy films can use such images freely, and serious films that stress an interior or subjective viewpoint may also use them very effectively.

Intrinsic similes, which are taken directly from the context of the scene itself, are more natural and usually more subtle. *Apocalypse Now* contains an intrinsic simile very similar to the extrinsic simile described above from Eisenstein's *Strike*. While Captain Willard (Martin Sheen) is in the temple carrying out his assignment—"terminating Kurtz (Marlon Brando) with extreme prejudice"—the camera cuts to the courtyard, where a giant bull is axed in a gruesome ritual sacrifice.

In his short story "Flight," John Steinbeck employs a subtle use of a simile that can be easily visualized in cinematic terms. The story's central character, the young man Pepé, has killed a man with his knife in Monterey, and is attempting to escape the pursuing posse alone. The following scene takes place near Pepé's home on the morning after the event, and focuses on Pepé's little brother and sister:

> Emilio and Rosy stood wondering in the dawn. They heard Mama whimpering in the house. They went out to sit on the cliff above the ocean. They touched shoulders. "When did Pepé come to be a man?" Emilio asked.
>
> "Last night," said Rosy. "Last night in Monterey." The ocean clouds turned red with the sun that was behind the mountains.
>
> "We will have no breakfast," said Emilio. "Mama will not want to cook." Rosy did not answer him. "Where is Pepé gone?" he asked.
>
> Rosy looked around at him. She drew her knowledge from the quiet air. "He has gone on a journey. He will never come back."
>
> "Is he dead? Do you think he is dead?"
>
> Rosy looked back at the ocean again. A little steamer, drawing a line of smoke, sat on the edge of the horizon. "He is not dead," Rosy explained. "Not yet."

The similes here depend primarily on the juxtaposition of the dialogue and image. When the ocean clouds turn red, we see the similarity to "last night in Monterey," a night of bloodshed. The image of the little steamer, all alone in the vast ocean and about to disappear over the edge of the horizon, becomes an effective simile that helps us to understand Pepé's predicament and his chances. Yet because they are intrinsic similes, drawn naturally from the scene's environment, they have a quiet subtlety and an understated power that would be impossible to achieve with an extrinsic image.

The dramatic power and communicative effectiveness of any symbol or simile are dependent also on its originality and freshness. A tired and worn-out symbol can no longer carry "heavy" meanings and a simile that has become a cliché becomes a hindrance rather than a help. This fact causes many problems in watching older films, for many of the similes and symbols used seem to be clichés today, although they might actually have been fresh and original when the film was made.

QUESTIONS

On Symbolism

1. What symbols appear in the film and what do they represent?
2. What universal or natural symbols are employed? How effective are they?
3. Which symbols derive their meaning solely from their context in the film? How are they charged with symbolic value? (In other words, how do you know they are symbols, and how do you arrive at their meaning?)
4. How are the special capabilities of film (the image, the soundtrack, and the musical score) employed to charge symbols with their meaning?
5. Which symbols fit into a larger pattern or progression with other symbols in the film?
6. How are the major symbols related to the theme?
7. Is the story structured around its symbolic meanings to the extent that it can be called an allegory?
8. Which of the symbols' meanings are clear and simple? Which symbols are complex and ambiguous? What gives them this quality?
9. Are visual similes employed effectively? Are they primarily extrinsic (imposed artificially in the scene by editing) or intrinsic (a natural part of the setting)?
10. How fresh and original are the film's symbols and similes? If they seem clichéd or time-worn, where have you encountered them before?

CHARACTERIZATION

If we are not interested in a film's most human elements, its characters, there is little chance that we will be interested in the film as a whole. To be interesting, characters must seem real, understandable, and worth caring about. For the most part, the characters in a story are believable in the same way that the story is believable; in other words, they either conform to the laws of probability and necessity (by reflecting externally observable truths about human nature), conform to some inner truth (man as we want him to be), or they are made to seem real by the convincing art of the actor.

If the characters are truly believable, it is almost impossible to remain completely neutral toward them. We must respond toward them in some way: We may admire them for their heroic deeds and their nobility, or pity them for their failures. We may love them or identify with them for their ordinary human qualities. And we may laugh at them for their ignorance, or laugh *with them* because theirs is a human ignorance that we all share. Or, if our reaction to them is negative, we may detest them for their greed, their cruelty, their selfishness, and their underhanded methods. Or we may scorn them for their cowardice.

Characterization by Appearance

Because most film actors project certain qualities of character the minute they appear on the screen, characterization in film has a great deal to do with the casting selection. Although some actors may be versatile enough to project completely different qualities in different roles, with most actors this is not the case. Thus the minute we see actors on the screen we make certain assumptions about them based on their facial features, dress, physical build, mannerisms, and the way they move. A major aspect of film characterization is therefore revealed visually and instantaneously by our first visual impression of each character. This first impression may be proven erroneous as the story progresses, but it is certainly an important means of establishing character. Consider the immediate reactions we have to Michael Pollard and Robert Redford when they appear for the first time in *Little Fauss and Big Halsey,* or to Jack Palance as the gunfighter Wilson in *Shane* (Fig. 3.21).

| 3.21 | Characterization by Appearance: The strange physical appearance, the unusual "uniform," and the exaggerated facial expressions immediately characterize the Gyro Captain (Bruce Spence) when we first meet him in *The Road Warrior.*

Characterization Through Dialogue

Characters in a fictional film naturally reveal a great deal about themselves by what they say. But there is also a great deal revealed by how they say it. Their true thoughts, attitudes, and emotions can be revealed in subtle ways through their choice of words and through the stress, pitch, and pause patterns built into their speech. Actors' use of grammar, sentence structure, vocabulary, and particular dialects (if any) all reveal a great deal about their characters' social and economic level, educational background,

| 3.22 | Characterization Through Dialogue: The quaint, formal, archaic Quaker dialogue of Mattie (Kim Darby) and the rough-hewn but stilted dialogue of Rooster Cogburn (John Wayne) add an unusual quality to their characters in *True Grit.*

and mental processes. Therefore, we must develop a keen ear, attuned to the faintest and most subtle nuances of meaning revealed through the human voice—not only by listening carefully to what is said, but also to how it is said (Fig. 3.22).

Characterization Through External Action

Although a character's appearance is an important measure of his or her personality, appearances are often misleading. Perhaps the best reflections of character can be found in a person's actions. It must be assumed, of course, that real characters are more than mere instruments of the plot, and they do what they do for a purpose, out of motives that are consistent with their overall personality. Thus there should be a clear relationship between a character and his or her actions so that the actions grow naturally out of the character's personality. If the motivation for a character's action is clearly established, the character and the plot become so closely interwoven that they are impossible to separate, and every action that a person takes in some way reflects the quality of the particular personality. As Henry James stated in *The Art of Fiction,* "What is character but the determination of incident? What is incident but the reflection of character?"

Of course, some actions are more important in revealing character than others, as Aristotle implied when he said the "character is manifested in those things which an individual chooses or rejects." Even the most ordinary kind of choice can be revealing, for some kind of choice is involved in almost everything we do. Sometimes the most effective characterization is achieved not by the large actions in the film, but by the small, seemingly insignificant ones. For example, a fireman may demonstrate his courage by saving a child from a burning building, yet such an act may be only a performance of duty rather than any choice on his part. His essential character might be more clearly defined by risking his life to save a little girl's doll, since such an action would not be imposed upon him by duty, but by his own value judgment on the importance a doll might have to a little girl.

Characterization Through Internal Action

There is also an inner world of "action" that normally remains unseen and unheard by even the most careful observer/listener. Yet the dimension of human nature that this world embraces is often essential to a real understanding of a character. Inner action occurs within characters' minds and emotions, and consists of secret, unspoken thoughts, daydreams, aspirations, memories, fears, and fantasies. People's hopes, dreams, and aspirations can be as important to an understanding of their character as any real achievement, and their fears and insecurities can be more terrible to them than any real catastrophic failure. Thus, although Walter Mitty is a dull, drab, insignificant creature, scarcely worth caring about when judged purely by his external behavior, he becomes an exciting and interesting personality when we "read" his mind and see his daydreams.

The most obvious way in which the filmmaker shows us this inner reality is by taking us visually or aurally into the mind so that we see or hear the things that the character imagines, remembers, or thinks about. This may be achieved through a sustained interior view, or through fleeting glimpses revealed by means of similes. Consider, for example, how the self-consciousness of T. S. Eliot's J. Alfred Prufrock[5] might be characterized by a simile:

5. See T. S. Eliot, "The Love Song of J. Alfred Prufrock." In *Collected Poems 1909–1962*. New York: Harcourt Brace Jovanovich, 1963. The lines that follow are reprinted by permission of Harcourt Brace Jovanovich, Inc.

And I have known the eyes already, known them all—
The eyes that fix you in a formulated phrase,
And when I am formulated, sprawling on a pin,
When I am pinned and wriggling on the wall . . .

In this image, Prufrock compares himself to an insect, "pinned and wriggling on the wall," as he is classified and dissected by the eyes of people watching him at a social gathering. The filmmaker might handle this inner characterization in one of two ways. He may simply cut from a subjective viewpoint (Prufrock's view of the people watching him) to a shot showing the same people examining and classifying a real insect "pinned and wriggling" on the wall. Or he may choose to interpret the image more literally, but cutting to a shot picturing Prufrock himself, reduced to insect size and with a huge pin through his middle, wriggling on a wall, helpless as he is analyzed by the same people.

Another scene taken from Eliot's poem illustrates other methods of conveying the inner story:

And indeed there will be time
To wonder, "Do I dare?" and "Do I dare?"
Time to turn back and descend the stair,
With a bald spot in the middle of my hair—
(They will say: "How his hair is growing thin!")
My morning coat, my collar mounting firmly to the chin,
My necktie rich and modest, but asserted by a simple pin—
(They will say: "But how his arms and legs are thin!")

This scene might be translated into film as follows: Tight close-up of Prufrock's head and shoulders from behind, as he's starting slowly upstairs toward social gathering. Stops after a few steps. Close-up of hand nervously gripping railing. Close-up of feet on stairs, posed to step up but not stepping. Close-up of top of Prufrock's head, with long thin fingers trying to brush hair over bald spot. Imaginary voice on soundtrack, over real buzz of conversation from top of stairs: "How his hair is growing thin." Close-up of front torso of Prufrock, now moving upstairs. Hands straightening lapels of coat, smoothing necktie, checking tiepin. Imaginary voice on soundtrack, rising again over blur of conversation: "But how his arms and legs are thin."

In this visualization, an important aspect of Prufrock's inner character is captured through a combination of carefully chosen close-ups and a few brief aural "glimpses" of the voices in his mind's "ear." In addition to providing glimpses into the inner action by revealing the sounds and sights the character imagines he sees and hears, the filmmaker may employ tight close-ups on an unusually sensitive and expressive face (reaction shots), or may utilize the musical score for essentially the same purpose.

Characterization by Reactions of Other Characters

The way other characters view a person often serves as an excellent means of characterization. Sometimes, a great deal of information about a character will already be provided through such means before he or she first appears on the screen, as is the case in the opening scene from *Hud*. In this sequence Lonnie (Brandon DeWilde) is walking along the main street of the little Texas town at around 6:30 in the morning, looking for his uncle, Hud (Paul Newman). As Lonnie passes a beer joint along the way, the owner is out front, sweeping up the pieces of glass that used to be his large front window. Lonnie notices the broken window and observes, "You must have had quite a brawl in here last night." The owner replies, "I had *Hud* in here last night, that's what I had." The man's emphasis on the name "Hud" and his tone of voice in saying it clearly expresses that "Hud" is a synonym for "trouble." An effective bit of reactive characterization is also seen in *Shane*, as the gunfighter Wilson (Jack Palance), a personification of pure evil, walks into a saloon, empty except for a mangy dog curled up under a table. As Wilson enters, the dog puts his ears back and his tail between his legs and slinks fearfully out of the room.

Characterization by Contrast: Dramatic Foils

One of the most effective techniques of characterization is the use of contrasting characters whose behavior, attitudes, opinions, life-styles, physical appearances, and so on are opposite to those of the main characters. The effect is similar to that achieved by putting black and white together—the black appears blacker, and the white appears whiter. The tallest giant and the tiniest midget might be placed side by side at the carnival sideshow, and the filmmaker sometimes uses characters in much the same way. Consider, for example, the effective contrasts in the characters played by Andy Griffith and Don Knotts on the old "Andy Griffith Show." Griffith, as Sheriff Taylor, was tall, a little heavy, and projected

| 3.23 | Dramatic Foils: In the film version of Herman Melville's allegory of good and evil, *Billy Budd,* Terence Stamp as the sweet, naive, and innocent Billy contrasts sharply with the grim, satanic Master of Arms Claggart (played by Robert Ryan). The striking opposites in their characters are emphasized by their features, facial expressions, clothing, and voice qualities. Stamp is baby-faced, his features soft and smooth, his expressions sweet, almost effeminate, his eyes light blue, wide open, innocent. Ryan's face is mature, lined, the jaw and mouth strong and hard set; his expressions sour and cynical, his eyes dark, narrow, piercing, malevolent. Billy's fair complexion, blond (almost white) hair, and white shirt also contrast with Claggart's dark hair and clothing. Billy's voice is soft, sometimes melodious; Claggart's is deep, unctuous, cold.

a calm, self-confident, easygoing personality. Knotts, as Deputy Fife, was the exact opposite: short, skinny, insecure, and a perpetual bundle of nerves (Figs. 3.23, 3.24, and 3.25).

Characterization by Caricature and Leitmotif

In order to etch a character quickly and deeply on our minds and memories, actors often exaggerate or distort one or more dominant features or personality traits, a device called *caricature* (from the technique used in cartooning). In television's "M*A*S*H," the perpetual womanizing of Hawkeye Pierce (Alan Alda), and the eternal naiveté, innocence, and keen hearing of Radar O'Reilly

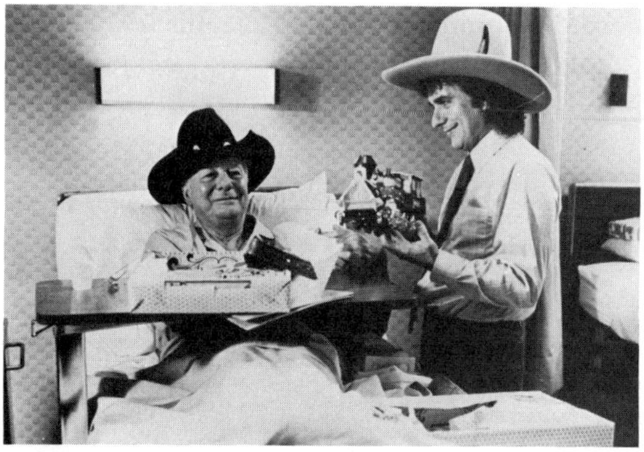

|3.24|

|3.25|

Dramatic Foils for Humor: Opposite character types are often brought together in a film for the purpose of intensifying humor, as is the case with the constantly inebriated playboy Arthur Bach (Dudley Moore) and his sober-sided valet Hobson (John Gielgud) in *Arthur* [3.24] and the strange "love story" of Harold (Bud Cort) and Maude (Ruth Gordon) in *Harold and Maude* [3.25]. As the ad for the movie described them: "Harold's 20 and in love with death . . . Maude's 80 and in love with life."

(Gary Burghoff) are examples of caricature, as are Felix Unger's obsession with neatness and Oscar Madison's messiness in "The Odd Couple." A physical feature, such as the way a person moves, may also be caricatured, as seen in Chester's exaggerated, stiff-legged limp on the old "Gunsmoke" series, or in Will Geer's half-limp shuffle as Grandpa in "The Waltons." Voice qualities and accents may also function in this way, as illustrated by the back-woods nasal voice employed by Ken Curtis as Festus Haigan on "Gunsmoke," and the New England aristocratic speech of Charles Ogden Stiers as Major Winchester on "M*A*S*H."

A similar means of characterization, called *leitmotif,* is the repetition of a single phrase or idea by a character until it becomes almost a trademark or theme song for that character. Because it essentially exaggerates and emphasizes (through repetition), such a device acts very much like caricature. Examples of *leitmotif* might be seen in the repeated Fred Astaire dance routines "performed" by the prosecuting attorney (Ted Danson) in *Body Heat,* or in the repeated phrase "sports fans" by Colonel Bull Meechum (Robert Duvall) in *The Great Santini.* One of the union henchmen in *On the Waterfront* adds dignity to his "yes man" role by constantly using the word "definitely." Perhaps Charles Dickens rates as the all-time master of both techniques. Recall Uriah Heep from

| 3.26 | Leitmotif: In *Popeye*, an obsession with hamburgers becomes a "theme song" for Wimpy (Paul Dooley).

David Copperfield, who continually wrings his hands (caricature) and says, "I'm so 'umble" (*leitmotif*). Modern films such as *Catch 22* still employ such techniques effectively, although not quite so extensively (Fig. 3.26).

Characterization Through Choice of Name

One important method of characterization often overlooked in film is the use of names possessing appropriate qualities of sound, meaning, or connotation to help describe the character, a technique known as *name-typing*. Since a great deal of thought goes into the choice of names, they should not be taken for granted, but should be carefully examined for the connotations they communicate. Some names, such as Dick Tracy, are rather obvious and clear connotations can be seen: Dick is a slang word for detective; Tracy derives from the fact that detectives "trace" criminals. Others may have only generalized connotations. Gomer Pyle has a small-town or country-hick ring to it, while Cornelius Witherspoon III has an opposite kind of sound. Certain sounds in names have generally unpleasant connotation. The "sn" sound, for example, evokes primarily unpleasant associations, since a large majority of the words beginning with that sound are unpleasant—snide, sneer, sneak, snake, snail, sneeze, snatch, snout, and snort are a few examples. Thus a name like Snerd or Snavely has an unpleasant ring automatically. Sometimes a name will draw its effect both from its meaning and its sound, such as Flem (read "phlegm") Snopes. In this vein, because of the connotative power of names, film actors' names are often changed to fit the image they project (Fig. 3.27). (John Wayne's real name was Marion Morrison; Cary Grant's was Archibald Leach.)

Stock Characters and Stereotypes

It is not essential, or even desirable, that every character in a film have a unique or memorable personality. *Stock characters* are minor characters whose actions are completely predictable. Typical of their job or profession (such as a bartender in a western), they are in the film simply because the situation demands their presence. Thus they serve more as a natural part of the setting than anything else, much as stage properties like a lamp or a chair might function in a play.

|3.27| Name Typing: Names in films are often chosen to suggest qualities of the character, as is the case here with Steve McQueen as Lieutenant Frank Bullitt in *Bullitt* (shown talking to the district attorney, played by Robert Vaughn).

Stereotypes, on the other hand, are characters of somewhat greater importance to the film who fit into preconceived patterns of behavior common to or representative of a large number of people, at least a large number of "fictional" people. Examples of stereotypes are the rich playboy, the western hero's sidekick, the pompous banker, and the old maid aunt. Our preconceived notions of such characters allow the director to economize greatly in treating them.

Static and Developing Characters

It is often useful to determine whether or not the most important characters in a film are static or developing characters. *Developing characters* are those who are deeply affected by the action of the plot (internal, external, or both) and who undergo some important change in personality, attitude, or outlook on life as a result of the action of the story. The change they undergo is an important, permanent one, not just a whimsical shift in attitude

| 3.28 |

| 3.29 |

Developing Characters: Some film characters undergo important character change or growth in the course of a film story, changes that alter their personalities, attitudes, or outlooks on life permanently, as is the case with T. S. Garp (Robin Williams) in *The World According to Garp* [3.28] and with Michael Corleone (Al Pacino) in *The Godfather* [3.29].

that will change back again tomorrow. The character will somehow never be the same person he or she was when the action of the film began. This change can be of any type, but is significant to the total makeup of the individual undergoing the change. Developing characters become sadder or wiser, or happier and more self-confident. They might gain some new awareness of life, or become more mature, more responsible, or more moral or less so. They may become simply more aware and knowing, and less innocent or naive. Examples of developing characters would include T. S. Garp (Robin Williams) in *The World According to Garp,* Tom Joad (Henry Fonda) in *The Grapes of Wrath,* and Michael Corleone (Al Pacino) in *The Godfather* (Figs. 3.28 and 3.29).

Static characters, as the term implies, remain essentially the same throughout the action of the film, either because the action does not have as important an effect on their lives (as might generally be the case with the hero of an action-adventure film), or simply because they are insensitive to the meaning of the action, and thus are not really capable of growth or change, as is the case with the title character in *Hud* (Paul Newman) and with Charles Foster Kane (Orson Welles) in *Citizen Kane* (Figs. 3.30 and 3.31).

Flat and Round Characters

Another important distinction is made between *flat characters* and *round characters. Flat characters* are two-dimensional, predictable characters who lack the complexity and unique qualities associated with what we call psychological depth. They often tend to be representative character types rather than real flesh and blood human beings. Unique, individualistic characters who have some degree of complexity and ambiguity and who cannot easily be categorized are called *round characters* or *three-dimensional characters.*

There is nothing inherently superior about round or developing characters over flat or static characters. The terms merely imply how different characters function within the framework of the story's theme or purpose. Static characters can be complex and vitally interesting without undergoing any character change. In fact, flat characters may function *better* than round characters when attention needs to be directed away from personalities and toward the meaning of the action, for example in an allegory such as *Lord of the Flies* or *Woman in the Dunes.*

|3.30|

|3.31|

Static Characters: Some film characters are not really capable of growth or change, and remain essentially unaffected by the important action of the film, as is the case with the Bo Derek character in *10* [3.30] and Tony Montana (Al Pacino) in *Scarface* [3.31].

QUESTIONS

On Characterization

1. Identify the central (most important) character or characters. Which characters are static and which ones are developing? Which characters are flat and which are round?
2. What methods of characterization are employed, and how effective are they?
3. Which of the characters are realistic, and which ones are exaggerated for effect?
4. What about each character's motivation? Which actions grow naturally out of the characters themselves, and where does the filmmaker seem to be manipulating the characters to fit the film's purpose?
5. What facets of the central character's personality are revealed by what he or she chooses or rejects?

6. Which minor characters function to bring out personality traits of the major characters, and what do these minor characters reveal?
7. Pick out bits of dialogue, images, or scenes that you consider especially effective in revealing character, and tell why they are effective.
8. Which characters function as stock characters and stereotypes, and how can the presence of each be justified in the film?

CONFLICT

In his essay "Why Do We Read Fiction?" Robert Penn Warren observes, "A story is not merely an image of life, but of life in motion . . . individual characters moving through their particular experiences to some end that we may accept as meaningful. And the experience that is characteristically presented in a story is that of facing a problem, a conflict. To put it bluntly: No conflict, no story." Conflict is the mainspring of every story, whether it be told on the printed page, on the stage, or on the screen. It is the element, then, that really captures our interest, that heightens the intensity of our experience, and that quickens our pulses and challenges our minds (Fig. 3.32).

|3.32| Conflict: The mainspring of practically any film is the dramatic tension created by scenes of human conflict like the one pictured here from *The Turning Point,* with Shirley MacLaine and Anne Bancroft.

Although there may be several conflicts within a story, some kind of *major conflict* at its core ultimately has the greatest importance to the story as a whole. This major conflict usually has some of the following characteristics, which can be helpful in identifying it.

To begin with, the major conflict is obviously of greater importance to the characters involved, and there is some worthwhile and perhaps lasting goal to be gained by the resolution of the conflict. Because it is highly significant to the characters, and because significant conflicts have important effects on people and events, the major conflict and its resolution almost always bring about some kind of important change, either in the people involved or in their overall situation.

The major conflict also has a reasonably high degree of complexity; it is not the sort of problem that can be quickly and easily resolved by an obvious or simple solution. Thus its outcome remains in doubt throughout the greater part of the film. The complexity of the struggle is also influenced by the fact that the forces that constitute the major conflict are nearly equal in strength, a fact that adds greatly to the dramatic tension and power of the work.

In some films, the major conflict and its resolution may also contribute greatly to the viewer's experience, for it is this conflict, and its resolution (or sometimes its lack of resolution), that does the most to clarify or illuminate the nature of human experience.

Types of Major Conflicts

Various types of major conflicts exist. Some may be primarily physical in nature, such as a fistfight or a shoot-out in a western. Others may be almost completely psychological, as is often the case in the films of Fellini or Bergman. In a large majority of films, however, the conflict has both physical and psychological implications, and it is often difficult to tell where one stops and the other begins. It is perhaps simpler and more meaningful to classify major conflicts under the broad headings of external and internal.

EXTERNAL CONFLICT

In its simplest form, an external conflict may consist of a personal and individual struggle between the central character and another character. On this level the conflict is nothing more than a contest of human wills in opposition or seeking similar goals, as might be illustrated by a prizefight, a duel, or even by two suitors seeking to win the affections of the same girl. Yet these basic and simple human conflicts have a tendency to be more complex than they first appear. Conflicts can seldom be isolated completely from other individuals, society as a whole, or the value systems of the individuals involved. Thus, they often grow into representative struggles between groups of people, different segments of society or social institutions, or different value systems.

Another type of external conflict is one that pits the central character or characters against some nonhuman force or agency, such as fate, the gods, the forces of nature, or the social system. Here the forces the characters face, though they may be man-made, are essentially nonhuman and impersonal. Jefferson Smith's (James Stewart) struggle against the political corruption and graft of the "Taylor machine" in *Mr. Smith Goes to Washington* is an example of this kind of external conflict, with a single individual pitted against "the system." A more physical type of external conflict might be seen in the legendary John Henry's pile-driving race with the steam hammer, where a human being struggles to prove his worth against the dehumanizing forces of technology.

INTERNAL CONFLICT

An internal conflict is one that centers on an internal, psychological conflict within the central character, so that the forces in opposition are simply different aspects of the same personality. For example, in Walter Mitty we have a conflict between what a man actually is (a small, timid, incompetent creature, henpecked viciously by an overbearing wife) and what he wants to be (a brave and competent hero). By escaping constantly into the world of his daydreams, Mitty reveals himself to be living in a permanent state of conflict between his heroic dreams and the drab reality of his existence. In all such internal conflicts, we see a character caught in a squeeze between two sides of his or her own personality, torn between equally strong but conflicting desires, goals, or value systems. In some cases, this inner conflict is resolved, and the character grows or develops as a result, but in many cases, like that of Walter Mitty, there is no resolution.

The standard Woody Allen character in such films as *Play It Again, Sam, Annie Hall,* and *Manhattan* is torn by internal con-

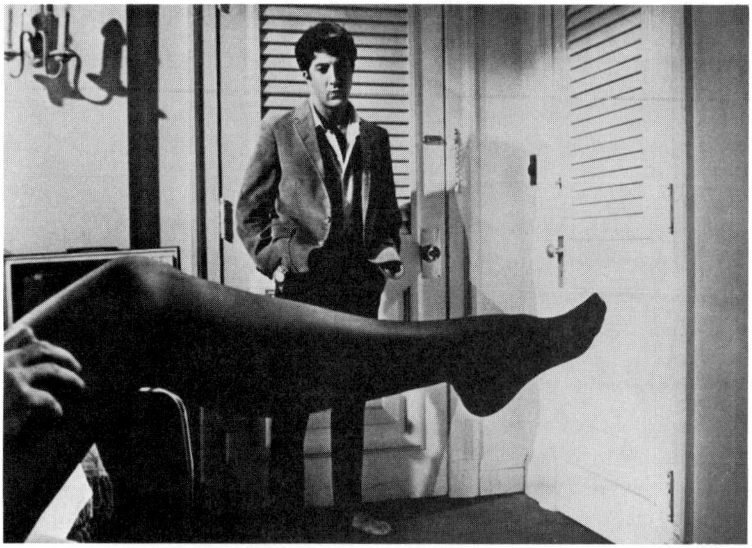

|3.33| Internal Conflict: Benjamin Braddock (Dustin Hoffman) gets all the internal conflict he can handle when he's seduced by the wife of his father's law partner in *The Graduate.*

flicts and insecurities. In *Play It Again, Sam,* the central character tries to overcome his self-doubts and insecurities by emulating his screen hero, Humphrey Bogart (Fig. 3.33).

Symbolic or Abstract Values in Conflicts

Although some conflicts in films are clearly self-contained and have no meaning beyond themselves, most conflicts tend to take on abstract or symbolic qualities so that the individuals or the forces involved represent something beyond themselves. It seems natural for the forces in opposition to align themselves with different generalized concepts or value systems, and even the most ordinary whodunit and typical western at least vaguely imply a conflict between law and order and lawlessness and chaos, or even simply between good and evil (Fig. 3.34). Other abstract ideas that might be represented by a film's conflict are civilization versus barbarism, sensual values versus spiritual ones, change versus tradition, idealism versus pragmatism, and the individual versus society. Thus almost any conflict can be stated in abstract or generalized terms. Because a comprehension of such abstract interpretations is often essential to determining and understanding a film's theme, the major conflict should be analyzed as carefully as possible on both the concrete and abstract planes.

|3.34| Abstract Values in Conflict: In *The Road Warrior,* the traditional western conflict between law and order and savagery and chaos is seen in a fresh environment and situation—a post-World War III environment where gasoline means survival. Like the western genre hero, Max (Mel Gibson) comes out of nowhere, and takes sides with the civilized community against the savages. He aids the "settlers" in their escape from the besieged fort, and then, with the savages momentarily subdued and the civilized group on its way to found a new settlement, Max goes his own way.

QUESTIONS

On Conflict

1. Identify the major conflict.
2. Is the conflict internal (man against himself), external, or a combination of both? Is it primarily a physical or a psychological conflict?
3. Express the major conflict in general or abstract terms (for example, brains versus brawn, man against nature).
4. How is the major conflict related to the theme?

SETTING

Simply stated, the setting is the time and place in which the film's story takes place. Although it may often seem unobtrusive or be taken for granted, setting is one of the essential ingredients in any story and thus makes an extremely important contribution to the film's theme or to its total effect. Because of its complex interrelationships with other story elements, such as plot, character, theme, conflict, and symbolism, setting should be analyzed carefully in terms of its effect on the story being told. And because of its important function on a purely visual plane, it must also be considered as a powerful cinematic element in its own right.

In examining the setting as it relates to the story, it is necessary to consider four factors in terms of the effect each has on the story as a whole:

1. **Temporal factors:** The time period in which the story takes place.
2. **Geographical factors:** The physical location and its characteristics, including the type of terrain, climate, population density (its visual and psychological impact), and any other physical factors of the locale that may have an effect on the story's characters and their actions.
3. **Social structures and economic factors.**
4. **Customs, moral attitudes, and codes of behavior.**

Each of these factors has an important effect on the problems, conflicts, and character of human beings. Therefore they must be considered as integral parts of any story's plot or theme.

Setting as Determiner of Character

The four aspects of setting listed above are especially important to understanding what might be called the naturalistic interpretation of the role of setting. This interpretation is based on the belief that our character, destiny, or fate are all determined by forces outside ourselves, that we may be nothing more than products of our heredity and environment, and that our cherished and precious freedom of choice is only an illusion. Thus, by considering the environment a significant shaping force or even a dominant controlling one, this interpretation forces us to consider carefully how their environment has made characters what they are—in other words, how their complete and total nature has been dictated by such factors as their time in history, the particular place on earth they inhabit, their place in the social and economic structure, and the customs, moral attitudes, and codes of behavior imposed upon them by their society. These environmental factors may be so pervasive that they serve as something much more important than a backdrop for the film's plot.

In some cases the environment may even function as an antagonist in the plot, as when the protagonists struggle against the environmental forces exerted upon them, seeking to express some freedom of choice, or to escape from an oppressive trap. Thus the serious consideration of the cruel, indifferent, or at least powerful forces of the environment is often a key to understanding a character and his or her dilemma.

Setting as Reflection of Character

The environment in which a person lives may also provide the viewer with clues to understanding his or her character. This is especially true in regard to the effect individuals have on those aspects of their environment over which they have some control. Houses, for example, may serve as excellent indications of character. Their usefulness is illustrated by the following examples of exterior views as they might appear in a film's opening establishing shot.

Picture a small, neat, white, green-shuttered cottage with red roses around the doorstep and bright and cheerful curtains at the windows. It is surrounded by a newly whitewashed picket fence. Such a setting has been traditionally used in films to suggest the happy honeymoon couple, full of youth, vigor, and optimism for a bright future.

On the other extreme, consider the image evoked by Poe's description of the Usher house in his classic short story "The Fall of the House of Usher": bleak, gray walls, vacant eye-like windows, crumbling stones, rotten woodwork, and a barely perceptible zigzag crack in the masonry from roof to foundation. This opening picture, a reflection of the Usher family's decadent state, becomes even more significant as the story progresses, for Roderick Usher and the house in which he lives are so closely interwoven symbolically and metaphorically that they become one: The house's vacant eye-like windows portray the eyes of Roderick Usher, and the zigzag crack in the masonry is equated with the crack in Usher's mind.

Thus, the filmgoer must be aware of any type of interaction between environment and character, whether setting is serving as a molder of character or merely as its reflection.

Setting for Verisimilitude

One of the most obvious and natural functions of the setting is to create a "semblance of reality" that gives the viewer a sense of a real time, a real place, and a feeling of being there. Because they recognize the great importance that an authentic setting plays in making a film believable, filmmakers may often search for months to find a proper setting, and then move crew, actors, and equipment thousands of miles in order to capture an appropriate backdrop for the story they are attempting to film.

To be thoroughly convincing, the setting chosen should be authentic in even the most minute detail. In a film set in the past, even the slightest anachronism may be detrimental. Thus a filmmaker shooting a story about the Civil War must be careful that the skies do not show jet vapor trails or the landscapes do not include high-tension power lines.

Some films are so effective in capturing the unique qualities of the time and place in which they are set that these factors become the most important elements of the film, being more powerful and memorable than the characters or the story line. *McCabe and Mrs. Miller, Ryan's Daughter,* and *The Last Picture Show* are good examples.

Setting for Sheer Visual Impact

When it is permissible within the limits of a film's theme and purpose, filmmakers will choose a setting with a high degree of visual impact. For example, the plot and structure of such westerns as *Shane* or *True Grit* do not demand great scenery, but the filmmakers realized that the sheer beauty of the wide western landscape, with its snowcapped mountains and rainbow-colored rock formations, is usually effective for its own sake, so long as it does not violate the overall tone or atmosphere of the film. David Lean is especially successful in choosing settings with a powerful visual impact, as demonstrated in *Dr. Zhivago, Ryan's Daughter,* and *Lawrence of Arabia.* The barren Australian desert provides an other-worldly backdrop for the action of *The Road Warrior* (Fig. 3.35).

| 3.35 | Setting for Visual Impact: The Australian high country provides a beautiful and powerful backdrop for Sigrid Thornton and Tom Burlinson in this scene from *The Man From Snowy River.*

| 3.36 | Setting for Emotional Atmosphere, Characterization, and Visual Impact: In sharp contrast to the drab, ordinary, rundown Bates Motel in *Psycho* is the Bates home, located on a hill behind the motel. Its strange, foreboding, haunted quality contributes immensely to the emotional atmosphere of the film. The house also contributes to the characterization of Norman Bates (Tony Perkins), both as reflection and determiner of his character. The starkness of the house, silhouetted against the sky, also contributes a strong visual impact to the film. In this picture, Perkins is shown standing against the same house as it appears in *Psycho II*.

Setting to Create Emotional Atmosphere

In certain specialized films, setting is extremely important in creating a pervasive mood or emotional atmosphere. This is especially true in horror films, and to some extent in the science fiction or fantasy film, where the unusually charged emotional atmosphere created and maintained by the setting becomes an important factor in achieving the "willing suspension of disbelief" on the viewer's part. Setting may also create a mood of tension and suspense in keeping with the overall tone of the film, in addition to adding credibility to plot and character elements (Fig. 3.36).

Setting as Symbol

The setting of a film story may also take on strong symbolic overtones when it is used to stand for or represent not just a location but some idea associated with the location. An example of such a symbolic environment may be seen in the garden setting for *Suddenly Last Summer.* The garden becomes a symbol for the world view reflected by the other symbols: that men are carnivorous creatures living in what is essentially a savage jungle, where they devour each other in a constant struggle of fang and claw, obeying only the jungle law of the survival of the fittest. That this world view is reflected in the setting is illustrated by Tennessee Williams' own description of the set:

> The interior is blended with a fantastic garden which is more like a tropical jungle, or forest, in the prehistoric age of giant fern-forests when living creatures had flippers turning into limbs and scales to skin. The colors of this jungle-garden are violent, especially since it is steaming with heat after rain. There are massive tree-flowers that suggest organs of the body, torn out, still glistening with undried blood; there are harsh cries and sibilant hissings and thrashing sounds in the garden as if it were inhabited by beasts, serpents and birds, all of a savage nature. . . .[6]

Setting as Microcosm

A special type of symbolic setting is the type known as a *microcosm,* meaning "the world in little," in which the human activity in a small and limited setting is actually representative of human behavior or the human condition in the world as a whole. In such a setting special care is taken to isolate the characters from all external influences, so that the "little world" of the setting seems self-contained. The limited group of people, which contains representative human "types" from various walks of life or levels of society, might be isolated on a desert island, an airplane, a stagecoach, or in a western town. The implication of the microcosm often comes very close to being allegorical: The viewer should see strong similarities to what happens in the microcosm in the world at large, and the film's theme should have universal implications. Such films as *Lord of the Flies, Ship of Fools* and *High Noon* can all be seen as microcosms; television's "Gilligan's Island," however, lacks the universal implications of a microcosm, though it possesses many microcosmic qualities.

6. Tennessee Williams, *Suddenly Last Summer.* Copyright © 1958 by Tennessee Williams. All rights reserved. Reprinted by permission of New Directions Publishing Corporation.

QUESTIONS

On Setting

1. Which of the four environmental factors (temporal factors, geographical factors, social structures and economic factors, and customs, moral attitudes, and codes of behavior) play significant roles in the film? Could the same story take place in any environment?
2. Which environmental factors are most important, and what effect do these factors have on the plot or the characters?
3. Why did the filmmaker choose this particular location for filming this story?
4. How does the film's setting contribute to the overall emotional atmosphere?
5. What kind of important interrelationships exist between setting and the characters, or between setting and plot?
6. Is the setting symbolic in any way? Does it function as a microcosm?

THE TITLE'S SIGNIFICANCE

In most films, the full significance of the title can be determined only after seeing the film. In many cases, the title will have one meaning to a viewer before seeing the film, and a completely different, richer and deeper meaning afterwards. Titles are often ironic, expressing an idea exactly the opposite of the meaning intended, and many titles allude to biblical passages, mythology, or other literary works. For example, the title *All the King's Men* is taken from "Humpty Dumpty," and serves to remind the reader of the whole nursery rhyme, which is actually a nutshell summary of the novel. *All the King's Men* concerns a southern dictator (king), who rises to a position of high power (sat on a wall), but is assassinated (had a great fall). As in the case of the egg, even "all the king's men" are unable to put him together again. On another level, the title literally tells us what the novel is about. Although Willie Stark, the politician, is the primary energy force in the novel, Jack Burden, his press secretary and right-hand man, is actually the focal character, and the novel is very much concerned with the lives of others who work for Stark in one capacity or another. Thus, the story is in a sense about "all the king's men." On yet another plane the title serves to link the character Willie Stark to Huey Long, on whose career the novel is loosely based. Long's favorite nickname for himself was "The Kingfisher," from a character on the old Amos and Andy radio show, and Long once wrote a song around his campaign slogan, "Every man a king, but no one wears a crown."

Some titles may call our attention to a key scene in the film that becomes worthy of especially careful study when we realize that the title has been taken from it. Although the title seldom names the theme, it is usually an extremely important clue in determining it. Thus, it is essential to think carefully about the possible meanings of the title after seeing any film.

QUESTIONS

On the Title's Significance

1. Why is the title appropriate? What does it mean in terms of the whole film?
2. How many different levels of meaning can you find in the title? How does each level apply to the film as a whole?
3. If the title is ironic, what opposite meanings or contrasts does it suggest?
4. If you recognize the title as being an allusion, why is the work or passage alluded to an appropriate one?
5. If the title calls your attention to a key scene, why is that scene important?
6. How is the title related to the theme?

IRONY

Irony, in the most general sense, is a literary, dramatic, and cinematic technique involving the juxtaposition or linking of opposites. By emphasizing the sharp and startling contrasts, reversals, and paradoxes of human experience, irony is capable of adding an intellectual dimension and achieving both comic and tragic effects at the same time. To be clearly understood, irony must be broken down into its various types and explained in terms of the contexts in which it appears.

Dramatic Irony

Dramatic irony derives its effect primarily through a contrast between ignorance and knowledge. The filmmaker will provide the audience with information a character remains ignorant of. Then, when the character speaks or acts in ignorance of the true state of affairs, the dramatic irony functions to create two separate meanings for each line of dialogue: (1) The meaning of the line as it is understood by the unenlightened character (a literal or face-value meaning), and (2) the additional meaning the line has to the enlightened audience (an ironic meaning, opposite to the literal meaning).

By knowing something that the character does not know, we gain pleasure from being in on the joke or secret. In *Oedipus Rex,* for example, Oedipus does not realize that he has already killed his father and married his mother when he refers to himself as "the child of Good Luck" and "the most fortunate of men." Since *we* are aware of the truth, however, we hear the line as a painful joke. On a less serious plane is an example from *Superman.* Although *we* know that Clark Kent is really Superman, Lois Lane does not. Therefore, every time Lois accuses Clark of cowardice because he disappears whenever trouble starts, we have to chuckle because of our inside knowledge.

Dramatic irony may also function in a purely visual way, either for comic effect or to build suspense, when the camera shows us something that the character on the screen can't see. For example, a character trying to elude a pursuer in a comic chase may be crawling toward the same corner as his pursuer, but only we will see and anticipate the coming shock of sudden confrontation (Fig. 3.37). Horror films employ similar scenes to both intensify and prolong suspense. Because of its great effectiveness in enriching both the emotional and intellectual impact of a story, dramatic irony has been a popular technique in literary and dramatic art since Homer employed it in *The Odyssey;* it remains popular and effective to this day.

13.37 Dramatic Irony: In this scene from *Indiana Jones and the Temple of Doom,* the fact that Indiana (Harrison Ford) doesn't know a palace assassin has designs on his Adam's apple increases our suspense and involvement in the action.

Irony of Situation

Irony of situation is essentially an irony of plot. It involves a sudden reversal or backfiring of events, so that the end result of a character's actions is exactly the opposite of his or her intentions. Almost the entire plot structure of *Oedipus Rex* involves irony of situation: Every move that Oedipus and Jocasta make to avoid the prophesies actually helps to bring them about. This particular type of irony is most often associated with O. Henry. An excellent example is his story "The Ransom of Red Chief," where two hoodlums kidnap a child who is such a demon that they end up having to pay his parents to get them to take the boy back.

Irony of Character

Irony of character occurs when characters possess strong opposites or contradictions within themselves, or when their actions involve sharp reversals in expected patterns of behavior. Oedipus, for example, is probably the most ironic character ever created, for the opposites built into his character constitute an almost endless list: He is both the detective and the murderer he is seeking; he sees, yet he is blind (in direct contrast to his foil, the blind "seer" Tiresias); he is the great riddle-solver, but doesn't know his own identity; his is his mother's husband, and his children's brother; and in the end, when he finally "sees," he blinds himself. Superman, in his alter ego as mild-mannered reporter Clark Kent, is another example of an ironic character, an irony intensified by Lois Lane's thinking him not only mild-mannered, but cowardly.

Irony of character may also be present when a character violates our stereotyped view of him, as illustrated by this imaginary scene. Two soldiers, played by Woody Allen and John Wayne, are pinned down in a foxhole by an enemy machine gun. When mortar shells start falling around the foxhole, the John Wayne character panics, buries his head under his arm, and begins sobbing uncontrollably. Meanwhile, the Woody Allen character puts his bayonet between his teeth, grabs a grenade in each hand, and charges the machine-gun nest alone.

Irony of Setting

Irony of setting occurs when an event takes place in a setting which is exactly the opposite of the setting we usually expect for such an event—for example, an orgy in a church, a birth in a graveyard, or a free-for-all in a Quaker meeting hall.

Irony of Tone

Because it communicates simultaneously on several different layers, film is especially suited for many types of irony, but irony of tone can be especially effective. In essence, irony of tone involves the juxtaposition of opposites in attitudes or feelings, as exemplified in literature by Erasmus's *The Praise of Folly,* in which the reader must read between the lines to discover that the work is actually a condemnation of Folly. Swift's classic essay, "A Modest Proposal," is another example. Here the author's proposal, put forth in rational, calm, and modest style, is actually an outrageous proposal—that the Irish people sell their year-old children to be eaten like suckling pigs by the wealthy English landlords. In film, such irony may be effectively provided through contrasting emotional attitudes communicated simultaneously by the soundtrack and the visual image. Consider, for example, the juxtaposition of an optimistic, Pollyanna-ish song such as "Everything Is Beautiful" with pictures of the mutilated victims of war atrocities.

Many different kinds of irony are possible in film because of film's ability to communicate on more than one level at a time. In fact, the multilayered nature can reach a point of complexity where its effect is difficult to describe. This is the case, for example, in the final scene of *Dr. Strangelove,* which combines three separate contrasting elements: (1) the visuals, composed of multiple shots of atomic mushroom clouds filmed in slow motion; (2) the soundtrack, where Vera Lynn's voice, sticky and sweet, sings "We'll Meet Again Some Sunny Day"; and (3) the significance of the action, which is the end of all life as we know it. The ironic effect is provided by the ingenious touch of the Vera Lynn song, which adds a sweet, haunting quality to the pictorial element, so that we become aware of the almost breathtaking beauty of the mushroom clouds. This ironic combination of beauty and horror creates an unbelievably powerful effect. Such effects are rare in film, but the filmgoer must be constantly aware of the potential for ironic expression in the musical score, juxtaposition of sight and sound, and in transitions of almost any kind.

Cosmic Irony

Although irony is basically a means of expression, the continuous use of ironic techniques might indicate that the filmmaker holds a certain philosophical attitude, constituting what might be called an ironic world view. Because irony pictures every situation as possessing two equal sides, or truths, that eventually cancel each other out or at least work against each other, the overall effect of ironic expression is to show the ridiculous complexity and uncertainty of human experience. Life is seen as a continuous series of paradoxes and contradictions, characterized by ambiguities and discrepancies, and no truth is ever absolute. Somehow, such irony reminds us that life is a game in which the players never win, and in which the players are aware of the impossibility of winning and the absurdity of the game, even while they continue to play. On the positive side, however, irony's ability to make life seem both tragic and comic at the same moment keeps us from taking things too seriously or too literally.

Looked at on a cosmic scale, an ironic world view implies the existence of some kind of supreme being or creator. Whether this supreme entity be called God, Fate, or Destiny, or The Force makes little difference. The implication is that the supreme being manipulates events in such a way as to deliberately frustrate and mock mankind, and derives supreme entertainment from what is essentially a perpetual cruel joke on the human race.

And although irony usually has a humorous effect, the humor of cosmic irony bites even deeper. It can bring a laugh, but not of the usual kind. It will not be a belly laugh, but a sudden outward gasp of air, almost a cough, that catches in the throat between the heart and mind. And we laugh perhaps because it hurts too much to cry.

QUESTIONS

On Irony

1. What examples of irony can be found in the film?
2. Is irony employed to such a significant degree that the whole film takes on an ironic tone? Is an ironic world view implied?
3. Do any particular examples of irony achieve comic and tragic effects at the same time?
4. Where in the film is suspense or humor achieved through dramatic irony?
5. How do the ironies contribute to the theme?

CHAPTER 4

VISUAL ELEMENTS

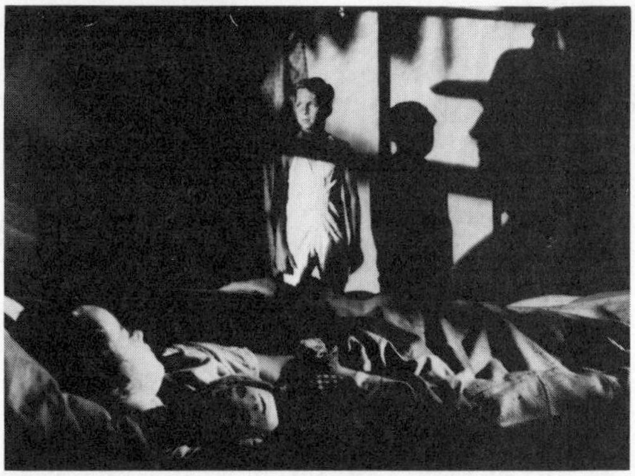

THE IMPORTANCE OF THE IMAGE

Because the visual element is the film's basic means of communication, it is the most important factor in distinguishing between the fictional film and the so-called "literary" forms of fiction and drama. The very term *literature* refers to the written word, and is defined as including all writings in verse or prose, especially those of an imaginative or critical nature. Even in colloquial use, literature means printed matter of any kind. Therefore, although it shares many of the techniques common to the literary form, film in itself is not literary. Its emphasis is on the moving image, which is generally what communicates a film's most significant or interesting aspects.

In the strictest sense of the word, drama is not literature either. For the spectator, drama has no reality as literature, aside from the fact that a play is written before the actors can memorize their lines. But a play's significance and its techniques can be understood through an intelligent and imaginative reading of the script, since drama relies primarily on the medium of words. Thus, though drama is intended to be performed rather than read, it can be studied from the printed page as literature. For the most part, the same is not true of film. So much is missing from the average screenplay, since the visual and aural elements are not there, that we almost need to have seen a film to make the reading of the screenplay worthwhile. Usually only about half of a film's running time is taken up with dialogue. So a major part of the story is communicated nonverbally, through images, music, and natural sounds.

Film speaks in a "language of the senses": its flowing and sparkling stream of images, its compelling pace and natural rhythms, and its pictorial style are all part of this nonverbal language. So it follows naturally that the aesthetic quality and dramatic power of the image are extremely important to the overall quality of a film. Although the nature and quality of the story, editing, musical score, sound effects, dialogue, and acting can do much to enhance the film's power, even these important elements cannot save a film whose images are mediocre or shoddily edited.

As important as the quality of the image may be, it must not be considered so important that the purpose of the film as an artistic, unified whole is ignored. A film's photographic effects should not be created for their own sake as independent, beautiful, or powerful images. They must, in the final analysis, be justified psychologically and dramatically as well as aesthetically in terms of the film as a whole, as important means to an end, not as ends in themselves. The creation of beautiful images for the sake of beautiful images violates a film's aesthetic unity and therefore may actually work against the film.

The same principle applies to an overly clever or self-conscious technique. Technique must not become an end in itself; any special technique must have some kind of underlying purpose related to the purpose of the film as a whole. Thus, every time a director or cinematographer employs an unusual camera angle or uses a new photographic technique, he or she should do so for the purpose of communicating (either sensually or intellectually) in the most effective way possible, not simply because he or she wants to show off or try out a new trick. A sense of naturalness, a feeling that it had to be done that way, is more praiseworthy than a clever camera trick.

Although the visual element is the motion picture's primary and most powerful means of communication, the cinematography can often completely dominate a film, taking it over by sheer force. When this occurs, the artistic structure of the film is weakened, its dramatic power fades, and watching the film becomes simply an orgy of the eyeballs. As cinematographer Vilmos Zsigmond puts it:

> I believe photography should never be dominating. The photography in *The Deer Hunter* doesn't look flashy to me; it doesn't overpower the film. It's with the story, never above it. It never tries to tell you how good I am or how good the lighting is. It's on the same level. The performances, the directing, the music, the camerawork are all on the same level. That's what I like about it, and that's what I think photography should be.[1]

THE CINEMATIC FILM

In the simplest terms, a cinematic film is a film that takes advantage of all the special properties and qualities that make the film medium unique. The first and most essential of these is the quality of continuous motion. The cinematic film is truly a "motion" picture—a flowing, ever-changing stream of images and sounds sparkling with a freshness and vitality all its own, a fluid blend of

1. "Dialogue on Film." *American Film*, June 1979, p. 41.

Films "noir" = films of the night (Black Cinema or black cinema)

Mise-en-Scene (the things you put on stage)

Visual (what it looks like)

theme (dark, somber) good & evil

Traced of German expressionism 1920-31 Berlin UFA Studios)

Chiaroscuro (interplay of light & shadow)

Orson Welles - Citizen Kane forerunner for film noir

Paul Shrader's 7 Recurring Char. of Film Noir

1. majority of scenes lit for night
2. Oblique & vertical lines preferred to horiz.
3. Actor & setting often given equal lighting
4. Comp. tensions pref. to physical action
5. Use of reflective surfaces (water mirrors windows)
6. Voice-over narration
7. Complex chronolog. order reinforces sense of hopelessness & lost time

add'l

1. Rain
2. neon lights
3. dimly lit nightclubs
4. Winding Hollywood hills road
5. Characters w/ physical handicaps

6. Sadists
7. double & triple cross
8. "Cosmic" irrationality

image, sound, and motion possessed by a restless compulsion to be vibrantly alive, to avoid the quiet, the still, and the static.

The second quality of the cinematic film evolves naturally out of the first. The continuous and simultaneous interplay of image, sound, and motion on the screen sets up varied, complex, and subtle rhythms. Clear, crisp visual and aural rhythms are created by the physical movements or sound of objects on the screen, by the pace of the dialogue, by the natural rhythms of human speech, by the frequency of editorial cuts, by the varying length of shots between cuts, and by the musical score. The pace of the plot also has distinct rhythms. All these serve to intensify the film's unique sense of pulsing life.

The cinematic film also makes maximum use of the great flexibility and freedom of the medium: its freedom from the spoken word, and its ability to communicate directly, physically, and concretely through images and sounds; its freedom to spirit us about on a kind of magic carpet ride, to show us action from any vantage point, and to vary our point of view at will; its capability to manipulate time and space, expanding or compressing them at will; and its freedom to make quick and clear transitions in time and space.

Although film is essentially a two-dimensional medium, the cinematic film overcomes this limitation by creating an illusion of depth. It creates the impression that the screen is not a flat surface, but a window through which we observe a three-dimensional world.

All these qualities are present in the truly cinematic film; if they are not present in the subject matter, it is up to the director, the cinematographer, and the editor to build them in. Otherwise, the film's dramatic scenes will not be communicated in all the fullness of the medium's potential.

ELEMENTS OF CINEMATIC COMPOSITION

Because the cinematic film is a unique medium, the problems in composition it poses for the director and cinematographer are also unique. First, both must be aware that every shot (a single uninterrupted running of the camera) is but a segment, a brief element in a continuous flow of images. Therefore, each shot must be created with a view to its contribution to the whole. The most difficult aspect of creating a shot is that the image itself will move, will in fact be in a constant state of flux, and the camera will be recording those images at a rate of twenty-four frames per second. So every frame in the shot cannot be set up according to the aesthetic principles of composition used in still photography. The cinematographer's choices in each shot are dictated by the nature of the film medium, and every shot must be designed with the goals of *cinematic* composition in mind. These goals are: (1) directing our attention to the object of greatest significance, (2) keeping the image in constant motion, and (3) creating an illusion of depth.

Focusing Our Attention on the Most Significant Object

Above all, the shot must be so composed that it draws our attention into the scene and toward the object of greatest dramatic significance. Only when this is achieved can the film's dramatic ideas be effectively conveyed. Several methods of directing our attention are open to the filmmaker.

1. Size and closeness of the object. Normally, the eye is directed toward larger, closer objects rather than toward smaller, more distant objects. Therefore, the image of an actor's face appearing in the foreground (closer to the camera, and therefore larger) would be more likely to serve as a focal point for our attention than a face in the background, which would appear smaller and more distant. In a normal situation, then, the size and relative distance of the object are important factors in determining the greatest area of interest (Fig. 4.1).

2. Sharpness of focus. On the other hand, the eye is also drawn almost automatically to what it can see best. Therefore, if a face in the foreground is slightly blurred and a face in the background, though smaller and more distant, is sharp and clear, our eyes are drawn to the background face, because it can be seen best. An object in sharp focus can divert our attention from a closer, larger object in soft focus, even if the larger object fills half the screen (Fig. 4.2).

3. Movement. The eye is also drawn to an object in motion, and a moving object can divert our attention from a static one. Thus, a single moving object in an otherwise static scene will draw our attention. Conversely, if movement and flow are a general part of

Handwritten margin notes:

Suspense ?
① may not know what's going to happen
mystery movies — you don't know what's going to happen? Who done it
Hitchcock started UFA Studios in Berlin then became English director.
Rebecca first American film won Academy award
comments on Hitchcock
— "was a purist"
— "actors are cattle"
— MacGuffin is that thing around which plot evolves.
— never looked thru a camera.
— view doesn't matter function it serves to motivate plot is important

his films had:
— "wrong man" theme
— good guy & bad guy hanging onto each other til death
— interwoven comedy w/ suspense
— transferred menace from film to audience
— pt of view of an individual would go back to person for reaction
— strong visual sense
— real suspense audience given info

— chase scene ends in theatre
— uses national monuments
— loved grandeur / splendor
— create emotion by style & manner story is told

Western

genre of order
Western, detective film, gangster
Genres of integration (people trying to pull things together

Characteristics
(1) Hero - male dominant
not romantic
1950's new kind of western
(2) Setting - contested space
1898 Triple Creek Barroom
first singing cowboy Ken Maynard
High Noon - Gary Cooper
(3) Conflict
(4) Resolution
(5) Themes
Mediation
Redemption
Revenge
Isolated Self Reliance
Utopia
Generic Iconography - White

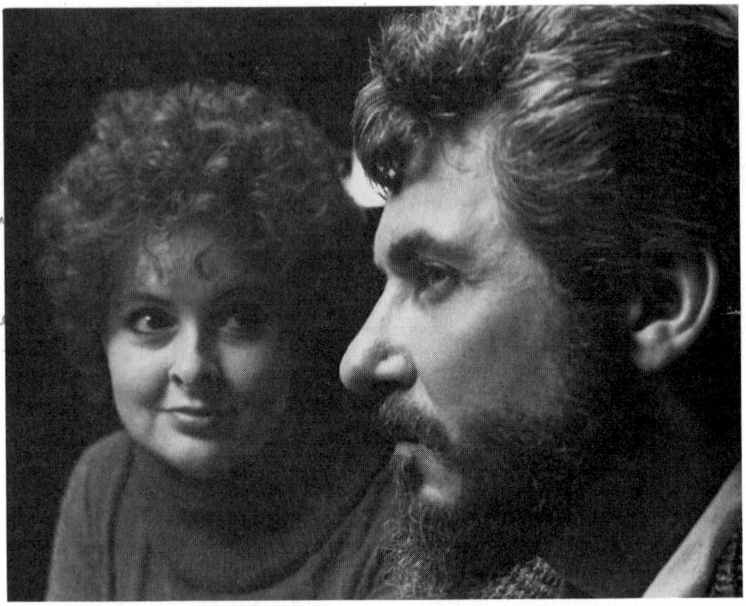

|4.1| Size and Closeness of Object: In most cases, our attention is naturally drawn to larger, closer objects or faces rather than toward smaller more distant objects or faces, such as the man's face in this picture.

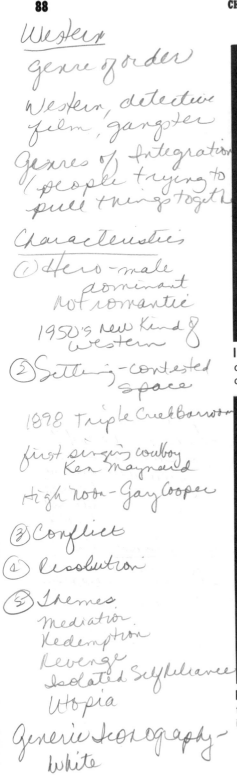

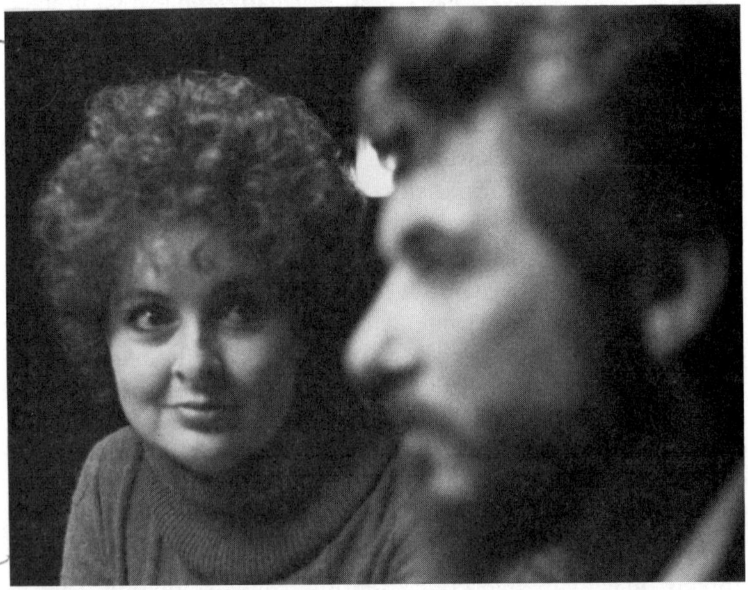

|4.2| Sharpness of Focus: When a larger, closer face in the foreground is in soft focus or blurred, our attention will be drawn to a smaller and more distant face in sharp focus: The eye is drawn almost automatically to what it can see best.

|4.3| Background in Motion: While the horse and carriage passing in the background are moving, they are part of a generalized traffic movement in the street, so our attention remains on the static but dramatically more important interaction between Julie Christie and Alan Bates in this scene from *The Go-Between.*

the background, moving objects will not divert our attention from static, but more dramatically important, objects (Fig. 4.3).

4. Extreme close-ups. Perhaps the most dictatorial control the cinematographer has on our attention is achieved by use of the tight or extreme close-up, which brings us so close to the object of interest (an actor's face, for example) that we cannot look elsewhere. The face so fills the screen that there is nothing else to see (Fig. 4.4).

5. Arrangement of people and/or objects. The director also focuses our attention by his or her arrangement of people (and/or objects) in relation to each other. Since each arrangement is determined largely by the nature of the dramatic moment being enacted and the complex interrelationships involved, the director must depend more on his or her intuitive sense of rightness than on any positioning "formulas" (Fig. 4.5).

6. Foreground framing. The director might even go so far as to frame the object of greatest significance with objects or people in the near foreground. To make sure that our attention is not distracted by the framing objects or people, the director will gener-

|4.4| Extreme Close-Up: There's no doubt about where our attention will be directed in this dramatic close-up of Tony Perkins in *Psycho II.*

|4.5| Dramatic Arrangement of People and Objects: There are no set formulas for positioning characters and objects within the frame. The director must rely on an intuitive sense of rightness in composing each shot to communicate the nature of the dramatic moment and in positioning actors to reveal subtle and complex interrelationships. The physical locations of the other characters, his position in the center of the architectural frame created by the grand foyer in the background, and the fact that his standing posture makes him dominant all focus our attention on Giancarlo Giannini in the scene from Lina Wertmuller's *Seven Beauties*.

ally emphasize the most important subject with brighter lighting and sharper focus (Figs. 4.6 and 4.7).

7. Lighting and color. Special uses of light and color also help to draw the eye to the object of greatest significance. High contrast areas of light and dark create natural centers of focal interest, as do bright colors present in a subdued or drab background (Figs. 4.8 and 4.9).

In composing each shot, the filmmaker continually employs these techniques, either separately or in conjunction with each other, to hold our attention on the object of greatest dramatic significance. Thus, the filmmaker can gently guide our thoughts and emotions where he or she wants them to go. Guiding our attention is certainly the most fundamental concern of cinematic composition but, as we shall see, not the only one.

|4.6| Foreground Framing: In *E.T., the Extra-Terrestrial* Peter Coyote and Dee Wallace talking in the foreground set up a frame that calls our attention to the listener, Henry Thomas. Subtle differences in lighting and his position in the center of the plastic tunnel also direct our attention to him.

|4.7| The Menacing Frame: Although Joey's (Shawn Carson) menacing figure dominates the screen, lighting and sharp focus draw attention to his sister Amy (Elizabeth Berridge) as he plays the old *Psycho* trick on her in this scene from *The Funhouse.*

|4.8|

|4.9|

High Contrast: These two pictures, from *Gandhi* and *29 Clues,* both use high contrast in very different ways to focus our attention. In the picture from *Gandhi* [4.8], the dark-skinned figure of Gandhi (Ben Kingsley) stands out against the bright sunlight on the parched Indian landscape beyond; in *29 Clues* [4.9] the almost total darkness of the basement interior draws our attention to the dark figure in the lighted doorway and the highlighted guns trained on him.

Keeping the Image in Motion

Since the essence of the cinematic film is its continuous motion—its flowing, ever-changing stream of images—the director or cinematographer must also build this quality of movement and flux into every shot. To create the flowing stream of constantly changing images, the cinematographer employs several techniques.

FIXED-FRAME MOVEMENT

The fixed camera frame approximates the effect of looking through a window. The camera remains in the same position, pointing at the same spot, as we might look at something with a frozen stare. Movement and variety are then worked into the shot by moving the subject. This movement can be rapid and frantic (like the physical action of a barroom brawl) or calm and subtle (like the changing facial expression of an actor speaking and gesturing normally).

Several types of movement are possible within the frame established by the fixed camera. Movement can be *lateral* (from the left to right of the frame), *in depth* (toward or away from the camera), or *diagonal* (a combination of lateral and in-depth movement). Purely lateral movement creates the impression of movement on a flat surface (which the screen is) and therefore calls attention to one of the medium's limitations: its two dimensionality. So, to create the illusion of three dimensions, the cinematographer will favor in-depth movement (toward or away from the camera), and/or diagonal movement, over purely lateral movement.

PANNING AND TILTING MOVEMENT

Usually when the camera remains in a fixed physical location, however, it also captures movement by approximating the head and eye movements of a human spectator. The camera's movements incorporate what is essentially a human field of view. With the body stationary, if we turn the head and neck from left to right, and add a corresponding sideward glance of the eyes, our field of view takes in an arc of something slightly wider than 180 degrees. And if we simply move the head and eyes up and down, our eyes span an arc of at least 90 degrees. Most movements of the camera—either horizontal (called *panning*) or vertical (called *tilt-*

ing)—fall within these natural human limitations. A closer look at these camera movements will clarify these limitations.

Panning The most common use of the camera pan is to follow the lateral movement of the subject. In a western, for example, the panning camera may function this way. The wagon train has been attacked by Indians and has moved into a defensive circle. The camera for this shot is set up in a fixed location looking over the shoulder of one of the settlers as she attempts to pick off circling Indians with a rifle. The movement of the circling Indians is from right to left. The camera (and the rifle) move to the right and pick up subject (target Indian). Then, both camera and rifle swing laterally to left as subject Indian rides by; when he reaches a center position, the rifle fires and we watch him fall off the horse and roll to the left of the center as he bites the dust. Then the camera either pans back to the right to pick up a new target, or an editorial cut starts the next shot with the camera picking up a new target Indian (far right) and the pattern is repeated.

Another type of pan is used to change from one subject to another. This might be illustrated by a stereotyped shoot-out scene in the middle of the street of a western town. The camera occupies a fixed position on the side of the street, halfway between the dueling gunfighters. After establishing the tense, poised image of the gunman on the right, the camera leaves him and slowly pans left until it focuses on the other man, also tensed and poised.

Since the eye normally jumps instantaneously from one object of interest to another, a pan must have a dramatic purpose or it will seem unnatural and conspicuous. There are several possible reasons for using a pan. In the gunfight scene, the slow fluid movement of the camera from one man to the other may help expand time, intensifying the suspense and the viewer's anticipation of the first draw. Also, it may reflect the tension in the environment as a whole by registering the fear and suspense on the faces of the onlookers across the street, who become secondary subjects, as we see their facial expressions in passing or catch glimpses of them frantically diving for cover. Finally, the pan may simply help to clearly establish the relative distance between the two men. Although this type of pan can be effective, it must be used with restraint, particularly if there is a great deal of dead screen (screen area with no objects of significance) between the two subjects.

On rare occasions, a complete 360-degree pan may be dramatically effective, especially when the situation calls for a sweeping panoramic view of the entire landscape. Such might be the case in a western where the fort is completely surrounded by Indians. A full 360-degree pan would clearly indicate the impossibility of escape and the helplessness of the situation. Also, a 360-degree pan might be useful in dramatizing the situation of a character waking up in an unfamiliar and unexpected environment. A person waking up in a jail cell, for instance, would turn his or her body enough to completely survey the surroundings.

Tilting The human quality of the camera is also illustrated by the camera movement known as *tilting,* which approximates the vertical movement of our head and eyes. The following hypothetical sequence illustrates how the tilt is used. The camera occupies a fixed position at the end of an airport runway, focused on a jet airliner taxiing toward the camera. As the plane lifts off, the camera tilts upward to follow the plane's trajectory to a point directly overhead. At this point, although it would be technically possible to create an axis to follow the plane in one continuous shot, the shot stops, and a new shot begins with the camera facing in the opposite direction. The second shot picks up the plane still overhead and tilts downward to follow its flight away from the camera. This movement approximates the way we would normally observe the incident if we were standing in the camera's position. As the plane turns right and begins to climb to altitude, the camera follows it in a diagonal movement which combines the elements of both panning and tilting. Thus, though the camera is in a fixed location, it is flexible enough to follow the movement of the plane as represented by the following arrows: take-off to directly overhead ↑, cross-over to turn ↘, turn and climb ↗.

In most panning and tilting shots, then, the movement of the camera approximates our normal *human* way of looking at things. Many shots in every film will be photographed in this manner, showing the story unfold as a person watching the scene might view it.

In the techniques described so far the camera has, in every case, remained in a fixed position. But the fixed camera, even though it can pan and tilt, lacks the fluidity necessary to create a truly cinematic film. The cinematic film depends, to a large degree, on a camera freed of its human limitations, a living camera with superhuman abilities. Thus the truly cinematic camera must function as a superhuman eye.

THE ZOOM LENS

The zoom lens frees the camera from its purely human limitations. Consisting of a complex series of lenses that keep the image in constant focus, the zoom lens gives the camera the apparent power to glide toward or away from the subject without requiring any movement of the camera.

Zoom lenses also can magnify the subject ten times or more, so that we seem to move ten times closer to the subject than the actual distance from the camera.

For example, to a camera stationed behind home plate in a baseball stadium, the center fielder, some four hundred feet away, will appear extremely small, the same size that he would appear to the naked eye. By zooming in on him, the lens elements move in exact relationship to each other, so that he stays in constant focus. The viewer, in effect, glides smoothly towards him until his figure almost fills the screen, as if we were seeing him from a distance of forty feet or closer (Figs. 4.10, 4.11, and 4.12). Though the camera is simply magnifying the image, the effect is one of moving toward the subject. By reversing the process, the effect is that of moving away from the subject.

Thus, through the use of zoom lens, the camera not only allows us to see things more clearly, but also gives us a sense of fluid motion in and out of the frame, thereby increasing our sensual

|4.10|

|4.11|

|4.12|

Zooming in on the Action: These three pictures represent different stages in a continuous shot on a single action using a zoom lens. At the start of the zoom, the cameraman picks up the center fielder as he starts after a fly ball. At this stage, the player's image fills a very small portion of the screen [4.10]. At the midway point in the zoom, the player's image is magnified so he appears about three times larger [4.11]. By the time he catches the ball, the zoom lens has continued to increase magnification until his figure fills almost the whole screen [4.12].

interest and involvement. And all of these variations are possible without even moving the camera.

THE MOBILE CAMERA

When the camera itself becomes mobile, the possibilities of movement increase tremendously. By freeing the camera from a fixed position, the cinematographer can create a constantly shifting viewpoint, giving us a moving image of a static subject. By mounting the camera on a boom or a crane (itself mounted on a truck or dolly), the cinematographer can move fluidly alongside, above, in front of, behind, or even under a running horse. The mobile camera can thus fulfill almost any demand for movement created by a story situation.

The mobile camera can also provide the tremendous sense of immediacy and dynamism that French director Abel Gance strove for in his 1927 *Napoleon*. As film historian Kevin Brownlow describes Gance and his film in the *Napoleon* program brochure:

> To him, a tripod was a set of crutches supporting a lame imagination. His aim was to free the camera, to hurl it into the middle of the action, to force the audience from mere spectators into active participants.
>
> Technicians in the German studios were putting the camera on wheels. Gance put it on wings. He strapped it to the back of a horse, for rapid inserts in the chase across Corsica; he suspended it from overhead wires, like a miniature cable-car; he mounted it on a huge pendulum, to achieve the vertigo-inducing storm in the convention.

Two recent developments have greatly increased the potential of the mobile camera. The first of these, called the Steadicam, is a portable, one-man camera with a built in gyroscope device that prevents any sudden jerkiness and provides a smooth, rock-steady image, even when the person carrying it is running up a flight of steps or down a rocky mountain path. The second development, the Skycam, is a small computerized remote-controlled camera that "flies" on wires at speeds up to 20 miles per hour, and can go practically anywhere cables can be strung.

EDITING AND MOVEMENT

The editing process also contributes greatly to the cinematic film's ever-changing stream of images. The editing, in fact, often creates the most vibrant visual rhythms in a film, as the editorial cuts and transitions propel us instantaneously from a long shot to a close-up, from one camera angle to another, and from one setting to another.

Thus the cinematographer uses a wide variety of techniques, either separately or in various combinations, to keep the visual image in constant motion:

- The movement of the subject within the fixed frame
- Apparent movement of the viewer toward or away from the objects in the frame (zoom lens)
- Vertical or horizontal movement of the camera (tilting and panning)
- Completely free movement of the camera and constantly changing viewpoint (mobile camera and editorial cuts).

Subject movement will also most likely be present in varying degrees in all of the above.

DEAD SCREEN AND LIVE SCREEN

The director must also be concerned with keeping the image alive in another sense. In almost every shot, he or she will attempt to

|4.13| The Packed Screen: The most obvious way to keep the screen alive is to pack almost every square inch of its surface with visual information, as is the case with this scene from *Murder on the Orient Express.*

|4.14| Background in Motion: The director will attempt to incorporate some kind of motion into almost every shot, and will often use a natural background movement to keep the screen alive. This type of background motion is a very subordinate type, which does not take our attention away from the primary subject. In this scene from *Suddenly Last Summer* a static shot of Elizabeth Taylor is kept alive by filming her against the gently lapping sea waves.

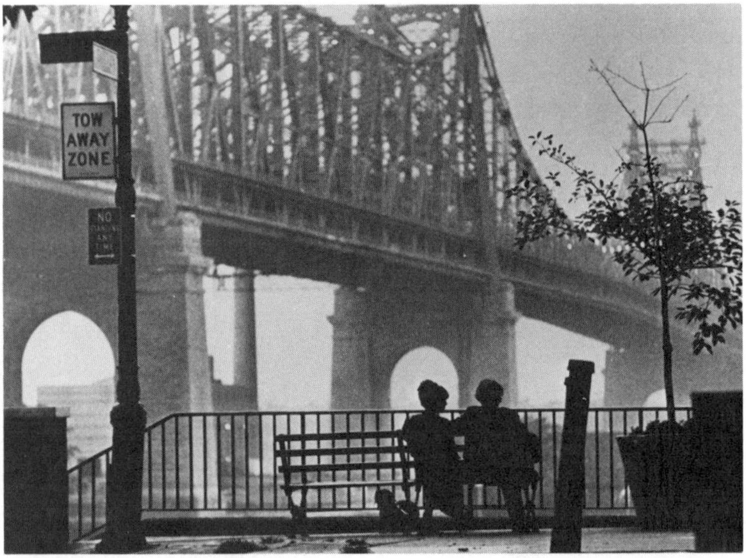

|4.15| Strong Visual Impact in a Static Background: The figures of Diane Keaton and Woody Allen occupy a very small portion of the frame in this scene from *Manhattan*, but the imposing architecture of the Queensborough Bridge in the background provides an esthetically pleasing composition and a strong sense of three dimensionality, as well as underscoring the "sense of place" that is such an integral part of the film.

communicate a significant amount of information in each frame. To achieve this, each shot must be composed so that the visual frame is loaded with cinematic information and large blank areas of "dead" screen are avoided—unless, as in some cases, there is a dramatic purpose for dead screen (Figs. 4.13, 4.14, and 4.15).

Creating the Illusion of Depth

Cinematic composition must also be concerned with creating an illusion of depth on what is essentially a two-dimensional screen. To achieve this, the cinematographer employs several different techniques.

1. Movement of subject. When using the fixed frame, the director sets up the movements of the subject to create an illusion of depth—by filming the subject moving toward or away from the camera, either head-on or at a diagonal angle. Purely lateral movement, perpendicular to the direction in which the camera is aimed, creates a purely two-dimensional effect and, to avoid a flat image, should be minimized.

2. Movement of camera. The mobile camera, mounted on a truck or dolly, may also create the illusion of depth by moving toward or away from a relatively static object. As it passes by or goes around objects on its way, we become more aware of the depth of the image. Since the camera "eye" actually moves, the objects on both sides of its path constantly change their position relative to each other. They change according to the changing angles from which they are viewed by the moving camera.

3. Apparent camera movement (zoom lens). The zoom lens, which by magnifying the image gives us the sensation of moving closer to or farther from the camera, is also employed to create the illusion of depth as well as that of movement. Because camera position does not change during zooming, there is no real change in perspective, meaning that the objects to the sides do not change their position in relation to each other as they do when the camera moves. For this reason, the zoom lens does not create the illusion of depth quite as effectively as the mobile camera.

4. Change of focal planes (rack focus). Most cameras, including still cameras, are designed to focus on objects at different distances from the lens. As we said earlier, the eye is ordinarily drawn to what it can see best—that is, the object in sharpest focus. So the cinematographer can create a kind of three dimensionality by focusing the camera lens, in turn, on objects in different depth planes. If the frame includes three faces, all at different distances from the camera, the cinematographer may first focus on the nearest face, and then, while the shot continues, focus on the second face, then on the third, thus, in effect, creating the illusion of depth within the frame (Figs. 4.16, 4.17, and 4.18).

5. Deep-depth focus or deep focus. In direct contrast to the change in focal planes is the use of special lenses that allow the camera to

|4.16|

|4.17|

|4.18|

Rack Focus—Moving Deeper into the Frame: Since our attention is naturally drawn to what we can see best, the illusion of depth can be created by changing the focal plane during a continuous shot. These three pictures represent different stages in a single running shot. In the first picture [4.16], our attention is drawn to the sharply focused image of the batter. As the shot continues, the camera next focuses on the pitcher [4.17], and then on the shortstop [4.18], giving us the feeling that we are being drawn deeper into a three-dimensional frame. (The order could also be reversed, beginning the shot with the shortstop in focus and ending with the batter in focus.)

focus simultaneously on objects anywhere from two feet away to several hundred feet away with equal clarity. This depth of focus approximates most clearly the ability of the human eye to see a deep range of objects in clear focus (Fig. 4.19).

6. Three-dimensional arrangement of people and objects. Perhaps the most important consideration in creating a three-dimensional image is how the people and objects to be filmed are arranged. If they are placed in separate planes, the cinematographer will have a truly three-dimensional scene to photograph. Without such an arrangement, however, there is no real purpose for the various effects and techniques described above (Fig. 4.20).

7. Foreground framing. A three-dimensional effect is also achieved when the shot is set up so that the subject is framed by an object or objects in the near foreground. With the object forming the frame in the focus, a strong sense of three-dimensionality is achieved. When the foreground frame is thrown out of focus or

| 4.19 | Deep Focus: In this picture from *The Right Stuff,* all seven of the actors playing the astronauts are in sharp focus, in spite of their varying distances from the camera.

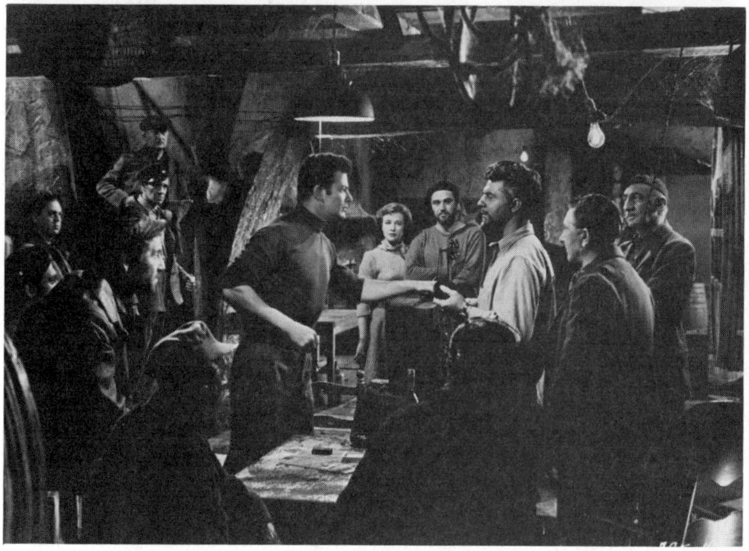

| 4.20 | Three-Dimensional Arrangement of People and Objects: The characters clustered around Cornell Wilde and Dan O'Herlihy are carefully positioned for a three-dimensional effect in this scene from *Operation Secret.*

seen in very soft focus, the three-dimensional effect is weakened somewhat but not lost, and the entire mood or atmosphere of the scene takes on a different character (Figs. 4.21 and 4.22).

8. Special lighting effects. By carefully controlling the angle, direction, intensity, and quality of the lighting, the director can further add to the illusion of depth (Figs. 4.23 and 4.24).

|4.21|

|4.22|

Foreground Framing: The wine glass and carafe in the foreground framing the woman's face are in focus in the picture on the left [4.21], and completely out of focus in the picture on the right [4.22].

|4.23|

|4.24|

Lighting for Depth: In the first photo [4.23], the flat lighting serves to minimize the sense of depth. By simply changing the direction, intensity, and quality of the light, the same scene provides a much stronger sense of depth and dramatic "punch."

Occasionally, the director may even control the source and direction of the lighting for the purpose of expanding the limits of the frame. By positioning the light source out of camera range—to either side or behind the camera—the filmmaker can cause the shadows of objects outside the frame to fall inside the frame, thus suggesting the presence of those objects. When these shadows come from objects behind the camera, they can add greatly to the three-dimensionality of the shot (Fig. 4.25).

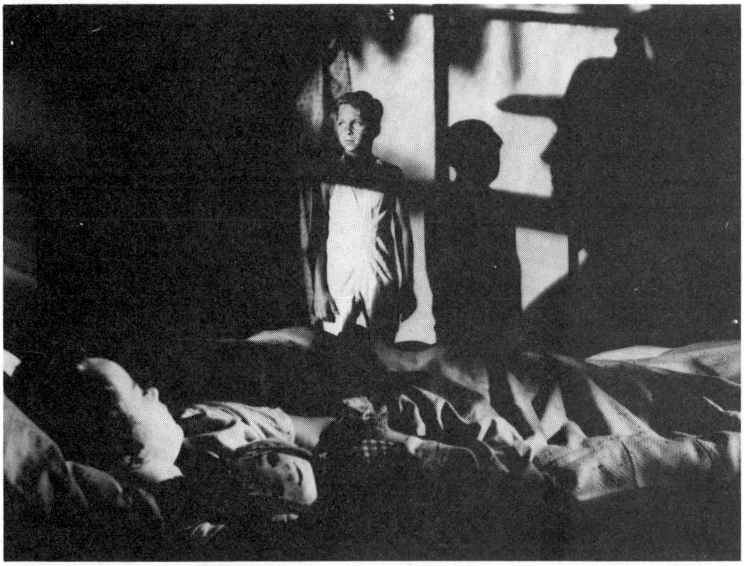

|4.25| Three-Dimensional Shadows: In this scene from Charles Laughton's *The Night of the Hunter,* the orphaned boy, John, stands guard over his sleeping sister Pearl and looks out the window at the villainous "preacher" Harry Powers (Robert Mitchum). Mitchum sits on a bench in the yard, a gas lamp behind him casting his shadow through the window and onto the room's back wall. If the scene were evenly lit, with no shadows, it would have only two important planes of depth: Pearl, sleeping in the foreground, and John, standing in the background. Although the shadows add only one *real* plane of depth (the wall), our mind's eye is aware of objects or shapes in five different planes: Mitchum seated in the yard, the window frame, Pearl sleeping on the bed, John, and the back wall. Even more important to the scene's dramatic power is the very real sense of Mitchum's presence in the room as his shadow looms over and threatens the shadow of John on the wall.

9. Use of reflections. Directors also make imaginative use of reflections to create a sense of depth and pack additional information into the frame. In *Grapes of Wrath,* for example, as the Joad truck travels across the Mohave desert at night, the camera looks out through the windshield at the strange world they are driving through. At the same time, the pale, ghostly reflections of Tom, Al, and Pa are seen on the glass as they talk about what they are seeing. In this way, the information which would usually require two shots is compressed into one. The same technique is used in *Hardcore,* where the worried face of George C. Scott (as the father) is reflected in the windshield as he tries to track his runaway daughter in a big-city porno district (Fig. 4.26).

|4.26| Use of Reflections: A worried father (George C. Scott) searches for his runaway daughter through a big-city porno district in this scene from *Hardcore.* By showing his reflected image on the car's windshield, director Paul Schrader has not only provided an additional plane of depth, but has, in effect, doubled the information in the frame: Not only do we see what the father sees, but also his reaction to it.

The effects described in this section, of course, have nothing to do with specialized three-dimensional projection systems such as 3-D and Cinerama. But most of these techniques do provide a fairly effective illusion of depth.

In spite of a recent revival of 3-D in films like *Jaws 3-D, The Spacehunter,* and *Friday the 13th, Part III,* and some new projection techniques, the effect has not been much improved, and the troublesome 3-D glasses are still required. And the quality of the films released in 3-D hasn't done much to help sell the product. Lily Tomlin perhaps sums up the problem best:

> *Bwana Devil* in 3-D was modestly billed as "The Miracle of the Age." On the poster it promised, "A Lion in Your Lap! A Lover in Your Arms!" . . . What more could one ask for? Well, a better script, perhaps. Is there a rule somewhere that says that for every giant techno-step we take forward we must take one step back and touch base with banality? So often, what we expect to be techno-leaps turn out to be techno-trash[2] [Fig. 4.27].

2. Lily Tomlin, as told to Jane Wagner, "Memoirs of an Usherette." *The Movies,* July 1983, pp. 41–42.

QUESTIONS

On Cinematic Qualities

1. To what degree is the film cinematic? Cite specific examples from the film to prove that the director succeeds or fails in (a) keeping the image constantly alive and in motion, (b) setting up clear, crisp visual and aural rhythms, (c) creating the illusion of depth, and (d) using the other special properties of the medium.
2. Does the cinematography create clear, powerful, and effective images in a natural way, or does it self-consciously show off the skills and techniques of the cinematographer?
3. Which methods does the director use to draw our attention to the object of greatest significance?
4. Does the director succeed in keeping the screen alive by avoiding large areas of dead screen?
5. What are the primary or most memorable techniques used to create the illusion of a three-dimensional image?

| 4.27 | 3-D Revival: Peter Strauss and Molly Ringwald in a scene from *Spacehunter,* one of 1983's attempts at reviving the 3-D "experience." Although these films produced some interesting three-dimensional effects, their overall quality was such that the "revival" never really had a chance.

PRODUCTION DESIGN/ART DIRECTION

> It's one thing to dress a set to represent Anytown, U.S.A., but a true aptitude for movie magic is needed to rebuild John Steinbeck's *Cannery Row* on a sound stage, make moviegoers feel at home far far away in another galaxy, turn New York City into a maximum security prison, or show how Los Angeles might look with a population of two hundred million in the year 2020.[3]

These are the challenges being met by modern production designers, who are finally being recognized for their critical contributions to the look of modern films. Actually, there is some confusion as to the difference between an art director and a production designer. The titles are synonomous when only one or the other is listed in the credits for a film. When both titles are listed, it means that the production designer conceives and plans the look, or visual texture, of a film, and the art director is responsible for supervising the work required in executing that plan. The production designer, or art director, will first make elaborate and detailed sketches and plans for the set, then supervise, down to the last detail, the construction, painting, furnishings, and decoration until he or she has achieved the exact look intended.

In every stage of this process the production designer consults with the other two people directly responsible for the visual texture of the film, the director and the cinematographer. All three must work closely, seeking each other's opinion, conferring, and coordinating their efforts toward a unified visual effect. In the modern film, this collaboration is often so integrated that art directors are often asked to suggest camera angles and lighting in their design, decisions that in the past have been left completely to the director and cinematographer. Such requests make very good sense, since production design has such a tremendous influence on the look of a film that it always affects the cinematographer's choice of lighting, angles, and focus. Likewise, the director's decisions may be subtly altered by the mood that a finely wrought set creates.

Even the actor's performances are enhanced and reinforced by production design. Settings are consciously designed as "personalized environments" that reflect a character and underscore or enhance the mood of each scene (Figs. 4.28 and 4.29). Yet while a good set is a perfectly integrated and powerful part of the

3. Bart Mills, "The Brave New World of Production Design." *American Film*, January-February 1982, p. 40.

|4.28|

|4.29|

Settings as Personalized Environments: In *Fanny and Alexander,* the production designer used rich, sensuous colors and luxurious but warm and comfortable furnishings in the Ekdahl family home [4.28] to reflect their sensitivity and warmth, setting up a sharp contrast to the cold, austere, and ascetic household of the children's fanatic stepfather, Bishop Vergerus [4.29].

magic on the screen, it must never be so dominant that it upstages the actors.

In recent years, production designers have been doing much of their work in studios, because many directors are returning to the sound stages, preferring to stylize a realistic background than go on location. There are two reasons for this. One seems to be that many of these directors were raised on the studio-made products of the '30s and '40s, and admired their look and feel so much that they are now trying to create similar styles in their own films. Another reason is the need to compete with made-for-television movies, usually filmed on location with smaller budgets and less attention to visual texture and production design. So a more impressive look is created for the big screen, where the attention, care, and expenditures necessary for obtaining that look can be better appreciated.

The production designer is also extremely important on location. He or she will be closely involved with the director in choosing the location on which the film will be shot, and will then design and oversee the construction of any sets that may be needed on location. For *Days of Heaven,* art director Jack Fisk worked closely with director Terrence Malick in scouting locations. When they finally found the perfect location in Canada (for a story set in Texas), the beauty of the rolling fields of wheat blowing in the wind reminded Fisk of the ocean, so he designed an unusual farmhouse with features that vaguely resembled a ship.

To build this set required a battle with the producers, who wanted an ordinary-looking ranch house. Fisk's theory is that audiences are disappointed with a truly realistic setting, and expect a kind of heightened reality, which he attempted to provide.

A more realistic, contemporary story like *The River* calls for a set that is completely authentic, and production designer Chuck Rosen was thrilled when a local man told him: "My Lord, Lord almighty, this farm here looks exactly like my grandaddy's farm." To achieve this look on location near Kingsport, Tennessee was no easy matter. Universal *purchased* 440 acres of mountain forest specifically for the movie. Sixty of those acres were leveled to create a river-bottom farm, and Rosen designed and constructed a two-story farmhouse, a main barn, an equipment building, and a double corncrib. A dam was built below the farm on the Holsten River, raising the water level by four feet, and a levee was built to keep the farm from flooding. Since filming continued into late November, bright autumn foliage had to be sprayed with green paint for summer scenes. A huge cornfield by the river, however, was planted late and so well-watered that four rows had to be sprayed brown or replaced with dead stalks for the autumn flood scene. Although this was the first "60-acre set" he'd ever done, Rosen achieved the main thing he had hoped for: "It looks like it belongs."[4]

The task of the art director is made especially challenging by an audience who demands that the world they see on the screen be completely convincing. For this reason, production designers must strive for a thorough illusion, creating transitions so smooth that viewers are unaware that in *Raiders of the Lost Ark* Harrison Ford outran the rolling ball through a cave interior set in England and escaped into a sunlit exterior in Hawaii (Fig. 4.30).

Perhaps the most serious kind of challenge faced by the production designer occurs when he's required to build a complete fantasy world. For *Blade Runner,* production designer Lawrence G. Paull created a complete futurescape for the year 2020 by what is called "additive architecture," that is, by building protrusions on to existing structures. The structures used were located on the familiar New York street set in the back lot of Burbank studios. *Blade Runner* also required twenty-five interior sets, one created inside an industrial refrigerator locker. Through inventive production design and the use of practically every technical trick in the book, Paull created a set that enabled director Ridley Scott

4. Linda Gross, "On Golden River." *Los Angeles Times Calendar,* 13 November 1983, p. 22.

|4.30| Composite Settings: Production designers are often required to create the illusion that two completely different sets in different locations are different parts of a single location. In this scene from *Raiders of the Lost Ark,* Harrison Ford is running away from the huge rolling boulder in a cave interior set in England. A few seconds later in the film he emerges from the cave into a sunlit exterior in Hawaii.

to "build layers of texture, so that visual information is imparted in every square inch of screen," and to convince the viewer that he has been transported to another time and another place[5] (Fig. 4.31).

|4.31| Inventive Production Design: Lawrence G. Paull built multiple layers of texture into his set for *Blade Runner,* so that director Ridley Scott could pack every square inch of the screen with visual information. The result was a set so powerful that it almost overwhelms the characters and the story, even in action scenes like this one showing Harrison Ford running across a rooftop.

QUESTIONS

On Production Design/Art Direction

1. How important is the set and/or location to the overall look of the film? Is it essentially a realistic or authentic set, or is it stylized to suggest a heightened reality?
2. Was the movie filmed primarily on location or in the studio? What effect does this have on the style or look of the film?
3. How do the settings serve as personalized environments to enhance or reinforce the actors' performances? To what degree do the settings underscore or enhance the mood or quality of each scene?
4. Is the setting so powerful and dominant that it upstages the actors?
5. If the film is a period piece, a fantasy, or a science fiction story taking place in a future time or on a strange planet, is the set convincing enough to make us believe (during the film) that we are really in another time and place? If so, what factors or details present in the set contribute to its convincing effect? If the set is not completely convincing, why does it fail?

5. Mills, p. 45.

EDITING

Also extremely important is the contribution made by the editor, whose function is to assemble the complete film, as if it were a gigantic and complex jigsaw puzzle, from its various component parts and soundtracks. The great Russian director V. I. Pudovkin, believing that editing is "the foundation of the film art," observed that "the expression that the film is 'shot' is entirely false, and should disappear from the language. The film is not *shot,* but built, built up from separate strips of celluloid that are its raw materials. . . ."[6] Alfred Hitchcock reinforces this viewpoint: "The screen ought to speak its own language, freshly coined, and it can't do that unless it treats an acted scene as a piece of raw material which must be broken up, taken to bits, before it can be woven into an expressive visual pattern."[7]

Because of the tremendous importance of the editing process, the editor's role can almost equal that of the director. Regardless of the quality of the raw material provided by the director, it may be worthless unless careful judgment is exercised in deciding when each segment will appear and how long it will remain on the screen. And this assembly of parts must be done with artistic sensitivity, perception, and aesthetic judgment as well as a true involvement in the subject and a clear understanding of the director's intentions. Therefore, for the most part, the director and the editor must be considered almost equal partners in the construction of a film. In some cases, the editor may be the true structuring genius, the master builder or architect of the film. In fact, the editor may have the clearest vision of the film's unity, and he or she may even make up for a lack of clear vision on the director's part.

Such would seem to be the case with many of Woody Allen's films. According to Ralph Rosenblum, who edited six of his films, Allen is obsessed with keeping a strain of seriousness running through practically any film he makes, much of which Rosenblum eliminates in the cutting room. *Annie Hall,* for example, was shot as a more philosophical film (working title—*Anhedonia*): The focal character was Alvy Singer, Annie was a secondary character,

6. V. I. Pudovkin, from the Introduction to the German edition, *Film Technique and Film Acting,* first Evergreen ed. New York: Grove Press, Inc., 1976, p. 24.

7. Richard Dyer McCann, ed., *Film: A Montage of Theories.* New York: E. P. Dutton and Co., Inc., 1966, p. 56.

and the mood fell somewhere between *Interiors* and *Manhattan*. In the editing process, Rosenblum refocused the film on the Alvy/Annie relationship by eliminating whole sequences and plot lines, and helped Allen develop and shoot a new ending to match the new focus. The end result was a film that won Academy Awards for best picture, director, actress, and original screenplay, but not even a nomination for the editor, who changed the whole emphasis and tone of the film from what was originally conceived and shot by the director.

The Editor's Responsibilities

To fully appreciate the important role that editing plays in film, we must look carefully at the basic responsibility of the editor: to assemble a complete film that is a unified whole, in which each separate shot or sound contributes significantly to the development of the film's theme and total effect. To fully understand the editor's function, it is also important that we comprehend the nature of the jigsaw puzzle. The basic unit with which the editor works is the *shot*, a strip of film produced by a single continuous run of the camera. By joining or splicing a series of shots so that they communicate a unified action taking place at one time and place, the editor assembles what is known as a *scene*. He or she then links a series of scenes to form what is called a *sequence*, which constitutes a significant part of the film's dramatic structure much in the same way that an act functions in a play. To assemble these parts effectively, the editor must successfully perform each of the following functions.

SELECTIVITY

The most basic editing function is selecting the best shots from several takes—choosing those segments that provide the most powerful, effective, or significant visual and sound effects—and eliminating inferior, irrelevant, or insignificant material. Of course, we cannot fully appreciate the editor's selectivity because we do not see the footage that ends up on the cutting room floor.

In deciding what actually ends up on the cutting room floor, the editor must consider several different takes of the same piece of action. While the film was being shot, the director began the selection process by telling the script girl which takes were good enough to be printed. Then each shot printed is screened shortly after the shooting at the "dailies," and the director may throw out more shots at that point, shots that contain flaws he or she was not aware of during the shooting. By the time the editor finally gets the film, the obvious bad footage has been culled out. But there are still difficult and subtle decisions to be made. For a given five seconds worth of action the editor may be working with ten "takes" or shots of that segment of action and dialogue, taken with three different cameras from three different angles. Assuming that the sound quality is adequate in each shot, the editor will choose the shot to fill that five-second slot in the finished film after considering the following factors: the camera technique (clear focus, smooth camera movement, and so on), composition, lighting, acting performance, and best angle to match the previous shot.

If each shot were equal in quality, the decision would be simple: Go with the best angle to match with the previous shot, and be done with it. But usually it's not that easy, and some of the editor's decisions amount to difficult compromises. The best shot in terms of lighting and composition may be the weakest in acting performance and dramatic impact. And the best acting performance may be poorly composed, or have lighting problems, or be slightly out of focus.

COHERENCE, CONTINUITY, AND RHYTHM

The film editor is also responsible for putting the pieces together into a coherent whole. To achieve this, he or she must guide our thoughts, associations, and emotional responses effectively from one image to another, or from one sound to another, so that the interrelationships between separate images and sounds are absolutely clear and so that transitions between scenes and sequences are smooth. To achieve this goal, the editor must carefully consider the aesthetic, dramatic, and psychological effect of the juxtaposition of image to image, sound to sound, or image to sound, and carefully place each piece of film and soundtrack together accordingly.

TRANSITIONS

In the past, filmmakers made widespread use of several special optical effects to create smooth and clear bridges between the film's more important divisions, such as transitions between two sequences that take place at a different time or place. Such formula transitions include the following:

- *Wipe*. A new image is separated from the previous one by a clear horizontal, vertical, or diagonal line that moves across the screen to "push" the previous image off the screen.
- *Flip-frame*. The entire frame appears to flip over to reveal a new scene, creating a visual effect very similar to turning a page.
- *Dissolve*. The gradual merging of the end of one shot into the beginning of the next, produced by superimposing a fade-out onto a fade-in of equal length, or imposing one scene over another.
- *Fade-out/fade-in*. The last image of the first sequence fades momentarily to black and the first image of the next sequence is gradually illuminated.

Each of these transitional devices has its own effect on the pace of the film and the nature of the transition taking place. Generally speaking, dissolves are relatively slow transitions, and are used to make the viewer aware of major scene changes or elapsed time. Flips and wipes are faster, and are employed when the logic of time-lapse or place change is more apparent to the viewer.

These devices are still used in films such as *The Sting* and *Pennies From Heaven* to suggest a film style typical of the period when the story takes place. But, for the most part, modern filmmakers have given up the extensive use of these traditional formulas, and often rely on a simple cut from one sequence to another without any clear transitional signal. The soundtrack has also taken on some of the transitional functions formerly handled through purely optical means.

Regardless of the nature of transitions, whether they be long and obvious (as in a slow dissolve), or short and quick (as in a simple instantaneous cut), the editor is the person who must put them together so they have continuity—that is, a logical flow from one sequence to another or merely from one image to another.

When possible, the editor will often use a *form cut* to smooth the visual flow from one shot, scene, or sequence to another. With this type of cut, the shape of an object in one shot is matched to a similarly shaped object in the succeeding shot. Since both objects appear in the same area of the frame, the first image flows smoothly into the second. In Kubrick's *2001*, for example, a piece of bone flung into the air dissolves into a similarly shaped orbiting bomb in the following sequence; in Eisenstein's *Potemkin*, the handle of a sword or dagger in one shot becomes the similarly shaped large cross around a priest's neck in the following shot. While form cuts like these provide smooth visual transitions, they also create ironic collisions of sharply contrasting ideas.

Similar to the *form cut* are cuts that use color or texture to link shots. For example, a glowing sun at the end of one shot may dissolve into a campfire at the beginning of the next. Of course, there are limitations to this type of transition, and when they are overdone they lose the sense of naturalness that makes them effective.

The editor must also assemble shots carefully for coherence *within* the sequence. For example, a great many sequences require an *establishing shot* at their beginning to provide us with a broad picture of the setting, so that we get a feel of the environment in which the scene occurs. The editor must decide if such an establishing shot is necessary for a clear understanding of the relationship of the closer and more detailed shots that follow it.

Two different editing procedures have become more or less standard in making transitions in time and space. The first of these, which we'll call the *outside/in pattern,* follows a very logical sequence, and concentrates on orienting us to the new setting. In it, we move in, as it were, to a new setting from the outside and gradually work our way inside to the details. The logical context of each step is clearly shown so that we always know exactly where we are: We get our bearings with an establishing shot of the whole setting, move into the setting itself, and then focus our attention on the details of that setting. This, the most traditional or typical kind of editing sequence, is the outside/in pattern.

The alternative to this editing formula, the *inside/out pattern,* is the exact opposite: Here we are jolted suddenly from one line of action that we completely understand to a close-up detail in another place, and we don't know where we are or really what is happening. Then, in a sequence of related shots, we back off from the detail of the first close-up and gradually find out where we are and what is happening in relation to the setting. Thus we move from a disorienting shot to more distant, more general shots that help us understand fully the action in the context of the new scene.

Airport '77, for example, begins with a couple of burglars breaking into an airport office at night and stealing information from a file cabinet. While that burglary is in progress, we jump immediately to a close-up of a hand pushing throttle levers forward. In the next shot, we back up to establish that the hand belongs to Jack Lemmon, who is in the pilot seat of a jetliner, with a view through the cockpit glass showing the runway in front of the plane. The next shot takes us one step further back and we see that Lemmon is not in a real cockpit at all but in a simulator training cockpit.

Thus we jolt the viewer with a transition first, and establish the overall location of the scene later. This creates a dynamic, explosive, exciting edit, which adds oomph and suspense to the transition. The accompanying series of illustrations (Figs. 4.32 and 4.33) demonstrate both methods as used for the coherent structuring of shots in an editorial sequence.

RHYTHMS, TEMPO, AND TIME CONTROL

A great many factors work together and separately to create rhythms in the motion picture: the physical objects moving on the screen, the real or apparent movement of the camera, the musical score, the pace of the dialogue and the natural rhythms of human speech, as well as the pace of the plot itself. All of these factors set up unique rhythms that blend into the whole. But these rhythms are natural, imposed on the film by the nature of its raw material. Perhaps the most dominant tempo of the film, its most compelling rhythm, is created by the frequency of editorial cuts and the varying duration of shots between cuts. The rhythms set up by these cuts are unique because, although they divide the film into a number of separate parts, they do so without interrupting the continuity and the fluid form of the medium. Thus editorial cuts set up clear rhythmic patterns that do not break the flowing stream of images and sound, but impart to it an externally controllable and unique rhythmic quality.

The rhythms established by editorial cutting are such a natural part of the film medium that we are often unaware of cuts within a given scene, yet we respond unconsciously to the tempo they create. One reason we can remain unconscious of such rhythms is that they often duplicate the manner in which we look at things in real life, by glancing quickly from one point of attention to another. Our emotional state is often reflected in how quickly our attention shifts from one point to another. Thus, slow cutting simulates the impressions of a tranquil observer, whereas quick cutting simulates the impressions of an excited observer. Our response to this built-in sense of "glancing" rhythms allows the editor to manipulate us, exciting or calming us almost at will.

Although the editor will generally alternate one tempo with another throughout the film as a whole, the cutting speed of each scene should be determined by the content of that scene, so that its rhythm corresponds to such things as the pace of the action, the speed of the dialogue, and the overall emotional tone.

4.32 EDITING SEQUENCE *A*—OUTSIDE/IN

The following editing sequence illustrates a very common pattern that we'll call the *outside/in pattern*. In this type of editing we get our bearings with an establishing shot of the new setting, and then move closer in to focus on the main characters and/or details of the new environment.

In editing sequence *A* there is almost no action and very little opportunity for dramatic visuals. But the editor has kept the visual image alive by providing a variety of viewpoints and creating a visual rhythm by varying the length of the shots. The editor also made the sequence clear by the order in which the shots have been joined.

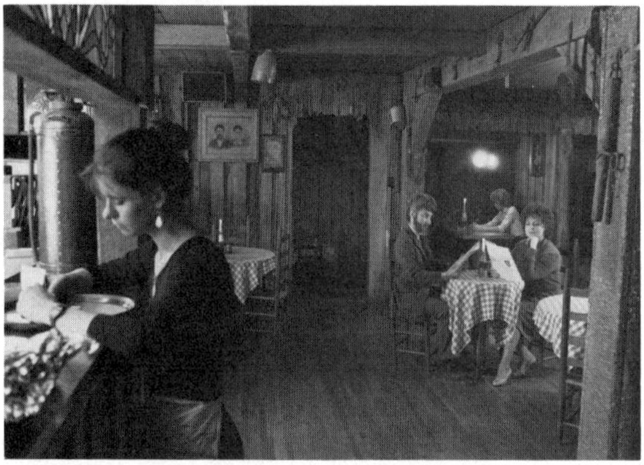

a. To help us get our bearings, the editor begins with a complete view of the setting and the actors' relative positions in that setting (an *establishing shot*).

b. In the second shot, the editor takes us closer to the actors, so that we can see them better and hear what they are saying. (This could also be accomplished with a slow zoom from shot 1a.)

c. The next shot takes us into the dialogue itself, and with the camera looking over the woman's shoulder, we see (and hear) the man as he talks.

d. To provide variety and visual rhythm in what is essentially a very static scene, the editor now cuts to a shot taken over the man's shoulder, focusing on the woman either reacting to his dialogue or responding verbally.

e. Now the editor cuts to a close-up of the man's face, providing an even more intimate viewpoint, capable of revealing subtle changes in expression. This kind of close-up is especially effective in a reaction shot, with the camera focusing on his face while the woman's voice is heard on the soundtrack.

f. Once again, for variety and rhythm, the editor cuts to a close-up of the woman's face, either speaking or reacting to the man's dialogue.

h. The next shot shows us what they are looking at: the waitress standing at the pickup counter, acknowledging the man's gesture (an *eye-line shot*).

g. Now the editor backs off to a two-shot to show both actors looking off-screen as the man tries to get the waitress's attention (a *look of outward regard*).

i. The editor then brings our attention back to the table with another over-the-shoulder shot of the woman talking, possibly commenting on the slow service.

j. As the waitress arrives to take the order, the editor cuts to a low-angle shot from behind the man's elbow, providing both variety and a clear view of the flirting waitress.

l. The next shot provides a viewpoint that combines both action and reaction, with the emphasis (and focus) on the woman's reaction. (To add intensity to the scene, this shot would be very short, perhaps a second or less.)

k. Next, the editor cuts to a shot that shows not only the man's response to the waitress, but the woman's reaction as well.

m. The editor then cuts to yet another viewpoint to record the waitress's reaction to the woman's reaction. This shot would also be of short duration, no longer than a second.

n. The editor then cuts quickly to a close-up of the woman's reaction, and her slow burn stretches out to about five seconds. The editor could then choose to continue this shot by a slow zoom away and a slow dissolve to another scene, a fade to black and then fading in the next scene, or a quick cut to another location. ▶

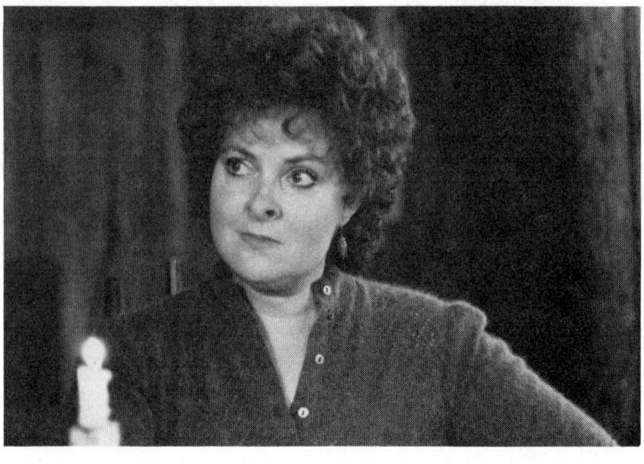

4.33 EDITING SEQUENCE *B*—INSIDE/OUT

The alternative to the outside/in pattern is the *inside/out pattern,* which jolts up suddenly from a line of action we completely understand to a close-up detail of some action in another place. With the first shot we are too close to know where we are, who the people are, or what's going on. Then, in a sequence of related shots, we back off from the detail of the first close-up shot and gradually find out where we are and what is happening in relationship to the setting.

a. The editor cuts immediately from the last shot of the previous scene into a totally unprepared-for detail in a different location.

b. In the next shot, we back off to a two-shot, which shows us the couple at a table in a restaurant.

c. If visual information in the larger setting is important to ▶ the action (like an important character entering through the door to the left), the third shot may back us off even further to show the necessary spatial relationships. If such details are not necessary, the editor may choose to show the wider set with a zoom out at the end of the scene, or may cut to another location without showing the table's surroundings at all.

EXPANSION OF TIME

Skillful editing can also greatly expand our normal concepts of time, through intercutting a normal action sequence with a series of related details. Take, for example, the brief action of a man walking up a flight of stairs. By simply alternating between a full shot of the man walking up the stairs with detailed shots of his feet, the scene and sense of time of the action are expanded. If close-ups of his face and his hand gripping the rail are added, our feeling of the time the action takes is even further expanded.

COMPRESSION OF TIME

By using fragmented flash-cutting, short "machine-gun bursts" of images sandwiched together, the editor can compress an hour's action into a few seconds. For example, by choosing representative actions out of the daily routine of a factory worker, the editor can, in a minute or two, suggest an entire eight-hour shift. By overlapping so that the first part of each shot is superimposed over the last part of the preceding one, a more fluid compression of time is achieved.

Another editorial technique used to compress time is the *jump cut,* which involves simply cutting out a strip of insignificant or unnecessary action from a continuous shot. For example, a continuous shot in a western follows the movement of the sheriff as he walks slowly across the street, from left to right, from his office to the saloon. If the continuous following of his movement slows the pace too much, the editor may cut out the section of film that shows him crossing the street, and jump cut from the point at which he steps into the street to his arrival at the sidewalk on the other side. Thus the jump cut speeds up the action by removing an unnecessary section of it, a section that is still easily understood when the scene, the moving subject, and the direction of movement are the same.

One of the most effective techniques of editorial cutting is *parallel cutting,* which is the quick alternating back and forth between two actions taking place at separate locations. Parallel cutting creates the impression that the two actions are occurring simultaneously, and can be a powerful suspense-building device. A common use of parallel cutting is seen in the "cavalry to the rescue" sequence, where the settlers in their circled wagons are under Indian attack, and the U.S. Cavalry is on the way. By cutting back and forth between the besieged settlers and the hard-riding Cavalry troops, the editor makes the eventual confrontation seem closer and closer, and effectively builds suspense between the two related scenes.

An entirely different kind of time compression is achieved by cutting to brief flashbacks or memory images, a technique that merges past and present into the same stream and often helps us to understand a character better.

CREATIVE JUXTAPOSITION: MONTAGE

Often the editor is called upon to communicate creatively within the film. Through unique juxtapositions of images and sounds, editors can often express an attitude or tone toward the material (as might be the case with an ironic transition). Or they may be called upon to create, through a brief series of visual and aural images, what is commonly known as *montage*. The term montage refers to an especially effective series of images and sounds that, without any clear, logical or sequential pattern, form a kind of visual poem in miniature. The unity of a montage is derived from complex internal relationships, which we understand instantly and intuitively.

In creating a montage, the editor uses a brief series of visual and aural images as impressionistic shorthand to create a certain mood, atmosphere, transition in time or place, or a physical or emotional impact. As defined by the great Russian director and film theorist Sergei Eisenstein, a montage is assembled from separate images that provide a "partial representation which in their combination and juxtaposition, shall evoke in the consciousness and feelings of the spectator . . . that same initial general image which originally hovered before the creative artist."[8]

An example of the montage concept can be borrowed from poetic imagery: in Shakespeare's *Sonnet 73,* he compares his time of life (old age) to three separate images: (1) winter: "When yellow leaves, or none, or few, do hang/Upon those boughs which shake against the cold"; (2) twilight: "As after sunset fadeth in the west"; and (3) a dying fire.

> That time of year thou mayst in me behold
> When yellow leaves, or none, or few, do hang
> Upon those boughs which shake against the cold,
> Bare ruined choirs where late the sweet birds sang.
> In me thou see'st the twilight of such day
> As after sunset fadeth in the west,

8. Jay Leyda, trans., *The Film Sense.* New York: Harcourt, Brace and World, Inc., 1947, pp. 30–31.

Which by and by and by black night doth take away,
Death's second self, that seals up all in rest.
In me thou see'st the glowing of such fire,
That on the ashes of his youth doth lie
As the deathbed whereon it must expire,
Consumed with that which it was nourished by.
This thou perceivest, which makes thy love more strong,
To love that well which thou must leave ere long.

A cinematic montage might be created around these images, all of which have universal associations with death and old age, with visual and aural images edited as follows:

Shot 1: Close-up of wrinkled faces of aged couple, both in rocking chairs. Their eyes are dim, and stare into the distance as their chairs rock slowly back and forth. *Sound:* Creaking of rocking chairs, loud ticking of old grandfather clock.

Shot 2: Slow dissolve to close-up of withered leaves, barely clinging to bare branches, light snow falling, thin layer of snow upon the black bare branches. *Sound:* Low moaning wind. Grandfather clock continues to tick.

Shot 3: Slow dissolve to seacoast scene, the sun's edge just barely visible on the horizon of the water; then it slips away, leaving a red glow and gradually darkening sky, light visibly fading. *Sound:* Soft rhythm of waves washing up on shore—grandfather clock continues ticking in the background.

Shot 4: Slow dissolve from red glow in sky to a glowing bed of coals in a fireplace . . . A few feeble fingers of flame flicker, then sputter out and die. The glowing coals, as if fanned by a slight breeze, glow brighter, then grow dimmer and dimmer. *Sound:* Continued sound link of ticking grandfather clock.

Shot 5: Return to same scene as shot #1, close-up of wrinkled faces of aged couple, rocking in their rocking chairs. *Sound:* Creaking chairs and the continuous tick of grandfather clock; gradual fade to black.

Montage is an especially effective technique when the director desires to compress a great deal of meaning into a very brief segment. In *The Grapes of Wrath,* John Ford used a montage that might be titled "The Joad's Journey Through Oklahoma" and another we might call "Invasion of the Big Cats" (tractors). Effective montages also occur in *Patton* (the "Winter Night Battle" montage), in *Rocky* (the "Training for the Big Fight" montage), and in *Mr. Smith Goes to Washington* (the "Patriotic Washington Tour" montage).

QUESTIONS

On Editing

1. How does the editing effectively guide your thoughts, associations, and emotional responses from one image to another so that smooth continuity and coherence are achieved?
2. Is the editing smooth, natural, and unobtrusive, or is it tricky and self-conscious? How much does the editor communicate through creative juxtapositions, such as ironic transitions, montages, and the like, and how effective is this communication?
3. What is the overall effect of editorial intercutting and transitions on the pace of the film as a whole?
4. How does the cutting speed (which determines the average duration of each shot) correspond to the emotional tone of the scene involved?
5. What segments of the film seem overlong or boring? Which parts of these segments could be cut without altering the total effect? Where are additional shots necessary to make the film completely coherent?
6. In the "stolen base" editing sequence that follows (Fig. 4.34), only minimal information has been provided. Analyze the sequence carefully, considering the following questions for each shot:
   a. What information does the shot convey, and what is its particular function in the editing sequence at this point?
   b. Why have the director and editor chosen to show us the action from this particular position? Does it represent the viewpoint of a player? Would another position or angle be equally good or better? Why?
   c. Which player do you identify with most strongly? Why?
   d. How does each shot relate to the shots before and after it in the sequence? Are other shots necessary to make the chain of events coherent? Is each shot made more meaningful by the shot that comes before it?
   e. Count out the number of beats (at two beats per second) that you would hold each shot on the screen. What is your total running time for the sequence? Which shots would be the longest and which the shortest? Why?
   f. Which shots could be relocated in the sequence? Which could be eliminated? Which could be repeated more than once? What effect would repeating them have?

4.34 "STOLEN BASE" EDITING SEQUENCE

(See question 6 of "Questions on Editing.")

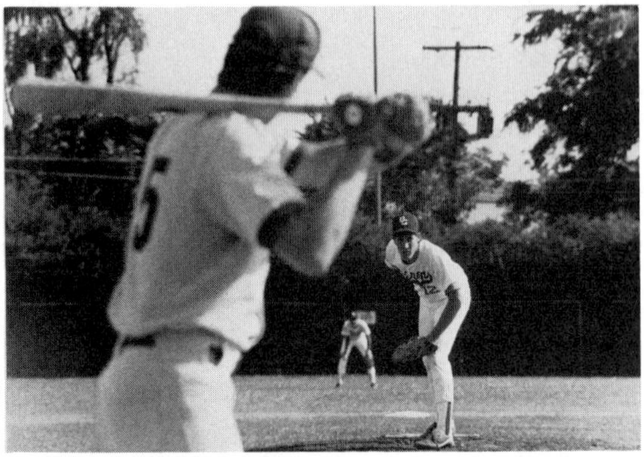

a. The pitcher looks in for the sign.

b. The batter studies the pitcher.

c. The pitcher studies the batter.

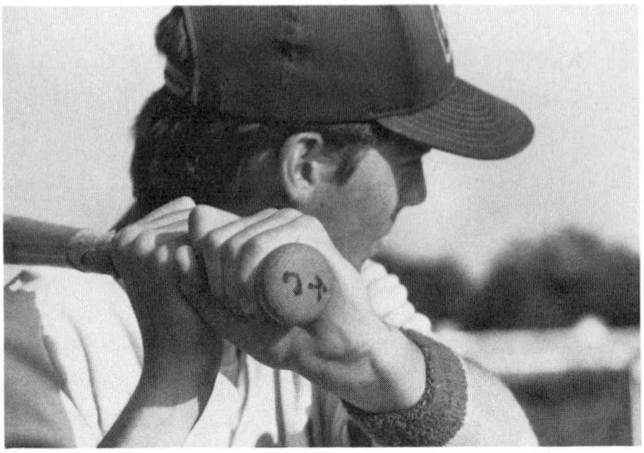

d. The batter tightens his grip.

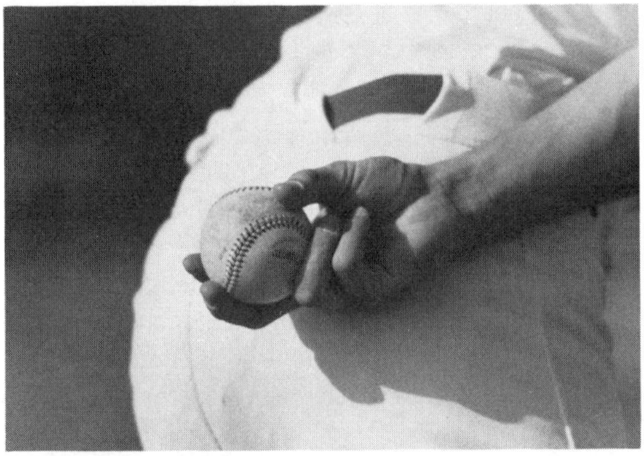

e. The pitcher sets his grip on the ball.

f. The pitcher checks the runner at first.

g. The first baseman holds the runner close to first.

h. The pitcher goes into his wind-up.

i. The runner breaks for second.

j. The pitcher throws the ball toward home plate.

k. The catcher throws the ball toward second.

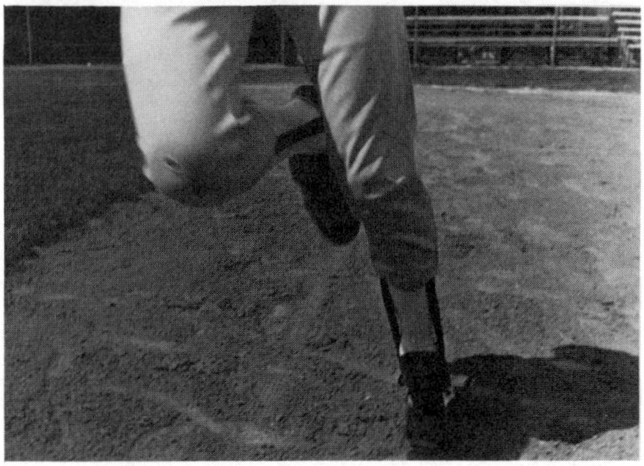

l. The runner moves on toward second.

m. The runner approaches second.

n. The runner slides into second.

o. The second baseman looks down at the dropped ball.

p. The umpire calls the runner "safe."

q. The runner's coach.

r. The pitcher.

CINEMATIC POINT OF VIEW

The term *point of view* must be considered in a rather specialized sense as it pertains to cinematography, for it differs significantly from the term as used in a literary sense. One primary difference is that there is no need for consistency in the cinematic viewpoint. Not only would true consistency of viewpoint be boring in a film, but it would also be too restricted for effective communication. What is important about point of view in film is that it maintain continuity and coherence. Thus, though we may be freely spirited about from one vantage point to another, we need only to respond intuitively to the different ways in which things are shown, so that the changing vantage points make sense to us visually, but not necessarily logically.

In considering cinematic point of view, the filmmaker is primarily concerned with the following matters:

1. From what position and through what kinds of "eyes" does the camera see the action?
2. What effect does the position of the camera and its particular ways of seeing the action have on our view of the action?
3. How is our response affected by changes in the point of view?

There are essentially four different points of view employed in the motion picture:

1. The objective point of view (camera as sideline observer)
2. The subjective point of view (camera as participant in the action)
3. The indirect-subjective point of view
4. The director's interpretive point of view

Generally, all four viewpoints can be used in every film to varying degrees, depending on the demands of the dramatic situation and the creative vision and style of the director.

Objective Point of View

The objective point of view is illustrated by John Ford's "philosophy of camera." He considered the camera to be a window, with the audience outside the window viewing the people and events within. We are asked to watch the actions as if they were taking place at a distance, but we are not asked to participate. Thus, the objective point of view employs a static camera as much as possible in order to produce this "window effect," and concentrates on the actors and the action without drawing attention to the camera. The objective camera suggests an emotional distance between camera and subject, as though the camera were simply recording, as straightforwardly as possible, the characters and actions of the story taking place. For the most part, the director uses the most natural, normal, straightforward types of camera positioning and camera angles to capture the action. Thus the objective camera does not comment on or interpret the action, but merely records it, letting it unfold before our eyes. We see the action from the viewpoint of an objective, impersonal observer. If the camera moves, it does so unobtrusively, calling as little attention to itself as possible.

There are distinct advantages to using the objective point of view. In most films, continuity and clear communication of the dramatic scene demand that some use be made of the objective point of view. But overuse of the objective view is dangerous, because its objective and impersonal qualities may cause us to lose interest. The objective viewpoint forces us to pinpoint subtle but perhaps significant visual details by ourselves (Fig. 4.35).

|4.35| Objective Viewpoint: In this objective shot of a baseball game in progress, we are clearly sideline observers, not really involved in the action.

Subjective Point of View

The subjective point of view provides us with the visual viewpoint and emotional intensity felt by a character participating in the action. Alfred Hitchcock, whose philosophy of camera is opposite to that of Ford, specializes in creating a strong sense of direct involvement on the part of the audience, and employs elaborate camera movement to create visual sequences that bring us into the suspense, literally forcing us to become the characters and experience their emotions.

An important tool in creating this kind of subjective involvement, according to Hitchcock, is skillful editing and a viewpoint close to the action, as the following passage from his essay "Direction" indicates:

> So you gradually build up the psychological situation, piece by piece, using the camera to emphasize first one detail, then another. The point is to draw the audience right into the situation—instead of leaving them to watch it from outside, from a distance. And you can do this only by breaking the action up into details and cutting from one piece to the other, so that each detail is forced in turn on the attention of the audience and reveals its psychological meaning. If you played the whole scene straight through, and simply made a photographic record of it with the camera always in one position, you would lose your power over the audience. They would watch the scene without becoming really involved in it, and you would have no means of concentrating their attention on those particular visual details which make them feel what the characters are feeling.[9]

With the more subjective point of view, our experience becomes more intense and more immediate as we become involved intimately in the action. Generally, this viewpoint is characterized by the moving camera, which forces us to see exactly what the character is seeing and in a sense to become the character (Fig. 4.36).

It is almost impossible to sustain a purely subjective point of view throughout a film, as was attempted in *Lady in the Lake*. The story of this film was told entirely through the eyes of its detective hero, and the only time the hero's face was seen was in a mirror's reflection. His hands and arms occasionally appeared, below eye level, as they might normally be seen from the hero's viewpoint.

9. McCann, p. 57. From "Direction" by Alfred Hitchcock, in *Footnotes to the Film*, edited by Charles Davy; reprinted by permission of Peter Davies Ltd., publishers.

|4.36| Subjective Viewpoint: In this subjective shot, the camera has put us in the game, giving us the catcher's view of the action.

The difficulty of sustaining such a viewpoint over an entire film, however, should be obvious, for clarity of communication and continuity usually demand that the film switch back and forth between the objective and subjective points of view.

This change in point of view from objective to subjective is often accomplished in the following manner. First, an objective shot which shows a character looking at something off screen (called a *look of outward regard*) cues us to wonder what he is looking at. Then the following shot, called an *eye-line shot,* shows us subjectively what the character is seeing. Because the simple logical relationship between the two shots provides a smooth and natural movement from an objective to a subjective point of view, this pattern is typical in film. The alternation of objective and subjective viewpoints, as well as the tight link between sight and sound, is further illustrated by the following scene:

1. *Establishing shot:* Objective camera view from street corner, focusing on a workman using an air hammer in center of street (apparent distance 50 to 75 feet). *Sound:* Loud chatter of air hammer mingled with other street noises.
2. *Cut to subjective view:* Close-ups of air hammer, and violently shaking lower arms and hands of workman, from workman's point of view. *Sound:* Hammer is almost deafening—no other sounds heard.

3. *Cut back to objective camera:* Heavy truck turns corner beyond workman, bears down on him at top speed. *Sound:* Loud chatter of air hammer, other street noises, rising sound of approaching truck.
4. *Cut to subjective view:* Close-up of air hammer and workman's hands as seen from his viewpoint. *Sound:* First, only deafening sounds of air hammer, then a rising squeal of brakes mixed with hammer noise.
5. *Quick cut to a new subjective view:* Front of truck closing quickly on camera from ten feet away. *Sound:* Squeal of brakes louder, hammer stops, woman's voice screaming, cut short by sickening thud, followed by darkness and momentary silence.
6. *Cut back to objective viewpoint* (from street corner): Unconscious figure of workman in front of stopped truck, curious crowd gathering into circle. *Sound:* Mixed jumble of panicked voices, street noises, ambulance siren in distance.

In this way the constant alternation between the objective and the subjective view provides both a clear understanding of the dramatic flow of events and also a strong sense of audience involvement.

Indirect-Subjective Point of View

The indirect-subjective point of view does not really provide a participant's point of view, but it does bring us close to the action so that we feel intimately involved and our visual experience becomes more intense. Consider, for example, a close-up that conveys the emotional reaction of a character. We recognize that we are not the character, yet we are drawn into the feeling that is being conveyed in a subjective way. A close-up of a face contorted in pain makes us feel that pain more vividly than an objective shot from a greater distance. Another example is the kind of shot that was common in the old western. With the stagecoach under attack by outlaws, the director inserts close-ups of pounding hoofs to capture the furious rhythm and pulsing excitement of the chase, bringing us close to the action and increasing the intensity of our experience. This point of view is called indirect-subjective, because it gives us the feeling and immediacy of participating in the action without showing the action through a participant's eyes (Fig. 4.37).

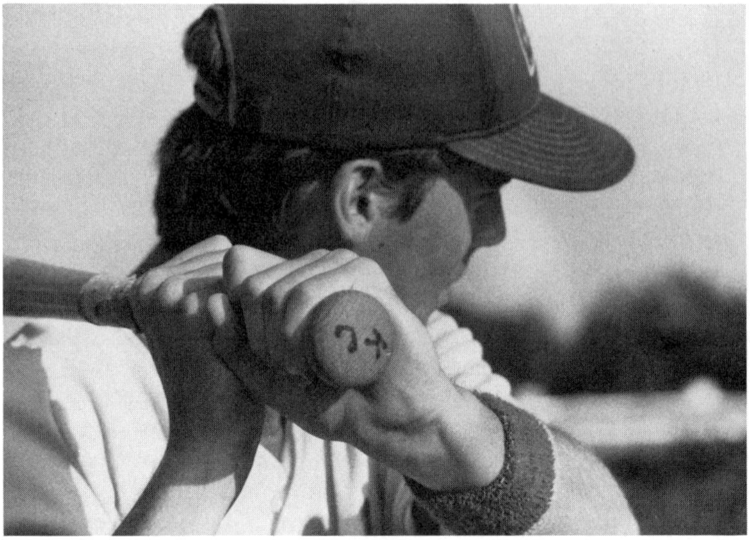

| 4.37 | Indirect-Subjective Viewpoint: Although we are not looking through any character's point of view, this indirect-subjective shot brings us close to the action and involves us in it, as we focus on the tension in the batter's hands as he awaits the pitch. Because we are so close to him, we are also identifying with the batter and feeling his tension.

| 4.38 | Director's Interpretive Viewpoint: By choosing an extremely low-angle view of the batter, the director has made us see him in a special or unusual way, perhaps to give us the pitcher's emotional perspective as he prepares to pitch to a powerful slugger in a close game.

Director's Interpretive Point of View

In other types of shots, the filmmaker chooses not only what to show us, but also how we will see it. By photographing the scene from special angles or with special lenses, or in slow or fast motion, and so on, he or she imposes upon the image a certain tone, emotional attitude, or style. We are thus forced to react emotionally in a certain way to what we see, thereby experiencing the director's point of view. The director is always manipulating our viewpoint in subtle ways, but with the director's interpretive point of view we are *consciously* aware that he wants us to see the action in some *unusual* way (Fig. 4.38).

There are examples of all four points of view in the following typical western sequence showing a stagecoach being attacked by bandits:

1. *Objective point of view:* Stagecoach and horses as seen from the side (from a distance of 50 to 75 feet) being pursued by bandits. Shot here could either be from a panning camera in fixed position or from a mobile camera tracking alongside or parallel to the path of the stagecoach.
2. *Subjective point of view:* Camera shot from the stage driver's point of view, looking out over horses' backs, with arms and hands holding and slapping reins seen below eye level.

3. *Indirect-subjective point of view:* Close-up of stage driver's face from side, as he turns his head to look back over his shoulder (a look of outward regard). His face registers fear, determination.
4. *Subjective point of view:* Camera shot of bandits in hot pursuit of stagecoach, from the point of view of driver looking back over top of stage.
5. *Indirect-subjective point of view:* Close-up of face of driver, now turned frontward again, registering strain, jaw set in determination, sweat streaming down face, screaming at horses.
6. *Director's interpretive point of view:* Slow-motion close-up of horses' heads in profile, their eyes wild with strain, mouths in agony straining at their bits, flecks of foamy sweat shaking from their necks. (By filming this shot in slow motion, the director in effect comments on the action, telling us how he wants us to see it. The slow-motion photography at this point conveys the horses' exhaustion, intensifies the tremendous effort they are putting out, and gives us a sense of the futility of the stage's chances for escape.)

TECHNIQUES FOR SPECIAL VISUAL EFFECTS

In conjunction with the four cinematic viewpoints described above, directors and cinematographers employ a variety of cinematic techniques to create special visual effects. The effects created by these techniques enhance certain qualities of the action or dramatic situation being filmed.

Hand-Held Camera

Related to the concept of cinematic point of view is the specialized dramatic effect achieved through use of the hand-held camera. Here the jerky, uneven movement of the camera heightens the sense of reality gained from the subjective viewpoint of a participant in motion. In *Alambrista!,* Robert Young employs an impressionistic hand-held camera, making the perspective jump madly to reflect the disassociation his Hispanic hero feels in a foreign country. If the viewpoint is not intended to be a subjective (participant) view, the same technique can give the sequence the feel of a documentary or newsreel. The hand-held camera, jerkiness and all, is especially effective in filming violent action scenes, where the random, chaotic camera movement fits in with the spirit of the action, as in a riot scene or in close-ups of fight scenes.

Camera Angles

Cinematographers, of course, do more with the camera than simply position it for one of the four basic viewpoints. The angle from which they photograph a certain event or object is also an important factor in cinematic composition. Sometimes they may employ different camera angles simply for the sake of variety or to create a sense of visual balance between one shot and another. But camera angles are also extremely effective at communicating special kinds of dramatic information or emotional attitudes. Since the objective point of view stresses or employs a normal, straightforward view of the action, unusual camera angles are employed primarily for other points of view, such as the subjective viewpoint of a participant in the action, or for the interpretive viewpoint of the director.

One type of objective camera angle is particularly worthy of mention. When an extremely high camera angle is combined with slow, fluid camera movement, as though the camera were slowly floating over the scene, the impression is that of a remote, external, detached spectator carefully examining the situation in an objective, almost scientific, manner (Fig. 4.39).

When the camera is placed below eye level, creating a *low-angle shot,* the size and importance of the subject are exaggerated. If a child is the principal figure in a film, low-angle shots of adults may be very much in evidence, as the director attempts to show us the scene from a child's perspective. For example, in *Night of the Hunter* two children are attempting to escape from the clutches of a Satanic itinerant preacher (Robert Mitchum) who has already murdered their mother. As the children attempt to launch a boat from the bank, Mitchum's figure is seen from a low angle as he crashes through the brush lining the bank and plunges into the water. The terror of the narrow escape is intensified by the low camera angle, which clearly communicates the helplessness of the children and their view of the monstrous Mitchum.

A different effect is achieved in *Lord of the Flies,* where Ralph, pursued to the point of exhaustion by the savage boys on the beach, falls headlong in the sand at the feet of a British naval officer. The low-angle shot of the officer, exaggerating his size and

|4.39| Extremely High Camera Angle: When the mobile camera seems to float slowly high above the action, as in this scene from *Midnight Express*, we become very remote and detached, as though our objectivity (like our viewpoint) is almost godlike.

solidity, conveys a sense of dominance, strength, and protectiveness to Ralph.

Thus, low camera angles effectively convey, in an exaggerated way, the participant's emotional perception of the adults.

An effect opposite to that of the low-angle shot is generally achieved by placing the camera *above* eye level (a *high-angle shot*), where the viewpoint seems to dwarf the subject and diminish its importance. Consider, for example, a subjective camera angle (high-angle shot) that would show Gulliver's view of the Lilliputians.

The director may also employ certain camera angles to suggest the feeling he or she wants to convey about a character at a given moment. In *Touch of Evil*, for example, Orson Welles employs a high camera angle to look down on Janet Leigh as she enters a prison cell, a shot that emphasizes her despair, her state of mind, and her helplessness. By making us see the character as he sees her, Welles interprets the emotional tenor and atmosphere of the scene for us (Figs. 4.40, 4.41, and 4.42).

In addition to the use of varying camera angles, directors have a great many other techniques at their command to aid in the creation of special dramatic effects. Although those discussed below are by no means the only techniques available, this list gives some idea of the tools at the filmmaker's disposal.

[4.40]

[4.41]

[4.42]

The Effect of Changing Camera Angles: In these three pictures, we see the effects created by three different camera angles on the same subject in the same position. The first picture is from what might be called a "normal" angle, with the camera looking directly at the pitcher at about eye level [4.40]. The second picture was taken with the camera slightly in front of the mound but located five or six feet above the pitcher's head, looking down on him in a *high-angle shot* [4.41]. For the third picture the camera was located on the ground in front of the pitcher, looking up at him in a *low-angle shot* [4.42].

Color, Diffusion, and Soft or Blurred Focus

A variety of filters are used to create a wide range of specialized effects. Directors may use special filters to darken the blue of the sky, thereby sharpening by contrast the whiteness of the clouds, or they may add a light-colored tone to the whole scene by filming it through a colored filter. For example, in *A Man and a Woman* a love scene was filmed with a red filter, which imparted a romantic warmth.

On rare occasions, a special filter may be used to add a certain quality to a whole film. An example is Zeffirelli's film version of

Taming of the Shrew, where a subtle light-diffusing filter (supposedly a nylon stocking over the camera lens) was used to soften the focus slightly and subdue the colors in a way that gave the whole film the quality of a Rembrandt painting. This technique, called the *Rembrandt effect,* was designed to give the film a mellow, aged quality, intensifying the sense that the action was taking place in another time period. A similar effect was employed in *McCabe and Mrs. Miller* and *Summer of '42,* but in the latter the quality suggested was not of an historical era but of the hazy images of the narrator's memory. For *Excalibur,* director John Boorman used green gel filters over his arc lamps to give the forest exteriors a lyric vernal glow, emphasizing the green of the moss and the leaves and creating a sense of other-worldliness.

Soft (slightly blurred) focus can also help to convey certain subjective states. In *The Graduate,* Elaine Robinson (Katharine Ross) is seen out of focus as she learns that the older woman Benjamin had an affair with "wasn't just another older woman." The blurred face expresses her state of shock and confusion, and her face comes back into focus only when she fully takes in what Benjamin (Dustin Hoffman) is trying to tell her. A similar technique is used earlier in the film to convey Benjamin's panic. After hearing Mr. Robinson's car pull up, Benjamin races hurriedly from Elaine's bedroom to return to the bar downstairs. As he reaches the foot of the stairs, Benjamin is shown in blurred focus as he dashes down the hall to the bar. He comes back into focus only as he reaches the relative safety of the barstool, just as Mr. Robinson enters the front door.

Soft focus is used in *Mr. Smith Goes to Washington* to reflect a warm, romantic glow (falling in love) that comes over Saunders (Jean Arthur) as Jeff Smith (Jimmy Stewart) describes the natural beauties of the Willet Creek country where he plans to build his boys' camp.

Special Lenses

Special lenses are often employed to provide subjective distortions of normal reality. Wide-angle and telephoto lenses, for example, distort the depth perspective of an image in opposite ways. A wide-angle lens exaggerates the perspective, so that the distance between an object in the foreground and one in the background seems much greater than it actually is. With the telephoto lens, depth is compressed, so that the distance between foreground

|4.43|

|4.44|

The Effects of Wide-Angle and Telephoto Lenses: These two pictures illustrate the different effects achieved by photographing the same scene with a wide-angle lens [4.43] and a telephoto lens [4.44]. The wide-angle shot makes the distance between the man and woman seem much greater, and the frame covers a much wider area in the background; the telephoto seems to bring the man and woman closer together and narrows the area of background in the frame.

and background objects seems less than it actually is (Figs. 4.43 and 4.44).

The effect of this distortion becomes more apparent when background-to-foreground movement is introduced. In *The Graduate,* for example, the hero was filmed running toward the camera in a frantic race to interrupt the wedding ceremony, and a telephoto distortion made him appear to gain very little headway in spite of his efforts, thus emphasizing his frustration and his desperation. Had a wide-angle lens been used in the same way, his speed would have been greatly exaggerated.

A special type of extreme wide-angle lens, called a *fish-eye,* which bends both horizontal and vertical planes and distorts depth relationships, is often used to create unusual subjective states such as dreams, fantasies, or drunk scenes (Fig. 4.45).

| 4.45 | Fish-Eye Lens: The nervous strain and tension created by men working and living in close quarters for long periods of time is expressed as a visual claustrophobic scream through the distortions of a fish-eye lens in this scene from *Dark Star.*

Slow Motion

If the action on the screen is to seem normal and realistic, the film must move through the camera at the same rate at which it is projected, which is generally twenty-four frames per second. However, if the scene is filmed at greater than normal speed and then projected at normal speed, the action will be slowed. This is called *slow motion,* and the use of slow-motion footage creates a variety of effects in film (Fig. 4.46). Ironically, the same basic technique can be used to create several very different effects.

1. To "stretch the moment" in order to intensify its emotional quality. One of the most common uses of slow-motion photography concentrates our attention on a relatively brief period of action and intensifies whatever emotion we associate with it by stretching out that fragment of time. Ironically, the same footage could be used either to make us savor the "thrill of victory" or suffer the "agony of defeat." For example, with the camera located just beyond the finish line, two runners could be photographed in slow motion as they run toward the camera, well ahead of the rest of the pack. The winner breaks the tape only a stride ahead of the second-place finisher. If the music builds into a joyous victory theme as the winner breaks the tape and is congratulated by teammates at the finish line (still in slow motion), we will tend to identify with the winner; we will share his joy and savor each handshake and embrace. On the other hand, if the same footage is

| 4.46 | Slow-Motion Showcase: Practically every sporting event pictured in *Chariots of Fire,* like the race shown here, makes some use of slow-motion cinematography to help us see parts of each event in some special way.

accompanied by discordant music played at a slow, dragging beat, we will tend to identify with the runner-up, and similarly share his disappointment as he congratulates the winner and turns to slowly walk away. In *Chariots of Fire* both kinds of moments are stretched by slow motion, with both victories and defeats further intensified by slow-motion replays of parts of each race.

2. To exaggerate effort, fatigue, and frustration. Slow motion is also very effective in conveying a subjective state by exaggerating a character's physical effort, fatigue, or frustration. Many of us have experienced slow-motion dreams where our feet become leaden when we're trying to escape danger or catch some fleeting object of desire. So we identify very subjectively with characters putting forth tremendous physical effort, experiencing fatigue, or even a general physical frustration. The context of the action, music, and sound all help to trigger the proper feeling, and slow-motion sound is particularly effective here (see "Slow-Motion Sound" in Chapter 5).

In *Chariots of Fire,* Eric Liddel (the Scotsman) is bumped off the track and falls into the grass infield. His fall, and the time-consuming effort of getting to his feet to begin running again, are exaggerated by slow motion. A similar effect is created in *Bang the Drum Slowly* as the terminally ill catcher Bruce (Robert DeNiro) circles under a high pop-up. Slow-motion photography combined with blurred sound makes the relatively simple act seem tremendously difficult, awkward, and tiring.

3. To suggest superhuman speed and power. The most ironic use of slow motion is its function as a cinematic formula for superhuman speed and power. Whereas fast motion would seem more logical to suggest speed, the herky-jerky movements created by fast motion are comical and even grotesque. Humans moving in fast motion seem like insects. But human beings photographed in slow motion appear serious, poetic, larger than life, as though they have slipped into some kind of superhuman gear that makes them move like gods. This formula is used effectively in films like *Chariots of Fire* and *Superman* as well as in television's "Six Million Dollar Man" and "The Bionic Woman."

4. To emphasize the grace of physical action. Even when the illusion of superhuman speed and power are not called for, slow motion can be used to impart a sense of great grace and beauty to almost any human or animal movement, especially rapid movement. In *Bang the Drum Slowly* this "poetry-in-motion" technique is used to enhance Arthur's (Michael Moriarty) pitching, creating the smooth, graceful, seemingly effortless motion of a major league pitcher.

5. To suggest the passage of time. By combining a series of slow-motion shots into a montage, with each shot slowly dissolving into the next, the impression is created that a relatively long period of time is passing. In *Bang the Drum Slowly* a series of slow-motion shots of unrelated baseball action are joined, compressing the feeling of a long, slow month or so of a baseball season into a few choice seconds on the screen.

6. To create a sharp contrast with "normal motion." Slow motion can also be used effectively to stretch time and build tension before the start of regular speed filming. In *Chariots of Fire,* the Olympic runners are pictured in slow motion as they walk into the stadium to prepare for their event. The anticipation of the race is increased as the runners remove outer garments, go through warm-up exercises, dig their starting holes in the dirt track, and settle into their starting positions. Then the tension and nervousness of preparing for the event is released suddenly as the starting gun sounds, and the runners explode off their marks in regular film speed. In this way a sharp contrast is created between the tension of waiting and preparing for a big event and the event itself.

Fast or Speeded Motion

If a scene is filmed at less than normal speed and then projected at normal speed, the result is called *fast* or *speeded motion.* Fast motion, which resembles the frantic, herky-jerky movements of the old silent comedies, is usually employed for comic effects or to compress the time of an event. Stanley Kubrick employed fast motion for comic effect in a scene from *A Clockwork Orange.* Alex (Malcolm McDowell) picks up two young girls and takes them both to his room for a frantic sex romp, which is filmed in fast motion and accompanied musically by the *William Tell Overture.*

An extreme form of fast motion is called *time-lapse photography,* and has the effect of greatly compressing time. In time-lapse filming, one frame is exposed at regular intervals, which may be as long as thirty minutes apart. This technique may be employed to compress something that normally takes hours or weeks into a few seconds, such as the blossoming of a flower or the construction of a house.

The Freeze Frame, the Thawed Frame, and Stills

The freeze frame, the thawed frame, and stills, by providing a sharp contrast to a film's dynamic motion, give the filmmaker powerful methods of providing a sense of ending, a sense of beginning, and clever transitions. Each is a special kind of emphasis that forces us to think about the significance of what we are seeing. Of course, these techniques, if not used sparingly—for special moments only—quickly lose their special emphasis or impact.

THE FREEZE FRAME

In the *freeze frame,* motion stops completely and the image on the screen remains still, as though the projector had stopped suddenly or the image had suddenly been frozen. The sudden use of a freeze frame can be stunning in its abruptness. The frozen image compels our attention because it is so shockingly still in comparison to the movement we have become accustomed to.

The freeze frame has a number of applications, but its most common use is to mark the end of a powerful dramatic sequence (and serve as a transition to the next), or to serve as the ending of the entire film. At the end of a powerful sequence, a freeze frame jolts us, as though life itself has stopped. Frozen, the image on the screen burns itself into our brain, and is locked into our memory in a way that moving images seldom are. At the end of a sequence, it is similar to the old tableau effect used in the stage, where the actors freeze in their positions for a brief moment before the curtain, creating a powerful image to be remembered during the time that elapses between scenes or acts.

When used as the movie's final image, the freeze frame can be even more powerful. By ending the movement on the screen, a sense of finality is achieved . . . a precious moment frozen for our memory. As the motion stops, it becomes like a snapshot. We can hold it in our minds, and savor its beauty or impact for several seconds before it fades forever from the screen. It also gives us time to resonate and reflect, to catch up with our emotions, our senses, and our thoughts. And we slowly drift back to earth from the magic carpet ride we've just taken.

The freeze frame can also be used to convey difficult information with taste, delicacy, and subtlety, either at the film's end or to mark the end of a scene. In the final scene of *Butch Cassidy and the Sundance Kid,* the images of Butch and the Kid are frozen in their last full moment of vitality as a deafening roar on the sound-

|4.47| The Freeze Frame Ending: Hopelessly outnumbered and totally surrounded by Bolivian soldiers, Butch (Paul Newman) and the Kid (Robert Redford) leave the "safety" of their barricade and come out shooting. *Butch Cassidy and the Sundance Kid* ends at this point on a freeze frame of the image above, as a deafening roar on the soundtrack suggests the fusillade of bullets that takes their lives.

track suggests the fusilade of bullets that takes their lives. Then the camera slowly pulls back from their frozen images and we remember them there, still frozen in their last moment of life (Fig. 4.47). A similar use occurs in *The World According to Garp*. As Garp's car careens up the dark asphalt toward the driveway accident, the camera zooms quickly in on Walt, then freezes him in close-up, which is accompanied by a brief moment of silence. As the next scene opens, only Walt is missing as the other members of the family are seen recuperating.

Freeze frames can also serve a transitional function. In *Chariots of Fire* a hurdler is caught and frozen in mid-hurdle. The colored freeze frame fades to black and white, and the camera pulls away to reveal it as a newspaper picture in a paper being read the next day, thus providing a quick time/place transition.

THE THAWED FRAME

The opposite effect, that of something beginning, is provided by what we might call the *thawed frame*. Here we *begin* with a frozen image, which quickly comes to life before our eyes. This technique can either be used at the beginning of a scene or the beginning of the whole film, or to serve a transitional function.

Sometimes, usually in the film's beginning, the frozen image begins as a painting or drawing, which slowly changes to a photograph and then thaws into life.

In *Citizen Kane,* the thawed frame serves a clever transitional function. Kane and one of his friends are seen looking through the front window of a rival newspaper, at a group picture of the paper's staff. The camera moves in for a close-up so we see only the picture, then there is a flash of light and the group members start to move, revealing that the flash of light was from a photographer taking a new group picture of the same people, who now work for Kane.

STILLS

Stills differ from the freeze frame and the thawed frame in that they are truly "stills," still photographs where the image never moves. Stills are usually combined creatively in a montage, and receive a sense of poetic motion as the camera pulls in or backs off from them, or moves over them. When used in a montage, each still will usually dissolve slowly into the next, creating the impression of information slowly unfolding or being remembered. In *Summer of '42,* a montage of stills under the credits opens the film, creating the impression of "snapshots" from the narrator's memory. In *Butch Cassidy and the Sundance Kid,* sepiatoned stills are combined in a "Happy Times in New York City" montage.

QUESTIONS

On Cinematic Viewpoint and Visual Effects

1. Although the director will probably employ all four cinematic viewpoints in making the film, one point of view may predominate to such a degree that it leaves the impression of a single point of view. With this in mind, answer the following questions:

   a. In terms of your reaction to the film as a whole, do you feel that you were primarily an objective, impersonal observer of the action, or did you have the sense of being a participant in the action? What specific scenes can you remember that used the objective point of view? In what scenes did you feel like a participant in the action? How were you made to feel like a participant?

b. In what scenes were you aware that the director was employing visual techniques to comment on or interpret the action, forcing you to see the action in a special way? What were the techniques used to achieve this, and how effective were they?

2. Although a thorough analysis of each visual element is impossible, make a mental note of those pictorial effects that struck you as especially effective, ineffective, or unique, and consider them in light of the following questions:

a. What was the director's aim in creating these images, and what camera tools or techniques were employed in the filming of them?

b. What made these memorable visual images effective, ineffective, or unique?

c. Justify each of these impressive visual effects aesthetically in terms of its relationship to the whole film.

LIGHTING

Lighting is as important as the camera positioning and other special techniques. By controlling the intensity, direction, and degree of diffusion (character) of the light, the director is able to create the impression of spatial depth, delineate and mold the contours and planes of the subject, convey emotional mood and atmosphere, and create special dramatic effects.

Thus, the way a given scene is lighted is an important factor in determining its dramatic effectiveness. Variation in lighting is used in extremely subtle ways to create moods and impart to the scene a suitable dramatic atmosphere for the action that is to take place. Because lighting should correspond to the mood of each scene, closely observing the nature of the lighting throughout the film should help in determining the film's overall mood or tone.

Two terms are employed to designate different general intensities of lighting. *Low-key* refers to lighting where most of the set is in shadow and just a few highlights define the subject. Since this type of lighting is effective in heightening suspense or creating a somber mood, it is used in the mystery or horror film. *High-key* lighting, on the other hand, has more light areas than shadows, and the subjects are seen in middle grays and highlights, with far less contrast. High-key lighting is suitable for comic and light

|4.48|

|4.49|

Low-Key and High-Key Lighting: Low-key lighting [4.48] puts most of the set in shadow and shows the couple with just a few highlights, increasing the intimacy and dramatic intensity of the scene. High-key lighting [4.49] opens up the frame with light in background areas and balances the lighting throughout the set. While high-key lighting diminishes the intimacy and dramatic intensity the scene had with low-key lighting, it provides us with more complete visual information on the couple and the setting.

moods, such as would prevail in a musical. Generally speaking, high-contrast scenes, with a wide range of difference between light and dark areas, create more powerful and dramatic images than scenes that are evenly lighted (Figs. 4.48 and 4.49).

The direction of the light also plays an important role in creating an effective visual image. Flat overhead lighting, for example, creates an entirely different effect from strong side lighting from floor level. Back lighting and front lighting also create strikingly different effects (Figs. 4.50, 4.51, 4.52, and 4.53).

Whether light is artificial or natural (as in exterior scenes) the director has the means to control what is commonly referred to as the *character* of the light. The character of light can generally be classified as one of three types: (1) direct, harsh, or hard; (2) medium and balanced; or (3) soft and diffused (Figs. 4.54, 4.55, and 4.56).

The three factors of light—intensity, direction, and character—all play a significant role in the dramatic effectiveness of the image. The director and cinematographer together will very carefully plan the look they want for the lighting. After that, the cinematographer assumes the primary responsibility for the lighting.

[4.50]

[4.51]

[4.52]

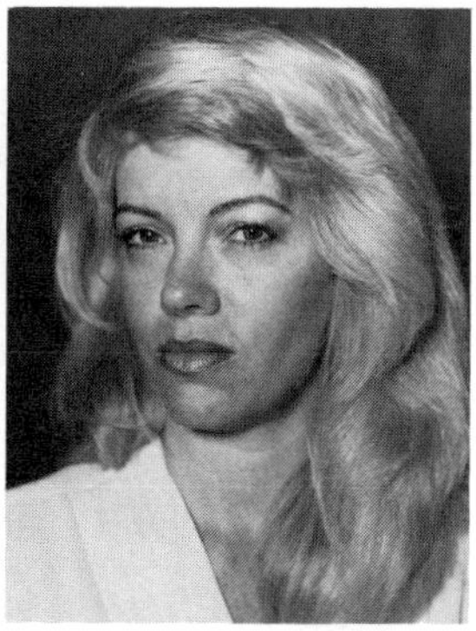

[4.53]

Direction of Lighting: Overhead, Side, Back, and Front Lighting: These pictures illustrate the different effects achieved by overhead lighting [4.50], side lighting [4.51], back lighting [4.52], and front lighting [4.53].

[4.54]

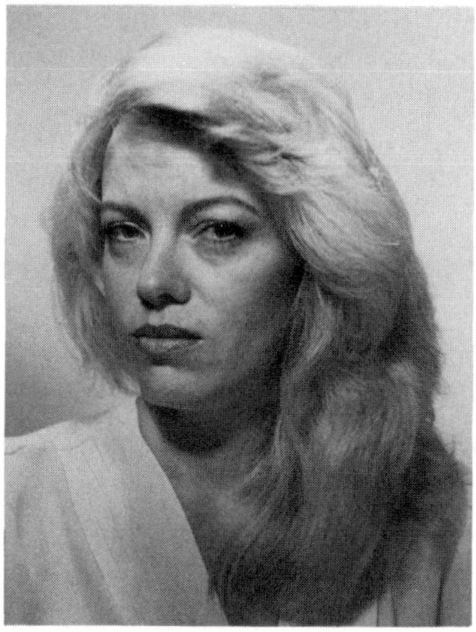

[4.55]

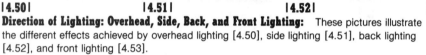

[4.56]

Character of Light: These pictures illustrate the different effects of changing the character of the light: direct, harsh, or hard lighting [4.54], balanced lighting [4.55], and soft and diffused lighting [4.56].

Today's filmmakers generally strive for a very natural effect in their lighting, which looks as though the cinematographer didn't use any supplemental light at all. Vilmos Zsigmond, one of the great current cinematographers, describes his philosophy in this way:

> I try to light so that it feels as if it comes from natural sources. That's why I like to have windows in my shots—windows, or candles or lamps. Those are my true light sources. Studying the Old Masters, Rembrandt, Vermeer, De la Tour, I found that they painted their best works relying on light effects coming from realistic sources. They even selected their subjects because they loved the light and the people. They were very selective and improved upon nature. They simplified and eliminated multiple shadows to concentrate on the dramatic. That is what a cinematographer does: improves on nature.[10]

Nestor Alemendros, another acknowledged master cinematographer, also stresses the importance of naturalness: "I use a minimum of artificial light . . . *Days of Heaven* was shot with very little light. Rather than create an artificial moment, I'd wait for the real one to happen. One great moment is worth waiting for all day."[11]

Even when he is working on interiors in a studio, for a film like *Kramer vs. Kramer,* Alemendros stresses a "natural light technique" by imagining the sun outside Kramer's apartment, justifying a back-lit subject with a window or lamp from behind, and making sure that all lighting seems to come from windows and table or floor lamps.

Special Lighting Effects

In *The Grapes of Wrath* John Ford employed a light reflected in the pupils of Tom Joad's (Henry Fonda) eyes at his first emotional meeting with Ma Joad (Jane Darwell) after four years in prison. Although it is done with such subtlety that it is not obvious to the casual viewer, it gives the moment a very special quality. Tom's eyes literally "light up" as he greets her.

Another special "moment of reunion" is created by lighting on the eyes of Lara (Julie Christie) in *Doctor Zhivago* when she sees Zhivago (Omar Sharif) in a remote village library after a year of separation. By highlighting her eyes, the emotional intensity of the scene is increased, for Ms. Christie's eyes either do not express the emotion fully enough or the change is so subtle that it needs to be pulled out from background details to create the desired effect.

Subtle changes in lighting are also employed in another touching scene from *The Grapes of Wrath.* As Ma Joad burns her souvenirs in preparing to leave for California, she discovers a pair of

10. "Zsigmond." *American Film,* September 1982, p. 55.
11. "Alemendros." *American Film,* December 1981, p. 19.

earrings she wore as a young woman. As she puts them up to her ears, subtle changes in the direction of light, accompanied by some gradual diffusion, make her seem to grow younger before our eyes. Then, as she takes them down again and the memory fades, we see the wrinkling and hard lines reappear as the original lighting returns.

Painterly Effects

As early as the 1920s, directors such as Cecil B. DeMille were attempting to use lighting to imitate the effects achieved by painters like Rembrandt. But, years later, Franco Zeffirelli perhaps achieved it most successfully in his *Taming of the Shrew* (1967), creating the soft, muted color of faded paintings by using a woman's nylon stocking over the camera lens, and lighting his interior scenes in the Rembrandt manner (Fig. 4.57).

In recent years, with cinematographers like Vilmos Zsigmond recognizing that cinematographers create mood with lighting and composition in the same way as painters, more emphasis seems to be placed on achieving painterly effects. The artists that cinematographers cite most often as influencing their work are Caravaggio, Georges de la Tour, Vermeer, and Rembrandt. For example,

| 4.57 | The "Rembrandt Effect": In *Taming of the Shrew* Director Franco Zeffirelli used special lighting and a woman's nylon stocking over the camera lens to soften the focus and mute the colors so that the image had the quality of a Rembrandt painting. The technique was especially effective in interior scenes like the one above, picturing Elizabeth Taylor as Katherine engaged in a shrewish "conversation" with her off-screen sister.

in preparing to shoot *The Verdict,* Sidney Lumet and his cinematographer, Andrzej Bartkowaik, spent an entire day studying a collection of prints of Caravaggio's paintings. They analyzed his treatment of backgrounds, foregrounds, and textured surfaces, with emphasis on light sources. Then they applied what they learned to *The Verdict,* with what Lumet called "extraordinary" results.

QUESTIONS

On Lighting

1. How would you characterize the lighting of the film as a whole: (a) direct, harsh, and hard, (b) medium and balanced, or (c) soft and diffused? Does high-key or low-key lighting predominate?
2. Does the lighting throughout the film seem artificial, coming from places where there would be no light sources, or does it seem to emanate naturally from sources visible or suggested on screen?
3. Are special lighting effects used for brief moments in the film? If so, what are the effects intended and how successful are they?
4. Does the lighting seem to create an effect designed to make the film have the look of a painting? How effective is this technique, and how well does the "painterly" style fit the subject matter of the film?
5. How does the lighting contribute to the overall emotional attitude or tone of the film?
6. In what individual scenes is the lighting especially effective, and what makes it effective?

OTHER IMPORTANT FACTORS

Even before some of the choices discussed above are made, at least two other extremely important factors will have been considered. The first of these is the very basic choice of whether the film should be shot in black and white or color. The second is the choice of screen shape or format in which the movie will ultimately be shown.

Color Versus Black and White

> I still think that black and white has a role in motion pictures, and not everything should be in color. In fact, unless the color is perfect to the idea, it can come between the beholder and the idea of the picture. One's eye can be deflected by the color. And one's thoughts as well. For instance, I cannot possibly see doing *Freud* in color or other pictures of a deeply psychological nature. Unless the palette and the values coincide or are part of the idea, why, it's better for it *not* to be in color.
> JOHN HUSTON, DIRECTOR[12]

> In most movies . . . I have restricted myself to a color or two only. Black-and-white is like a tuxedo, always elegant. Color, if you're not careful with it, can be vulgar.
> NESTOR ALEMENDROS, CINEMATOGRAPHER[13]

Although there is a continuing theoretical argument about the relative merits of color versus black and white film, on a practical level there is very clearly no longer a real struggle. Because a vast television audience awaits almost any decent film, the great majority of films today are made in color to better their chances for eventual sale to this medium. The apparently insatiable desire of the TV audience to see absolutely everything in color has drastically reduced the number of black and white films being produced. So few black and white films are produced today that when one does come out (like *Manhattan, Stardust Memories,* or *The Elephant Man*) it is praised for its daring.

For some films black and white is simply a more powerful and effective medium, but this has almost been entirely overlooked. Of course, the director's decision to use black and white or color *should* be determined by the film's overall spirit or mood. A clear demonstration of the correct use of color and black and white can be seen by comparing Sir Laurence Olivier's productions of *Henry V* and *Hamlet. Henry V,* a heroic or epic drama, much of which is set outdoors with battlefield action, colorful costuming, and much pagentry, was ideally suited for color, and was so produced by Olivier. The mood of the entire film is positive; it emphasizes the glorious heroic character of King Henry V, who emerges victorious. *Hamlet,* on the other hand, which Olivier chose to make in black and white, is a tragedy, a somber, serious play of the mind. Most of the settings are interior ones, and some are at night. The brooding, serious, intellectual quality of the hero himself

12. "Dialogue on Film." *American Film,* January-February 1984, p. 22.
13. "Alemendros." *American Film,* December 1981, p. 19.

has a starkness to it, a pensive gloom that could not have been captured nearly so well in color as it was in black and white.

The overall effect of black and white can be somewhat paradoxical, for somehow it often seems more true to life, more realistic, than color—in spite of the fact that we obviously do not see the world around us in black and white. For example, it is difficult to imagine that *Dr. Strangelove* in color would be quite as "real" as it is in black and white. And one wonders if *Catch 22* might not have been much more powerful in black and white for the same reason. The warmth of the color images in *Catch 22*—a warmth that is difficult to avoid when working with color—fights the cold, bitterly ironic tone that underlies the story. Perhaps its sense of starkness is what makes the black-and-white treatment suitable for such film subjects.

The essentially opposite effects of color and black and white might also be explained in terms of another pair of films, *Shane* and *Hud,* both of which are set in the west. Color is perfectly suited for *Shane,* a romantic western in the epic tradition set in a magnificently huge and beautiful landscape with snowcapped mountains ever present in the background. *Hud,* on the other hand, is a contemporary character study of a heel, set in a drab, barren, and sterile landscape. The film emphasizes the harsh realities and glorifies nothing; this story could find adequate expression only in black and white.

The difference in seriousness and overall tone in *Annie Hall* (color) and *Manhattan* (black and white) would also justify the choices of different film types for those films.

Generally, films that seem to demand color treatment are those with a romantic, idealized, or light, playful, or humorous quality, such as musicals, fantasies, historical pageants, and comedies. Also, those with exceptionally beautiful settings might be better filmed in color. But the more naturalistic, serious, somber stories stressing the harsh realities of life and set in drab, dull, or sordid settings cry out for black and white. There are those, of course, that fall into a middle ground and can be treated equally well either way.

Some films have made effective use of mixtures of black and white *and* color, such as *The Wizard of Oz,* which employed black and white for the story's frame in Kansas (reality) and changed to color for the dream sequence in Oz, or *A Man and a Woman,* which used a large variety of different film types and effects.

Directors and cinematographers are more and more beginning to think of film as being similar to painting. In addition to their attempts to achieve "painterly" effects with lighting, a great deal of experimentation is being done to create a kind of palette in color film, so that the actual nature of the color can be mixed to achieve the same kinds of effects the artist achieves with subtle blendings of the colors on his palette.

Color experimentation has actually been going on for some time. In *Greed* (1923), Eric von Stroheim experimented with coloring all the golden objects in the film a bright yellow using the Handschlegl process, a stencil-coloring operation. But critics objected to the technique, which they felt betrayed the otherwise pure realism of picture. As early as 1935 Rouben Mamoulian used the then-new Technicolor process creatively in *Becky Sharp* to express the panic accompanying the news of Napoleon's advance: As dancers flee the ballroom after hearing the news, they are photographed in a montage of changing colors, starting with black and white, progressing through the other colors of the spectrum, and climaxing in red.

In *Moulin Rouge* John Huston attempted what he called "a wedding of black-and-white and color" in an attempt to give the entire film the look of a Toulouse-Lautrec painting. To achieve this look, it was necessary to flatten the color (rendering it in planes of solid hues) and eliminate highlights and the illusion of three dimensionality created by the lighting of rounded, three-dimensional forms. He achieved this by using a filter that was designed for simulating fog in exterior scenes, and added smoke to the set so that a flat, monochromatic quality prevailed. As Huston puts it: "It was the first picture that succeeded in dominating the color instead of being dominated by it."[14] Huston further experimented with color in *Reflections in a Golden Eye*, where an amber, golden look was given to the whole picture through a laboratory process.

John Boorman and cinematographer Vilmos Zsigmond also used special color techniques in *Deliverance*. When colors as naturally recorded on the film created an image that was too happy and cheerful looking, they printed black and white into the material, combining a black and white print with a color print. This technique is extremely effective in creating the impression that the woods, with bright green leaves and all, are essentially dark and foreboding. A similar but less subtle effect was achieved in *Sophie's Choice*. During the concentration camp scenes in that film, the color is muted so much that it almost completely disap-

14. John Huston, *John Huston: An Open Book*. New York: Alfred A. Knopf, 1980, p. 211.

pears, thus effectively conveying the grimness of those scenes and setting them apart from the bright and cheerful colors of the present-time sequences.

Directors and cinematographers are continually struggling to create the perfect look for the period piece, but never seem to find the perfect solution. Zeffirelli created a fairly effective sense of time past by filtering *Taming of the Shrew* through a woman's nylon stocking, muting the colors and softening sharp edges so that the whole film resembles a faded Rembrandt painting; similar filtering effects have since been used frequently to create a sense of hazy, remembered experiences. But Laszlo Kovacs, cinematographer for *F.I.S.T.*, describes the difficulty of achieving the perfect period look:

> I would have loved if somehow we could have discovered how to do sepia in color. That's the hardest thing to do; I mean, it's easy to go to amber or to yellowish and reddish tones, but sepia is a brown which is not a color. It's a dirt. It's a combination of everything. Somehow it's almost impossible to create that sepia tone, all that faded quality. It's always a problem. You see a period picture, and it looks too new. It should look as if it was really made in the thirties and was pulled out from a drawer, like old faded prints.[15]

As experimentation continues, this difficulty will probably be overcome, for film technology has advanced rapidly in recent years.

By using all the technology and know-how now available, whether it's done by special lighting, diffusion filters, special film in the camera, or by processing the film in a certain way in the laboratory, modern filmmakers are able to create practically any color effect they want to achieve. This special color effect must of course be consistent in the film from beginning to end, unless it is used only for a specialized segment set off from the rest of the film—like a flashback, a dream, or a fantasy.

Size and Shape of the Projected Image

Similar to the choice of black and white or color for a film is the choice among different sizes and shapes of the final projected image. Essentially, there are two basic shapes for the projected image: the *standard screen*, the width of which is 1.33 times its height, and *wide screen* (commonly known by a variety of trade names, such as Cinemascope, Panavision, and Vistavision), the width of which varies from 1.85 to 2.55 times its height. The

15. "Dialogue on Film." *American Film*, June 1979, p. 43.

different dimensions and shapes of these screens cause different types of compositional problems, but generally speaking, the wide screen lends itself naturally to a panoramic view of a vast landscape or large numbers of people, as well as rapid motion such as might be characteristic in westerns, war dramas, historical pageants, or fast-paced action-adventure dramas. The standard screen is more suited for an intimate love story set in a small apartment, requiring the frequent use of tight close-ups and with very little movement of subjects in space. A wide screen can actually distort an image and detract from the visual effectiveness if it is confined to a physical set too narrow for its field of view (Figs. 4.58 and 4.59).

Smooth- Versus Rough-Grain Film

The type of film stock used may also have an important effect on the nature of the visual image. Some film stock is capable of reproducing an image which is extremely smooth or "slick." Such film also registers a wide range of subtle differences between light and dark, enabling the director to create fine tones, artistic shadows, and contrasts. Such images often have a more powerful visual effect than reality, due to their clarity and artistic perfection.

Another type of film stock, rough- or high-grain, produces an opposite effect: a rough, grainy-textured image with harsh contrasts between blacks and whites, and almost no subtle differences in contrast. Because newspaper pictures and newsreels also have this coarse, rough-grained effect, this type of film has become associated with a documentary "here and now" quality, as though the "reality" had to be captured quickly, with little concern for clarity and artistic perfection. The same film may employ both types of stock for different effects. For example, a romantic love scene would probably be done in slow or smooth-grain film, whereas a riot or a furious battle scene may be done with rough-grain film (Figs. 4.60 and 4.61).

QUESTIONS

On Color, Black and White, and Screen Size

1. Was the filmmaker's choice of black and white or color film correct for this story? What factors do you think influenced this decision? Try to

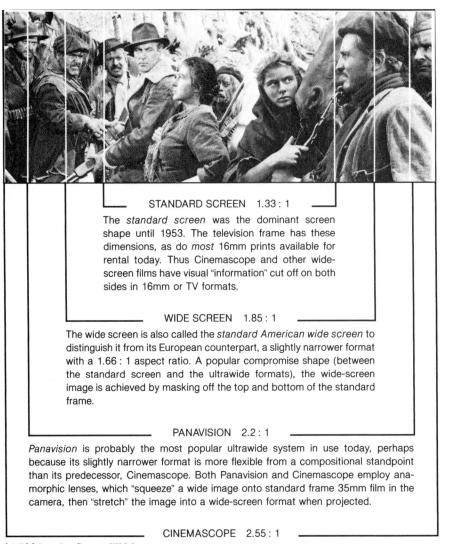

STANDARD SCREEN 1.33 : 1

The *standard screen* was the dominant screen shape until 1953. The television frame has these dimensions, as do *most* 16mm prints available for rental today. Thus Cinemascope and other wide-screen films have visual "information" cut off on both sides in 16mm or TV formats.

WIDE SCREEN 1.85 : 1

The wide screen is also called the *standard American wide screen* to distinguish it from its European counterpart, a slightly narrower format with a 1.66 : 1 aspect ratio. A popular compromise shape (between the standard screen and the ultrawide formats), the wide-screen image is achieved by masking off the top and bottom of the standard frame.

PANAVISION 2.2 : 1

Panavision is probably the most popular ultrawide system in use today, perhaps because its slightly narrower format is more flexible from a compositional standpoint than its predecessor, Cinemascope. Both Panavision and Cinemascope employ anamorphic lenses, which "squeeze" a wide image onto standard frame 35mm film in the camera, then "stretch" the image into a wide-screen format when projected.

CINEMASCOPE 2.55 : 1

| 4.58 | Popular Screen Widths Cinemascope actually can be said to have two aspect ratios. In the '50s its dimensions were 2.55 : 1; it has since been narrowed slightly (to 2.35 : 1) to accommodate an optical sound track. When theaters began installing special screens for Cinemascope in the '50s, many of these screens were curved slightly to enhance the three-dimensional effect. Although popular with the public, the system had many critics, among them director George Stevens, who claimed "the wide screen is better suited to a boa constrictor than a man." The lines drawn on the photo above from *For Whom the Bell Tolls* show the amount of side information lost when any of the wide screen films are reduced to the 16mm or TV format.

| 4.59 | The Projected Image: The four different screen sizes and shapes as illustrated by four different croppings of the same scene from *The Terror.*

a. Standard screen 1.33 : 1

b. Wide screen 1.85 : 1

c. Panavision 2.2 : 1

d. Cinemascope 2.55 : 1

| 4.60 | Smooth-Grain Film Stock: A romantic love story like *Doctor Zhivago,* which strives for an artistically heightened reality, calls for the use of slow or smooth-grain film stock that produces clear, sharp images like the one above, with Omar Sharif as Zhivago and Julie Christie as Lara.

| 4.61 | Rough-Grain Film Stock: The look of rough-grain film stock is simulated by the frame enlargement above from the 1976 coal strike documentary *Harlan County, U.S.A.* Rough-grain film stock is sometimes used in feature films in sequences where the director wants to convey a kind of "here-and-now" immediacy, or to create a TV news, newsreel, or documentary effect.

imagine the film as it would appear in the other film type. What would the important differences in total effect be?

2. Are any special color effects attempted? If so, what was the director or cinematographer trying to achieve with the unusual effect? How successful is the overall effect achieved?
3. Is the film designed for standard or wide-screen projection? What factors do you think influenced this decision?

MOVIE MAGIC: SPECIAL EFFECTS IN THE MODERN FILM

As admission prices escalated and the lure of television kept more and more people at home for their entertainment, motion pictures began to incorporate elements that television could not provide. One such element was the special effect, which created visual spectacle on a grand scale and showed audiences things they had never seen before.

Advances in recent technology have made elaborate special effects an important part of the modern film. Given proper time and money, there are few things the modern special effects technician cannot realize on screen—though truly top-quality visuals can be prohibitively expensive. This capability has opened an entirely new frontier to the filmmakers; it allows them to use the medium to its fullest extent, and enables them to really *show* their audience what they wish to show, instead of just telling them about it. This increased flexibility is a great asset to the industry; too often, however, innovations have become a liability as well, as elaborate visual effects in certain films have not just served to enhance the story, but have themselves become the focus of the film.

4.62 Special Effect Miniature: Creating the illusion that a miniature model is a full-sized jet fighter/bomber is essential to making us believe the incredible speed and other capabilities of the stolen Russian MIG 31 and the "dog fight" with its twin pursuer in *Firefox*.

Special effects have been an integral part of film throughout its history. But only recently has technology produced effects so sophisticated that the audience often cannot distinguish between footage of a real object and a special effect miniature, as is the case with the jet aircraft in 1982's *Firefox* (Fig. 4.62). Nor are all of these effects of the flashy laser-blast variety. The nature of any given special effect is one of three types: "credible" effects, which simply recreate in dramatic form a familiar, historic, or real event; "incredible" effects, which simulate potentially real events in a

|4.63| "You'll Believe a Man Can Fly": A real effort was made in *Superman* to make us believe the flying sequences like the one above, with Superman (Christopher Reeve) taking Lois Lane (Margot Kidder) on a romantic demonstration flight over Metropolis. In *Superman II* and *III*, however, less attention was paid to the flying effects and the results were not as convincing.

heightened or extreme fashion; and "amazing" effects, which create people, creatures, places, or occurrences that are beyond what is presently considered possible. "Credible" effects include elaborate stunts, such as those in 1982's *The Road Warrior,* the miniaturized sinking of the American navy at Pearl Harbor on December 7, 1941 in *Tora! Tora! Tora!,* and even extreme make-ups, such as that worn by actor John Hurt to portray *The Elephant Man.* Incredible effects, often the backbone of disaster films, can simulate the destruction of Los Angeles by an *Earthquake!,* the destruction by aging of the Genesis planet in *Star Trek III: The Search for Spock,* and even the powerful burning of Atlanta in *Gone With the Wind.*

While such special effects can be original and highly sophisticated, the "amazing" special effect is often the most eye-catching, if only for the very impossibility of its subject matter. The wide variety of "amazing" effects can be classified into several distinct categories.

Superhuman ability effects help *Time Bandits'* Evil Wizard cast lightning bolts from his fingertips, *Excalibur*'s Merlin weave his magic, and Clark Kent defy gravity as *Superman* (Fig. 4.63). Flying vehicle effects, a staple of many science fiction films, can range from the frenetic outer-space dog fights in *Star Wars,* to the majestic lift-off of the Mothership from *Close Encounters of the Third Kind,* to the spectacular shift to warp speed by *Star Trek*'s Starship *Enterprise.* This type of effect, called an optical, is created in the printing process where the primary image (such as a spaceship) is superimposed on another image (such as a starfield background) and the two are composited onto one strip of film by an optical printer. Modern optical printers are guided by computer, affording precise matching of a tremendous number of different images.

Another amazing effect with a long history is the creature effect. These unnatural monsters can be as crude as *Godzilla* (a man in a rubber suit) or as convincing as *Alien* (likewise, a man in a rubber suit); they may be remote-controlled (as was the title creature in *E.T., the Extra-Terrestrial*), or a sophisticated puppet (as was the Jedi master Yoda [Fig. 4.64] from the *Star Wars* sequels *The Empire Strikes Back* and *Return of the Jedi*), or stop-motion animated (as was the original *King Kong* [Fig. 4.65]), or a combination of all these techniques and more (as was the dragon Vermithrax Pejorative [Fig. 4.66] in *Dragonslayer*). They may be subtly inhuman, like the vampire *Dracula,* or unmistakably monstrous, like the giant snake in *Conan the Barbarian.*

|4.64|

|4.65|

Evolving "Life" Forms: Creature effects are becoming more and more sophisticated in modern films, progressing from the rather primitive but effective single-frame animation in the original *King Kong* [4.64] to the wise and highly expressive puppet face of the Jedi master Yoda from *The Empire Strikes Back* [4.65] to a combination of animation and remote-controlled movement in the truly frightening dragon in *Dragonslayer* [4.66].

|4.66|

A variant of the creature effect is the transformation effect, where the audience actually gets to see man become monster. This effect has come far since Lon Chaney Jr. became the Wolfman (Fig. 4.67); recent transformations have turned men and women into snakes (*Conan the Barbarian*), black panthers (*Cat*

| 4.67 | Transformations: In 1941's *The Wolf Man,* Lon Chaney Jr. became the Wolfman at the full moon by having his Wolfman makeup applied in six or seven stages while the camera was turned off, creating the illusion of a slow, miraculous transformation when the film was run continuously. The man-becomes-beast techniques used today in such films as *The Howling, An American Werewolf in London,* and *Altered States* are much more complex and employ sculpted, remote-controlled latex models of the actors' heads.

People), reptilian monsters (*The Sword and the Sorceror*), primates and amorphous super-conscious beings (*Altered States*), and, of course, werewolves (*The Howling* and *An American Werewolf in London*)—all on screen. Curiously, many of these makeup effects were not makeups in the traditional sense at all, but rather sculpted remote-controlled models (such as the transforming head from *American Werewolf*). So unorthodox were the transformation effects for 1982's *The Thing* that an effort was made to have artist Rob Bottin's work classified as visual effects instead of makeup.

The last major category of "amazing" effects is the broad heading of unknown locations. Such effects, which transport an audience to a place they could never actually go, can create such diverse locales as the glittering crystalline world of Krypton in *Superman,* the drug-induced, hallucinogenic reality of *Altered States,* the interior of the human body in *Fantastic Voyage,* the sparkling high-tech starship bridge of *Star Trek: The Wrath of Khan,* or the oppressive, smog-shrouded futurescape of *Blade Runner.*

Consider the use of these different types of effects in 1982's *Poltergeist:* the duel of television remote controls is a barely noticeable but difficult to achieve "credible" effect; the sudden tornado is a natural but extreme event, an incredible effect achieved through simple animation; and the flaring hellmouth, the imploding house, and the ghostly poltergeison themselves are all different kinds of "amazing" effects—though all are quite believable within the context of the film.

That has become the real measure of an effect's success—how well the effect is integrated into the storyline of the film. No longer is it a challenge to make the effect itself believable; in the modern film, proper integration of special effects, as opposed to the domination of special effects, is the proper measure of that film's relative success.

The number of special effects in a film does not necessarily determine how effectively those effects are used. *Star Wars* incorporated some 365 individual visual effects, all of which serve to propel the story forward. *Time After Time* uses only a few simple optical effects to send H. G. Wells into the future, but they effectively establish that film's whimsical nature. Tremendous time and money was devoted to the flying sequences for 1978's *Superman* because it was crucial to the film's credibility that the audience really believe a man can fly.

These films use their special effects as little—or as much—as necessary, and no more. The visuals create the atmosphere for the story and impel that story forward. In that way, they become simply one properly integrated element of the film. *E.T., the Extra-Terrestrial* is filled with dazzling effects from beginning to end; E.T. itself is on screen for a great portion of the picture. Yet all these dazzling effects do not impair the warm, friendly ambience of the film because they are properly integrated.

The potential power of such visuals, however, often tempts film-makers to overuse them, to let them overwhelm the story they are designed to help tell. Walt Disney's *Tron* introduced computer animation—images designed and executed through computers—to American audiences, yet failed to craft characters or a story as interesting as their computer effects; the result was a dry light-show. Similar criticism can be leveled at *The Black Hole* and *The Howling*. "Gore" effects, the ability to simulate so many different kinds of deaths, decapitations and eviscerations, are at least partly responsible for the recent upsurge of murder movies in the "hack 'n slash" horror vein. *The Thing* featured such a plethora of transformation sequences that it destroyed the internal suspense it was striving for; and so much focus was placed on *Blade Runner*'s grimly detailed futurescape that its characters drowned in it.

The first two Star Trek films offer a graphic contrast of how special effects can dominate a film or be integrated with its other elements. *Star Trek: The Motion Picture* (1979) boasted a budget in excess of $40 million, involved almost every major effects house in Hollywood, featured several innovative, spectacular effects shots, and yet was universally criticized, particularly for its plodding pace, which included actors staring silently for long minutes at the film's expensive effects. The first sequel, *Star Trek: The Wrath of Khan* (1982), on the other hand, was budgeted at a modest $11 million, featured standard but effective spaceship effects plus some innovative but inexpensive computer animation, and focused its plotline on its characters rather than its technology; this film opened to critical praise and set a record for the most money grossed in a single weekend (June 4–6, 1982). (*Star Trek III* has also found a proper integration of effects and story.)

There is a final role special effects can play: to achieve the novel or nontraditional effect, often called a "gimmick," called for by certain films. Recent novelty effects have included the use of clips from classic films to allow Steve Martin to interact with stars like

|4.68|

|4.69|

Novelty Effects: A blend of past and present has been achieved in recent films like *Dead Men Don't Wear Plaid* where Steve Martin's image was superimposed over the foreground figure in shots like the one above from *Dark Passage* [4.68], creating the illusion that Martin and Humphrey Bogart were "playing" a scene together, and *Zelig* [4.69] where Woody Allen seems to appear between Calvin Coolidge and Herbert Hoover in newsreel footage.

Humphrey Bogart in 1982's *Dead Men Don't Wear Plaid* (Fig. 4.68) and Woody Allen with Calvin Coolidge and Herbert Hoover in 1983's *Zelig* (Fig. 4.69).

Doubtless further innovations, revisions, and experiments will continue to bring new and even more amazing special effects off the screen and into the audiences' figurative and literal laps.

QUESTIONS

On Special Effects

1. How effective are the special effects employed in the film? Do they dominate the film to the point that the film is just a showcase for the effects, or are they an integrated part of the film as a whole?
2. Identify the types of special effects used in the film as "credible" effects, "incredible" effects, and "amazing" effects. Which kind of effects are used most often?
3. To what degree does the credibility of the entire film depend on the audience believing in its special effects? Do special effects overshadow the major characters so much that they seem secondary to the effects?

CHAPTER 5

SOUND EFFECTS AND DIALOGUE

SOUND AND THE MODERN FILM

Film is primarily a visual medium, and its areas of greatest significance and interest are generally communicated through visual means. But sound plays an increasingly important role in the modern film, because its here-and-now reality relies heavily on the three elements that make up the soundtrack: sound effects, dialogue, and the musical score. These elements create additional levels of meaning and provide sensual and emotional stimuli that increase the range, depth, and intensity of our experience far beyond what can be achieved through visual means alone.

Since we are more *consciously* aware of what we see than what we hear, we generally accept the soundtrack without much thought, responding intuitively to the information it provides while ignoring the complex techniques employed to create those responses. The intricacy of a finished soundtrack is illustrated by Leonard Bernstein's description of the sound mixer's contribution to a single scene from *On the Waterfront:*

> For instance, he may be told to keep the audience unconsciously aware of the traffic noises of a great city, yet they must also be aware of the sounds of wind and waves coming into a large, almost empty church over those traffic noises. And meantime, the pedaling of a child's bicycle going around the church must punctuate the dialogue of two stray characters who have wandered in. Not a word of that dialogue, of course, can be lost, and the voices, at the same time, must arouse the dim echoes they would have in so cavernous a setting. And at this particular point no one (except the composer) has even begun to think how the musical background can fit in.[1]

Five different layers of sound are at work simultaneously in the brief scene that Bernstein describes, and each one contributes significantly to the total effect. Compared to many scenes in the modern film, the sounds in this one are simple and traditional. They are not nearly as complex as the soundtrack for the film *M*A*S*H,* for example, where sound is at least as significant as the visual element, if not more so. Thus, the modern soundtrack demands more and more of our conscious attention, so much so in fact, that if we want to fully appreciate a modern film we should perhaps go prepared as much to hear the film as to see it.

1. Leonard Bernstein, *The Joy of Music.* New York: Simon and Schuster, 1959, p. 66.

DIALOGUE

A major part of our attention to sound in the modern film will naturally be directed toward understanding the dialogue, for dialogue gives us a great deal of important information in most films. But we should also be aware of the unique characteristics of film dialogue, and especially those ways in which film dialogue is different from stage dialogue.

In a typical stage play, dialogue is an extremely important element, and it is essential that almost every word be heard. To accomplish this end, stage actors use a certain measured rhythm, carefully speaking their lines in turn and incorporating brief pauses in the question-response pattern, so that each line of dialogue can be clearly heard by the person occupying the worst seat in the house. This limitation does not apply to film, however, and so dialogue can be treated much more realistically. In *Citizen Kane*, for example, Orson Welles employed the overlapping dialogue, fragmented sentences, and interruptions common to everyday conversation without loss of essential information or dramatic power. This was achieved, as it is now in most films, through careful microphone positioning and recording, skillful editing and mixing of the recorded sound, and subtle variations in sound quality (volume, clarity, reverberation, and tonal qualities). Through such means, the modern filmmaker creates the impression of a highly selective ear turned to what it wants or needs to hear. The most important sounds are singled out, emphasized, and made clear; those of less importance are blurred or muted.

Because it can be heard distinctly in every theater seat, film dialogue can also be delivered at a much more rapid pace than stage dialogue. This capability is put to good use by Frank Capra in *Mr. Smith Goes to Washington* and *Mr. Deeds Goes to Town* where he uses compressed, machine-gun paced dialogue in phone conversations that get necessary but non-dramatic exposition out of the way as fast as possible so he can get down to the serious business of telling his stories.

The old adage that a picture is worth a thousand words is especially true in the film medium. Filmmakers must, first of all, use dialogue with great restraint to avoid repeating what has already been made clear visually. Furthermore, film's dramatic power and cinematic qualities are both diminished if dialogue is used to communicate what could be expressed more powerfully through visual means. In some cases, the most dramatically effective results are achieved through sparse or monosyllabic dialogue, and in a few films, dialogue is dispensed with entirely. This is not to say that dialogue should never dominate the screen. But it should do so only when the dramatic situation demands it. As a general rule, dialogue in film should be subordinate to the visual image, and seldom assume the dominant role it has on the stage.

THREE DIMENSIONALITY IN SOUND

In *Citizen Kane* (1941), which is generally conceded to be the first modern sound film, Orson Welles created a strong impression of three-dimensional sound without the benefit of the multiple soundtracks and speakers required for true stereo. Perhaps more conscious of the importance of sound and its potential for subtleties because of his radio experience, Welles achieved this effect by varying the sound quality (volume, clarity, reverberation, and tonal qualities) of voices or sound effects in terms of their relative distance from the camera, so that a sense of aural three dimensionality was achieved to match the three-dimensional image of Gregg Toland's deep-focus cinematography. This three dimensionality was achieved on one "track" (monaural sound) by making voices or sounds sound close up or far away—without the left and right separation of stereo (which is achieved by recording on two separate tracks and then playing back what was recorded on two or more speakers).

In 1952, true three dimensionality of sound was achieved by combining the techniques pioneered by Welles with a six-track stereophonic system—in the triple wide-screen *This Is Cinerama*. A four-track system was introduced to match the Cinemascope image of *The Robe* in 1953. But as the number of wide-screen films being produced declined and the studios and independent producers returned to the standard screen format, the interest in stereophonic sound declined also.

In the mid-'70s, a different attempt was made to achieve spectacular sound effects in theaters with Sensurround. The Sensurround system derived its sound from two large closet-sized speaker cabinets located at the rear corners of the theater. These powerful speakers were designed to literally shake the entire theater, but the system was used for relatively few films, such as *Earthquake* (1974) and *Midway* (1976). In *Midway*, the rear speakers effectively provided a realistic 360-degree sound environment by using techniques such as the following. The camera is positioned on one side of an aircraft carrier looking up toward a kamikaze plane diving toward the carrier. The soundtrack in front grows louder until the plane roars right overhead. Then the huge speaker boxes in the rear take over to complete the roar, and give us the sounds and shock waves of the explosion on the deck behind us.

At about the same period (1974) the Dolby system was introduced. An audio recording system that reduces background noise and increases frequency range, it has been combined with a system called "surround sound" from Tate Audio Ltd. to produce a multitrack stereophonic system for theaters. This unique system employs an encoding process that achieves a 360-degree sound field, and creates the effect of a greater number of separate speakers than are actually required.

Dolby-Surround Sound has been used with great power and effectiveness in recent films, achieving the effect of hissing snakes all around us in *Raiders of the Lost Ark* (Fig. 5.1), and the cheering fight crowd, managers, and trainers in *Raging Bull.*

In *Das Boot,* an incredible sense of a 360-degree sound environment is created both inside the confined quarters of the German U-boat and the sea around and above it. The quality of each sound is unique: a strumming guitar, a radio, a phonograph, men talking and laughing, clanging horns, engine noises—all seem to come from different sources and give us a sense of being there. It is a film full of listening. As the crew first strains to hear the creaking of collapsing bulkheads on a ship they sink; then later, with the sub nestled on the bottom in hiding from a destroyer on the surface, the crew grows deathly quiet so as not to give away their position. Their silence emphasizes every noise, which the Dolby Stereo locates with pinpoint accuracy. We hear the destroyer's pinging sonar, and every turn of its screw as it passes overhead, growing louder and then softer. As the sub sits on the bottom, at a great depth, we hear the rivets straining, then popping, and the sound of water spraying in as parts of the boat fail to withstand the tremendous pressure (Fig. 5.2).

Ironically, despite the care lavished on crafting soundtracks these days, many filmgoers never fully experience them. About 60 percent of the theaters in this country (most of which are older theaters and small suburban theaters) simply do not have the capability to reproduce the quality or the dimensions of the sound recorded in the films they show.

|5.1| |5.2|
Three-Dimensional Sound: Snakes hiss all around us in *Raiders of the Lost Ark,* and destroyers rumble menacingly overhead in *Das Boot,* thanks to the three-dimensional sound effects in Dolby stereo.

VISIBLE AND INVISIBLE SOUND

In the early days of the sound film, the emphasis was naturally placed on recorded sound that was synchronized with the visual image. As the popular term *talking pictures* indicates, the audience of that time was fascinated by the reproduction of the human voice. Although sound effects were employed, they were generally limited to sounds that would naturally and realistically emanate from the images on the screen, that is, to *visible sounds.*

Although the dramatic power of the human voice and the sense of reality conveyed through sound effects certainly contributed new dimensions to the film art, the tight link between sound and image proved very confining, and filmmakers began to experiment with other uses of sound. They soon discovered what stage directors had known all along: that *invisible sound,* or sound emanating from sources *not* on the screen, could be used to extend the dimensions of film beyond what is seen, and to achieve more powerful dramatic effects as well. Once they realized the unique and dynamic potential of invisible sound, they were able to free sound from its restricted role of simply accompanying the image. Invisible sounds now function in a highly expressive or even symbolic way as independent "images," sometimes carrying as much significance as the visual image, and occasionally even more.

This creative use of invisible sound is important to the modern film for a variety of reasons. To begin with, many of the sounds around us in real life are invisible, simply because we find it unnecessary or impossible to look at their sources. Realizing this, filmmakers now employ sound as a separate storytelling element capable of providing information by itself. Sound used in this way complements the image instead of merely duplicating its effects. For example, if we hear the sound of a closing door, we can tell that someone has left the room even if we do not see an accompanying image. Thus the camera is freed from what might be considered routine chores, and can focus on the subject of the greatest significance. This is especially important when the emphasis is on reaction instead of action, when the camera leaves the face of the speaker to focus on the face of the listener.

In some cases invisible sound can have a more powerful effect alone than would be possible with an accompanying image. The human mind is equipped with an "eye" much more powerful than that of the camera. An effective sound image can trigger a response in our imagination much stronger than any visual image. In the horror film, for example, invisible sounds can create a total, terror-charged atmosphere. Story elements that heighten and intensify our emotional response—the clank of chains, muffled footsteps on a creaking stair, a stifled scream, the opening of a creaking door, the howl of a wolf, or even unidentifiable sounds—are much more effective when the sources are *not* seen (Fig. 5.3).

As demonstrated by the description of the scene from *On the Waterfront* earlier, invisible sounds (such as the sounds of city traffic, wind and waves, and the child's bicycle) are routinely used to intensify the filmgoer's sense of really "being there." Thus, by encircling the viewer with the natural sounds of the scene's immediate environment, the soundtrack suggests a reality beyond the limits of the visual frame.

In comedy, sound can be effectively substituted for the visual image, and is usually used to "depict" comic catastrophes set up and made completely predictable through the visual means. For example, in a scene picturing a crazy inventor trying out a homemade flying machine, the picture may show the launching, while the predictable crash is left to be illustrated by the soundtrack. A dual purpose is achieved here: Our imaginations intensify the humorous effect of the crash by forming their own

15.3 | Off-Screen Sound: In *M*, an early sound film, an inventive use of off-screen sound builds mystery and suspense as the child-killer (Peter Lorre) announces his presence by whistling bits of a classical theme before he appears on screen.

picture of it, while the camera focuses on the reactions registered on the faces of the onlookers, which become the focal point of comic interest. Such use of sound also has clear practical benefits, considering the danger to the stuntman and the destruction of expensive properties that go along with showing the crash visually. By using sound for the crash, the would-be pilot needs only to stagger on screen, battered and dirty, draped in a few recognizable fragments of the plane.

Thus sound effects achieve their most original and effective results not through simultaneous use with the visual image, but as independent "images," enhancing and enriching the picture rather than merely duplicating it.

POINTS OF VIEW IN SOUND

In the objective point of view the characters and the action of a scene are perceived as if by a somewhat remote observer, who looks calmly on the events without becoming emotionally or physically involved. Camera and microphone perceive the characters externally, from the sidelines, without stepping in to assume the role of participants. The subjective viewpoint, on the other hand, is that of one who is intensely involved, either emotionally or physically, in the happenings on the screen. In the completely subjective view, therefore, camera and microphone become the eyes and ears of a character in the film, and see and hear exactly what that character sees and hears. As already noted, since maintaining the subjective point of view consistently is difficult if not impossible in film, most directors choose to alternate between the two viewpoints, first establishing each situation clearly from an objective viewpoint, then cutting to a relatively brief subjective shot, then repeating the same pattern. Since, in each shot, the camera and the microphone *together* create the unified impression of a single viewpoint, the volume and quality of the sound will vary in direct relationship to camera positioning. For example, sounds audible in a subjective close-up may not be audible in an objective long shot, and vice versa. This alternation between the objective and subjective viewpoints, and the tight link between camera and microphone, are illustrated by the following scene:

1. Establishing shot: Objective camera view from street corner, focusing on a workman using an air hammer in center of street (apparent distance 50 to 75 feet). *Sound:* Loud chatter of air hammer, mingled with other street noises.

2. Cut to subjective view: Close-ups of air hammer, and violently shaking lower arms and hands of workman, from workman's point of view. *Sound:* Hammer is almost deafening—no other sounds heard.

3. Cut back to objective camera: Heavy truck turns corner beyond workman, bears down on him at top speed. *Sound:* Loud chatter of air hammer, other street noises, rising sound of approaching truck.

4. Cut to subjective view: Close-up of air hammer and workman's hands as seen from his viewpoint. *Sound:* First only deafening sounds of air hammer, then a rising squeal of brakes mixed with hammer noise.

5. Quick cut to new subjective view: Front of truck closing quickly on camera from ten feet away. *Sound:* Squeal of brakes louder, hammer stops, woman's voice screaming, cut short by sickening thud . . . darkness and momentary silence.

6. Cut back to objective viewpoint (from street corner): Unconscious figure of workman in front of stopped truck. Curious crowd gathering into circle. *Sound:* Mixed jumble of panicked voices, street noises, ambulance siren in distance.

Sometimes the soundtrack is used to provide an even more intensely subjective point of view, one that communicates what goes on in a character's mind. The link between camera and microphone is slightly different here, for the camera will usually only suggest the subjective view by picturing the character's face in tight close-up, and rely on the soundtrack to make the subjectiv-

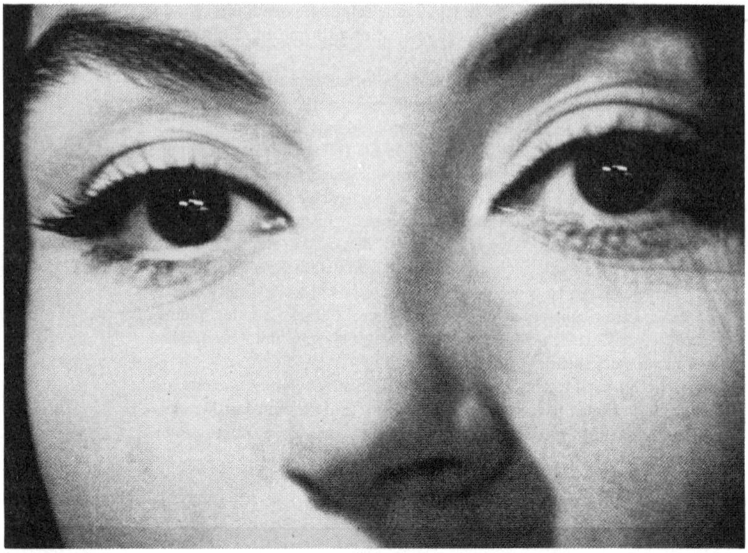

|5.4| The Eyes as a "Window of the Mind": Director Claude Lelouch moves the camera in for a tight close-up on the eyes of Anouk Aimee as he prepares for a memory voice-over or a visual flashback in *A Man and a Woman.*

ity of the viewpoint clear. Just as the image is in close-up, the sound is in close-up, too. In most cases the sound quality will be distorted slightly to signal that the sounds being heard are not a part of the natural scene, but come from inside the character's mind. The camera also serves to make this clear by focusing tightly on the character's eyes. The eyes loom large enough to fill the entire screen, and thus become a window of the mind through which we "read" the character's inner state. The camera in such a sequence can remain in tight close-up while the soundtrack communicates the character's thoughts or sounds and voices from his or her memory. Or the sequence may merely act as a transition to a *visual* flashback. These sequences are frequently filmed in soft focus, another clue to their subjective nature (Fig. 5.4).

Unusual inner emotional states are also represented by the soundtrack, through use of variations in volume, reverberation, or other distortions in the voices or natural sounds heard by the character. Physical reactions such as extreme shock, excitement, or even illness are sometimes suggested by drumbeats, which supposedly represent internal symptoms of these reactions, such as high pulse rate, or a pounding heart. Extreme amplification and distortion of natural sounds are also used to suggest a hysterical state of mind.

SPECIAL USES OF SOUND EFFECTS AND DIALOGUE

In addition to the sound formulas described above, which have been used over and over again, innovative filmmakers have creatively used sound effects and dialogue for a variety of specialized purposes.

Sound Effects to Tell an Inner Story

Directors also manipulate and distort sound for artistic ends—to put us "inside" a character so that we can understand what he or she is feeling. In a powerful scene from *On the Waterfront,* Elia Kazan employs the sounds of the waterfront to dramatize the emotions of Terry Malloy (Marlon Brando) and Edie Doyle (Eva Marie Saint). The priest (Karl Malden) has just convinced Terry to confess to Edie (whom he now loves) that he was involved in setting up the murder of her brother by corrupt union officials. The priest and Terry stand on a hill overlooking the waterfront, and when Edie appears walking toward them on the flats below, Terry hurries down the steep hill to meet her. Almost imperceptibly at first, the rhythmic hammering of a pile driver, which has been a part of the natural sound environment, grows increasingly louder as Terry approaches Edie, thus making us aware of the fear he feels about leveling with her. As he reaches the crucial part of his "confession," the steam whistle on a nearby ship shrieks loudly, obscuring his words as we watch his anguished face trying to tell the story we already know. With the deafening shriek of the whistle, we are suddenly "inside" Edie, feeling the shock, the horror, and the disbelief of what she has just heard, as she covers her ears with her hands to protest a truth she cannot accept. The steam whistle stops just before Terry finishes his story, and as he finishes, Edie stares at him a moment in disbelief, then turns and runs away from him in panic, her action accompanied by high, wailing violins. The scene's dramatic intensity is literally "beyond words"—the faces and the internalized sounds alone tell the entire "story."

In *All That Jazz,* Bob Fosse takes a totally different approach in his directing of Joe Gideon's "heart attack warning" scene. At the opening of the scene, everything is normal. A room full of cast members for a new musical are sitting around reading dialogue from a very funny script, for the entire cast periodically breaks into laughter. Suddenly, without warning, we no longer hear the laughter—we still see the faces laughing, but the sound is gone. The soundtrack carries only the close-up sounds of Joe Gideon (Roy Scheider). We hear him striking a match, his finger drumming on the table, a labored breathing, his wristwatch ticking, and his shoe grinding out a cigarette on the floor. With all sound external to Gideon cut off (in spite of constant visual reminders that we should be hearing it) and every close-up sound of Gideon magnified, Fosse has literally grabbed us by the ears and pulled us inside Joe Gideon's circulatory system, and sent a clear message that "something's terribly wrong here." After Gideon holds a pencil in both hands behind the chair, snaps it in two and drops the pieces, the sound returns to normal, the reading ends, and the room is vacated. The next scene shows three of the producers in the back of the cab discussing his symptoms, and the fact that he is now in the hospital undergoing tests.

Distortion of Sound to Suggest Subjective States

In *When a Stranger Calls,* Carol Kane, as a teenage babysitter, receives threatening phone calls from a psychopathic killer, who repeatedly asks her the question, "Why haven't you checked the children?" The call is finally traced by the police to another phone *within* the house. Before the police can get there, the children are brutally murdered, but the killer is captured and imprisoned. Seven years later, Kane is married with two children of her own. On the same evening that the killer escapes from prison, Kane's husband takes her out for a special dinner celebrating a job promotion, and they leave their children in the care of a babysitter. As they settle down to their meal in the restaurant, Kane is told by a waiter that she has a telephone call at the cashier's desk. She unsuspectingly answers the phone, assuming the babysitter has called with a question. We do hear a question in the receiver—but

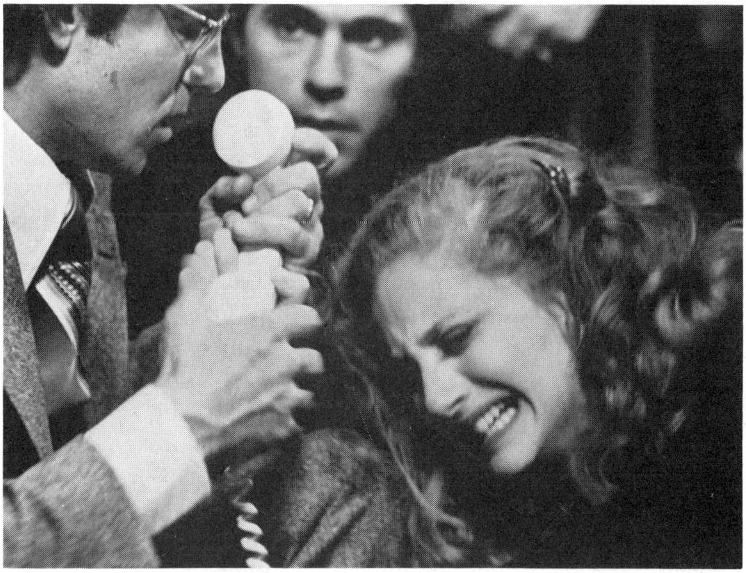

|5.5| Distortion of Sound: The cold, metallic voice of the killer on the phone sets up terrifying echoes of the past for Carol Kane in *When a Stranger Calls.*

it's the killer's voice, cold and metallic: "Have you checked the children . . . ildren . . . dren . . . ren?" The familiar but distorted voice echoes louder and louder, blending into her hysterical scream as we are suddenly yanked inside her fear and horror (Fig. 5.5).

The "Personality" of Mechanical Sounds

Mechanical sounds can even be integrated into the overall tone of a specific scene by giving them "personalities." In *The Grapes of Wrath,* John Ford uses the different personalities of two auto horns to underscore the emotions in a scene. As the Joad family stand around the yard in welcoming Tom back from prison, Tom's brother Al drives up in the old Joad truck, and joins in the happy scene with a bright cheerful *uugga!* from the truck's horn. The celebration continues for a minute or so, until it is suddenly interrupted by an ominous, low-pitched, and insultingly loud horn, as the convertible driven by the land and cattle company representative pulls up. The horn freezes the Joads as it sounds, and they wait meekly for the reminder they know is coming: that they must be off the land by the next day.

Slow-Motion Sound

Walter Hill matches slow-motion sound to slow-motion action in the final shoot-out scene of *The Long Riders*. After robbing a bank in Northfield, Minnesota, the James Gang find themselves trapped: As the gang attempts their getaway, gunmen on top of buildings and behind barricades throw up a wall of bullets. At first, the action is a mixture of normal and slow motion. As outlaws or townsmen are wounded, the action goes slow motion as they reel or fall, and the sound slows down also. However, these brief, "slow" scenes are alternated with scenes shown at normal speed. But as the action intensifies and focuses on the outlaws as they are riddled with bullets, the *whole sequence* goes into slow-motion picture and sound. The surreal slowness of the image draws us closer to the gang members, and the slow-motion sound makes us feel their pain as the bullets tear into their flesh. The total effect is eerie, with low whistling sounds, muffled roars, grotesquely slowed horse whinnies, and low-pitch human grunts and groans (Fig. 5.6).

| 5.6 | Slow Motion Sound: Unusual effects are achieved by the use of slow motion sound as members of the James Gang are shot up by townspeople as they try to make their escape after a bank robbery in *The Long Riders*.

Martin Scorsese similarly used slow-motion sound in *Raging Bull* to portray Jake LaMotta's (Robert DeNiro) fatigue in a difficult fight and to isolate the effect of a single, crucial blow.

Ironic Juxtaposition of Sound and Image

Usually picture and sound work together to carry a single set of impressions. It is occasionally effective, however, to create ironic contrasts between them. In *The Grapes of Wrath,* the Joads have just stopped along the road to look down on a lush green valley of California orchards, their first look at the "land of milk and honey" they expected. There are cries of glee, excitement, and amazement, accompanied by birds chirping. The camera cuts to Ma Joad as she appears around the back of the truck. We know that Grandma is dead, and that Ma Joad has concealed this from the others until they could reach the "promised land" of California. The cheerful noises that continue provide an ironic counterpoint to Ma's tired, grief-stricken face, serving to strengthen its impact.

Placing Unusual Emphasis on Sound

A director who wishes to place some unusual kind of emphasis on sound has several options. Two obvious methods involve de-emphasizing the visual image: (1) drop the image altogether, by fading to black, or (2) purposely make the image uninteresting or dull, by holding a meaningless shot for a long period or by prolonged use of "dead scenes."

In *Reds,* to catch our attention and introduce us to the unusual device of "the witnesses" (old people who actually knew John Reed and Louise Bryant), Warren Beatty starts the witnesses' testimony before the images begin. The voices start about halfway through the opening credits, as we watch white credits unfold over a black screen. At the end of the film, the witnesses continue their interesting and significant comments as the visual image fades and is followed by the ending credits, shown again white against black.

In *Citizen Kane,* Orson Welles employs the "dead screen" technique during one of the Susan Alexander Kane's (Dorothy Commingore) opera performances. The camera cuts from the performance and begins a long, slow tilt upward, following a pair of cables up the bare gray walls behind the scenery. Faced with looking at this incredibly boring dead screen, we are forced to listen to the painfully off-key voice. The slow tilt is stretched out just the right amount of time so that we properly appreciate our reward at the end, when the camera finally stops at the two technicians on the catwalk. We gain relief from our pain (and our suspense at where this long journey upward over the dead gray background is leading) as one of the technicians holds his nose to indicate his response to the "music" we have all been suffering through.

The simplest and most obvious way to emphasize a sound is to increase its volume. In *Bonnie and Clyde,* Arthur Penn underscores the violence by amplifying the roar of the gunfire and the constant shrieking of Blanche Barrow (Estelle Parsons) (Fig. 5.7). A similar amplification of sound to underscore violence occurs in *Shane,* where gunshots and the sounds of a fistfight are exaggerated. An effective use of amplified sound occurs in the fight between Shane (Alan Ladd) and Joe Starret (Van Heflin) to see

| 5.7 | Exaggerated Sound Effects: The amplified sounds of gunfire and Blanche Barrow's (Estelle Parsons') constant hysterical screaming add greatly to the intensity of action scenes in *Bonnie and Clyde.*

which of them will go to town for a showdown with the Ryker clan. The fight is filmed from an extremely low angle, with the combatants framed under the belly of a panicked horse. As the fighters struggle, the horse prances, with the pounding of each hoof amplified to match its closeness to the camera. The violence panics other animals, who join in the chorus: A barking dog and a bawling cow trying to break out of her stall join in to accompany the snorts, the whinnies, and the pounding hoofs of the panicked horse. Although the sounds of the fistfight in the background are audible, they are somewhat de-emphasized by the loudness of the closer horse hoofs, but the violence of that fight is actually intensified by the exaggerated sound environment.

Using Sound for Texture

In *McCabe and Mrs. Miller,* Robert Altman experimented with a new approach to dialogue and sound recording. His goal in this and later films seems to be away from the dramatic enhancement of dialogue and sound and toward a thick, realistic sound texture in which dialogue can become a series of fragmented, blurred, and unseparated utterings, equal to but not dramatically more important than the ambient sounds (sounds natural to the scene's environment). By blurring the sharp edges of dialogue, and thereby de-emphasizing the words, Altman makes us more conscious of the visual elements and weaves visual and aural elements into a more equal blend, creating a unique texture in the film. The ambient sound is thick, rich, and detailed, but not dramatically enhanced. In *McCabe and Mrs. Miller,* the stomping and shuffling of boots against a rough wooden floor are there right along with the mumbled, naturalistic dialogue. Typical of the difference in Altman's approach is a scene in which McCabe (Warren Beatty) and another man pass through a crowded saloon on their way upstairs. Someone is telling a joke at the bar, and we hear fragments of it as they pass through, but as they start up the stairs, their loud footsteps obscure the punch line.

Everything in *McCabe and Mrs. Miller* sounds real: the rain, a chair scraped across a floor, mumbled poker-game dialogue, moaning wind, a jug skidding across the ice, gunshots and their reverberation. Sound is often stacked on sound, voice on voice, but stacked in a new way so that we get an incredible sense of being there—in a different place and a different time. The texture is so real that we feel the rain and the cold wind and even smell the smoke.

SOUND AS A TRANSITIONAL ELEMENT

Sound is also an extremely important transitional device in films, serving either to show the relationship between shots, scenes, or sequences, or to make a change in image from one shot or sequence to another seem more fluid or natural.

A fluid and graceful transition between sequences is achieved through the slight overlapping of sound from one shot into the next, where the sound from a shot continues even after the image fades or dissolves into an entirely new image. This overlapping usually represents a passage of time, a change of setting, or both. A similar effect is created by the converse, where the sound of an *upcoming* sequence slightly precedes its corresponding image. In many cases, sound may overlap sound, with the sound from one image fading under the rising sound of the succeeding image. This provides a smooth flow of sound from one sequence to another when abrupt changes in sound are not desirable (although they sometimes are).

Sound links, which are bridges between scenes or sequences (changes in place or time), are created through the use of similar or identical sounds in both sequences. For example, a buzzing alarm clock at the end of one sequence becomes a buzzing telephone switchboard at the start of the next. Sound is thus used as a somewhat artificial link between the two sequences to create a sense of fluid continuity. Sometimes even dialogue links provide transition between two sequences: A question asked by a character at the close of one sequence may be answered by another character at the start of the following sequence, even though the two scenes may be set in a different time and place.

Sometimes dialogue transitions are ironic, resulting in a sharp or startling contrast between the scenes being joined. Consider, for example, the effect if one scene's last line of a dialogue had a character say: "I don't care what happens! Nothing on the face of the earth could entice me to go to Paris!" and the next scene opened with the same character walking by the Eiffel Tower.

Dozens of examples of dynamic and unusual uses of sound can be found in *Citizen Kane,* where Orson Welles employs a variety of sound links to blend scenes and explosive changes in volume to propel us from one scene to another.

VOICE-OVER NARRATION

The filmmaker can also employ sound that has no *direct* relationship to the natural sounds and dialogue involved in the story. A human voice off screen, called voice-over narration, has a variety of functions. It is perhaps most commonly used as an expository device, conveying necessary background information or filling in gaps for continuity that cannot be dramatically presented. Some films use voice-over narration only at the beginning to give necessary background, place the action in historical perspective, or provide a sense of authenticity. Others may employ voice-over at the beginning, occasionally in the body of the film for transition or continuity, and at the end.

The flavor of a novelistic first-person point of view is often provided through the use of voice-over. This can be accomplished by setting the story in a frame: A narrator is visually introduced who then tells the story through a series of flashbacks (as in *Little Big Man* and *The Glass Menagerie*); or else the narrator is never introduced visually, but only as the voice of a participant recalling past events. In *To Kill A Mockingbird,* for example, the voice-over is obviously that of an adult relating childhood recollections, but the narrator is never pictured. The adult narrator of that film, in a soft, southern voice, provides a sense of time and place, describing the pace and style of life of Macomb, and then, by ending the introductory voice-over with "that summer I was six years old" just as Scout Finch appears on the screen, slips easily from the adult remembering the past into young Scout's viewpoint and the present tense of the film (Figs. 5.8 and 5.9).

The narrator for *Summer of '42* performs a similar function (establishing place, time, and point of view) but comments more philosophically on the significance of the events to Hermie, the point-of-view character. Both *To Kill a Mockingbird* and *Summer of '42* employ great restraint in their use of voice-over narration.

The film versions of some novels must depend on voice-over to tell a story that cannot be told effectively through cinematic

|5.8| **|5.9|**
Voice-Over Narration—Remembering: Effective and restrained use of voice-over narration provides a framework for journeys into the past in both *To Kill a Mockingbird* (with an adult narrator speaking as a grown-up Scout Finch) and *Julia* (with Jane Fonda speaking as Lillian Hellman).

means. Such is the case with *The Old Man and the Sea,* where the most important part of the story takes place in the old man's mind, in his reactions to what happens rather than in the events themselves. The voice-over becomes a noncinematic compromise, as Spencer Tracy, who plays the old man Santiago, simply reads passages from the novel that communicate the character's thoughts and feelings about the action.

A similar problem occurs in *Cannery Row,* where John Huston's rich voice and skillful narration add a certain style and quality to the film, but the narration is forced to carry far too much of the burden. The literary style of the narration and its excessive use combine to make us feel that we're "reading" a movie.

In *Apocalypse Now,* Martin Sheen's narration, necessary to glue together an otherwise incoherent film, flattens the dramatic impact of the visuals by overinterpreting and overexplaining, by telling us too many things we can see for ourselves. Here the voice-over gets in the way. By telling us too much about "the horror," the film prevents us from discovering it for ourselves. As a result, we never really feel that horror (Fig. 5.10).

| 5.10 | Voice-Over Narration as Structural Glue: With the voice-over provided by Martin Sheen (seen here with Marlon Brando), Director Francis Ford Coppola tries to plug holes in the script of *Apocalypse Now,* but succeeds only in diminishing the film's dramatic punch.

The voice-over technique is sometimes employed in direct contrast to the image for an ironic effect. For example, in *Two for the Road,* Albert Finney writes a letter to his wife while he is traveling alone. As he writes the letter, its content (which describes an ordinary humdrum day on the road, lonely without her) serves as a voice-over narration for the visual sequence that shows the day he really had—a very exciting one where he meets and beds a beautiful girl.

Perhaps the most powerful voice-over narration in film to date is that provided by Linda Manz for *Days of Heaven.* There is a distinctive style to her narration, a poetic rhythm, a texture that permeates the entire film. The unique vocal quality and "verbal essence" provide more than just the narrative glue to hold the story's structure together; combined with the strange woman-child philosophical reflections and childish utterings, they are integrated so beautifully that they become a major element of the film's unique style and texture (Fig. 5.11).

Generally, voice-over narration can be very effective if used with restraint. It is not, however, a truly cinematic technique, and overusing it can be seriously detrimental to the quality of the film.

| 5.11 | Narration as an Integral Part of Texture: Linda Manz's poetic and ironic narration for *Days of Heaven* functions almost as a part of the musical score. The "personality" of her voice becomes a dominant factor in the film's unique style and texture.

SILENCE AS A "SOUND" EFFECT

In certain situations a short *dead track,* the complete absence of sound, may be as effective as the most powerful sound effect. There is a ghostly, unnatural quality about film without sound that forces us to look more intently at the image. Because the natural rhythms of sound effects, dialogue, and music become as natural to the film as the rhythms of breathing, when these rhythms stop we immediately develop a feeling of almost physical tension and suspense, as though we are holding our breath and can't wait to start breathing again. This effect is used to great advantage in conjunction with the freeze frame. The sudden change from vibrant, noisy movement to silent, frozen stillness can stun us for a moment.

The most common use of dead track is simply to increase, by contrast, the impact and shock effect of sudden or unexpected sounds that follow these moments of silence.

In *Still of the Night,* psychiatrist Sam Rice (Roy Scheider) is following a woman he believes to be Brooke Reynolds (Meryl Streep) through Central Park. The soundtrack is alive with environmental noises: wind, muffled music, and traffic, all blended into a kind of "big-city-alive-in-the-distance" hum. As Rice walks into an underpass and stops, the soundtrack goes dead, providing a few moments of silence to set up the aural shock of a mugger's switchblade springing from its handle a few inches from his face. The opposite of this, the shock of silence after violent sound, is experienced during the moments of almost dead track that immediately follow the final fusilade in *Bonnie and Clyde.*

RHYTHMIC QUALITIES OF DIALOGUE AND SOUND EFFECTS

Both dialogue and sound effects are also important for the rhythmic patterns or cadences they create, for these rhythmic elements often match the visual rhythms and reflect the mood, emotion, or pace of the action. Thus the pace of the dialogue and the rhythmic qualities of the sound effects influence the pace of the film as a whole.

QUESTIONS

On Sound Effects and Dialogue

1. Where in the film are off-screen or invisible sounds effectively employed to enlarge the boundaries of the visual frame, or to create mood and atmosphere?
2. What sound effects in particular contribute to a sense of reality and a feeling of being there?
3. Does the film attempt to provide a sense of three dimensionality or depth in sound? If a stereophonic soundtrack is used, what does it contribute to the overall effect of the film?
4. Where is sound employed to represent subjective states of mind, and how effective is it?
5. Where is unusual emphasis placed on sound in the film and what is the purpose of such emphasis?
6. Is sound used to provide important transitions in the film? Why is sound needed to provide these transitions?
7. If voice-over soundtracks are used for narration or internal monologues (thoughts of a character spoken aloud), can you justify their use, or could the same information have been conveyed through purely dramatic means?

8. Is dialogue used unnecessarily, repeating information already adequately communicated by the image? Where?
9. Where in the film is silence employed as a sound effect to intensify suspense, to increase the impact of sounds which follow, or to create other special dramatic effects?
10. Where in the film is sound used for other specialized purposes, and how effective is each use?
11. How do the pace of the dialogue and the rhythmic qualities of the sound effects influence the pace of the film as a whole?

CHAPTER 6

THE MUSICAL SCORE

THE REMARKABLE AFFINITY OF MUSIC AND FILM

Music has such a remarkable affinity to film that the addition of what we call the *musical score* was almost an inevitability. Even in the earliest films, the audience felt a very real vacuum of silence because the pulsing vitality provided by the moving image seemed unnatural, almost ghostly, without some form of corresponding sound. But by the time it became possible to use recorded dialogue and sound effects, music had already proven itself as a highly effective accompaniment for the emotions and rhythms built into the images.

Music has made possible an artistic blending of sight and sound, a fusing of music and movement so effective that composer Dimitri Tiomkin was moved to remark that a good film is "really just ballet with dialogue." Muir Mathieson, in *The Technique of Film Music,* put it this way: "Music, having a form of its own, has ways of doing its appointed task in films with distinction, judged purely as music, and with subtlety, judged as a part of the whole film. It must be accepted not as a decoration or a filler of gaps in the plaster, but a part of the architecture."[1]

Both film and music divide time into rather clearly defined rhythmic patterns; perhaps that provides the most important common bond. There are certain natural rhythms inherent in the physical movements of many objects on the screen. Trees swaying in the breeze, a walking man, a galloping horse, a speeding motorcycle, or a machine capping bottles on an assembly line—all establish natural rhythms that create an almost instinctive need for corresponding rhythmic sounds. Another rhythmic pattern is provided by the pace of the plot, by how quickly or slowly it unfolds. Still another is created by the pace of the dialogue and the natural rhythms of human speech. Tempo is also established by the frequency of editorial cuts and the varying duration of shots between cuts, which gives each sequence a unique rhythmic character. Although editing divides the film into a number of separate parts, the continuity and the fluid form of the medium remain, since the cuts create clear rhythmic patterns but do not break the flowing stream of images and sound.

1. Roger Manvell and John Huntley, *The Technique of Film Music.* London: Focal Press Ltd., 1957, p. 210.

Because music possesses these same qualities of rhythm and fluid continuity, it can be easily adapted to the film's basic rhythms, to its liquid contours or shapes. This affinity between music and film has led us to accept them almost as unity, as part of the same package, as though music somehow exists magically alongside every film.

THE IMPORTANCE OF THE MUSICAL SCORE

Although we often accept film music without question and sometimes even without noticing it, this does not mean that its contribution to the film experience is insignificant. Music has a tremendous effect on our response, greatly enriching and enhancing our overall reaction to almost any film. It accomplishes this in several ways: by reinforcing or strengthening the emotional content of the image, by stimulating the imagination and the kinetic sense, and by suggesting and expressing emotions that cannot be conveyed by pictorial means alone.

Because it has a *direct* and very significant effect on our reaction to film, the term *background music*, which is so often applied to the musical score, is a misnomer. Music actually functions as an integral or complementary element. In spite of its direct effect on us, however, there is general critical agreement on one point: The role of music in film should be a subordinate one.

Two schools of thought exist on the proper degree of this subordination. The older, traditional view is that the best film music performs its various functions without making us consciously aware of its presence. In other words, if we don't notice the music, it's a good score. Therefore, the music for a "good" score shouldn't be *too* good, for really good music draws attention to itself and away from the film.

The modern view, by contrast, allows the music, *on appropriate occasions*, not only to demand our conscious attention but even to dominate the picture, so long as it remains essentially integrated with the visual, dramatic, and rhythmic elements of the film as a whole. At such moments, we may become conscious of how intrinsically beautiful the music is, though we should not be so moved that we lose sight of its appropriateness to the image on the screen.

Both modern and traditional views are therefore in agreement on one essential point: Music that calls *too much* attention to itself at the expense of the film as a whole is not effective. Regardless of the *degree* of subordination, a good score will always be a significant structural element, performing its proper functions in a perfectly integrated way, serving as a means to an end rather than an end itself.

GENERAL FUNCTIONS OF THE MUSICAL SCORE

The two most general and basic functions of the musical score are to create structural rhythms and to stimulate emotional responses, both of which greatly enhance and reinforce the effect of the image.

The film score creates a sense of structural rhythm in both the film as a whole and in its individual shots by developing a sense of pace corresponding to the pace of the movement within each shot and to the pace of the editing. In this way, the composer articulates and underscores the basic rhythms of the film.

The film score also serves to complement and enhance the narrative and dramatic structure by stimulating emotional responses that parallel each individual sequence and the film as a whole. Since even the most subtle moods are established, intensified, maintained, and changed through the effective use of film music, the musical score becomes an accurate reflection of the emotional patterns and shapes of the film as a whole. This does not mean that a film's structured visual rhythms can be separated from its emotional patterns, for both are closely interwoven into the same fabric. Effective film music will therefore usually parallel one and complement the other.

The simplest and oldest method of adding music to film is simply the selection of a piece of familiar music (classical, pop, folk, jazz, blues, rock, and so on) that fits the rhythmic, emotional, or dramatic demands of the sequence at hand. An excellent example of the use of familiar music was the choice of the *William Tell Overture* for the old "Lone Ranger" radio show. The classical overture provided not only a perfect rhythmic counterpart to the galloping hoof beats and served as a stimulus to the visual imagination, but also gave the program a seriousness of tone that it would not have possessed otherwise. In similar manner, Stanley Kubrick employed such diverse types of music as *Thus Spake Zarathustra*, *The Blue Danube*, and *When Johnny Comes Marching Home* to very effective ends in *2001* and *Dr. Strangelove*.

Many directors, however, prefer to use music specially created and designed for the film—music composed either after the film and its accompanying sound effects track are completed, or while the film is being made so that composer and director can work together in the same creative atmosphere. Many films, of course, use a combination of familiar and original music.

Film music especially composed for a film can be divided into two types:

1. Mickey Mousing. So named because it grew out of animation techniques, *Mickey Mousing* is the exact, calculated dovetailing of music and action. This ballet-like synchronization precisely matches the rhythm of the music with the natural rhythms of the objects moving on the screen, and requires a meticulous analysis of the filmed sequence by the composer. Although some sense of emotional tone, mood, or atmosphere can be included in Mickey Mouse scoring, the primary emphasis is on the kinetic (the sense of movement and action) and rhythmic elements of the sequences in which it is used.

2. Generalized or implicit. In this technique, no attempt is made to precisely match music and movement; instead the emphasis is on capturing the *overall* emotional atmosphere or mood of a sequence or of the film as a whole. Often, this is achieved through recurring rhythmic and emotive variations of only a few main motifs or "themes." Although basic rhythms in such scores are varied to *suggest* the rhythmic structure of individual action sequences, their primary function is to convey an emotion that parallels the story.

QUESTIONS

On the Musical Score: General Functions

1. Where in the film is music used to match exactly the natural rhythms of the moving objects on the screen? At what points in the film does the music simply try to capture a scene's overall emotional mood?
2. Where does the film employ rhythmic and emotive variations on a single musical theme or motif?
3. Does the musical score remain inconspicuous in the background, or does it occasionally break through to assert itself?
4. If the music does demand your conscious attention, does it still perform a subordinate function in the film as a whole? How?

5. Where in the film is the main purpose of the music to match structural or visual rhythms? Where is it used to create more generalized emotional patterns?
6. How would the total effect of the film differ if the musical score were removed from the soundtrack?

SPECIAL FUNCTIONS OF FILM MUSIC

In the modern film, music is used to perform many varied and complex functions, some of which are rather specialized. Although it is impossible to list or describe all these functions, some of the most basic ones are worthy of our attention.

Covering Weaknesses or Defects in the Film

A nonstorytelling function of the music score is to disguise or cover up weaknesses in acting and dialogue. When such defects are evident, the director or composer can use heavy musical backing to make weak acting or banal dialogue appear more dramatically significant than it otherwise would. Television soap operas use organ music for this purpose with great frequency (and little sense of shame).

Heightening the Dramatic Effect of Dialogue

Music is often employed as a kind of emotional punctuation for the dialogue, expressing the feeling underlying what is said. Generally, the musical accompaniment of dialogue must be extremely subtle and unobtrusive, stealing in and out so quietly that we respond to its effects without conscious awareness of its presence.

Telling an "Inner Story"

Music often moves beyond a merely subordinate or complementary role to assume a primary storytelling function, enabling the director to express things that cannot be expressed through verbal or pictorial means. This is especially true when a character's state of mind undergoes extreme and rapid changes that neither words nor action can adequately express. A good example of this occurs in *On the Beach.* An American submarine captain, played by Gregory Peck, takes an Australian woman (Ava Gardner) to a mountain resort for a final fling at trout fishing before the lethal radioactive clouds reach Australia. The American, whose family was killed in the nuclear war, has failed to adapt to the reality of the situation, and continues to think and talk of his family as though they were alive, making it impossible for him to accept the love of the Australian. The two are in their room in the lodge, listening to the dissonant, off-key voices of the drunken fishermen downstairs singing "Waltzing Matilda." In an underplayed dramatic scene, Peck finally realizes the futility of his ties with the past and accepts Gardner's love. As they embrace, the loud and drunken voices become soft, sober, and melodious, and blend into perfect harmony, reflecting not any actual change in the voices downstairs, but the inner story of the change in Peck's state of mind (Fig. 6.1). The use of massed voices of choirs to express an inner mystical or spiritual transformation is a more obvious example of the same function.

|6.1| Music to Tell an Inner Story: An important change in a character's state of mind is conveyed by music in this scene from *On The Beach* (Culver Pictures).

Providing a Sense of Time and Place

Certain pieces of music or even musical styles are associated with specific time periods and locations, and composers can utilize such music to provide the emotional atmosphere that a given setting normally connotes. For example, a sense of scenic spaciousness is conveyed by standard western songs, such as "The Call of the Faraway Hills" from *Shane;* completely different qualities, such as the hustle and bustle of people having a good time and a merry, more communal feeling, is conveyed by "town" or "saloon" music. Therefore, when the locale in a western changes from the range to the town or saloon, the visual transition is often preceded slightly by a switch to standard saloon music (player piano accompanied by shouting, laughter, general crowd noises, and an occasional gunshot or two). Thus the music not only tells us that a change of scene is coming, but also prepares us mentally for the visual scene before it appears, thereby serving a transitional function.

Music associated with different countries or even different ethnic groups can be used in a similar way. Certain instruments are also associated with definite settings or groups of people: the zither, the mandolin, the guitar, the banjo, the Spanish guitar, and the Hawaiian guitar all have fairly concrete geographical connotations, and these connotations can be varied or even changed completely by the style in which the instruments are played.

The time period in which the film is set is also made realistic through the use of appropriate music and instrumentation, as illustrated by the use of the quaint, old sound of a harpsicord for a "period piece," or other-worldly or futuristic electronic music for a science fiction film.

Evoking Nostalgic Feelings

When the time frame of a story is within most viewers' memories, recent American films have loaded the soundtrack with popular recordings from the era, thus evoking a strong "remembered flavor" of the time. Not only does such music underscore the past-tense quality of the story for the viewer, but by triggering built-in associations, it intensifies and personalizes the viewer's involvement with the story itself.

Nostalgic music is used effectively in such films as *The Big Chill, Coming Home, The Last Picture Show,* and *American Graffiti,* which is literally built around such music. In many cases such music is heard coming from some on-screen source such as a radio or record player, but it usually is used as part of the off-screen musical score as well.

Foreshadowing Events or Building Dramatic Tension

Any time a surprising change of mood or an unexpected action is about to occur on the screen, we will almost always be prepared for that change by the musical score. By preparing us emotionally for a shocking turn of events, the score does not soften the effect of the shock, but actually intensifies it by signaling its approach. In its own way, the music says, "Watch carefully now. Something shocking or unexpected is going to happen," and we respond to the musical signal by becoming more attentive. Even the fact that we know what is going to happen does not relieve the tension thus created, for suspense is as much a matter of "when" as it is of "what." Music used in this way does not coincide exactly with what is happening on the screen, but precedes it, introducing a feeling of tension while the images on the screen retain their calm.

Foreshadowing or tension-building music deliberately plays on our nerves in a variety of ways: by gradually increasing in volume or pitch, switching from a major to a minor key, or introducing percussion instruments and dissonance. The introduction of dissonance into a musical score that has been harmonious to that point automatically creates a sense of nervousness and anxiety. Dissonance in such a situation expresses disorder, chaos, and a breakdown of the normal patterned order of harmony, causing us to become nervous and insecure, exactly the state of mind desired for effective foreshadowing or the building of dramatic tension.

Adding Levels of Meaning to the Visual Image

Sometimes music makes us see the visual scene in a fresh, unusual way by combining with the image to create additional levels of meaning. Take, for example, the opening scene in *Dr. Strangelove,* which shows a B-52 bomber refueling in flight. Extremely delicate maneuvering is required to correctly place the refueling boom, trailing like a giant winged hose from the tail of the tanker plane, into the fuel-tank opening in the nose of the giant B-52 bomber, which is flying slightly behind and below the tanker. The music accompanying this sequence is the familiar love song "Try a Little Tenderness," played on romantic violins. If we are alert enough to recognize the song and think of its title, the music not only seems very appropriate to the delicate maneuvering required for the refueling operation, but could also lead us to see the whole thing as a gentle love scene, a tender sexual coupling of two giant birds. Since this is the opening sequence of the film, the music also helps to establish the satiric tone that runs throughout the film as a whole.

Highly ironic levels of meaning can be achieved by using music that suggests a mood exactly opposite to the mood normally suggested by what is occurring on the screen. This technique is illustrated at the conclusion of *Dr. Strangelove,* in which the sticky-sweet voice of Vera Lynn singing "We'll Meet Again Some Sunny Day" accompanies the image of a nuclear holocaust as it destroys the world.

Characterization Through Music

Music also can play a role in characterization. Mickey Mouse scoring may be used, for example, to emphasize a peculiar or rhythmic pattern set up by a certain character's physical movement. The score for *Of Human Bondage*, for example, utilized a "crippled" theme, which rhythmically paralleled the main character's limp, thus reinforcing that aspect of his character. Some actors and actresses, such as John Wayne, Robert Mitchum, and Marilyn Monroe, have distinctive walks that exhibit definite rhythmic patterns and can therefore be reinforced musically.

Instrumentation can also be used to aid in characterization in an effect which might be called "Peter and the Wolfing." Here instruments and types of music represent and signal the presence of certain characters. Many films of the '30s and '40s used this technique, causing the audience to associate the villain with sinister-sounding music in a minor key, the heroine with soft, ethereal violins, and the hero with strong, "honest" music. Although such heavy-handed treatment is not common today, *leitmotifs* (the repetition of a single musical theme or phrase to announce the reappearance of a certain character) are still employed to some extent.

A good composer may also use the musical score to add qualities to an actor or actress which that person does not normally have. In the filming of *Cyrano de Bergerac*, for example, Dimitri Tiomkin felt that Mala Powers did not really look French enough for the part of Roxanne. Therefore he "Frenchified" her by using French-style thematic music whenever she appeared on the screen, thus building up associations in the viewer's mind to achieve the desired effect.

Triggering Conditioned Responses

The composer also takes advantage of the fact that we have been conditioned to associate certain musical stereotypes or musical codes with certain situations, and such codes can be used with great economy and effectiveness. The sudden introduction of a steady tom-tom beat accompanied by a high, wailing, wind instrument ranging through a simple four- or five-tone scale effectively signals the presence of Indians even before they appear. The familiar "cavalry to the rescue" bugle call is an equally familiar example. Such musical codes cannot be treated in a highly creative way, for to do so would cause them to lose some of their effectiveness as code devices. Composers do, however, try to make them *seem* as fresh and original as possible.

Even stereotyped musical codes can create unusual reactions when they are used ironically. In *Little Big Man,* for example, a lively fife and drum "good guys victorious" score accompanies scenes of General Custer's troops as they brutally massacre an Indian tribe. The ironic effect catches us in a tug-of-war between the music and the image: So compelling is the rhythm of the heroic music that we can scarcely resist tapping our toes and swelling with heroic pride, while our visual sensibilities are appalled by the unheroic action taking place on the screen.

Traveling Music

Film music is at its best when used to characterize rapid movement. Such music, sometimes called "traveling music," is often employed almost as a formula or a shorthand code to give the impression of various means of transportation, and these formulas are varied to fit the unique quality of the movement being portrayed. Thus stagecoach music is different from horse-and-buggy music, and both differ essentially from lone-rider music. The old steam engine even requires a different type of railroad music from the diesel locomotive (Fig. 6.2). On rare occasions, traveling music performs a wide variety of functions, as is illustrated by the use of Flatt and Scruggs's "Foggy Mountain Breakdown" to accompany the famous chase scenes in *Bonnie and Clyde.* The strong, almost frantic sounds of the fast-fingered five-string banjo create a desperate yet happy rhythm that captures precisely the derring-do and spirit of the Barrow Gang, the slapstick comedy, desperation, and blind excitement of the chases themselves, and the nostalgic, good-old-days flavor of the film as a whole.

|6.2| Traveling Music: In *Breaking Away* an excerpt from *The Barber of Seville,* a stirring opera by the Italian composer Rossini, provides traveling music for Dave (Dennis Christopher) as he prepares for the big race, and it reinforces the character's obsession with things Italian as well as underscoring the heroic effort involved in his training.

Accompanying Titles

The music that accompanies the main titles of a film usually serves at least two functions. First, it often articulates rhythmically the title information itself, making it somehow more interesting than it is. If the music consciously captures our attention anywhere in the film, it is during the showing of the titles and credits. Second, music is especially important here, for at this initial stage it usually establishes the general mood or tone of the film. It may even introduce story elements through the use of lyrics, as was done in *High Noon* and *Cat Ballou*. Since the opening or establishing scene is generally under way before the credits are completed, it can also dramatically or rhythmically match the visual image behind the credits.

Musical "Sounds" as a Part of the Score

Certain sound effects or noises from nature can be used in subtle ways for their own sake, to create atmosphere in the same way that music does. Crashing waves, rippling streams, bird calls, and moaning winds all possess clear musical qualities, as do many man-made sounds such as foghorns, auto horns, industrial noises of various kinds, steam whistles, clanging doors, chains, squealing auto brakes, and engine noises. Such sounds can be built up and artistically mixed into an exciting rhythmical sequence that, because of its naturalness, may be even more effective than music in conveying a mood.

Music as Interior Monologue

In the modern film, songs with lyrics that have no clear or direct relationship to the scenes they accompany are increasingly used as part of the soundtrack. In many cases, such songs are used to reveal the private moods, emotions, or thoughts of a central character, as was the case with the lyrics of "The Sounds of Silence" in *The Graduate* and the song "Everybody's Talkin' at Me" in *Midnight Cowboy*. Such lyrics function on a more or less independent level as a highly subjective and poetic means of communication, capable of expanding the meaning and emotional content of the scenes they accompany.

Music as a Base for Choreographed Action

Usually the director composes, photographs, and edits the images first and adds music later, after the visual elements are already assembled. In a relatively small number of films, however, such as *A Clockwork Orange*, music is used to provide a clear rhythmic framework for the action, which essentially becomes a highly stylized dance performed to the music. A similar technique is used when the music originates from some on-screen source, such as a radio or record player, and the actor coordinates the rhythms of his movements to it. In *Hopscotch,* Walter Matthau, playing an ex-CIA agent writing his memoirs, comically structures his typing and related tasks to match the rhythms of a Mozart symphony on the record player.

An extreme use of this technique of "music first" is *The Wall,* Alan Parker's film version of Pink Floyd's 1979 hit album. Pink Floyd's music provided the narrative framework, and combines with Parker's images to create a "nonstop assault on the senses." Some parts of the film, such as the "We Don't Want No Education" segment, are choreographed to the music, combining both live action and animation. Although much of the action in *The Wall* is not so completely choreographed as this section, there are only a few lines of dialogue in the entire film, and the dynamic rhythms of the action and the editing are designed to correspond to, reinforce, or complement the words and music of the Pink Floyd songs (Fig. 6.3).

Action that has no essential rhythmic qualities can be edited to music to create an effect very similar to that of choreographed action. The Little League baseball action in *The Bad News Bears* was apparently edited to match the "heroic" rhythms of orchestral music from the opera *Carmen,* creating the impression of a comic/heroic dance.

|6.3| Choreographed Action: The song "We Don't Need No Education" was recorded on an album released long before the film *Pink Floyd: The Wall* was conceived. The action shown here was choreographed to match the ideas and rhythms of that song.

| 6.4 | Musical Interlude: The scene pictured above from *Butch Cassidy and the Sundance Kid* was accompanied by the song "Raindrops Keep Fallin' on My Head." The song had nothing whatsoever to do with the film and served only as a musical interlude to separate the film's two very different halves.

The examples just described represent only the most common and obvious uses of music in the modern film; it would be impossible to comment on them all. The important point is that we must be aware of the various emotions and levels of meaning that music communicates (Fig. 6.4).

ECONOMY IN FILM MUSIC

Generally speaking, economy is a great virtue in film music, both in duration and instrumentation. The musical score should do no more than is necessary to perform its proper function clearly and simply. However, because of some irresistible temptations to dress up scenes with music whether they need it or not, the normal dramatic film usually ends up with too much music rather than not enough. The proper amount of music employed largely depends, of course, on the nature of the picture itself—some films require a lot of music; others are so realistic that music would only interfere with the desired effect. The fact remains that in many cases the most dramatically effective musical score is that which is used most sparingly.

So far as economy of instrumentation is concerned, the Hollywood tendency seems to be more toward large orchestras, even though smaller combinations can be more interesting and colorful, or even more powerful in their effect on the film as a whole.

SYNTHESIZER SCORING

A fairly recent trend is the use of electronic synthesizers for instrumentation on film scores. A synthesizer is essentially a musical computer, played on a piano-like keyboard, and equipped with various knobs and buttons that permit all sorts of variation in pitch, tone, and decay. It can imitate the sounds of a large variety of other instruments while still retaining its own distinct quality.

Because of its tremendous flexibility, it is the fastest, most efficient way to score a film. A two-person team, one playing the keyboard, the other controlling the sound qualities, can create a full sound comparable to that provided by a complete orchestra.

Synthesizers have played a part in film scores for some time, at least since *A Clockwork Orange* in 1971, but they have become much more prevalent since 1978's *Midnight Express,* with a complete "synth" score by Giorgio Moroder. Recent films with synthesizer scores include *Sorcerer, Thief, American Gigolo, Foxes, Blade Runner,* and *Cat People,* but the great versatility of "synth" scoring was most evident in 1981's *Chariots of Fire,* a period piece that seemed an unlikely choice for an electronic score. *Chariots* composer Vangelis' challenge was to compose a "score which was contemporary, but still compatible with the time of the film," a challenge he met successfully by mixing synthesizer and a grand piano.[2]

Sometimes it is difficult to know whether to classify electronic "scores" as music or sound effects. In *Cat People* for example, the synthesizer often functions as an almost subliminal animal presence behind the image, creating the effect of "listening in on the vital processes of other organisms—of other places, other worlds."[3] Horror movies have been less subtle in their overuse of the tension-building, nervous-pulse sounds, which are repeated over and over without musical development.

Electronic scores are still relatively rare in major films, however, because the eight or nine top composers still prefer to use orchestra. But some critics predict that synthesizers will provide the music for most movies by 1990.

QUESTIONS

On the Musical Score: Special Functions

1. Which of the following functions of film music are used in the film, and where are they used?

a. To cover weaknesses and defects.
b. To heighten the dramatic effect of dialogue.
c. To tell an "inner story" by expressing a state of mind.
d. To provide a sense of time or place.
e. To evoke remembered experiences or emotions.
f. To foreshadow events or build dramatic tension.
g. To add levels of meaning to the image.
h. To aid characterization.

2. Terry Atkinson, "Scoring with Synthesizers." *American Film,* September 1982, p. 70.
3. Ibid., p. 68.

   i. To trigger conditioned responses.
   j. To characterize rapid movement (traveling music).

2. Does the music accompanying the titles serve basically to underscore the rhythmic qualities of the title information, or to establish the general mood of the film? If lyrics are sung at this point, how do these lyrics relate to the film as a whole?
3. Where are sound effects or natural noises employed for a kind of rhythmic or musical effect?
4. If lyrics sung within the film provide a kind of interior monologue, what feeling or attitude do they convey?
5. If music is used as a base for choreographed action, how appropriate is the piece selected? How appropriate are its rhythms to the mood and the visual content? How effectively is the choreographed sequence integrated into the film as a whole?
6. Does the score use a full orchestra throughout, a smaller number of well-chosen instruments, or a synthesizer? How well suited is the instrumentation chosen to the film as a whole? If it is not well chosen, what kind of instrumentation should have been used? How would your choice of instrumentation change the quality of the film, and why would it be an improvement?
7. Does the amount of music used fit the requirements of the film, or is the musical score overdone or used too economically?
8. How effectively does the score perform its various functions?

CHAPTER 7

ACTING

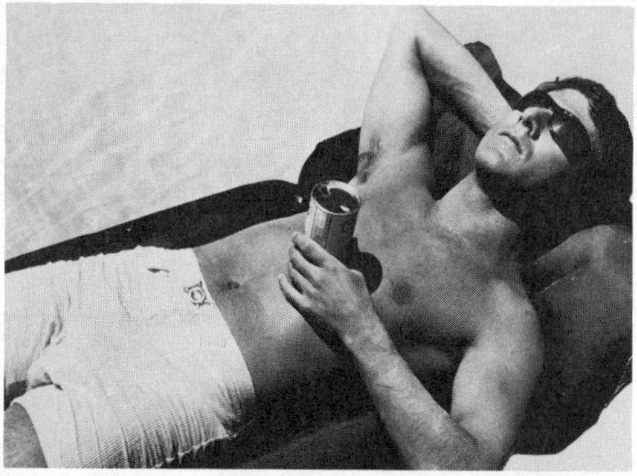

THE IMPORTANCE OF ACTING

> All we are is a very sophisticated recording device whose job is to record an event that has to be created by the actors. No matter how brilliantly you record something, if the event stinks, then you have a brilliant recording of a lousy event. So the crucial element is the actor.
>
> MARK RYDELL, DIRECTOR[1]

When we consider going to a movie, the first question we usually ask has nothing to do with the director or the cinematographer, but with the actors: "Who's in it?" This is a natural question, because the art of the actor is the most clearly visible one. The actor's work commands most of our attention, overshadowing the considerable contributions of the writer, director, cinematographer, editor, and composer of the score. As Kernodle puts it in *An Invitation to the Theatre:*

> Whether the picture is *Tom Jones, Thunderball, The Sound of Music, Ship of Fools,* or *The Collector,* it is the star that draws the crowds. The audience may be amused, thrilled, or deeply moved by the story, fascinated by new plot devices, property gadgets, and camera angles, charmed by backgrounds that are exotic, or captivated by those that are familiar and real, but it is the people on the screen, and especially the faces, that command the center of attention.[2]

Therefore, because we naturally respond to film's most human ingredient, the actor's contribution is extremely important.

Yet in spite of our tendency to focus attention on the actor, there is general agreement among critics and directors that the actor's role in film should be a subordinate one, one of many important elements contributing to a greater aesthetic whole, the film itself. As Alfred Hitchcock states it, "Film work hasn't much need for the virtuoso actor who gets his effects and climaxes himself, who plays directly to the audience with the force of his talent and personality. The screen actor has got to be much more plastic; he has to submit himself to be used by the director and the camera."[3]

1. "Dialogue on Film." *American Film,* June 1982, p. 23.
2. George R. Kernodle, *An Invitation to the Theatre.* New York: Harcourt, Brace and World, Inc., 1967, p. 259.
3. Richard Dyer McCann, ed., *Film: A Montage of Theories.* New York: E. P. Dutton and Co., Inc., 1966, p. 57.

THE GOAL OF THE ACTOR

The ultimate goal of any actor should be to make us believe completely in the reality of the character. If this goal is to be achieved, actors must either develop or be blessed with several talents. First of all, they must be able to project sincerity, truthfulness, and naturalness, and to project these qualities in such a way that we are never aware that they are only acting a part. In a sense, then, good acting must seem not to be acting at all.

Sometimes the actors achieve a certain naturalness through tricks and gimmicks. Knowing that the character of Ratso Rizzo being played by Dustin Hoffman in *Midnight Cowboy* had a distinct limp, a fellow actor advised Hoffman on how to make the limp consistent: "Once you get the limp right, why don't you put rocks in your shoe? You'll never have to think about limping. It will be there; you won't have to worry about it." There are a number of similar tricks actors use to create a trademark for their characters and to keep the characters consistent. But good acting demands much more than tricks and gimmicks. To project the sincerity that a really deep, complex, and demanding role requires, actors must be willing to draw on the deepest and most personal qualities of their inner being. As director Mark Rydell (a former actor himself) puts it:

> I find that acting is one of the bravest professions of all. An actor has to remain vulnerable. The entire process of learning to act necessitates a kind of peeling away of layers of insulation that we develop from the time we're children, when we were innocent and exposed. The actor has to sandpaper his feelings and his vulnerabilities. He has to be open to assault from circumstances, events, relationships. I suspect that any time you see a great performance, it's because some actor has been courageous enough to allow you to peek at a very personal, private secret of his.[4]

Actors must also possess the intelligence, imagination, sensitivity, and insight into human nature necessary to fully understand the characters they play—their inner thoughts, motivations, and emotions. Furthermore, actors must have the ability to express these things convincingly through voice, body movements, gestures, or facial expressions, so the qualities seem true to the characters portrayed and to the situation in which the characters find themselves. And actors must maintain the illusion of reality in

4. "Dialogue on Film." p. 23.

their characters with complete consistency from beginning to end. It is also important that actors keep their egos under control, so that they can see their roles in proper perspective to the dramatic work as a whole. Actors who do not possess these capabilities must be willing and able to take direction well enough so that they will *appear* to have them.

DIFFERENCES BETWEEN FILM ACTING AND STAGE ACTING

Acting for motion pictures and acting for the stage have in common the goals, traits, and skills described above, yet there are important differences in the acting techniques required for the two media. The primary difference involves the relative distance between the performer and the spectator. As mentioned earlier, when acting in the theater, actors must always be sure that every member of the audience can see and hear them distinctly. Thus, stage actors must constantly project the voice, make gestures that are obvious and clear, and generally move and speak so they can be clearly heard and seen by the most remote observer. This is no problem in a small, intimate theater, but the larger the theater and the more distant the spectator in the last row, the further the actor's voice must be projected and the broader the gestures must be. As these adjustments are made, the depth and reality of the performance suffer, since louder tones and wider gestures lead to generalized form and stylization. Therefore, the finer, subtler shades of intonation are lost as the distance between actor and audience increases.

The problem of reaching a remote spectator does not exist in films, since the viewer is moved (in effect) to the best possible location for hearing and viewing the actor. With the mobility of the recording microphone, the film actor may speak softly, or even whisper, with full confidence that every word will be heard and every subtle tone of voice perceived. The same holds true for facial expression, gesture, and body movement, for in close-ups even the subtlest facial expressions are clearly visible for the most remote spectator. And the mobility of the camera further assures the actor that the scene will be viewed from the most effective angle. Thus film acting can be, and in fact *must be,* more subtle and restrained than stage acting.

Henry Fonda learned this lesson when director Victor Fleming accused him of "mugging" while filming a scene from Fonda's first movie, *The Farmer Takes a Wife*. Henry had played the role on Broadway, and Fleming explained the problem to him in terms he clearly understood: "You're playing the farmer the way you did in the theater. You're playing to the back row of the orchestra and the rear row of the balcony. That's stage technique." The understated Fonda style, using as little facial mobility as possible, began at that moment and served him well in almost a hundred films:

> I just pulled it right back to reality because that lens and that microphone are doing all the projection you need. No sense in using too much voice, and you don't need any more expression on your face than you'd use in everyday life.[5]

Actor Robert Shaw put it this way: "Here's the difference: On stage, you have to dominate the audience. You don't have to *think* the way you do when you're in the movies. Stage acting is the art of *domination*. Movie acting is the art of *seduction*."[6]

This is not to say that film acting is less difficult than stage acting. The film actor must be extremely careful in every gesture and word, for the camera and microphone are unforgiving and cruelly revealing, especially in close-ups. Since complete sincerity, naturalness, and restraint are all-important, a single false move or phony gesture or a line delivered without conviction, too much conviction, or out of character will shatter the illusion of reality.

Thus, the most successful film actors either possess or can project, with seeming ease and naturalness, a truly genuine personality, and somehow appear to be completely themselves without self-consciousness or a sense of strain. This rare quality generally seems to depend as much on natural talent as disciplined study and training.

Another difficulty faces film actors because they perform their roles in discontinuous bits and pieces, rather than in a continuous flow with one scene following the next, as is done in theater. Only later, in the cutting room, will the fragments be assembled in proper sequence. For this reason, assuming the proper frame of

5. Henry Fonda, as told to Howard Teichman, *Fonda: My Life*. New York: The New American Library, Inc., 1981, p. 104.
6. "Ask Them Yourself." *Family Weekly*, 11 June 1972.

mind, mood, and acting style for each segment of the film becomes a problem. For example, actors required to speak in a dialect remotely removed from their own natural speech patterns may have difficulty capturing the dialect in exactly the same way they did in a scene filmed two weeks earlier, a problem they would not have had in a continuous stage performance. But a clear advantage also arises from this difference. The performance of the film actor can be made more nearly perfect than that of the stage actor, for the editor and director can choose the best and most convincing performance from several "takes" of the same sequence. That way, the film becomes a continuous whole of best performances.

Another disadvantage in film acting is that actors have no direct link with the audience as stage actors do, and therefore must act for an imagined audience. Since film actors cannot draw on audience reaction for inspiration, whatever inspiration they receive must come from the director, the crew, and the fact that their work will have more permanence than that of the stage actor.

Film is also for the most part a more physical medium than drama; that is, film actors must use more nonverbal means of communication than stage actors. Julian Fast discusses this aspect of film acting in his book *Body Language:* "Good actors must all be experts in the use of body language. A process of elimination guarantees that only those with an excellent command of the grammar and vocabulary get to be successful"[7] (Figs. 7.1 and 7.2).

The grammar and vocabulary of body language include a vast array of nonverbal communication techniques, but the motion picture is perhaps unique in its emphasis on the eloquence of the human face. Although the face and facial expressions play a part in other story forms, such as fiction and drama, in film the face becomes a medium of communication in its own right. Magnified on the screen, the human face with its infinite variety of expressions can convey both a depth and subtlety of emotion that cannot be approached through purely rational or verbal means. As Hungarian film critic and theorist Béla Balázs so aptly puts it, "What happens on the face and in facial expression is a spiritual experience which is rendered immediately visible without the intermediary of words"[8] (Figs. 7.3, 7.4, and 7.5).

7. Julian Fast, *Body Language*. New York: M. Evans and Company, Inc., 1970, p. 185.

8. Edith Bone, trans., *Theory of the Film: Character and Growth of a New Art.* New York: Dover Publications, Inc., 1970, p. 168.

|7.1| Body Language: In *Cat People* Malcolm McDowell's every movement has a graceful, catlike quality that suggests "the cat within." Here, he assumes a feline pose as he watches his sister sleep.

|7.2| Postures of Endearment: The developing relationship between the playboy ex-astronaut (Jack Nicholson) and Aurora Greenway (Shirley MacLaine) is apparent in their body language in this scene from *Terms of Endearment.*

The human face is a marvelously complex structure, capable of transmitting a tremendously wide range of emotions through slight changes in mouth, eyes, eyelids, eyebrows, and forehead. This helps to explain another important difference between film acting and stage acting: the film's emphasis on "reacting" rather than acting. The *reaction shot* achieves its considerable dramatic

The Actor's Face as a Means of Communication: In *The Caine Mutiny,* Humphrey Bogart's face clearly reveals the inner thoughts and feelings of Captain Queeg. In the first picture, the seeds of paranoia have been planted. Bogart's eyes are anxious and worried, and his jaw is a little slack, suggesting Queeg's bewilderment as his self-control slips away. In the second picture (during the storm sequence) all control is gone. Queeg's psychotic state is revealed in the stark terror in the eyes; the jaw is slack, and the face is that of a terrified, cornered animal (Culver Pictures).

|7.3|

|7.4|

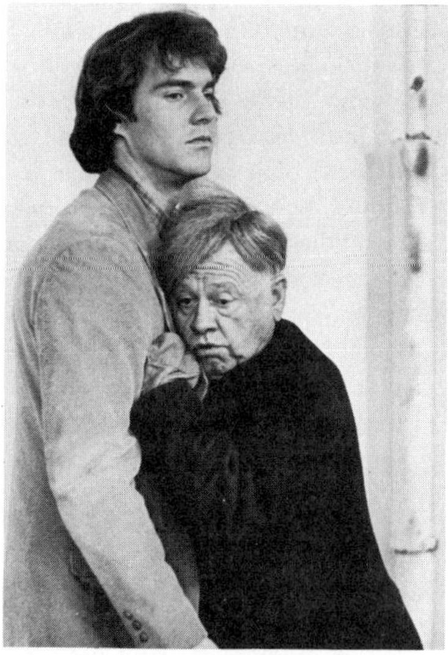

|7.5| Sustained Expression: In the television movie *Bill*, Mickey Rooney convincingly portrays the mentally retarded title character by maintaining a "retarded look" throughout the film.

|7.6| The Reaction Shot: In this shot from *The War Lover*, there is no reason for the camera to show us the scene inside the crash-landed bomber—the gruesome horror of what lies inside is clearly reflected on the faces of Robert Wagner and his crew (Culver Pictures).

impact through a close-up of the character most affected by the dialogue or action. The actor's face, within the brief moment that it is on the screen, must register clearly yet subtly and without the aid of dialogue the appropriate emotional reaction. Some of the most powerful moments in film are built around such "facial acting." The stage actor's facial reactions, on the other hand, are seldom if ever quite so important to a play's dramatic power (Fig. 7.6).

But even in reaction shots the film actor is often assisted by the nature of the medium, for in film much of the powerful and expressive quality of the human face is created by the context in which it appears, and the meanings of many expressions are determined by skillful editing. Thus the actor's face may not be so beautifully expressive as the visual context makes it appear. This phenomenon was demonstrated in an experiment conducted in the early 1920s by the young Russian painter Lev Kuleshov and film director V. I. Pudovkin:

> We took from some film or other several close-ups of the well-known Russian actor Mosjukhin. We chose close-ups which were static and which did not express any feeling at all—quiet close-ups. We joined these close-

> ups, which were all similar, with other bits of film in three different combinations. In the first combination the close-up of Mosjukhin was immediately followed by a shot of soup standing on a table. It was obvious and certain that Mosjukhin was looking at this soup. In the second combination the face of Mosjukhin was joined to shots showing a coffin in which lay a dead woman. In the third the close-up was followed by a shot of a little girl playing with a funny toy bear. When we showed the three combinations to an audience which had not been let into the secret, the result was terrific. The public raved about the acting of the artist. They pointed out the heavy pensiveness of the mood over the forgotten soup, were touched and moved by the deep sorrow with which he looked on the dead woman, and admired the light, happy smile with which he surveyed the girl at play. But we knew in all three cases the face was exactly the same.[9]

This experiment is not cited to prove that film acting is only an illusion created by editing. But it does show that we are eager to respond to faces, whether those faces are really projecting what we think we see or not.

Film actors must also be able to communicate more with bodily movements and gestures than stage actors. Since the stage actor's chief instrument of expression is the voice, his or her movements are mainly an accompaniment to or an extension of what is said. In film, however, physical movement and gesture may communicate effectively without dialogue. The magnification of the human image on the screen enables the actor to communicate with extremely subtle movements. A slight shrug of the shoulders, the nervous trembling of a hand viewed in close-up, or the visible tensing of the muscles and tendons in the neck may be much more important than anything said. A classic example of the power of body language in film acting is Jack Palance's portrayal of the gunfighter Wilson in *Shane*. Palance plays Wilson as the personification of pure evil: Every movement, every gesture is slow, deliberate, yet tense, so that we get the feeling that Wilson is a rattlesnake, moving slowly and sensuously but always ready to strike in a split second. When he slowly performs the ritual of putting on his black leather gloves in order to practice his profession, Palance makes us sense with horror Wilson's cold, cruel indifference to human life.

Film acting also differs from stage acting in that it actually requires two different kinds of acting. The first of these is the kind of acting required for the action/adventure film, what we might

9. V. I. Pudovkin, *Film Technique and Film Acting,* memorial edition. Translated and edited by Ivor Montagu. New York: Grove Press, Inc., 1958, p. 168.

refer to as *action acting*. While this type of acting requires a great deal in the way of reactions, body language, physical exertion, and special skills, it does not draw on the deepest resources of the actor's intelligence and feelings. The other type, which might be called *dramatic acting*, involves sustained, intense dialogue with another person, and requires an emotional and psychological depth seldom called for in action acting. Action acting is the art of doing, whereas dramatic acting involves feeling, thinking, and communicating emotions and thoughts. Action acting is on the surface, with little need for nuance. Dramatic acting is just the opposite: beneath the surface, full of subtlety. Each type of acting requires its own particular gift or talent. While some actors can do both, most are better suited for one or the other, and are usually cast accordingly. Clint Eastwood, for example, is essentially an action actor, while Richard Burton was a dramatic actor (Figs. 7.7 and 7.8).

Film acting is thus an art in itself that, although it shares its basic goals with stage acting, utilizes fundamentally different techniques to achieve them.

TYPES OF ACTORS

In addition to classifying actors into the two broad categories of action and dramatic actors, it is meaningful for us to view them in terms of how the roles they play relate to their own personalities.

|7.7| Action Acting: Clint Eastwood as Dirty Harry in *Sudden Impact* telling a would-be robber, "Make my day."

|7.8| Dramatic Acting: Richard Burton in a scene from the 1953 epic, *The Robe.*

In *A Primer for Playgoers,*[10] Edward A. Wright and Lenthiel H. Downs provide a useful breakdown of these types as follows.

Impersonators

Impersonators are actors who have the talent to completely leave their real personality behind, to assume the personality of a character with whom they may have few characteristics in common. Such actors can completely submerge themselves in a role, altering their personal, physical, and vocal characteristics to such a degree that they seem to become the character. We actually lose sight of the impersonator's real identity. The roles such actors can perform are almost unlimited.

Interpreters and Commentors

Interpreters and commentors play characters closely resembling themselves in personality and physical appearance, and interpret these parts dramatically without wholly losing their own identity. Although they may slightly alter themselves to fit the role, they do not attempt to radically change their individual personality traits, physical characteristics, or voice qualities. They choose instead to color or interpret the role by filtering it through their own best qualities, modifying it to fit their own inherent abilities. The end result is an effective compromise between actor and role, between the real and the assumed identity. The compromise adds a unique creative dimension to the character being portrayed, for in their delivery of the lines these actors reveal something of their own thoughts and feelings concerning the character being played, but do so without ever falling out of character. Thus, these actors may simultaneously comment on and interpret the role. Although the range of roles such actors can play is not as wide as that open to impersonators, it is still relatively broad. If they are cast wisely within this range, they can bring something new and fresh to each role they play, in addition to their own best and most attractive qualities.

10. Edward A. Wright and Lenthiel H. Downs, *A Primer for Playgoers.* Englewood Cliffs, New Jersey: Prentice Hall, 1969, pp. 217–220.

Personality Actors

Actors whose primary "talent" is to be themselves and nothing more are called *personality actors*. They project the essential qualities of sincerity, truthfulness, and naturalness, and they generally possess some dynamic and magnetic mass appeal through a striking appearance, a physical or vocal idiosyncrasy, or some other special quality strongly communicated to us on film. These actors, however popular, are incapable of assuming any variety in the roles they play, for they cannot project sincerity and naturalness when they attempt to move outside their own basic personality. Thus, they must either fit exactly the roles in which they are cast, or the roles must be tailored to fit their personality.

THE STAR SYSTEM

In the past many personality actors and some interpreter and commentor actors were exploited in what became known as the *star system*, an approach to filmmaking based on the assumption that the average moviegoer is more interested in personalities than in great stories or, for that matter, in film art. The stars were, of course, actors with great mass appeal. The big studios did everything in their power to preserve as carefully and rigidly as possible all those qualities of the stars that appealed to the public, and created films around the image of the star personality. Often the star's presence in a film was the main guarantee of financial success, and such films became nothing more than a suitable package in which to display and market the attractive wares of the actors, who had only to project the charm of their personality.

However, once these stars realized the commercial advantages of their presence in a film, they demanded to be paid accordingly. As a result, the star system began to lose favor within the industry. Producers now often prefer to use lesser known actors who have the range and flexibility to play a variety of roles and who, of course, demand less money than established stars. However, there is some evidence that a new star system may be in the making—one in which a certain name on the marquee will promise not the repetition of a tested and tried personality, but the guarantee of a high-level performance in a fresh and exciting role. A great many of the older actors and actresses whose images were created and frozen solid under the star system have broken free of their confining image and proved themselves to be highly capable as interpreters and commentors instead of merely the personalities that the star system required them to become.

For some directors, the star system had certain clear advantages. John Ford and Frank Capra, for example, used the star system as a myth-making apparatus, building their films around such stars as John Wayne, Henry Fonda, James Stewart, and Gary Cooper. These stars projected fairly consistent personalities, and embraced a constant set of values in each film they did, so that they came into each new Ford or Capra film trailing clouds of associations and reverberating strong echoes of earlier parts. By surrounding these stars with their stock company of top-notch secondary actors—also in predictable roles echoing earlier parts—Ford and Capra were, in a sense, using pre-established symbols for the values they wanted their characters to represent, and could more easily build the mythic world of their films on the shoulders of actors who had already established their mythic dimensions.

Although it has changed greatly over the last thirty or forty years, the star system is certainly not dead. The personality cults that spring up periodically around charismatic actors provide ample evidence to the contrary. We will always be attracted to familiar faces and personalities, for we seem to have a psychological need for the familiar, the predictable, and the comfortable. But possibly because the television weekly series has helped satisfy that need, modern moviegoers not only demand more flexibility in film acting, but have begun to realize that many actors they once considered the same in every role were actually commenting on and interpreting the roles they played.

CASTING

> Casting is one of the most important aspects in making a film. A film can live or die on it. The cast has to bring those characters to life. If you miscast a character, or one stands out wrong, you can throw the whole picture out of whack.
>
> CLINT EASTWOOD, DIRECTOR[11]

Acting skills aside, the casting of actors in roles right for them is an extremely important consideration. If their physical character-

11. "Eastwood." *American Film*, December 1982, p. 47.

istics, facial features, voice qualities, or the total personality they naturally project are not suited to the character, their performance will probably not be convincing. Thus, in spite of their great ability as impersonators, Alec Guinness or Peter Sellers could not have effectively played the roles assigned to John Wayne, for example, nor could Burt Lancaster be very effective in roles played by Woody Allen.

Less extreme problems in casting can be solved by sheer genius or camera tricks. For example, in the film *Boy on a Dolphin*, Alan Ladd, who measured 5′6″, was cast opposite Sophia Loren, who towered over him at 5′9″. But in one scene, which showed them walking side by side, Ladd seemed at least as tall or slightly taller than Loren. What the camera didn't show was that the actress was actually walking in a shallow trench especially dug for the purpose (Fig. 7.9). When the male lead is to be something other than the traditional macho hero, relative size does not seem so important. No effort was made to conceal that Dudley Moore is shorter than both Mary Tyler Moore in *Six Weeks* and Elizabeth McGovern in *Lovesick* (Fig. 7.10). And in the film version of *Who's Afraid of Virginia Woolf?*, the character named Honey (Sandy

Casting Problems: Because Sophia Loren is so much taller than Alan Ladd, she is photographed standing a step below him in this scene from *Boy on a Dolphin* (Culver Pictures). When the story is a comedy, however, the romantic lead can be shorter than his leading lady, as is apparent in this scene with Dudley Moore and Elizabeth McGovern from *Lovesick.*

|7.9|

|7.10|

Dennis) is repeatedly referred to as "slim-hipped" in spite of visual evidence to the contrary. The discrepancy here is obscured by Ms. Dennis's acting; she projects a psychological type of "slim-hippedness" that is more convincing than the physical semblance of it.

It is also extremely important that the cast of any film be viewed as a team, not simply as a hodgepodge of separate individuals, for each actor will not appear on the screen alone, but in interaction with the other actors. Therefore some thought has to be given to the way they will look on the screen with each other. When casting two male leads such as Robert Redford and Paul Newman, for example, the casting director will make certain that they have certain contrasting features, so that they stand out clearly from each other.

Actors of the same sex will be cast with the idea of contrasting their coloring, builds, heights, voice qualities, etc. If such differences are not apparent, they can be created through such artificial means as costuming, hair style, and facial hair (clean-shaven, mustaches, or beards).

But superficial visual differences are only part of the requirements. The actors must also project, either naturally or through their skill as actors, significantly different personality traits so that they can effectively play off each other as separate and distinct personalities. This is especially important in what is called *ensemble acting,* which involves a number of leading roles (with none of these roles "starring"—that is, standing out or dominating the others), as is the case in many modern films such as *The Big Chill, The Right Stuff, Four Friends,* and *Diner* (Figs. 7.11 and 7.12).

One of the most difficult jobs in casting is finding the combination of actors that will create chemistry between them—preferably a chemistry so powerful that the audience wants to see them together again in another film. Most important in Hollywood productions is what is known as the he/she chemistry. Spencer Tracy was paired with a bevy of actresses (Lana Turner, Hedy Lamarr, Jean Harlow, and Deborah Kerr) before he was cast with Katherine Hepburn to form a winning team that could be repeated for success after success (Fig. 7.13). The James Stewart/June Allyson combination also proved very successful (Fig. 7.14). The Woody Allen/Diane Keaton team has certainly worked well in recent times. Burt Reynolds has been paired with Jill Clayburgh and Sally Field, but it looks like the best potential team in recent years is the Reynolds/Goldie Hawn combination first tried in *Best Friends* (Fig. 7.15). Ironically, Katherine Hepburn and Henry

|7.11|

|7.12|

Ensemble Acting: In some films, such as *The Big Chill* and *Diner*, four or more actors are cast in roles of almost equal importance, and none of them actually dominate the film enough to be considered in the "starring" role.

Fonda had never been paired until *On Golden Pond* brought them together for the first (and last) time (Fig. 7.16).

Physical characteristics and natural personality traits are especially important in casting actors in roles where we have clear mental images of the character before we see the movie, as in the case of films about familiar historical figures or those based on popular novels. We often have a difficult time believing in the actors who violate our preconceived notions of such characters, and even outstanding performances seldom overcome this handicap.

Financial considerations also play an important part in casting. A well-known actor may be the perfect choice for a starring role, but may be too high-priced for a film with a limited budget. Or she may have other commitments that prevent her from taking the part. Thus casting becomes a matter of selecting the best available talent within the limits of the film's budget and shooting schedule.

For actors that already have an established and loyal following, producers may take a chance in casting them in a role unlike their established image, hoping that they will automatically draw their special fans. Thus Mary Tyler Moore was cast as the mother in *Ordinary People*, Robin Williams in *The World According to Garp*, and Steve Martin in *Pennies From Heaven*.

Billy Wilder's methods of casting are perhaps unique because he also writes many of the stories he directs, but he does provide an excellent example of the importance of casting to a film. Instead of selecting a cast to fit an existing story, Wilder often starts with a story idea alone, and then proceeds to select and sign up his

|7.13|

|7.14|

|7.15|

|7.16|

Acting Teams—"He/She" Chemistry: Studios are constantly searching for the perfect couple, so that they can be played opposite each other in film after film. So far, few modern teams have enjoyed the kind of success experienced by Katherine Hepburn and Spencer Tracy [7.13] or James Stewart and June Allyson [7.14]. Burt Reynolds and Goldie Hawn showed real potential in *Best Friends* [7.15], and Katherine Hepburn and Henry Fonda seemed a good match in *On Golden Pond* [7.16].

cast. Only after the actors he wants agree to do the film does the actual writing of the script begin. As Wilder himself puts it, "What good is it to have a magnificent dramatic concept for which you must have Sir Laurence Olivier and Audrey Hepburn if they're not available?"[12]

Casting Problems

Casting a feature film can often be a more difficult matter than just visualizing the right actor for the part and signing him to a contract. German director Werner Herzog's experiences with casting *Fitzcarraldo* are certainly not typical, but they do illustrate a variety of problems that can occur on almost any production. Jack Nicholson had originally expressed interest in playing the lead, then lost interest. Later, Warren Oates agreed to play the title role. However, Oates, who had never signed a contract, backed out four weeks before shooting was to begin because he didn't relish spending three months in a remote jungle location. After a two-month delay, with Jason Robards replacing Oates, and Mick Jagger in a supporting role, shooting finally got under way. Six weeks later Robards came down with amoebic dysentery and flew home. Shortly after that, Mick Jagger had to drop out to honor other commitments. Unable to find a suitable replacement for Jagger, Herzog wrote him out of the script. Production was then suspended for two months while the director searched for a new leading man. Although he was not an ideal choice because he could not project the warmth and charm of the obsessed Irishman, Herzog hired Klaus Kinski for the part because further delay would certainly kill the project.

Fate seems to play a hand in casting also, for often actors become stars in roles that were turned down by others. Robert Redford got the part of the Sundance Kid only after Marlon Brando, Steve McQueen, and Warren Beatty had turned down the role. During a very brief period, Montgomery Clift turned down four starring roles that virtually made stars of the actors who finally played the parts: the William Holden role in *Sunset Boulevard*, the James Dean role in *East Of Eden*, the Paul Newman role in *Somebody Up There Likes Me*, and the Marlon Brando role in *On The Waterfront*. Gene Hackman was offered the part of the father

12. Tom Wood, *The Bright Side of Billy Wilder, Primarily*. New York: Doubleday and Co., Inc., 1970, p. 140.

|7.17| The "Starless Cast": Occasionally, a film can be a big hit even when all of the stars are relatively unknown, as was the case with Irene Miracle and Brad Davis in *Midnight Express.*

in *Ordinary People,* and wanted to do it, but could not work out the kind of financial deal he wanted. Richard Dreyfuss was originally set to play Joe Gideon in *All That Jazz,* but was afraid of the dancing the role would require and was used to working with directors who allowed the actor more freedom than Fosse. So the role went to Roy Scheider.

While the names on the marquee are usually important factors in the success of a film, there are exceptions. *Midnight Express* is one. The film did not have any "name" stars, and the director, Alan Parker, had made only one film before that, so his name was not exactly a household word, either. Yet the film succeeded because its great intensity and excellent performances (from relatively unknown actors) stimulated audience interest (Fig. 7.17).

The Type-Casting Trap

There is danger of a type-casting trap even today, a natural result of two logical patterns. First, the studios have a great deal of money invested in every film they do. For that reason it is natural that they would want to cast an actor in the same kind of role that was successful before, in the hopes of repeating the earlier success. Second, if an actor repeats a similar role two or three times, the qualities that the actor projected in the role may take on mythic proportions, and the actor may become a figure on which moviegoers hang their fantasies. If this happens, the moviegoing audience not only expects, but demands, that the role be repeated again and again, with only slight variations. To the fans, anything else is a betrayal, a personal affront to those who have developed what to them is a very personal relationship with a fictional character on the silver screen. For example, Sissy Spacek has projected a fairly consistent screen image: a young, innocent, intelligent, sensitive, but somewhat unsophisticated small town or country girl. In fact, she played Loretta Lynn so convincingly in *Coal Miner's Daughter* that people actually believe that Sissy Spacek *is* that character, "just plain folks" in real life. The fact is that Sissy Spacek is an extremely versatile actress capable of playing practically any part, probably even the sophisticated city girl roles formerly played by Audrey Hepburn. Thus there is a real danger that an actor who is too convincing in an early role will be type-cast for the rest of his career. (Fig. 7.18) Robert DeNiro created such a strong impression with his Georgia Cracker farm boy as Bruce in *Bang The Drum Slowly* that people were saying how sad it was that he had such a strong Georgia accent, for he'd really be limited to roles that called for that kind of a character. DeNiro, who is now well-known for his meticulous research, had taken a tape recorder to Georgia to study the speech patterns of the residents—so he could capture the exact dialect of the character he was cast to play. By carefully choosing his roles, DeNiro has completely broken the type-casting trap. He has shown not only that he can play a variety of roles but that he can alter himself both mentally and physically to project entirely different qualities in each part he plays. In *Bang The Drum Slowly,* playing the second-rate big league catcher with Hodgkin's disease, he projects a kind of fragile quality, a small man among giants. In *The Deer Hunter,* he stands tall and strong, a quiet, confident leader among men. In *Raging Bull* he changes his image within the film itself, playing a young, trim, perfectly conditioned fighter (Jake LaMotta) in the beginning and then ballooning his weight sixty pounds to play the middle-aged LaMotta at the film's end. His transformations are so perfectly executed, his character so completely transformed, that we lose sight of the fact that we're seeing the same actor in all three roles. Dustin Hoffman shares this rare ability, as seen in the extreme differences in the characters he plays in *The Graduate, Midnight Cowboy, Papillon,* and *Tootsie* (Figs. 7.19, 7.20, and 7.21).

|7.18| Type-Casting: Sissy Spacek was so convincing in her Oscar-winning portrayal of Loretta Lynn in *Coal Miner's Daughter* that she has found it difficult to break away from the "country girl" image and demonstrate her versatility as an actress.

|7.19|

|7.20|

|7.21|

The Actor as Chameleon: One of the most versatile actors in films today is Dustin Hoffman, who is capable of transforming himself into totally different personalities as he moves from one role to another. Hoffman is shown as he appears in *Papillon* [7.19], *The Graduate* [7.20], and *Tootsie* [7.21].

Many young actors are wary of falling into the type-casting trap, and plan their careers accordingly, doing everything possible to avoid the dangers. Gary Busey, who like DeNiro has altered his weight and his appearance greatly in some of the roles he's played, expresses his philosophy this way: "My idea is to look for roles that make right-angle turns from one film to the next. I try to bring a freshness and spontaneity to each part and scene I play."[13]

So far as casting is concerned, there are often disadvantages for the male actor who is too handsome or the female actor who is exceptionally beautiful, because the strength of their attractiveness cuts down somewhat on the number of roles they can play. There is a limited group of fine leading actors who might be called "the ordinary people," actors who have everyday kinds of faces. Such actors do not really have the star quality to become fantasy objects or matinee idols. But their special "gift" of blandness frees them to become actors of great range and flexibility. Chameleon-like, they can blend into any surroundings to make them seem convincing and natural in almost any part they choose to play. Actors such as Gene Hackman (Fig 7.22), Robert Duvall (Fig 7.23), Jane Alexander (Fig 7.24), and Mary Steenburgen (Fig. 7.25) have perhaps a wider range of roles open to them simply because they are not stereotypically glamorous Hollywood stars. Although they are very attractive in their own ways, there is still an "everyman" or "everywoman" quality to their appearance that prevents them from becoming locked into an image. Gene Hackman, who never worries about the fact that he is seldom recognized in public, doesn't really want to be a star: "I like to be thought of as an actor. It could be conceived as some kind of a cop-out, I guess. But I'm afraid that if I start to become a star, I'll lose contact with the normal guys I play best."[14]

Supporting Players

The casting process does not begin and end with the casting of stars in the leading roles. Almost as important as the leading players in any production are the supporting players. Although they may not provide the box-office draw of the big names, the supporting players may be even less interchangeable from movie to movie than the major stars. For example, George Raft was originally chosen to play Sam Spade in *The Maltese Falcon*, and it is fairly easy to imagine him in the role. But could anyone other than Peter Lorre play the part of Joel Cairo?

13. Thomas Wiener, "Carny: Bozo Meets Girl." *American Film*, March 1980, p. 28.
14. Quoted in Robert Ward, "I'm Not a Movie Star; I'm an Actor!" *American Film*, March 1983, p. 42.

Ordinary People: The extraordinary talent concealed behind these rather "ordinary" faces helps to give Gene Hackman [7.22], Robert Duvall [7.23], Jane Alexander [7.24], and Mary Steenburgen [7.25] a greater flexibility in the roles they play than the more glamorous "stars."

|7.22|

|7.23|

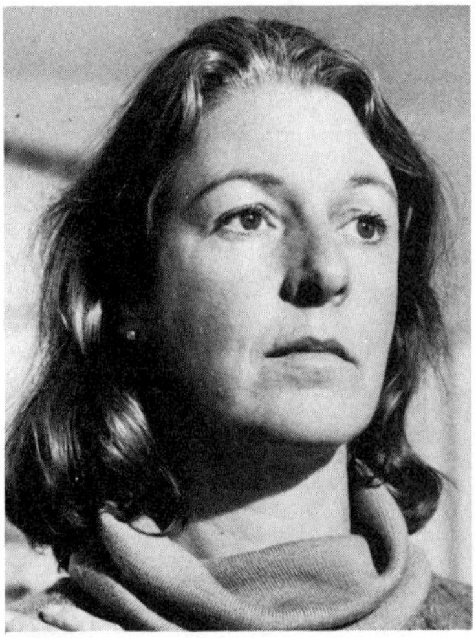

|7.24|

|7.25|

Supporting players do exactly that—*support* the major roles. The major stars play off them, as friends, adversaries, employers, employees, leaders, or even dramatic foils. And the supporting players make the stars shine brighter, sharper, and more clearly, providing a sounding board that both helps to bring out all the dimensions of the star's character and makes the most important facets stand out in bold relief.

But supporting players often do much more. Sometimes they create characters that are brilliant in their own right. Although their glow may be less radiant than that of the star players they support, the supporting players often create, usually with (but often without) the star, some of the most memorable moments in film. Consider, for example the contributions of Gene Hackman, Estelle Parsons, Dub Taylor, Gene Wilder, and Michael J. Pollard to *Bonnie and Clyde*, Butterfly McQueen to *Gone With The Wind*, Thomas Mitchell to *Mr. Smith Goes to Washington* and *Stagecoach*, Sterling Hayden and Slim Pickens to *Dr. Strangelove*, Ben Johnson to *The Last Picture Show*, Strother Martin to *True Grit*, *Butch Cassidy and the Sundance Kid*, and *Cool Hand Luke*, Thelma Ritter to practically anything, and Lucille Benson to *Slaughterhouse Five* and *Silver Streak*, Paul Dooley to *Popeye* (as Wimpy) and to *Breaking Away* (as the father), Scatman Crothers to *Silver Streak*, *The Shining*, and *One Flew Over the Cuckoo's Nest*. These great performances highlight how important a contribution supporting actors make to the overall quality of any film (Figs. 7.26, 7.27, 7.28, and 7.29).

Although the modern film does not have child stars of the magnitude of Shirley Temple, Judy Garland, or Mickey Rooney, children still make important contributions in supporting roles, and often steal the show from the starring actors. Most of these young actors seem to have a gift for projecting the naturalness and sincerity so essential for film acting. Recent performances by child actors in films like *E.T.*, *Poltergeist*, *The Black Stallion*, *Shoot the Moon*, and *Once Upon a Time in America* indicate the quality that can be achieved with careful casting (Figs. 7.30 and 7.31).

Extras and Small Parts

The casting of extras is another important consideration, for extras are often called on to perform some very important scenes. If they are not reacting properly, if their faces do not show what is being called for by the scene they are observing, the scene may be ruined. Therefore, extras are, in a sense, actors in their own right, not just background for the story. They may be called on to react to some very emotional material, and unless they can react with some degree of sincerity, for that brief moment that they are on the screen the film will lose its effectiveness.

For that reason studios hire casting directors specifically for the job of hiring extras to fit the film's requirements. And often this job is done on the actual shooting location. The "extra" casting director will go to the location in advance of the crew and spend a great

|7.26|

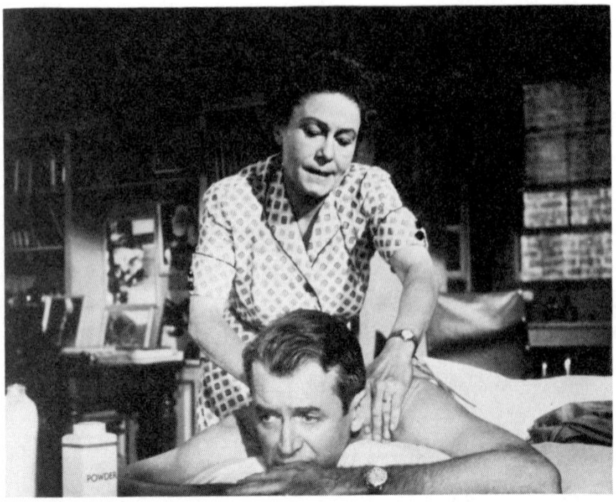

|7.27|

|7.28|

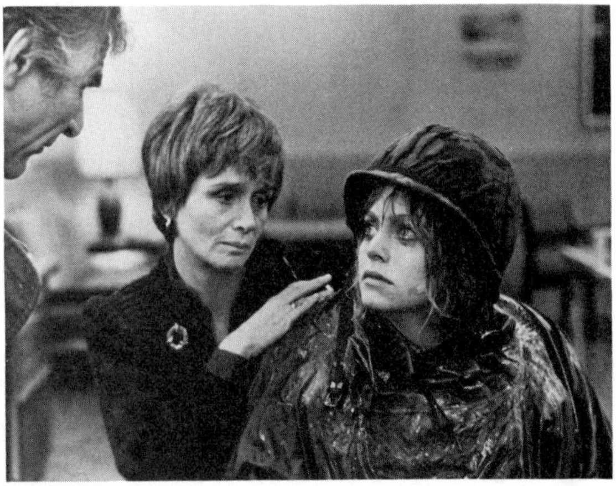

|7.29|

Supporting Players: By interacting with the stars playing leading roles, supporting players help define the most important aspects of the stars' character, and often create some of the most memorable moments in film in the process. Pictured above are Dub Taylor and Michael J. Pollard in *Bonnie and Clyde* [7.26], Thelma Ritter ministering to James Stewart in *Rear Window* [7.27], Strother Martin being "taken" by George C. Scott in *The Flim Flam Man* [7.28], and Barbara Barrie mothering Goldie Hawn in *Private Benjamin* [7.29].

deal of time finding the right faces, backgrounds, and personalities to fit the story. Jody Hummell, location casting director for *The River,* needed two different sets of extras for that film. One group consisted of farmers, who were to assemble at an auction of a farm that had to be sold. Many of the farm extras in the scene had been through such an auction themselves and responded with great sadness and even tears, and their sincerity showed through.

|7.30| The Little People: The stark realism of *Shoot the Moon* owes much to convincing performances by Diane Keaton's on-screen children (left to right): Tracy Gold, Tina Yothers, and Viveka Davis.

|7.31| Growing Up: Great care is taken in casting children to portray the young versions of characters who will mature during the film's story. The picture above shows the incredible job done in casting children for *Once Upon a Time in America*, with Scott Schutzman as the young Noodles (Robert De Niro), Jennifer Connelly as the young Deborah (Elizabeth McGovern), and Rusty Jacobs as the young Max (James Woods).

A second set of extras was needed to play a group of drifters who are hired by the film's villain to break down the levee protecting the riverside farms from flooding. For the drifters, Hummel assembled a group of rough-looking unemployed men who looked desperate enough to take any kind of a job. In the casting of extras, each face must be right, matching our preconceived notions of what a farmer looks like, what a truck driver looks like, or what a drifter looks like. And each face should be interesting in its own right, with each extra fitting the type but looking different from every other individual in the group. An impression is thus created of a representative sampling of the particular group, but such that we do not feel that each individual has been stamped from a mold (Fig. 7.32). In fact, extras are not always cast only on the basis of appearance, because often their part may require a special skill. Even in the brief moment they are on screen, they must do their assigned tasks with naturalness, a lack of self-consciousness, and a competence that will show. Bob Fosse, who demands absolute realism in his films, exemplifies this point: If a scene calls for waiters to serve drinks, instead of actors he will use real waiters "because only they know how to put a glass down on a table."

Andy Stahl, who has a small part in *The River* as a next-farm neighbor of star Mel Gibson, feels he was chosen by casting expert Lynn Stalmaster on the basis of several factors: professional acting experience, a kind of ordinary handsomeness that puts him between Mel Gibson and the real farmers cast as extras, a farm background, and experience with operating farm equipment (the role required operating a small bulldozer) (Fig. 7.33).

| 7.32 | Extras—Striking Truck Drivers: In this scene from *F.I.S.T.*, a gang of well-chosen extras march into battle with union leaders Johnny Kovak (Sylvester Stallone) and Abe Belkin (David Huffman).

Movies are actually a series of brief moments woven into a whole by the editing process. Great movies are therefore movies that achieve as many great moments as possible, and those great moments in many cases are not created by the stars, but by the supporting players or the extras. If we are so dazzled by the performance of the stars that we fail to be fully conscious of the rich moments provided by the supporting actors, bit players, and extras, we will miss an important part of the film experience. Zeffirelli's *Taming of the Shrew*, for example, literally packs the screen with fascinating faces, from the major supporting roles to the briefest appearance by an extra.

Thus, in a well-cast movie there are no weak links. Each member of the cast contributes significantly to the film, whether he or she is on the screen for five seconds, five minutes, or two hours.

17.33 Casting—New Faces: Andy Stahl, a promising newcomer, feels that his farm background and his experience with operating farm equipment were factors leading to his small role as Mel Gibson's next-farm neighbor in *The River*.

ACTORS AS CREATIVE CONTRIBUTORS

While Alfred Hitchcock supposedly felt that actors should be treated as cattle, and came to production with a complete, detailed plan for every shot, the modern trend is more and more toward not just allowing the actors a significant role in determining the nature of their characters, but giving them a great deal of input into the total creative process. After directing Susan Sarandon in *The Tempest*, director Paul Mazursky paid tribute to her value as a collaborator: "In working on *Tempest*, Susan helped make the character more dimensional than the one I wrote. She had a lot of good criticisms, and I did some rewriting because of her input . . . Susan would often say to me, 'There's something wrong here; I really think this is a cliché.' She was usually right." Sarandon enjoys a lively give and take with her directors, preferring to act in films where "whatever comes into your head you can express. I don't think I've ever worked on a film where I haven't also worked on rewriting the script—except maybe *The Front Page*. Billy Wilder has a very set idea of a film, and everything has to be done to the letter, to the comma."[15] Dustin Hoffman, who is credited by director Mike Nichols with making several significant

15. Stephen Farber, "Who Is She This Time?" *American Film*, May 1983, pp. 32–33.

contributions to his character in *The Graduate,* believes that the relationship between the actor and the director should be "a real partnership, not the classically imagined situation where a supposedly 'solid, objective' director simply 'handles' a 'neurotic, subjective' actor." As Hoffman explains it:

> I think that some directors are closed minded about what an actor can contribute. You'll hear directors say sometimes "Yes. I got a performance out of that actor: I had to push him. I had to push him further that he thought he could go." Well, there are probably a lot of uncredited occasions where actors have pushed directors into areas that they haven't gone into before, and I think there have been more than a few occasions where a picture is better because of the actor who is in it. They will say, "The actor is subjective—only cares about his own part." Not so. An actor is as capable of considering "the whole" as the director, and often does. Sure we care about our own parts, but we have a responsibility to the entire film also, and I don't think many of us ignore that responsibility.[16]

Hoffman's problems with director Sydney Pollack on *Tootsie* have been well-documented. In his struggle with Pollack over who had final control over *Tootsie,* Hoffman, who conceived the idea for the film and wanted to produce it, finally worked out a bargain with the director, giving Pollack the ultimate power of "final cut." But Hoffman maintained script and cast approval, as well as the right to go into the cutting room, watch the film being edited, and disagree and show alternatives before the final cut was made.

Perhaps the most extreme example of an actor's influence on the overall direction of a film is that of Jon Voight's creative input in *Coming Home.* After two days of shooting, director Hal Ashby saw where Voight was coming from with his character, and threw the first script out. From that point on, the script was written as they shot. As Ashby describes the process,

> I would talk with the actors the night before and say, "Here's what I think we ought to do tomorrow," and give the reasons why I thought we should do it. And they'd all come in with their lines, and they were great. They were terrific. And that all was guided by Jon's character—I threw out a screenplay because of where he was. That man received incredible amounts of resistance—down to everybody, including Jane Fonda, wanting him to play it more macho.

And all of this creative input came from the actor that Ashby had to fight United Artists to cast. When told by Ashby that he wanted

16. "Dialogue on Film." *American Film,* April 1983, p. 27.

Jon in the cast, Mike Medavoy simply said, "No way. Absolutely. The man has no sex appeal." He then proceeded with "a whole big line of reasons not to cast Jon Voight in the role."[17] Voight, of course, won an Academy Award for the part (Fig. 7.34).

| 7.34 | Rewriting the Script: Jon Voight's concept of his character in *Coming Home* so differed from the first script that director Hal Ashby threw the screenplay away and the actors rewrote their lines each night for the next day's shooting. Voight also had to overcome resistance from his co-star Jane Fonda (shown here with Voight in a scene from the film), who thought his character should be played "more macho."

SUBJECTIVE RESPONSES TO ACTORS

We should also remember that our response to actors is very subjective and personal, and often our views will be diametrically opposed to those of our friends or our favorite critics. And critics themselves will disagree violently in their personal response to acting performances. Meryl Streep, an actor to whom people respond in various ways, summarizes this problem herself: "Once a year I come out in a film and go around and listen to people or read people who tell me what they think of me. It's a revelation. I have too many mannerisms . . . or not enough mannerisms . . . to become a real movie star. Someone says I don't put enough of my own character into my roles." Those who think she has "too many mannerisms" apparently see them as acting gimmicks, techniques that make the viewer aware she is acting, not "being" the character she is playing. Others accept the "mannerisms" (her nervous tics or twitches) as perfectly natural for the character and accept her *as* the perfect embodiment of the personality of the character she is playing. Whether Streep's acting style works or not may be a matter of casting. Her mannerisms seemed to fit perfectly in *The Still of the Night,* where the audience suspected her all along of being a murderess. The nervous mannerisms made us suspect that the *character* she played was acting as she tried to deceive Roy Scheider (playing a psychiatrist). But *Time* critic Richard Schickel objects to her technique in *Silkwood:*

> She is an actress of calculated effects, which work well when she is playing self-consciously intelligent women. But interpreting a character who abandoned three children, shares a house with a rather shiftless boyfriend and a lesbian, and shows her contempt for authority by flashing a bare breast at its representative, she seems at once forced and pulled back.[18]

17. "Dialogue on Film." *American Film,* May 1980, p. 55.
18. Richard Schickel, "A Tissue of Implications." *Time,* 19 December 1983, p. 73.

|7.35| What Stars Project: Most real stars project essential qualities of their personalities on the screen. Lily Tomlin describes Warren Beatty's essential image as follows: "Warren has this lovable, slightly perplexed look, like he's worried about something . . . You don't know if he's lost his girl or his car keys and it doesn't matter because whatever is bothering him bothers you. He has this kind of automatic audience rapport. Also, he's got this subjective almost talking-to-himself speech style that makes you feel like you're overhearing something very private. His voice is breathy, sexy, . . ."[19]

Although some actors seem to create a wide range of responses, most stars project some essential image, some profound quality of their personality that comes through on the screen in every role they play (Fig. 7.35). These are basic qualities that cannot be changed, and intelligent casting will never ask this kind of star to move outside his or her essential being. For this reason, it is impossible to imagine Humphrey Bogart as Jefferson Smith in *Mr. Smith Goes to Washington* or James Stewart as Rick in *Casablanca.*

QUESTIONS

On Acting

1. Which actors did you feel were correctly cast in their parts? Which actors were not cast wisely? Why?
2. How well were the physical characteristics, facial features, and voice qualities of the actors suited to the characters they were attempting to portray?
3. If a performance was unconvincing, was it because the actor was miscast in the role to begin with, or did he simply deliver an incompetent performance?
   a. If faulty casting seems to be the problem, what actor would you choose for the part if you were directing the film?
   b. If the actor proved incompetent in the part, what were the primary reasons for his failure?
4. What kind of acting is required of the actors in the starring roles—action acting or dramatic acting? Are the actors well-suited to the type of acting demanded by the roles they play? If not, why not? Where are their weaknesses or limitations most evident? If they are well-suited, in what scenes is their special type of acting skill most apparent?
5. Based on your knowledge of their past performances, classify the actors in the major roles as "impersonators," "commentors and interpreters," or "personalities."
6. Try to determine whether the following actors and actresses are impersonators, interpreter/commentors, or personalities: George C. Scott, Cary Grant, Laurence Olivier, Steve McQueen, Robert Duvall, John Wayne, Marlon Brando, Sophia Loren, Elizabeth Taylor, Faye Dun-

19. Lily Tomlin, as told to Jane Wagner, "Memoirs of an Usherette." *The Movies,* July 1983, p. 37.

away, Dustin Hoffman, Anne Bancroft, Shirley MacLaine, Clint Eastwood, Gene Hackman, James Stewart, Raquel Welch, Glenda Jackson, Peter O'Toole, Woody Allen, Diane Keaton, Humphrey Bogart, Peter Sellers, Harrison Ford, William Hurt, Debra Winger, Jack Lemmon, Jane Fonda, Jack Nicholson, Henry Fonda, Doris Day, Joan Crawford, Gary Cooper, Sean Connery, Al Pacino, Mia Farrow, etc. Justify your decision in categorizing each actor by describing the degree of similarities or differences in his or her roles in at least three movies. Which of the actors are most difficult to categorize and why?

7. Consider the following questions with respect to each of the starring actors:
   a. Does the actor seem to depend more on the charm of his or her own personality, or does he or she attempt to "become" the character?
   b. Is the actor consistently believable in the portrayal of the character, or does he or she occasionally fall out of character?
   c. If the actor seems unnatural in the part, is it because he or she tends to be overdramatic, or wooden and mechanical? Is this unnaturalness more apparent in the way he or she delivers the lines, or in his or her physical actions?

8. In which specific scenes is the acting especially effective or ineffective? Why?

9. In which scenes are the actors' facial expressions used in reaction shots? What reaction shots are particularly effective?

10. How strong is the cast of supporting actors, and what does each contribute to the film? How does each help bring out different aspects of the star's personality? Do the supporting players create memorable moments or "steal the show" in spots? If so, where in the film do such moments occur?

11. What contributions do the small parts and extras make to the film? Are the faces and bodies well-chosen to fit our preconceived notions of what they should look like? Are their "working tasks," if any, performed with confidence and naturalness?

12. Taking as your model Lily Tomlin's description of what Warren Beatty[19] projects (see the caption to Fig. 7.35), describe the qualities projected by the following: Marilyn Monroe, James Stewart, Henry Fonda, Debra Winger, Richard Gere, Humphrey Bogart, Bette Davis, Goldie Hawn, Burt Reynolds, Robin Williams, Sophia Loren, Jill Clayburgh, Katherine Hepburn, Spencer Tracy, Sidney Poitier, Marlon Brando, James Dean.

CHAPTER 8

THE DIRECTOR'S STYLE

A motion picture is always a cooperative effort, a joint creative interaction of many artists and technicians working on diverse elements, all of which contribute to the finished film. Because of the technical and physical complexity of the task of filmmaking and the large number of people involved, it might seem misleading to talk of any single individual's style. However, since the director generally serves as the unifying force and makes the majority of the creative decisions, it is perhaps proper to equate the film's style with the director's style.

The actual amount of control that directors have over the films they direct can vary widely. At one extreme is the director who functions primarily as a hireling of a big studio. The studio buys a story or an idea, hires a script writer to translate it into film language, and then assigns the script to a director who more or less mechanically supervises the shooting of the film.

At the other extreme is the concept of the director as *auteur*, or "author," of the film. An *auteur* is a complete filmmaker: He or she conceives the idea for the story, writes the script or the screenplay, and then carefully supervises every step in the filmmaking process, from selecting the cast and finding a suitable setting down to editing the final cut.

Most directors fall into the gray area between these two extremes, since the degree of studio involvement or control and the director's dependence on other creative personalities can vary considerably. Nevertheless, regardless of the actual degree of control, the director has the greatest opportunity to impart a personal artistic vision, philosophy, technique, and attitude into the film as a whole, thereby dictating or determining its style. In analyzing or evaluating a director's style, therefore, we assume that he or she has exercised aesthetic control over at least the majority of complex elements that make up a finished film.

A meaningful assessment of any director's style requires the careful study of at least three of his or her films, concentrating on those special qualities of the work that set the individual apart from all other directors. Since some directors can go through a long evolutionary period of stylistic experimentation before they arrive at anything consistent enough to be called a style, the study of six or more films may be necessary to characterize their style.

THE CONCEPT OF STYLE

In simplest terms, a director's style is the manner in which his or her own unique personality is expressed through the language of the medium. "Style" is actually an all-embracing term, for it is reflected in almost every decision the director makes. Every single element or combination of elements may reveal a unique creative personality that shapes, molds, and filters the film through intellect, sensibility, and imagination. If we assume that all directors strive to communicate clearly with the audience, then we can further assume that directors want to manipulate our responses to correspond with their own, so that we can share that vision. Thus, almost everything the directors do in making a film becomes a part of their style, because in almost every decision they are in some subtle way interpreting or commenting upon the action, revealing their own attitudes, and injecting their own personality indelibly into the film.

Before analyzing the separate elements that reveal style in film, it is worthwhile to make some general observations about the film as a whole. In this first general overall analysis, we might consider which of the following terms best describe what is stressed or emphasized by the film:

1. Intellectual and rational *or* emotional and sensual
2. Calm or quiet *or* fast-paced and exciting
3. Polished and smooth *or* rough and crude-cut
4. Cool and objective *or* warm and subjective
5. Ordinary and trite *or* fresh, unique, and original
6. Tightly structured, direct, and concise *or* loosely structured and rambling
7. Truthful and realistic *or* romantic and idealized
8. Simple and straightforward *or* complex and indirect
9. Grave, serious, tragic, and heavy *or* light, comical, and humorous
10. Restrained and understated *or* exaggerated
11. Optimistic and hopeful *or* bitter and cynical
12. Logical and orderly *or* irrational and chaotic

An accurate assessment of these values will provide at least a beginning in the analysis of the director's style; a complete analysis must, of course, break down into segments of his or her treatment of individual film elements.

SUBJECT MATTER

Perhaps no single element of a director's style is more important than the choice of subject matter. If the director is truly an *auteur*—one who both conceives of the idea for a film and then writes the script or supervises the writing to conform to his or her own vision of the film—the subject is an essential aspect of his or her style. But even when this is not the case, directors who are free to choose the stories they want to film express their style by their choices of subject. Even studio assignments may reveal the director's style if such assignments are made in accordance with an already established style.

In studying a director, the first thing to determine is whether any common themes thread through all the films under study. One director may be concerned primarily with social problems, another with man's relationship to God, and yet another with the struggle between good and evil. Directors' choices of subject matter may be related to their tendency to create similar emotional effects or moods in everything they do. Alfred Hitchcock, for example, is clearly identified with the terror-suspense film, in which the mood becomes a kind of theme. Similarly, some directors specialize in a genre, such as the western, historical pageant, or comedy, while others specialize in adapting novels or plays to film.

The types of conflicts that directors choose to deal with constitute an extremely important thematic thread. Some directors lean toward the serious examination of subtle philosophical problems concerning the complexities of human nature, the universe, or God; others may favor simple stories of ordinary people facing the ordinary problems of life. Still other directors may prefer to treat conflict on a purely physical plane, as in the action-adventure film.

The subject chosen may also show some consistency with respect to the concepts of time and space. Some directors may work only in compressed time, and prefer a story that is compressed into a very short time period—a week or less—while others may prefer historical panoramas covering a century or more. Spatial concepts may be equally diverse: Some directors specialize in the epic film, with casts of thousands and a broad sweeping landscape as a canvas. Others may restrict themselves to a limited physical setting and keep the number of actors in the cast to a bare minimum.

In some cases, our study of a director's style may reveal a unified world view, a consistent philosophical statement on the nature of man and the universe. Even irony, which is generally thought of as a technique, can take on philosophical implications reflecting the director's world view if it is used enough (see the section "Irony" in Chapter 3).

CINEMATOGRAPHY

As far as the visual elements of style are concerned, the cinematographer, who actually oversees the camera work, plays a very significant role. But we cannot be present on the set, and lack the inside knowledge necessary to accurately assess the cinematographer's contribution. We can't really know how much of the visual style of *Birth of a Nation* was the work of Billy Bitzer, how much imagery in *Citizen Kane* was conceived by Gregg Toland, or how much of *The Seventh Seal* resulted from the creative vision of Gunnar Fischer. Therefore, because directors usually choose the cinematographer they want, we can assume their selections are based on a compatibility of "visual philosophies," and for simplicity's sake we usually attribute the film's visual style to the director.

In analyzing visual style we must first consider the composition. Some directors will use composition very formally and dramatically; others will prefer a more informal or low-keyed effect. One director may favor a certain type of arrangement of people and objects in the frame, while another may place special emphasis on one particular type of camera angle. Important differences may also be noted in "philosophies of camera." For example, some directors stress the *objective camera* (one that views the action as a remote spectator); others may lean toward the other end of the spectrum—the *subjective camera,* which views the scene from the visual or emotional point of view of a participant. Other marks of style include the consistent use of certain stylistic devices (such as unusual camera angles, slow or fast motion, colored or light-diffusing filters, or distorting lenses) to interpret the visual scene in some unique way.

Lighting also expresses directorial style: Some directors prefer to work mostly with high-key lighting, which creates stark contrasts between light and dark and leaves large portions of the set in shadow, while others favor low-key lighting, which is more even and contains many subtle shades of gray. Even the lighting's character contributes greatly to the director's visual style, since a director may favor either harsh, balanced, or diffused lighting throughout a series of films.

Treatment of color may also be an element of style. Some directors use sharp, clear images with bright, highly contrasting hues dominating the image; some favor soft, muted, pastel shades and dim or even blurred tones.

Directors also reveal their style through the use of camera movement. The possibilities range from favoring the static camera, with as little camera movement as possible, to favoring the fixed camera, moving mostly through panning and tilting. Another choice is the "poetic" camera—slow, liquid, almost floating movements executed with the camera mounted on a dolly or boom crane. And while one director may favor the freedom and spontaneity of the jerky hand-held camera, another may make great use of the zoom lens to simulate movement in and out of the frame. The type of camera movement favored is an important stylistic element, for it creates its own sense of pace and rhythm, and greatly affects the film's overall impression.

Some directors are also more concerned with achieving three dimensionality in their images than others, and their techniques of achieving this effect automatically become an integral part of their visual style.

EDITING

Editing is also an extemely important stylistic element, especially as it affects the overall rhythm or pace of the film. The most obvious element of editorial style is the average shot length in the film. Generally the longer the time between editorial cuts, the slower the pace of the film. Editorial cuts that make time-place transitions also may take on a unique rhythmic character. For example, one director may favor a soft, fluid transition, such as a slow dissolve, where another may simply cut immediately from one sequence to the next, relying on the soundtrack or the visual context to make the transition clear. When editorial juxtapositions are used creatively, the director's style may also be seen in the nature of the relationships between shots. Directors may stress an intellectual relationship between two shots by using ironic or metaphorical juxtapositions, or may emphasize visual continuity by cutting to similar forms, colors, or textures. They might also choose to emphasize aural relationships by linking the two shots solely through the soundtrack or the musical score.

Other special tricks of editing, such as the use of parallel cutting, fragmented flash-cutting, and dialogue overlaps are also indicators of style. Editing may also be characterized by whether it calls attention to itself or not; thus, one director may lean toward editing that is clever, self-conscious, and tricky, whereas another may favor editing that is smooth, natural, and unobtrusive. Use of montages and the nature of the images also help to characterize editing style.

CHOICE OF SETTING AND SET DESIGN

Closely related to the choice of subject or genre in revealing directorial style is the choice of setting and the degree to which it is emphasized. The visual emphasis placed on the setting may be an important aspect of the director's style. One director may lean toward settings that are stark, barren, or drab; another may choose only settings of great natural beauty. Some may use setting to help us understand character, or as a powerful tool to build atmosphere or mood; others may simply allow it to slide by as a backdrop to the action, giving no particular emphasis to the setting at all.

By choosing to photograph certain details in the setting the director may stress either the sordid and the brutal, or the ideal and the romantic. This type of emphasis may be very important in determining the director's style, for it may reflect an overall world view. Other significant factors of setting may also reflect the director's style: for example, which social and economic classes are focused on, whether or not the settings are rural or urban, and whether contemporary, historical past, or futuristic time periods are favored. Also, when elaborate or unusual sets have obviously been constructed especially for a film, the director's taste will often be apparent in the set design.

SOUND AND SCORE

Directors also make use of the soundtrack and the musical score in unique and individual ways. Whereas one may simply match natural sounds to the corresponding action, another may consider sound almost as important as the image, and use off-screen sound imaginatively to create a sense of total environment. Yet another director may use sound in an impressionistic or even symbolic manner; still another might stress the rhythmic and even musical properties of natural sounds and use them instead of a musical score.

With respect to screen dialogue, some directors want every word to be clearly and distinctly heard, and record with this aim in mind. Others allow—even encourage—overlapping lines and frequent interruptions, for the realism these effects produce.

Loudness or softness of the soundtrack as a whole may also reflect something of a director's style. One director may employ silence as a "sound" effect, while another may feel a need to fill every second with some kind of sound. Similarly, some may use a minimum of dialogue, while others fill the soundtrack with dialogue and depend on it to carry the major burdens of the film's communication.

Directors also may vary greatly in their utilization of the musical score. One director may be completely dependent on music to create and sustain mood; another may use it sparingly. One may use music to communicate on several levels of meaning, while another may use music only when it reinforces the rhythms of the action. Whereas one director may desire the music to be understated or even completely inconspicuous, so we are not even aware of the score, another may employ strong, emotional music that occasionally overpowers the visual elements. Some favor music scored expressly for the film; others employ a variety of familiar music as it fits their purpose. Instrumentation and size of orchestra used is also an element of style: Some directors prefer a full symphony sound; others find a few instruments or even a single instrument more effective.

CASTING AND ACTING PERFORMANCES

Most directors have a hand in selecting the actors they work with, and it must be taken for granted that they can have a strong influence on individual acting performances. In the choice of actors, one director may take the safe, sure way, by casting established stars in roles very similar to those they have played before; another may prefer to try relatively unknown actors who do not already have an established image; another director may like to cast an established star in a role entirely different from anything he or she has played before. Some directors never work with the same actor twice, while others employ the same stable of actors in almost every film they make.

In their choice of actors, directors may also reveal an emphasis on certain qualities. For example, a director can have a remarkable feel for faces, and choose stars and even bit players who have faces with extremely strong visual character, that is, faces that may not be beautiful or handsome, but are strikingly powerful on the screen. On the other hand, a director might prefer to work with only the "beautiful people." Whereas one director may seem to stress the actors' voice qualities, another may consider the total body, or the physical presence of the actor more important.

The director may have a tremendous influence on the acting style of the actors in the cast, although this may be difficult to determine even in a study of several films. Almost every aspect of an actor's performance can be influenced by the director—the subtlety of the facial expressions, the quality of the voice and physical gestures, and the psychological depth of the interpretation of the role. Thus an actor who has a tendency to overplay for one director may show more subtlety and restraint with another. Whether a director has the ability to influence the acting style of each actor under his or her direction is, of course, impossible to detect, but in some cases the director's influence may be obvious.

NARRATIVE STRUCTURE

The way a director chooses to tell the story—the narrative structure—is also an important element of style. A director may choose to build a simple, straightforward, chronological sequence of events as in *Shane* or *High Noon*, or a complex elliptical structure, jumping back and forth in time, as in *Slaughterhouse Five* or *Citizen Kane*. He or she may choose to tell the story objectively, putting the camera and the viewer in the vantage point of a sideline observer, bringing the action just close enough so that we get all the necessary information without identifying with any single character. On the other hand, a director may tell the story from the viewpoint of a single character, and manipulate us so that we essentially experience the story as that character perceives it. Although the camera will not limit itself to subjective shots, we will emotionally and intellectually identify with the viewpoint character and see the story through his or her eyes. A director may even structure the film so that we get a multiple viewpoint, seeing the same action repeated as it is perceived from the different viewpoints of several characters. Along the way, there may even be side trips into the characters' minds, into fantasies and/or memories as in *Midnight Cowboy*, *Garp*, and *Annie Hall*.

Sometimes there may even be some confusion as to whether what we are seeing is reality or illusion. The dividing line between those two worlds may be clear or blurred. Time may be compressed in montages or clever transitions that jump huge segments of time. Changing time frames may be made clear with newsreel inserts, TV news segments, or popular music on radio, phonograph, or tape players.

Unusual techniques, like the "witnesses" in *Reds,* may be inserted into the narrative to provide both background information and varying viewpoints. Voice-over narration may be provided from the point-of-view character to set up a frame at beginning or end and to fill in gaps in the filmed narrative. Or voice-over narration may be employed not just to help structure the film, but to provide a style and humor, or the sense of an author telling the story (as in *Cannery Row*).

Beginnings may be slow and leisurely; the director may prefer to establish characters and exposition before conflict develops. Or he or she may prefer exciting, dynamic *in medias res* beginnings, where conflict is already developing when the film opens. Some directors may prefer endings where all loose ends are tied up, providing a sense of completeness; others may prefer endings that are left in the air, without clear-cut resolution—endings that leave questions unanswered, and give us something to puzzle about long after the film is over. Some directors prefer upbeat endings—that is, endings on a heroic note, with strong, uplifting music; some prefer downbeat endings that offer little or no hope. There are spectacular endings, quiet endings . . . happy endings, and sad endings. Some directors may use trick endings where information is withheld from the audience until the end, with strange and unusual twists of plot leading to endings we're really not prepared for.

Some directors will create a tight structure, so that every single action, every word of dialogue advance the plot in some way, with no side trips; others prefer a rambling, loosely structured plot with side trips that may be interesting for themselves but actually have little or nothing to do with stream of the action. Some structures let the audience in on the secrets but keep the characters guessing, creating a sense of dramatic irony, while others withhold information from the audience and create suspense with mystery. Repeated patterns of character are often used, where the entire film may end with the resolution of one problem and establish the fact that the character has simply taken on another similar problem at the end, so that we get a sense that the character has not really learned anything from the experience, but will continue going about his crazy business (as in *Breaking Away*).

Directors also differ in the way they handle films with multiple narrative levels. Complex plots, with several lines of action occurring simultaneously at different locations, can be broken into fragments jumping quickly back and forth from one developing story to another, or can develop each stream of action rather completely before switching to another stream of narrative.

A director may prefer a lazy, slow-paced gradual unfolding of character or information, focusing on each single detail, or compressed machine-gun dialogue and quick images to get exposition out of the way as quickly as possible and introduce characters quickly so that he can use more time later to focus on the most dramatic scenes.

What actually carries the narrative forward may also vary greatly from one director to the next. Some may provide dialogue for the most important bits of story and action, and others may prefer to tell the story in strictly visual terms with a bare minimum of dialogue. Some narrative structures use traditional formulas for beginnings and endings, emphasizing set patterns like the hero arriving at the beginning and leaving at the end. Others use a structure where the characters of the story are already there in the beginning and the camera leaves at the end, leaving them there to continue their lives. We leave, they stay, but we leave with a strong sense that their story goes on, their lives continue.

The sense of what makes a story and how to tell it, of course, is often determined by the screenwriter, but it should be remembered that many directors simply look at the screenplay as a rough outline for a movie, and impose their own feel for narrative structure on it, expressing themselves creatively in terms of the film's overall shape and form.

EVOLVING STYLES AND FLEXIBILITY

Some directors do not arrive at a mature, static style, but continue to evolve and experiment throughout their careers. Three prominent directors serve as examples of constant experimentation, and artistic growth. Robert Altman is perhaps one of the most experimental of the present time. Although a certain freedom of form and an emphasis on texture permeates everything he does, the films Altman has directed show little in common in terms of subject matter, world view, or even visual style: *M*A*S*H, Buffalo Bill and the Indians, Nashville, Three Women, A Wedding, McCabe and Mrs. Miller, Popeye,* and *Come Back to the Five and Dime, Jimmy Dean, Jimmy Dean.*

Woody Allen has also experimented with a wide diversity of styles: Although his most successful films have focused on the familiar Allen persona (*Take the Money and Run, Bananas, Sleeper,* and *Annie Hall*), experimentation and artistic growth are evident in *Interiors, Manhattan, Stardust Memories, A Midsummer's Sex Comedy,* and *Zelig.*

Mike Nichols, Alan Parker, Martin Scorsese, and Stanley Kubrick are also experimental directors, who do films with entirely different kinds of subject matter and narrative structure. As their careers progress, the films directed by such innovators may become either more formal or less formal, more serious or less serious. A filmmaker who directs a comedic farce after having directed a serious drama has not automatically taken a stylistic step backward. The growth comes about by taking on some new kind of challenge, tackling an entirely new genre, or perhaps even by bringing new styles to bear on a familiar genre. Or the director may simply break out of genre films altogether.

Such innovators are often Hollywood outsiders, who maintain a high degree of independence perhaps because they also write and produce, or who achieve such a high degree of financial success that they can afford a gamble or two, and put their own money into their experiments. But such experiments are often not successful with the public. Audiences were so enamored with the familiar Woody Allen persona that they were unable to accept his Bergmanesque *Interiors,* where Allen served as director only and attempted to make a serious and profound "art" movie. However, audiences *could* accept the serious art of *Manhattan,* mainly because it featured the familiar Allen persona and its humor did not take it too far from the popular *Annie Hall.* It is perhaps much easier for a director like Alan Parker to avoid the trap of audience expectations, because all of the films he has directed have been radically different kinds of stories with very different styles.

Directors thus face the same kinds of type-casting that actors fall into. And this type-casting, like that of actors, depends on these two factors: the expectations of moviegoers, who feel a sense of betrayal if a director does not continue to deliver the same kind of popular fare that they associate with his or her name, and conservative thinking by studios, production companies, and financial backers, who are unwilling to gamble huge amounts of money on a director who wants to stretch his or her creative wings. It is much easier to get financing for a director to do the tried and true for which he or she has a proven track record.

One wonders if even Alfred Hitchcock could have succeeded with a film like *Interiors,* or with any other film that did not contain the suspense element audiences grew to expect from him in film after film after film. Or even if he would have been allowed to direct it in the first place.

QUESTIONS

On the Director's Style

1. After viewing several films by a single director, what kinds of general observations can you make about his or her style? Which of the adjectives listed below describe his or her style?
    a. Intellectual and rational *or* emotional and sensual.
    b. Calm and quiet *or* fast-paced and exciting.
    c. Calm and quiet *or* rough and crude-cut.
    d. Cool and objective *or* warm and subjective.
    e. Ordinary and trite *or* fresh and original.
    f. Tightly structured, direct, and concise *or* loosely structured and rambling.
    g. Truthful and realistic *or* romantic and idealized.
    h. Simple and straightforward *or* complex and indirect.
    i. Grave, serious, tragic, and heavy *or* light, comical, and humorous.
    j. Restrained and understated *or* exaggerated.
    k. Optimistic and hopeful *or* bitter and cynical.
    l. Logical and orderly *or* irrational and chaotic.
2. What common thematic threads are reflected in the director's choice of subject matter? How is this thematic similarity revealed in the nature of the conflicts he or she deals with?
3. In the films you have seen, what consistencies do you find in the director's treatment of space and time?
4. Is a consistent philosophical view of the nature of man and the universe found in all the films studied? If so, describe the director's world view.
5. How is the director's style revealed by the following visual elements: composition and lighting, philosophy of camera, the nature of the camera movement, and methods of achieving three dimensionality?
6. How does the director use special visual techniques (unusual camera angles, fast motion, slow motion, distorting lenses, and so on) to

interpret or comment on the action, and how do these techniques reflect overall style?

7. How is the director's style reflected in the different aspects of the editing in the films, such as the rhythm and pacing of editorial cuts, the nature of transitions, montages, and other creative juxtapositions? How does the style of editing relate to other elements of the director's visual style, such as the philosophy of camera or how the point of view is emphasized?
8. How consistent is the director in using and emphasizing setting? What kind of details of the natural setting does the director emphasize, and how do these details relate to his or her overall style? Is there any similarity in the director's approach to entirely different kinds of settings? How do the sets constructed especially for the film reflect the director's taste?
9. In what ways are the director's use of sound effects, dialogue, and music unique? How are these elements of style related to the image?
10. What consistencies can be seen in the director's choice of actors and in the performances they give under his or her direction? How does the choice of actors and acting styles fit in with the style in other areas?
11. What consistencies do you find in the director's narrative structure?
12. If the director seems to be constantly evolving instead of settling into a fixed style, what directions or tendencies do you see in that evolution? What stylistic elements can you find in all his or her films?

The pictures on the following pages represent films by four different directors. Although it is difficult, if not impossible, to capture a director's visual style in a limited number of still pictures, most of the pictures here contain strong stylistic elements. Study the pictures listed below as representative of each director's style, and try to answer the questions that follow about each director.

Ingmar Bergman: Figs. 8.1a, b, c, and d

Woody Allen: Figs. 8.2a, b, c, and d

Federico Fellini: Figs. 8.3a, b, c, and d

Alfred Hitchcock: Figs. 8.4a, b, c, and d

13. What does each set of pictures reveal about the director's visual style, as reflected by such elements as composition and lighting, "philosophy of camera" or point of view, use of setting, methods of achieving three dimensionality, and choice of actors?
14. The pictures represent four films by each director. Study the pictures *from each film* and see what you can deduce about the nature of the film.

a. What do the pictures reveal about the general subject matter of the film or the kind of cinematic theme being treated?
b. Characterize as clearly as possible the mood or emotional quality suggested by the stills from each film.
c. If you are familiar with other films by the same director, how do these thematic concerns and emotional qualities relate to his other films?

15. Considering all the stills from each director, characterize each director as to how he fits the following descriptive sets:
a. Intellectual and rational *or* emotional and sensual.
b. Naturalistic and realistic *or* romantic, idealized, and surreal.
c. Simple, obvious, and straightforward *or* complex, subtle, and indirect.
d. Heavy, serious, and tragic *or* light, comical and humorous.

16. Which directors represent *extremes* of each of the descriptive sets above?

17. Which director seems most formal and structured in composition? Which director seems most informal and natural in composition?

18. Which director seems to be trying to involve us emotionally in the action or dramatic situation portrayed in the stills? How does he attempt to achieve this effect? Which director's viewpoint seems most objective and detached, and why do the pictures have that effect?

19. Which director relies most on lighting for special effects, and what effects does he achieve?

20. Which director places the most emphasis on setting to create special effects or moods?

21. Compare the visual styles of the foreign directors (Bergman and Fellini) with the styles of the American directors (Allen and Hitchcock). Can you see any basic differences between the foreign and American directors' styles? If so, what is the nature of those differences?

22. Based on your answers to all the preceding questions, what general observations can you make about each director's style?

23. For additional pictures representing the style of these four directors, see the following figures: 3.12, 4.15, and 4.69 (Allen); 2.28, 4.28, and 4.29 (Bergman); 7.27 (Hitchcock); and 13.3 (Fellini).

a. *The Seventh Seal* (Culver Pictures)

b. *The Magic Flute*

c. *Wild Strawberries* (Culver Pictures)

d. *Through a Glass Darkly*

8.2 THE DIRECTOR'S STYLE

a. *Interiors*

b. *A Midsummer Night's Sex Comedy*

c. *Broadway Danny Rose*

d. *Manhattan*

8.3 THE DIRECTOR'S STYLE

a. *Amarcord*

b. *8½* (Culver Pictures)

c. *La Dolce Vita* (Culver Pictures)

d. *La Strada* (Culver Pictures)

8.4 THE DIRECTOR'S STYLE

a. *North by Northwest* (Culver Pictures)

b. *The Trouble with Harry*

c. *Rear Window*

d. *Vertigo*

CHAPTER 9

ANALYSIS OF THE WHOLE FILM

New Hollywood Cinema
Begins 1960-67
Psycho (1960)
The Hustler 1961
Lonely are the Brave 1962
Dr. Strangelove (or how I
learned to Stop Worrying
& Love the Bomb) 1963
The Pawn Broker 1965
Who Afraid of V. Woolfe 1966
Bonnie & Clyde 1967
The Graduate (1967)
more
sex & violence in movies

Elements.
① offbeat lead protagonist
② Sterile societal surroundings
③ explicit treatment of
 sexual conflicts)
 psychological perversities
④ Glorification of the past &
 open spaces
⑤ Mixing of comic & serious
 (often jarringly)
⑥ Self conscious use of
 cinematic effects
⑦ lots more sex &
 violence

Evolved because:
① Fewer people attending movies
 TV came along)
② younger audience
③ more success of European dir.
④ Greater success underground
 films.
⑤ 1st video generation
⑥ Film school
⑦ TV
⑧ change in movie rating sys.
 (G, m, R, X)
 duty of censorship on parents or theatre owners
⑨ nonconformity & sex-themes

In the previous chapters, we broke the film down into its separate parts, and considered several questions after each section to help us reach a better understanding of each separate film element. Now we must attempt to put the separate parts together, to relate them to and consider them in terms of their contribution to the whole film. Before we begin to put the pieces back together, however, we need to consider the whole process involved in the art of watching films, because the process begins in most cases long before we see the film.

OVERCOMING VIEWER-CENTERED PROBLEMS

Before we begin the actual process of analysis, the first thing we should consider are the various obstacles to objective analysis and maximum enjoyment that we ourselves create through our prejudices and misconceptions and by the particular set of circumstances under which we watch the film. Each of us reacts in a unique and complex way to internal and external forces that are beyond the filmmaker's control. Although these forces lie outside the film itself, they can have a very negative effect on how we experience a film. A conscious awareness of these problems should encourage us to try to overcome them or at least minimize their effect.

Categorical Rejection

One of the most difficult types of prejudice to overcome is that which forces us to approach certain types of films with a grim determination to dislike them. While it is natural to prefer some types of films over others, most of us can appreciate or enjoy some aspects of almost any film. We should also keep in mind that some films simply do not fit our preconceived notions of the standard categories. For example, one person might stay away from *Bonnie and Clyde* because he or she does not like gangster movies, another may shun *Patton* out of dislike for war movies, and a third may ignore *Blazing Saddles* because it's a western. All would lose a memorable film experience in the process, for all three films are more than simple genre pieces.

Even professional critics are subject to this form of prejudice, but they must see all kinds of films and are often pleasantly

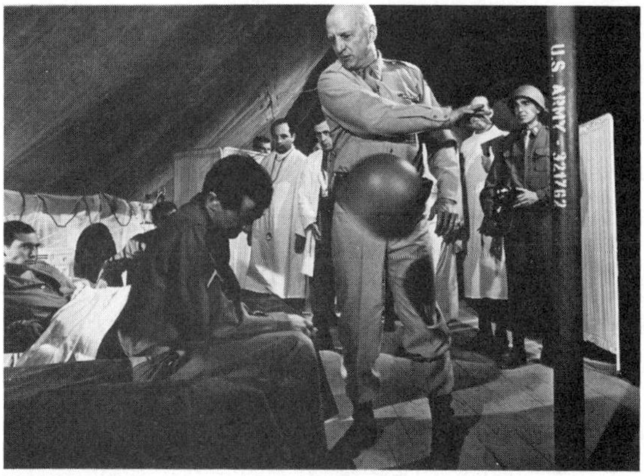

|9.1|

|9.2|

Beyond Genre: Not every film set against a backdrop of war is a formula war film, as evidenced by the brilliant character study of General George S. Patton in *Patton* (starring George C. Scott as Patton) [9.1] and the zany black comedy *M*A*S*H*, with Donald Sutherland as Hawkeye Pierce [9.2].

surprised, as illustrated by the following excerpt from Rex Reed's *Holiday* review of *Patton* and *M*A*S*H*:

> When Hollywood goes to war, it usually drops nothing but bombs. The movies rarely use the theater of war as a theater of ideas; most war films are, in fact, only mere excuses for various studio technical departments to flex their muscles with the latest developments in scar tissue, heavy machinery, and explosions. It was with more than a fair degree of sound loathing, therefore, that I approached the screenings of both *Patton* and *M*A*S*H*. Two new 20th Century Fox war flicks, I moaned, from the studio that bored us all to death with *The Longest Day?* Now I'm eating crow. They are both extraordinarily fine pictures that do more to raise the artistic level of the war-movie genre in the direction of serious filmmaking than anything I've seen in quite some time.[1] [Figs. 9.1 and 9.2].

Perhaps even narrower in their outlook are those filmgoers who have an inflexible attitude about what movies are supposed to be. This type of categorical rejection might be illustrated by two extreme examples. At one extreme are filmgoers who say, "I just want to be entertained," and are offended if they see a film that is grim and depressing. Ironically, these same filmgoers may desire and even expect a stage play to be grim and depressing, but they

1. "Rex Reed at the Movies: From Blood and Guts to Guts and Blood." *Holiday Magazine*, vol. 47, no. 4, April 1970, p. 24. Permission to reprint granted by Travel Magazine, Inc., Floral Park, New York 11001.

Innovations (cliches)
new Hollywood cinema

(A) Protagonist: social
 misfits, deviates
 (Graduate Cool Hand Luke
 China Town)

(B) Guys in Badges repre-
 sent "order"
 tend to be inhuman,
 inhumane & humorless
 (Easy Rider, Cool Hand Luke)

(C) Death of a Protagonist is
 almost obligatory
 (Cool Hand Luke, China town)

(D) Law triumphs over
 lawlessness that is
 not the triumph of
 good over evil

(E) not to be taken as
 reality (camera tricks)
 slow motion, sound
 manipulation,

70's aiming toward
romantic nostalgia
film:
 Love Story
 Summer of 42
 Great Gatsby
 American Graffiti

feel that the motion picture should function only to provide light entertainment. Viewers at the other extreme are equally narrow in outlook; they expect every film to make some deep, serious, profound, and highly artistic statement on the human condition, and are often disappointed if the film is *not* grim and depressing, for a film that is not grim and depressing may be entertaining, and for them that just is not the proper function of the motion picture.

Closely related to those who reject films categorically are those who set up their own rigid ground rules for certain films and ignore the intentions and artistic aims of the director. This kind of narrowness can easily be seen in *Time's* first review of *Bonnie and Clyde*, where the reviewer condemned the film purely on the grounds that it was not an historically accurate portrayal of the career of Bonnie and Clyde. In making such a judgment, he simply ignored the intentions of the director, Arthur Penn, and judged the film according to his own narrow critical framework.

Others may reject films because of equally ridiculous minor reasons. Some may stay away from black and white films because of their preference for color; others may shun foreign-language films because they have difficulty reading subtitles or because they cannot get used to dubbing that is not perfectly synchronized with mouth movement.

Mistaking the Part for the Whole

Almost as detrimental as categorical rejection is the blindness caused by overresponding to individual elements rather than to the film as a whole. An extreme example of this prejudice is offered by viewers who are infected with a near-fatal case of actor worship or antipathy: "I just love all Roddy McDowell's pictures!" or "I can't stand Doris Day movies!" Such extreme reactions are very common with some viewers, who fail to see the actor as subordinate to the film.

Less extreme examples of this same blindness include the over-response to certain film elements, especially those elements capable of causing a strong audience response. The two ingredients most likely to cause this kind of reaction are sex and violence. Some films are certainly guilty of exploiting these ingredients, and of overemphasizing them to the point of the ridiculous. But this is not *always* the case. Some films may demand the use of nudity and/or violence to tell honestly the story they have to tell. The point is simply that the use of sex or violence should not be condemned per se, without considering the film as a whole, and the perceptive filmgoer should neither reject nor praise a film simply with respect to its treatment of sex or violence. For example, the violent ending of *Bonnie and Clyde* did not, by itself, determine the overall quality of that film. And such films as *Reds* or *The World According to Garp* actually require some emphasis on sexual encounters to honestly tell their stories.

Filmgoers may also overrespond to such elements as the musical score or the visual beauties of the natural landscape. In *Dr. Zhivago,* for example, the song "Lara's Theme" and the beautiful ice palace made vivid and lasting impressions, and perhaps convinced many viewers that the film was better than it actually was.

Great Expectations

Another subjective factor that greatly influences film evaluation is simply expecting too much from a film. We may develop great expectations for a film from a variety of influences. It may be that the film has received a lot of publicity for winning awards from such prestigious groups as the Academy of Motion Picture Arts and Sciences, the New York Film Critics, or the Cannes Film Festival. Even if the film has not won any awards, we may be aware that it has generally won widespread critical acclaim. We may also base our high expectations on the past performances or achievements of the film's actors or its director, or simply on their reputations if we have not seen their work before. And perhaps the most difficult factor to ignore is the word-of-mouth raves of our friends. The result is that our expectations are built up so high that the film can't possibly measure up, and our disappointment causes a negative reaction to a film we would have liked immensely if we had never heard of it until we saw it. Expectations may also run too high if we are particularly fond of a novel that is later adapted to film. Film can never completely reproduce the experience of a novel, and the more we like a novel the more likely we are to be disappointed with the film version.

Our own memory even plays tricks on us, and influences our reactions to a film that may have been a favorite many years before. With the passage of time, we sometimes build the remembered experience up in our minds to the point that the actual film, when viewed, seems rather drab by comparison. Although this self-indulgent nostalgia and glorification of the past is a rather natural human trait, we might simply try to see the wisdom of the person who, when told that "*Gone with the Wind* just isn't as good as it used to be," replied, "It never was."

An Excess of Expertise

Although filmmakers go to great pains to make their films as realistic in every detail as possible, and usually hire technical advisors to help with special problems, there will still be a relatively small number of us who simply know too much for our own good, at least inasmuch as our reaction to a given film is concerned. If we possess special technical skills or inside knowledge about subjects dealt with, we are often unable to enjoy the film because of minor technical errors to which most viewers would be completely oblivious. Take for example a concert violinist viewing a film about a great violinist. The actor playing the part could be trained to finger the violin well enough to convince the average viewer, but the concert violinist would see at a glance how awkward or inept the actor's fingering actually was. More likely than not, her reaction to this minor detail would completely destroy her chances of enjoying the film. In such cases, the solution is simple: The expert viewer should not expect such a high degree of realism, and should try to enjoy other aspects of the film as much as possible.

The Influence of External Factors

Our response to any film is also determined to a large degree by external factors that have nothing to do with either our own prejudices or the film itself. Some of these factors can be controlled to some degree, while others lie completely beyond our power. To begin with, our mood, mental attitude, and physical condition at the time we see a film have a great deal to do with our responses to it. If we are tired or sleepy, have eaten too much, or had a few drinks, we may lack the concentration required to understand or appreciate the film fully. If we have had to stand in line for an extended period, we may develop a grim set to our jaws and a "This better be worth it!" attitude, a prejudice that no film ever made could overcome.

Once inside the theater, other external factors come into play. We may find ourselves in uncomfortable seats, located directly behind the world's tallest man and directly in front of the world's loudest popcorn box rattlers. A poor soundtrack may make the dialogue difficult to hear, and a scratchy print may take something away from the visual effect. Waiting for the nearsighted projectionist to focus the image may also be taxing. For the most part, however, the theatergoer has it over the film student, who must often watch films in hard classroom seats located in the worst acoustical environment imaginable. In either case we have little choice but to try to make the best of the situation.

Another factor that cannot be overlooked is the reaction we have to the audience around us. A crying baby or a talkative group nearby can certainly keep us from becoming totally immersed in the experience. On the other hand, the reactions of the audience around us may have certain positive effects that are capable of actually intensifying our pleasure in the film. This is especially true with comedy; laughter is contagious, and we enjoy laughing more in a group than we do alone. Imagine the difference between seeing such a picture as *Changing Places* in an almost empty theater, and seeing it in a theater packed with a highly responsive audience. This "herd instinct" may also work to some degree with fear and pathos, but if members of the audience overreact it may have adverse effects. One who laughs too hard at things that really aren't funny may make some viewers self-conscious about their own responses, and loud sobbing or sniffling may cause others to resort to laughter.

When watching films either on television or at a drive-in theater, we lose the positive effects of the theater audience, and must face different types of external obstacles. With network television, complete immersion in the film experience is impossible; if the drastically reduced size of the image and the frequent commercial interruptions can be tolerated, there are generally enough normal household distractions to make viewing films on television somewhat less than satisfactory.

The facts that the drive-in screen is larger and there are no commercial interruptions do not atone for the drawbacks of drive-in viewing. Although the drive-in must certainly be recognized as a great American institution, and certain arts can be practiced there, it leaves much to be desired as a place to practice the art of watching films. Dirty windshields, fog, rain, insects flying through the projection light, car lights occasionally fading out the image on the screen, ridiculously poor-quality in-car speakers, discomforts caused by various weather conditions, and a multitude of other distractions all work against the drive-in as an ideal place for watching movies. Still, it must be admitted that seeing a great movie on television or at the drive-in is better than not seeing it at all.

Since the drive-in theaters still specialize in double features, we might consider how one feature may affect our response to the other. Although the drive-ins usually schedule two films of the same genre in their double features (two horror films, two comedies, and so on), studies have shown that such programming weakens the effect of the second feature. The less alike the two films are, the stronger our reaction will be to the second feature. In other words, ideally a light comedy and a horror show should be shown on the same bill so that we will have not only a fresh but also a contrasting emotional reaction to the second feature. If both films are of the same type, we will be drained of whatever emotional response is called for by the first feature, and our response to the second feature will be weakened.

The art of watching films, therefore, involves increased awareness of our responses as uniquely individual and complex, and that we react to internal and external forces that are completely beyond the filmmaker's control. We should attempt to minimize the effect of such factors whenever possible, for they may interfere with our analysis and our enjoyment of the film as well.

QUESTIONS

On Viewer-Centered Problems

1. Do you have any strong prejudices against this particular type of film? If so, how did these prejudices affect your responses to the film? Does this film have any special qualities that set it apart from other films of the same genre?
2. How much do your personal and highly subjective responses to the following aspects of the film affect your judgment: actors and actresses in the film, treatment of sexual material, and scenes involving violence? Can you justify the sex and violence in the film aesthetically, or are these scenes included strictly for the box-office appeal?
3. What were your expectations before seeing the film? How did these expectations influence your reaction to the film?
4. Do you have some specialized knowledge about any subject dealt with by the film? If so, how does it affect your reaction to the film as a whole?
5. Was your mood, mental attitude, or physical condition while seeing the movie less than ideal? If so, how was your reaction to the film affected?
6. If the physical environment in which you watched the film was less than ideal, how did this influence your judgment?

PRECONCEPTIONS: REVIEWS AND OTHER SOURCES

How much should we know about the film before we see it? There is, of course, no simple answer to this question. Sometimes we have little control over how much we know about a movie before we see it, but some general guidelines on how to prepare for seeing a film might be helpful.

To begin with, we don't usually go to see a film that we know absolutely nothing about, for several sources exist from which we pick up general ideas and attitudes about each film. If we handle this information properly and do not let it overinfluence us, it can greatly enhance our viewing experience. On the other hand, if we allow these influences to completely dominate our thinking, the richness of our experience may be diminished.

One of the most common ways to gain some knowledge about a film before seeing it is to read reviews. In addition to helping us decide what films we want to see, reviews provide us with several different kinds of information and opinions. One of the most valuable functions of a review is to provide us with some essential factual information about the film. It gives us the name of the film, its director, the actors in leading roles, a brief summary of its subject matter and its plot, and even whether it's in color or black and white.

In addition to this factual information, most reviews mention or single out those elements in the film that are most significant and most worthy of special attention. They may also help us place the film in context by relating it to similar films past or present, or by relating it to other films by the same director. The review may even employ analysis, breaking the film into its parts and examining the nature, proportions, functions, and interrelationship of these parts. The review will almost always include some kind of value judgment on the film, some negative or positive opinions on its overall worth or merit. But we must watch very carefully how we read reviews at this point.

Before seeing the film, we should be primarily interested in a single question: whether the film will be interesting and enjoyable enough to be worth seeing. To answer this question, all we need to do is read several reviews of the film in a very superficial way, looking for the basic kinds of information all reviews provide, such as who directed the film, who the major actors are, what the basic plot or subject matter is. We will also pick up a very good general picture of the reviewers' reactions to the film—that is, generally speaking, whether the critics liked the film. If we are interested in seeing the film, we should also take note of those elements or high points that the reviewers singled out as worthy of special attention, as well as how they place the film in context with other films, past or present.

But we should generally ignore or forget the other ideas, opinions, analyses, interpretations, and subjective reactions presented in the reviews. Most importantly, we should not look too deeply into any single critic's evaluation or subjective reactions to the film. To do so may seriously hamper or limit our own response, so that we see the same things that the critic has seen, but nothing more. Not only does taking a critic's opinion too seriously restrict our personal and subjective response, it often destroys the independence of our judgment on the film's worth and weakens our critical perception in the process. Thus, we should prepare ourselves for seeing a film by reading some reviews before we go, but we should not overprepare to the point that our personal response to the film is overly influenced by the opinions of others.

Imagine how our view of *Bonnie and Clyde* would be distorted and limited if we paid serious attention to *Time's* first review of that film, and restricted ourselves to seeing what the reviewer has seen.

> Producer Beatty and Director Arthur Penn have elected to tell their tale of bullets and blood in a strange and purposeless mingling of fact and claptrap that totters uneasily on the brink of burlesque. Like Bonnie and Clyde themselves, the film rides off in all directions, and ends up full of holes. . . .
>
> Faye Dunaway's Sunday-social prettiness is at variance with any known information about Bonnie Parker. The other gang members struggle to little avail against a script that gives their characters no discernible shape. . . .
>
> The real fault with *Bonnie and Clyde* is its sheer, tasteless aimlessness. Director Penn has marshalled an impressive framework of documentation: a flotilla of old cars, a scene played in a movie theater while *Gold Diggers of 1933* runs off on the screen, a string of dusty, fly-bitten Southwestern roads, houses and farms. (One booboo: the use of post-1934 dollar bills.) But repeated bursts of country-style music punctuating the bandits' grisly adventures and a sentimental interlude with Bonnie's old Maw photographed through a hazy filter, aims at irony and misses by a mile. And this, if you please, was the U.S. entry in this year's Montreal Film Festival.[2]

2. "Low-Down Hoedown." *Time*, 25 August 1967, p. 78.

|9.3|

|9.4|

From Real to Reel: The film version of *Bonnie and Clyde,* starring Faye Dunaway and Warren Beatty, glamorized the images of Bonnie Parker and Clyde Barrow, the real characters on whom the film was based.

Viewers who followed this reviewer's lead could end up focusing their attention on the historical inaccuracies, and miss the real experience of that film. Too much emphasis on the trees (or the post-1934 dollar bills) may cause us to miss the entire forest (Figs. 9.3 and 9.4).

A similar phenomenon occurs in John McCarten's *New Yorker* review of *Shane,* in which the critic becomes so upset about the fact that Shane sides with the homesteaders that he builds his review around his defense of the cattlemen, mentioning them three different times in the review and thus neglecting more important elements in the film:

> High among Hollywood's articles of faith . . . is the doctrine that the gentlemen running cattle in the Old West were somehow criminal because they objected to having their grazing land invaded by homesteaders, bean patches, and Monday workers. I was moved to reflect on these beliefs, all of which strike me as cockeyed. . . .
>
> Stevens (the director) deals with the entirely orthodox notion that the homesteaders in Wyoming were given a highly unfair shake by the cattlemen. I'm not at all sure that he really believes this, however, because he takes so much pleasure in filming the cattlemen's noble, unfenced demesne. . . .

> My original feeling about the glorification of homesteaders and the vilification of their betters on the range still holds, however tenuously. It is certainly an odd thing when pictures about the cow country do their best to eliminate their principal ingredient.[3]

In reading reviews, we must always remember that criticism is a highly subjective process, and if we take any single review or series of reviews too seriously before seeing a film we will restrict our ability to judge the film independently. Also, if we rely too much on the reviews, we may completely lose faith in our own judgment and end up in a tug-of-war between critical opinions. Consider the dilemma we might face if we took all the reviews on *Bonnie and Clyde* seriously before seeing the film. *Time* summarizes the critical views on *Bonnie and Clyde* as follows:

> *Bonnie and Clyde* also stirred up a battle among movie critics that seemed to be almost as violent as the film itself. Bosley Crowther of the *New York Times* was so offended by it that he reviewed it—negatively—three times. "This blending of farce with brutal killings is as pointless as it is lacking in taste," he wrote. *Time's* review made the mistake of comparing the fictional and the real Bonnie and Clyde, a totally irrelevant exercise. *Newsweek* panned the film, but the following week returned to praise it.
>
> The *New Yorker* ran a respectful appreciation by Guest Critic Penelope Gilliatt, followed nine weeks later with an ecstatic 9,000 word analysis by another guest critic, Pauline Kael. In Chicago, the *Tribune's* reviewer sided with the nay-sayers. He called it "stomach churning"; the *American* said it was "unappetizing." But the *Daily News* acclaimed it as one of the most significant motion pictures of the decade; the *Sun Times* said it was "astonishingly beautiful." It seemed as if two different Bonnie and Clydes were slipping into town simultaneously.[4]

Reviews, of course, are not the only source of information and attitudes about films. The great amount of publicity released on almost every film can also influence our reactions. Television talk shows frequently feature interviews with actors or directors of recently released films. A great deal of important information is also picked up from the grapevine, the word-of-mouth "reviews" by friends who have seen the movie. We should certainly consider all this information before seeing a film, but none of it should be taken too seriously.

3. John McCarten, "Up the Cattlemen." *The New Yorker,* 2 May 1953. From a review in *The New Yorker.* Reprinted by permission; © 1953, 1981 The New Yorker Magazine, Inc.
4. "The Shock of Freedom in Films." *Time,* 8 December 1967, p. 73.

Although it is almost impossible to do, and often highly impractical even when it is possible, seeing a movie "cold"—without knowing anything at all about it—can be highly desirable. Without any kind of information about the film, we can watch it completely free from others' opinions and judge it purely on its own merits. But given the increased price of movies, few of us can simply walk into a theater on impulse, saying, "I think I'll take in a movie." If we get a chance at all to see a film this way, it is usually when the theater schedules an unannounced sneak preview of a newly released film along with something we want to see anyway.

THE BASIC APPROACH: WATCHING, ANALYZING, AND EVALUATING THE FILM

When we actually enter the theater to watch the film, we need to keep certain things in mind. The first of these is that we cannot freeze the film for analysis—only in its continuous flowing form is it truly a motion picture. Therefore, we must concentrate most of our attention on responding sensitively to what is happening on the screen—the simultaneous interplay of image, sound, and motion. Yet at the same time, in the back of our minds, we must be storing up impressions of another sort, asking ourselves "How?" "Why?" and "How effective is it?" about everything we see and hear. We must make an effort to become totally immersed in the reality of the film, and at the same time maintain some degree of objectivity and critical detachment.

As discussed earlier, if we can see the film twice, our analysis will be a much easier task. The complexity of the medium makes it difficult to consider all the elements of a film in a single viewing; too many things happen on too many levels to allow for a complete analysis. Therefore, we should try to see the film twice whenever possible. In the first viewing, we can watch the film in the usual manner, concerning ourselves primarily with plot elements, the total emotional effect, and the central idea or theme. Ideally, after the first viewing, we will have some time to reflect on and clarify the film's purpose and its theme in our minds. Then, in a second viewing, since we are no longer caught up in the suspense of what happens, we can focus our full attention on the hows and whys of the filmmaker's art. The more practice we have in the double-viewing technique, the easier it will become for us to combine the functions of both viewings into one.

It is sometimes possible in film classes to view the entire film and then screen selected segments that illustrate the function and interrelationship of the different elements to the film as a whole. Then the film can be viewed again in its entirety so that the parts can be seen in the continuous stream of the whole. This practice can be very helpful in developing the habits and skills of film analysis.

Double viewing not only helps with our analysis, but in the cases of exceptional films, it should also increase our appreciation. For example, critic Dwight Macdonald wrote, in regard to Fellini's *8½*, "The second time I saw *8½*, two weeks after the first, I took more notes than I had the first time, so many beauties and subtleties and puzzles I had overlooked."[5]

However, regardless of which option we have, single viewing, double viewing, or breaking the film into segments, we can follow basically the same procedure in approaching the film for analysis.

Theme and the Director's Intentions

The first step in analysis should be to get a fairly clear idea of the film's primary concern, focus, or theme and to establish the director's intentions. To begin with we might try to classify the film in terms of its primary concern. Is the film structured around its action or plot, a single unique character, the creation of a specialized mood or feeling, or is it designed to convey an idea or make a statement? Once this decision has been made, we can move on to a clearer and more specific statement of theme or central focus, trying to pinpoint it and state it as concisely as possible. What we really want to know here is: *What is the director's purpose or primary aim in making the film, what is the true subject of the film, and what kind of statement, if any, does the film make about that subject?*

The Relationship of the Parts to the Whole

Once we have tentatively made our decision about the film's theme or central concern and the director's intentions in the film, and have stated the theme as concisely and precisely as possible,

5. Dwight Macdonald, *On Movies*. New York: Berkley Medallion Books, 1971, p. 15. Reprinted by permission of Dwight Macdonald. Copyright © 1969 by Dwight Macdonald.

we should move on to see how well our decisions stand up under a complete analysis of all film elements. After we have tried to answer all the applicable and relevant questions relating to each separate element, we are prepared to relate each element to the whole. The basic question here is this: *How do all the separate elements of the film relate to and contribute to the theme, central purpose, or total effect?* Answering this question involves at least some consideration of all the elements in the film, although the contribution of some will be much greater than others. Every element should be considered at this point: story, dramatic structure, symbolism, characterization, conflict, setting, title, irony, cinematography, editing, film type and size, sound effects, dialogue, the musical score, the acting, and the film's overall style.

If we can see clear and logical relationships between each element and the theme or purpose, then we may assume that our decision on the film's theme was valid. If we cannot see these clear relationships, however, we may need to reassess our original understanding of the theme and modify it to fit the patterns and interrelationships we see among the individual film elements.

Once our analysis at this level is complete and we have satisfied ourselves that we understand the film as a unified work of art, ordered and structured around a central purpose of some kind, we are almost ready to move on to an evaluation process. In other words, once we feel that we understand the director's intentions and have a pretty clear idea of how he or she went about carrying out those intentions, we are free to make some kind of judgment on whether the director succeeded or failed, to what extent he or she achieved the original intentions.

The Film's Level of Ambition

Because it is closely related to the director's intentions, however, there is one factor to consider before beginning an objective evaluation. That is the film's level of ambition. It is grossly unfair to judge a film that seeks only to entertain as though it were intended as the ultimate in serious cinematic art. Thus, we must adjust our expectations to what the film aims to do. Renata Adler describes the need for this adjustment:

> If a movie stars Doris Day, or if it is directed by John Wayne, the reviewer tries to put himself in a Day or Wayne sympathetic frame of mind and argue, on other grounds, that the film is better Day or lesser Wayne, but once the ingredients are fairly named, the reader knows and is freed to his taste. The

> same with Luis Buñuel—and comparable situations with great directors do arise—the critical inventory part gets complicated.
>
> I think it is absolutely essential in a review to establish the level of ambition that a film is at, to match it, if possible with the level of your own, and then to adjust your tone of voice. There is no point in admiring an Elvis Presley film in the same tone as a George C. Scott—or in treating simple lapses of competence with the same indignation one has for what seem to be failures of taste and integrity.[6]

This is not to say that we should give up our own standards or ground rules for what makes a good film. But we should make some attempt to judge the film in terms of what the director was trying to do and the level on which he or she was trying to communicate before we apply our own yardsticks of evaluation. Therefore, before we make any kind of objective evaluation we must consider this question: *What is the film's level of ambition?*

Objective Evaluation of the Film

Once we have clearly established the theme, the director's intentions, and the level of ambition, and have seen how the elements function together to contribute to the theme, we are ready to begin our objective evaluation of the film. The overall question to consider is simply this: *In terms of the director's intentions and the film's level of ambition, how well does the film succeed?* After considering this question, we must review our earlier assessment of the effectiveness of all individual film elements to determine the effect each element has on our answer to this question. Once we have done this, we can proceed to the next question: *Why does it succeed or fail?* In attempting to answer this question, we should be as specific as possible, determining not only "Why?" but "Where?" Here we should look into individual elements for strengths and weaknesses, deciding which parts or elements of the film contribute the most to the film's success or failure: *Which elements or parts make the strongest contribution to the theme and why? Which elements or parts fail to function effectively in carrying out the director's intentions? Why do they fail?* We must be careful here to weigh each strength and weakness in terms of its overall effect on the film, avoiding petty nit-picking such as concentrating on slight technical flaws and the like.

6. Renata Adler, *A Year in the Dark*. New York: Berkley Medallion Books, 1971, p. 330.

And, since we are making an objective evaluation of the film, we should be prepared to defend each decision with a logical argument, based on or supportable by our analysis as a whole. We must explain *why* something works well or *why* a given scene fails to achieve its potential. Every part of this evaluation should be as logical and rational as possible and we should be able to defend each judgment with a just argument based on a viable framework of critical standards.

Subjective Evaluation of the Film

Up to this point, we have been using a systematic and reasonable critical method. But, hopefully, we have done so with the full awareness that we cannot reduce art to reason, or make it as simple as $2 + 2 = 4$. Our reaction to films is much more complex than this, for we are human beings, not analytical computers, and we know that much of art is intuitive, emotional, and personal. Thus our reaction to it will include strong feelings, prejudices, and biases. It will be colored by our own experiences in life, by our moral and social conditioning, our degree of sophistication, our age, the time and place in which we live, and by every other unique aspect of our personality. Now that we have completed our objective analysis and evaluation, we are ready to allow ourselves the luxury of leaving the rationally ordered framework to describe the nature and intensity of our own response to the film. *What were your personal reactions to the film? What are your personal reasons for liking it or disliking it?*

QUESTIONS

On Analysis of the Whole Film

1. What is the director's purpose or primary aim in making the film?
2. What is the true subject of the film, and what kind of statement, if any, does the film make about that subject?
3. How do all the separate elements of the film relate to and contribute to the theme, central purpose, or total effect?
4. What is the film's level of ambition?
5. In terms of the director's intentions and the film's level of ambition, how well does the film succeed in what it tries to do? Why does it succeed or fail?

6. What elements or parts make the strongest contribution to the theme and why? What elements or parts fail to function effectively in carrying out the director's intentions? Why do they fail?
7. What were your *personal* reactions to the film; what are your *personal* reasons for liking or disliking it?

OTHER APPROACHES TO ANALYSIS, EVALUATION, AND DISCUSSION

Once we have completed our personal and subjective evaluation of the film's worth, we may want to approach the film from several rather specialized angles or critical perspectives. These exercises in criticism might be especially meaningful as guidelines for classroom discussion. Each of the approaches described has its own focus, bias, perspective, and intentions, and each looks for something a little different in the film.

The Film as a Technical Achievement

If we have sufficient understanding of the film medium and the techniques of filmmaking, we may want to focus our attention on the technical devices that the filmmaker uses and the importance of these techniques to the film's overall impact. In evaluating the film in this manner, we are more concerned with *how* the director communicates, not what he or she communicates or why. By these standards, the most perfect film is the one that best utilizes the potential of the medium. Films such as *Citizen Kane* and *2001: A Space Odyssey* both rate very high on this respect. Questions that we should consider with this kind of focus in mind follow:

1. How well does the film utilize the full potential of the medium?
2. What inventive techniques are employed, and how impressive are the effects they create?
3. Judged as a whole, is the film technically superior or inferior?
4. Technically speaking, what are the film's strongest points and what are its weakest?

The Film as a Showcase for the Actor—the Personality Cult

If our primary interest is in actors, acting performances, and screen personalities, we may want to focus our attention on the performances of the major actors in the film, especially the established stars or film personalities. In this approach, we assume that the leading actor has the most important effect on the quality of the film, that he or she carries the film on the basis of his or her acting skill or personality. Judged through this framework the best film is that in which the basic personality, acting style, or personal idiosyncrasies of the leading actor in the cast are best projected. In this approach, then, we look on the film as a showcase for the actor's talent, and think of it as a "John Wayne movie," or a "Bogart movie." To give this approach validity, we must of course be familiar with a number of other films starring the same actor, so that we can evaluate his performance in comparison with the roles he has played in the past. To evaluate a film through this approach, we might consider the following questions:

1. How well are the actor's special personality traits or acting skills suited to his or her character and to the action of the film?
2. Does this role seem tailored to fit his or her personality and skills, or does the actor "bend" his or her personality to fit the role?
3. How powerful is the actor's performance in this film compared with his or her performance in other starring roles?
4. What similarities or significant differences do you see in the character the actor plays in this film and the characters played in other films?
5. Judging in terms of past performances, how difficult and demanding is this particular role for the actor?

The Film as a Product of a Single Creative Mind—the Auteur Approach

In this approach we focus on the style, technique, and philosophy of the film's dominant creative personality—the director, the *auteur,* the complete filmmaker whose genius, style, and creative personality are reflected in every aspect of the film. Since all truly great directors impose their personalities on every aspect of their films, the film in this approach is viewed not as an objective sort of art, but as a reflection of the person who made it, especially in terms of his or her artistic vision or style. A good movie, according to this theory, is therefore one whose every element bears the director's trademark—the story, the casting, the cinematography, the lighting, the music, the sound effects, the editing, and so on. And the film itself must not be judged alone, but as part of the director's whole canon. In evaluating a film from this approach, then, we should consider the following questions:

1. In terms of this film and other films by the same director, how would you describe the directorial style?
2. How does each element of this film reflect the director's artistic vision, style, and overall philosophy of film or even his or her philosophy of life itself?
3. What similarities does this film have to other films by the same director? How is it significantly different?
4. Where in the film do we get the strongest impressions of the director's personality showing through, of his or her unique creativity being imposed on the material?
5. What is the special quality of this film as compared to the other works in the director's canon? As compared to the other films, how well does this film reflect the philosophy, personality, and artistic vision of the person who made it?
6. Does this film suggest a growth in some new direction away from the other films? If so, describe the new direction.

The Film as a Moral, Philosophical, or Social Statement

In this approach, often called the *humanistic approach,* we focus our attention on the statement the film makes, and in this respect the best films are those built around a statement that teaches us something. In this kind of evaluation, we must determine if the acting and the characters have significance or meaning beyond the context of the film itself—significance in a moral, social, or philosophical sense—that helps us gain a clearer understanding of some aspect of life, human nature, the human experience, or the human condition. In the humanistic approach, therefore, we judge the film for the most part on its power as an idea with intellectual, moral, social, or cultural importance, and on how effectively it moves us to a different belief or action that will somehow influence our lives for the better. Acting, cinematography, lighting, editing, sound, and so on are all judged in terms of how effectively they contribute to the communication of the film's message, and the overall value of the film depends on the significance of its theme. We might consider the following questions in evaluating a film by the humanistic approach:

1. What is the statement the film makes, and how significant is the "truth" we learn from it?
2. How effectively do the different film elements function to get the film's message across?
3. How does the film attempt to influence our lives for the better? What changes in our beliefs and actions does it attempt to bring about?
4. Is the message stated by the film universal, or is it restricted to our own time and place?
5. How relevant is the theme to our own experience?

The Film as an Emotional or Sensual Experience

In this approach, which is the opposite of the more intellectual humanistic approach, we judge a film in terms of the reality and intensity of its impact on the viewer. The stronger the emotional or sensual experience provided by the film, the better the film is. Generally, with this approach the preference is for films that stress fast-paced action, excitement, and adventure. Since a strong physical or visceral response is desired, a film is judged good if it is simply hard-hitting and direct, like a punch in the jaw.

Those who favor this approach show a clear anti-intellectual bias, for they want no message in their films, no significance beyond the immediate experience. They prefer pure action, excitement, and the simple, direct, unpretentious telling of a story. If the experience provided by the film is extremely realistic, vivid, and intense, the film is considered good. In evaluating a film by these standards, we might consider the following questions:

1. How powerful or intense is the film as an emotional or sensual experience?
2. Where in the film are we completely wrapped up and involved in its reality? Where is the film weakest in emotional and sensual intensity?
3. What role does each of the film elements play in creating a hard-hitting emotional and sensual response?

The Film as a Conventionalized Form—the Genre Approach

In the genre approach, we judge a film according to how it fits into a body of "formula" films having essentially the same setting, characters, conflict, resolution, and values reaffirmed. In approaching this type of film we should begin our analysis and evaluation by determining in what ways the film conforms to the standard formula of the genre it represents, as well as how it deviates from it.

Since we have probably seen a great many films from this genre before viewing the film under present study, we will also probably have clear expectations. As we watch the film, we will be disappointed if our expectations are not fulfilled. At the same time, we should look for variations and innovations that make this film stand out from others in the same genre, for we will be disappointed if the film offers no variety or innovations. Thus a good genre film not only fulfills our expectations by following the traditional patterns and providing complete and totally satisfying resolutions, but provides enough variations to satisfy our demand for novelty. Since genre films are made for a truly mass audience and reinforce the values and myths sacred to that audience, we might also consider how well the genre film reflects and reinforces basic American beliefs. We might consider the following questions in evaluating the film through the genre approach:

1. What are the basic requirements of the formula for this particular genre, and how well does this film fit the formula?
2. Does the film fit the formula in such a way that all your expectations for the films of this type are fulfilled?
3. What variations and innovations on the standard formula are incorporated into the film? Are these variations fresh enough to satisfy your need for novelty? What variations make the film stand out from other films of the same genre?
4. What basic American beliefs, values, and myths are reflected and reinforced by the film? Are these beliefs, myths, and values outdated, or are they still applicable at the present?

It would be impractical to approach every film we see from the same narrow critical framework drawn strictly from one or another of the approaches discussed here. To do so would severely hamper our evaluation. To be fair in any approach, we must consider the director's intentions and attempt to match our approach to them. Consider the result, for example, if we were to apply the humanistic approach to a James Bond film or an Alfred Hitchcock film.

Vincent Canby's *New York Times* review of Hitchcock's *Frenzy* demonstrates the difficulty in judging a Hitchcock film through a humanistic frame of reference:

> Alfred Hitchcock is enough to make one despair. After 50 years of directing films, he's still not perfect. He refuses to be serious, at least in any easily recognizable way that might win him the Jean Hersholt Award, or even an Oscar for directorial excellence. Take, for example, his new film, "Frenzy," a suspense melodrama about a homicidal maniac, known as the Necktie Killer, who is terrorizing London, and the wrong man who is chased, arrested and convicted for the crimes. What does it tell us about the Human Condition, Love, the Third World, God, Structural Politics, Environmental Violence, Justice, Conscience, Aspects of Underdevelopment, Discrimination, Radical Stupor, Religious Ecstasy or Conservative Commitment? Practically nothing.
>
> It is immensely entertaining, yet it's possible to direct at "Frenzy" the same charges that have been directed at some of his best films in the past, meaning that it's "not significant," that "what it has to say about people and human nature is superficial and glib," that it "does nothing but give out a good time," that it's "wonderful while you're in the theater and impossible to remember 24 hours later."[7]

Because Hitchcock is a strong personality and a strong director, who imposes his own stylistic trademark on every film he makes, his films can be profitably discussed from the auteur viewpoint, and "the film as emotional or sensual experience" approach would be equally if not more appropriate to the Hitchcock film. Because he stresses the subordinate role of the actor to the film ("all actors should be treated like cattle"), the personality cult approach would be totally worthless, and, as seen above, the humanistic approach leads nowhere. Again, the point here is that the most valid of these approaches is the one that best matches the director's intentions.

The Eclectic Approach

One approach to film evaluation, however, is more valid than any one of the narrow critical approaches described above. This is the *eclectic approach,* which accepts the fact that all six approaches have some validity, and simply uses whatever aspects of these

7. Vincent Canby, "Hitchcock: The Agony Is Exquisite." *New York Times,* 2 July 1972. © 1972 The New York Times. Reprinted by permission.

approaches are appropriate and useful for the evaluation of a film under consideration. In the eclectic evaluation, we might begin by asking ourselves simply whether the film is good or not, and then trying to support our decision with our answers to several of these questions:

1. How technically sound and sophisticated is the film, and how well does it utilize the full potential of the medium?
2. How powerful is the star's performance?
3. How well does the film reflect the philosophy, personality, and artistic vision of the person who made it?
4. How worthwhile or significant is the statement made by the film, and how powerfully is it stated?
5. How effective is the film as an emotional or sensual experience?
6. How well does the film conform to the patterns of its genre, and what variations or innovations does it introduce into that format?

REREADING THE REVIEWS

Now we are ready to return to the reviews. We have seen the film, analyzed it, and interpreted it for ourselves. We have formed our own opinions on its worth, and have noted our own very personal and subjective reactions to it. Now the review takes on another function, and should be read in an entirely different way from that in which we read it before seeing the film. Now we can read all parts of the review in depth, entering into a mental dialogue (perhaps even an argument) with the reviewer, as we compare our mental notes and opinions on the film with the written review. Here we may agree with the critic on many points, and disagree completely on others. Reader and critic may analyze or interpret the film in the same way, and yet reach opposite conclusions as to its worth. In essence, what results here is a learning experience, with two separate minds—our own and the critic's—coming together on the same work, seeking agreement perhaps but also relishing argument. While we should be open minded, and try to see the critic's points and understand his or her analysis, interpretation, or evaluation, we must be independent enough not to be subservient to them.

EVALUATING THE REVIEWER

We might also evaluate the reviewers we read, determining how well we think they have carried out their duties. The key function of the reviewer is to lead us toward a better understanding or a keener appreciation of specific films and of the medium in general. Pauline Kael put it this way:

> He is a good critic if he helps people understand more about the work than they could see for themselves; he is a great critic, if by his understanding and feeling for his work, by his passion, he can excite people so that they want to experience more of the art that is there, waiting to be seized.

Therefore, after rereading the review in depth, we might first ask ourselves how well the reviewer succeeds in carrying out this function. In other words: *Does the critic succeed in helping you understand more about the film than you could see for yourself? Does he or she make the film medium itself seem exciting, so that you want to experience its art more deeply and intensely?*

After answering these basic questions, we can move on to a thorough evaluation of the review by considering the following questions:

1. In what parts of the review is the critic merely providing factual information, things that cannot possibly be argued with? How thorough is this information, and how clear an idea does it give of the nature of the film?
2. In what parts of the review does the critic serve as an objective interpreter or guide by pointing out elements of the film that are worthy of special attention, by explaining the director's intentions, by placing the film in context, or by describing the techniques employed? Does he or she try to analyze or interpret the film objectively?
3. In what part of the review does the critic make relatively objective value judgments on the film's worth? How does the critic support judgments with critical ground rules? Does the critic make these critical ground rules clear? Does the critic provide a logical, convincing argument in support of the evaluation, or does he or she judge the film dogmatically?
4. Where in the review does the critic reveal his or her subjectivity, prejudices, and biases? How much does the critic reveal about his or her own personality in this part of the review? How valuable are these subjective parts of the review in stimulating

your interest in the film or providing material for mental dialogue or argument? What critical weaknesses, limitations, or narrow attitudes are reflected in this review? Does the critic bother to warn us about his or her prejudices?

5. Which critical method or approach does the critic emphasize? Does he or she place emphasis on how the film was made (film as technical achievement), who stars in the film (film as showcase for the actor), who made the film (the auteur approach), what the film says (the humanistic approach), the reality and intensity of the experience of the film (the film as an emotional or sensual experience), or how well the film conforms to and/or introduces variations on a conventionalized form (the genre approach)?
6. Does the critic carefully consider the director's intentions and the level of ambition of the film, and then select an approach to adjust for these expectations? If not, how does this affect the review?

So that we will not be overly influenced by the critics' opinions, we need to develop the discipline of independent thinking, which requires confidence in our skills of observation and analysis, and some degree of faith in our own critical judgment. This is extremely important in developing the confidence to know what we like and the ability to tell why we like it.

Above all, we must develop enough confidence in our own taste, our own insight, our own perception, and our own sensitivity so that, although we may be influenced by the critics' opinions or their arguments, we will never be intimidated by them. We must continually question and weigh every opinion the critics state, and we may even question their personalities—their intelligence, emotional balance, judgment, and even their humanity. For the fact is that, in spite of the valuable services provided by the critics, criticism remains a very secondary and subjective art. No work of criticism ever written has provided the last word on film, and none should be accepted as such.

DEVELOPING PERSONAL CRITERIA

In achieving confidence in our critical abilities, it might be very helpful to develop some kind of personal criterion for film evaluation. The difficulty of this task is illustrated by the fact that few professional critics have a hard and fast set of rules to judge films that they have any real faith in. Dwight Macdonald discusses this in the introduction to his collected reviews. *On Movies:*

> I know something about cinema after forty years, and being a congenital critic, I know what I like and why. But I can't explain the *why* except in terms of the specific work under consideration, on which I'm copious enough. The general theory, the larger view, the gestalt—these have always eluded me. Whether this gap in my critical armor be called an idiosyncrasy or, less charitably, a personal failing, it has always been most definitely there.
>
> But people, especially undergraduates hot for certainty, keep asking me what rules, principals or standard I judge movies by—a fair question to which I can never think of an answer. Years ago, some forgotten but evidently sharp stimulus spurred me to put some guidelines down on paper. The result, hitherto unprinted for reasons which will become clear was:
>
> **1.** Are the characters consistent, and in fact, are there characters at all?
> **2.** Is it true to life?
> **3.** Is the photography cliché, or is it adapted to the particular film and therefore original?
> **4.** Do the parts go together; do they add up to something; is there a rhythm established so that there is a form, shape, climax, building up tension and exploding it?
> **5.** Is there a mind behind it; is there a feeling that a single intelligence has imposed its own view on the material?
>
> The last two questions rough out some vague sort of meaning, and the third is sound, if truistic. But I can't account for the first two being here at all, let alone in the lead-off place. Many films I admire are not "true to life" unless that stretchable term is strained beyond normal usage: *Broken Blossoms, Children of Paradise, Zero de Conduite, Caligari, On Approval,* Eisenstein's *Ivan the Terrible.* And some have no "characters" at all, consistent or no: *Potemkin, Arsenal, October, Intolerance, Marienbad, Orpheus, Olympia.* The comedies of Keaton, Chaplin, Lubitsch, the Marx Brothers and W. C. Fields occupy a middle ground. They have "consistent" characters all right, and they are also "true to life." But the consistency is always extreme and sometimes positively compulsive and obsessed (W. C., Groucho, Buster), and the truth is abstract. In short, they are so highly stylized (cf. "the Lubitsch touch") that they are constantly floating up from *terra firma* into the empyrean of art, right before my astonished and delighted eyes. . . .
>
> Getting back to general principles, I can think offhand (the only way I seem able to think about general principles) of two ways to judge the quality of a movie. They are rules of thumb, but they work—for me anyway:
>
> **A.** Did it change the way you look at things?
> **B.** Did you find more (or less) in it the second, third, *N*th time?
>
> (Also, how did it stand up over the years, after one or more "periods" of cinematic history?)

> Both rules are *post facto* and so, while they may be helpful to critics and audiences, they aren't of the slightest use to those who make movies. This is as it should be.[8]

Although Macdonald has little faith in *rigid* principles or guidelines, guidelines of some sort seem necessary for a foundation on which to build and develop the complex art of watching, analyzing, interpreting, and evaluating films.

The basic problem of set ground rules or guidelines for judging art is that they are often inflexible, and fail to expand or contract to fit the work being evaluated. What we need is a general but flexible set of guidelines or critical principles that apply to most films. But any such guidelines must provide for exceptions. A highly innovative or groundbreaking film may come along that does not conform to any of the basic guidelines, even though it is a great film. If we are equipped with a very flexible, wide-ranging set of guidelines, in which absolute consistency of approach is seen as neither necessary nor desirable, we can modify our old guidelines to cover its greatness or create now ones to include it. Since we are constantly experiencing new types of films, our guidelines must be constantly changing and growing to meet our needs.

In developing our personal criteria for film evaluation, we might begin (as Dwight Macdonald did) by trying to formulate a series of questions to ask ourselves about each movie that we see. Or we may simply try to list those qualities we think are essential to any good movie. Whichever course we choose, the task is not an easy one. But just making the effort should add to our understanding of why some movies are better than others. Even if we do come up with a set of guidelines we consider adequate, however, we should resist the temptation to carve them into stone. The cinema is a dynamic, evolving art form, still capable of providing us with new films that won't fit the old rules. And it is equally important that we keep our minds and eyes open for discovering new things in old films.

But, perhaps most important of all, we must keep our hearts open to films of all sorts, so that we may continue to respond to movies emotionally, intuitively, and subjectively. Watching films is an art, not a science.The analytical approach should complement or deepen our emotional and intuitive responses, not replace or destroy them. Used properly, the analytical approach will

8. Dwight Macdonald, *On Movies*. New York: Berkley Medallion Books, 1971, pp. 9–12. Reprinted by permission of Dwight Macdonald. Copyright © 1969 by Dwight Macdonald.

add rich, new levels of awareness to our normal emotional and intuitive responses, and help us to become more proficient in the art of watching films.

QUESTIONS

On Developing Personal Criteria for Film Evaluation

1. Try to construct a set of five or ten questions that *you* think should be answered in judging the merits of a film, *or* list the five to ten qualities *you* think are essential to a good movie.
2. If you fall short on the question asked for above, or lack confidence in the validity of the qualities you're listed as essential, try another approach: List ten all-time favorite films.
3. Now answer the following questions about your list, and see what your answers reveal about your personal criteria for film evaluation:
   a. Consider each film on the list carefully, and decide what three or four things you liked best about the film.Then decide which of these played the most important role in making you like or respect the film.
   b. How many of the films on your list share the qualities that most appeal to you? Which films seem to be most similar in the characteristics you like best?
   c. Do the qualities you pick show an emphasis on any single critical approach, or are you eclectic in your tastes? To decide this, answer the following:
      (1) How many of the films listed do you respect primarily for their technique?
      (2) Do several of the films you chose feature the same actor?
      (3) How many of your favorite films are done by the same director?
      (4) Which of the films listed make a significant statement of some kind?
      (5) Which of the films have a powerful, intense, and very real emotional or sensual effect?
      (6) Which of the films listed could be classified as genre or formula films, and how many of them belong to the same genre?
   d. What do your answers to questions (1) through (6) above reveal about your personal preferences? Do your tastes seem restricted?
   e. How does your list of favorite films measure up against your first attempt at establishing a personal criteria for evaluation? How can your standards be changed, perhaps added to, in order to better match your list of film favorites?

CHAPTER 10

ADAPTATIONS

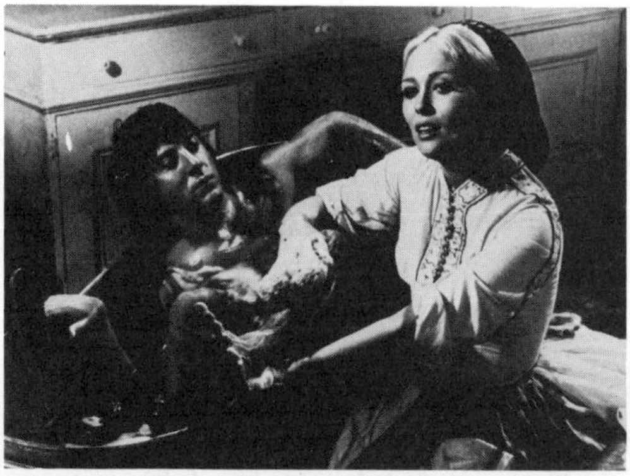

THE PROBLEMS OF ADAPTATION

One of the most difficult problems of film analysis arises when we see a film adaptation of a play we have seen or a novel we have read, for we generally approach such films with completely unreasonable expectations. Usually we expect the film to duplicate exactly the experience we had in seeing the play or in reading the novel, which is, of course, completely impossible. Since we have already experienced the story once, and are familiar with the characters and events, the adaptation is bound to lack some of the freshness of the original. But there are a great many other factors that should be considered if we are to approach an adaptation with the proper frame of mind. To know what we can reasonably expect from the film adaptations of either a play or a novel requires foresight into the kinds of changes that will occur, as well as an understanding of the relative strengths and weaknesses of the mediums involved.

Change in Medium

First of all, we must expect some changes, since the medium in which a story is told has a very definite effect on the story itself. Since each medium has its own strengths and limitations, any adaptation from one medium to another must take these factors into account and adapt the subject matter to fit the strengths of the new medium. Thus, if we are to judge a film adaptation fairly, we should recognize that a novel, a play, or a film can tell generally the same story, but that each is a distinct work of art representing a different medium. And in spite of the fact that some properties are shared by all three, each medium has its own distinctive techniques, conventions, consciousness, and viewpoint. We do not expect an oil painting to have the same effect as a statue or a woven tapestry picturing the same subject, and we should look on the film adaptation of a novel or a play in much the same manner.

Change in Creative Artists

The influence that any change in creative talents will have upon a work of art must certainly be considered. No two creative minds are alike, and once the reins have been turned over from one creative hand to another the end product will be different. Some kind of creative shift occurs in almost any kind of adaptation: Even when the novelist or the playwright adapts his or her own work for the screen, changes (sometimes rather drastic) are sure to be made. Some of these changes may be required by the new medium. For example, the average novel contains more material than a film could ever hope to include, so the screenwriter or director must be highly selective in choosing what to leave in and what to take out. Because the novel cannot be translated intact, its emphasis may have to be changed, even if the novelist is writing the screenplay. The most significant changes, however, will come about because the novelist or playwright must surrender some artistic control to the director and the actors (Fig. 10.1).

To expect an exact carry-over from one medium to another where different creative artists are involved seems especially irrational when we consider our attitudes toward different versions of the same vehicle within the same medium. For example, we fully expect the same play staged or filmed by different directors and with different actors to differ vastly in emphasis and interpretation. Consider Sir Laurence Olivier's *Hamlet,* Nicol Williamson's *Hamlet,* and even Richard Chamberlain's *Hamlet* (the latter made for television). All are different and all are praised for being different, for we expect and perhaps even demand that they be different. As filmgoers, we must develop an equally tolerant attitude toward all film adaptation, and freely grant the new creative talent some poetic license.

| 10.1 | Passing the Torch: Novelist John Irving (right) discusses a point about his best-selling novel, *The World According to Garp,* with screenwriter Steve Tesich, who wrote the film version.

Of course, there are limits to which poetic license can justifiably be carried. If a work is changed so much that it is almost unrecognizable, it should probably not even bear the same title as the original. It has been said, perhaps with justification, that Hollywood frequently distorts the meaning of a novel so thoroughly that nothing is left but the title. Two brief examples may illustrate the validity of that statement, though it probably does not apply to the two films mentioned.

John Ford, when asked about his indebtedness to the novel in making *The Informer* supposedly replied, "I never read the book." In a similar vein, Edward Albee was once asked whether or not he was pleased with the screen adaptation of *Who's Afraid of Virginia Woolf?* He replied ironically that, although it omitted some things he felt were important, he was rather pleased with the adaptation, especially in light of the fact that a friend had called him to pass on the rumor that the filmmakers were seeking someone to cast in the role of George and Martha's nonexistent son.

Cinematic Potential of the Original Work

Renata Adler wrote, "Not every written thing aspires to be a movie." And, indeed, some plays and novels are more adaptable to the film medium than others. The style in which a novel is written, for example, certainly affects its adaptability to film. Randall Stewart and Dorothy Bethurum point out important differences in the novelistic styles of Ernest Hemingway and Henry James:

> It is interesting to observe that two such influential prose writers as Hemingway and Henry James should be at the opposite poles of style: one (Hemingway) giving us the rhythms of speech, the other (James) literary convolutions found only on the printed page, one (Hemingway) elemental and sensuous, the other (James) complex and infinitely qualifying. Each style is admirably fitted for the purpose for which it is intended. James is concerned primarily with the intellectual analysis of experience. Hemingway's aim is the sensuous and emotional rendering of experience.[1]

Because of these differences in their style, a Hemingway novel would be more easily adapted to the screen than a novel by Henry James. The last point made is especially important: Hemingway's sensuous and emotional rendering of experience is cinematic, James's intellectual analysis of experience is not. The difference

1. Randall Stewart and Dorothy Bethurum, *Modern American Narration.* Chicago: Scott, Foresman and Co., 1954, pp. 66–67.

in the two writers' styles and their adaptability to the screen can be observed in the following samples of their work:

> Mrs. Gereth had said she would go with the rest to church, but suddenly it seemed to her that she should not be able to wait till church-time for relief: breakfast, at Waterbath, was a punctual meal, and she had still nearly an hour on her hands. Knowing the church to be near, she prepared in her room for the little rural walk, and on her way down again, passing through corridors and observing imbecilities of decoration, the aesthetic misery of the big commodious house, she felt a return of the tide of last night's irritation, a renewal of everything she could secretly suffer from ugliness and stupidity. Why did she consent to such contacts, why did she so rashly expose herself? She had had, heaven knew, her reasons, but the whole experience was to be sharper than she had feared. To get away from it and out into the air, into the presence of sky and trees, flowers and birds was a necessity of every nerve. The flowers of Waterbath would probably go wrong in color and the nightingales sing out of tune; but she remembered to have heard the place described as possessing those advantages that are usually spoken of as natural. There were advantages enough it clearly didn't possess. It was hard for her to believe that a woman could look presentable who had been kept awake for hours by the wall-paper in her room; yet none the less, as in her fresh widow's weeds she rustled across the hall, she was, as usual, the only person in the house incapable of wearing in her preparation the horrible stamp of the exceptional smartness that would be conspicuous in a grocer's wife. She would rather have perished than to have looked *endimanchee*.
>
> OPENING PARAGRAPH FROM *THE SPOILS OF POYNTON* BY HENRY JAMES

> Nick stood up. He was all right. He looked up the track at the lights of the caboose going out of sight around the curve. There was water on both sides of the track, then tamarack swamp.
>
> He felt of his knee. The pants were torn and skin was barked. His hands were scraped and there were sand and cinders driven up under his nails. He went over to the edge of the track down the little slope to the water and washed his hands. He washed them carefully in the cold water, getting the dirt out from the nails. He squatted down and bathed his knee.
>
> FIRST TWO PARAGRAPHS OF "THE BATTLER" BY ERNEST HEMINGWAY[2]

Although the problems of adapting a play to the screen are not generally as great as those presented by the James novel, playwrights also have styles that affect the ease with which their plays can be adapted to film. Tennessee Williams, for example, is a more cinematic playwright than Edward Albee, basically because his verbal imagery is more concrete and sensual and because his

2. Reprinted from "The Battler" by Ernest Hemingway with the permission of Charles Scribner's Sons.

plays contain speeches that lend themselves to visual flashbacks—such as the one describing Sebastian's death in *Suddenly Last Summer.*

Problems Created by the Viewer

When we see a film adaptation of a favorite play or novel, we as viewers create many problems that work against our enjoyment of the film. First, our own experience of the play or novel is itself a creative process. We have locked very vividly in our minds strong visual images and impressive bits of dialogue from the play or novel. In a play, we may even remember the inflections with which the actors delivered the lines. Because we experienced them first, these images or bits of dialogue become the standard by which we measure all further efforts.

What's more, we are not aware of the degree of our own selectivity. Because remembering is a very selective process, it is also a creative act. Unconsciously and a bit unfairly perhaps, we demand that the adaptation single out for emphasis, or at least treat, all of those things that are important to us—that is, everything our memory has selected from the original. We do not always mind if things are left out, so long as they are not our favorite things. In a sense, we have the same reaction to many film adaptations that we might have toward a friend we haven't seen for a long time, and who has changed greatly over the intervening years. Mentally prepared to meet an old friend, we meet a stranger, and take the changes as a personal affront, as though the friend had no right to undergo them without our knowledge or permission.

ADAPTATIONS OF NOVELS

The general problems discussed above influence our reactions to film adaptations of both novels and plays. But a complete understanding of the problems involved requires a deeper examination of the specific difficulties posed by the nature of the medium being translated into film. Therefore, to fully grasp the difficulties of translating a novel into film, we must look specifically at several characteristics of the novelistic form.

Novelistic Versus Cinematic Point of View

Point of view is an extremely important factor in any novel, for the fictional point of view controls and dictates the form and shape the novel takes, and determines its area of emphasis, tone, strengths, and limitations. A change in point of view is almost as important in a work of fiction as a change from one medium to another, for the point of view in a novel determines to a large degree what the novelist can and cannot do. To appreciate the difficulties the filmmaker faces in translating a novel into film requires some familiarity with literary viewpoints. A basic understanding of each of the five fictional viewpoints should be provided by the brief descriptions and examples that follow.

1. First person point of view. A character who has participated in or observed the action of the story gives us an eyewitness or firsthand account of what happened and his or her responses to it.

> Yes sir. Flem Snopes has filled the whole country full of spotted horses. You can hear folks running them all day and all night, whooping and hollering, and the horses running back and forth across them little wooden bridges ever now and then kind of like thunder. Here I was this morning pretty near halfway to town, with a team ambling along and me setting in the buckboard about half asleep, when all of a sudden something come swurging up outen the bushes and jumped the road clean, without touching hoof to it. It flew right over my team big as a billboard and flying through the air like a hawk. It taken me thirty minutes to stop my team and untangle the harness and the buckboard and hitch them up again.
>
> OPENING PARAGRAPH OF "SPOTTED HORSES," BY WILLIAM FAULKNER[3]

2. Omniscient narrator point of view. An all-seeing, all-knowing narrator, capable of reading the thoughts of all the characters and capable of being several places at once if need be, tells us the story.

> There was a woman who was beautiful, who started with all the advantages, yet she had no luck. She married for love, and the love turned to dust. She had bonny children, yet she felt they had been thrust upon her, and she could not love them. They looked at her coldly, as if they were finding fault with her. And hurriedly she felt she must cover up some fault in herself. Yet what it was that she must cover up she never knew. Nevertheless, when her children were present, she always felt the center of her heart go hard. This troubled her, and in her manner she was all the more gentle and anxious for her children, as if she loved them very much. Only she could not feel love,

3. William Faulkner, "Spotted Horses," from *The Faulkner Reader*. New York: Random House, Inc., 1959.

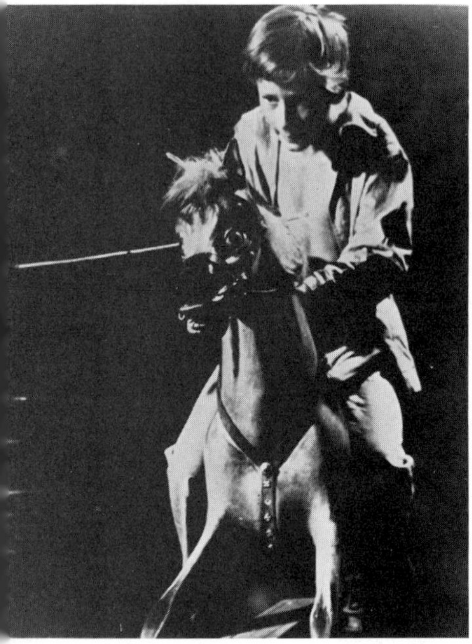

|10.2| Short Story into Film: John Howard Davies rides his rocking horse into a mystical trance where the winners of horse races are revealed to him in the film version of D. H. Lawrence's "The Rocking-Horse Winner."

no, not for anybody. Everybody else said of her: "She is such a good mother. She adores her children." Only she herself, and her children themselves, knew it was not so. They read it in each other's eyes.

There was a boy and two little girls. They lived in a pleasant house, with a garden, and they had discreet servants, and felt themselves superior to anyone in the neighborhood.

Although they lived in style, they felt always in anxiety in the house. There was never enough money [Fig. 10.2].

OPENING PARAGRAPHS OF "THE ROCKING-HORSE WINNER," BY D. H. LAWRENCE[4]

3. Third-person limited point of view. The narrator is omniscient except for the fact that his or her powers of mind-reading are limited to or at least focused on a single character. This character's thoughts are extremely important to the novel, for he or she becomes the central intelligence through which we view the action.

Although Bertha Young was thirty she still had moments like this when she wanted to run instead of walk, to take dancing steps on and off the pavement, to bowl a hoop, to throw something up in the air and catch it again, or to stand still and laugh at nothing—at nothing, simply.

What can you do if you are thirty and, turning the corner of your own street, you are overcome, suddenly, by a feeling of bliss—absolute bliss!—as though you'd suddenly swallowed a bright piece of that late afternoon sun and it burned in your bosom, sending out a little shower of sparks into every particle, into every finger and toe? . . .

Oh, is there no way you can express it without being "drunk and disorderly?" How idiotic civilization is! Why be given a body if you have to keep it shut up in a case like a rare, rare fiddle?

OPENING PARAGRAPHS OF "BLISS" BY KATHERINE MANSFIELD[5]

4. Dramatic point of view (also called the concealed—or effaced—narrator point of view). We are not conscious of a narrator, for the author does not comment on the action, but simply describes the scene, telling us what happens and what the characters say, so we get a feeling of being there, observing the scene as we would in a play.

The door of Henry's lunchroom opened and two men came in. They sat down at the counter.

"What's yours?" George asked them.

"I don't know," one of the men said. "What do you want to eat, Al?"

4. From "The Rocking-Horse Winner," *The Complete Short Stories of D. H. Lawrence,* vol. 3. Copyright 1933 by The Estate of D. H. Lawrence, © 1961 by Angelo Ravagli and C. M. Weekley, Executors of the Estate of Frieda Lawrence Ravagli.

5. Copyright 1920 by Alfred A. Knopf, Inc., and renewed 1948 by John Middleton Murry. Reprinted from *The Short Stories of Katherine Mansfield* by permission of the publisher.

"I don't know," said Al. "I don't know what I want to eat."

Outside it was getting dark. The street light came on outside the window. The two men at the counter read the menu. From the other end of the counter Nick Adams watched them. He had been talking to George when they came in.

"I'll have a roast pork tenderloin with apple sauce and mashed potatoes," the first man said.

"It isn't ready yet."

"What the hell do you put it on the card for?"

"That's the dinner," George explained. "You can get that at six o'clock."

George looked at the clock on the wall behind the counter. "It's five o'clock."

"The clock says twenty minutes past five," the second man said.

"It's twenty minutes fast."

"Oh, to hell with the clock," the first man said. "What have you got to eat?"

OPENING PARAGRAPHS OF "THE KILLERS," BY ERNEST HEMINGWAY[6]

5. Stream of consciousness or interior monologue. This is a kind of first-person narrative, except the participant in the action is not consciously narrating the story. What we get instead is a unique kind of inner view, as though a microphone and a movie camera in the fictional character's mind were recording for us every thought, image, and impression that passes through his brain, without the conscious acts of organization, selectivity, or narration.

Stay mad. My shirt was getting wet and my hair. Across the roof hearing the roof loud now I could see Natalie going through the garden among the rain. Get wet I hope you catch pneumonia go on home Cowface. I jumped hard as I could into the hog-wallow the mud yellowed up to my waist stinking I kept on plunging until I fell down and rolled over in it. "Hear them in swimming, sister? I wouldn't mind doing that myself." If I had time. When I have time. I could hear my watch. *Mud was warmer than the rain it smelled awful. She had her back turned I went around in front of her. You know what I was doing? She turned her back I went around in front of her the rain creeping into the mud flatting her bodice through her dress it smelled horrible. I was hugging her that's what I was doing. She turned her back I went around in front of her. I was hugging her I tell you. I don't give a damn what you were doing. . .*

FROM *THE SOUND AND THE FURY* BY WILLIAM FAULKNER[7]

6. Reprinted from "The Killers" by Ernest Hemingway with the permission of Charles Scribner's Sons.

7. Reprinted by permission of Random House, Inc., from William Faulkner, *The Sound and the Fury*. Copyright 1929 by William Faulkner. Copyright renewed 1956 by William Faulkner.

Of the five points of view possible in a novel, three require of the narrator an ability to look inside a character's mind to "see" what he or she is thinking. Omniscient, third-person limited, and stream of consciousness all stress the thoughts, concepts, or reflections of a character—elements that are difficult to depict cinematically. The basic problem is that these three fictional points of view have no natural cinematic equivalents. George Bluestone discusses this problem in *Novels into Film:*

> The rendition of mental states—memory, dream, imagination—cannot be as adequately represented by film as by language . . . The film, by arranging external signs for our visual perception, or by presenting us with dialogue, can lead us to *infer* thought. But it cannot show us thought directly. It can show us characters thinking, feeling, and speaking, but it cannot show us their thoughts and feelings. A film is not thought; it is perceived.[8]

Another problem arises from the fact that in three of the viewpoints—first person, omniscient, and third-person limited—we are aware of a narrator, of someone telling a story. The sense of a narrator, or a novelistic point of view, can be imposed (or superimposed) upon a film through voice-over narration added to the soundtrack. But this is not a natural cinematic quality, and it is rarely completely successful in duplicating or even suggesting the novelistic viewpoints. In film we usually simply see the story unfold. The dramatic point of view, then, is the only novelistic viewpoint that can be directly translated into cinema. But few if any novels are written in the strict dramatic point of view, because this viewpoint requires so much of the reader's concentration; he or she must read between the lines for the significance or meaning. Thus this viewpoint is usually restricted to short stories.

The usual "solution" to these problems of adaptation is to ignore the novel's point of view, omit the prose passages stressing thought or reflection, and simply duplicate the most dramatic scenes. The problem, of course, is that the prose passages and the point of view often constitute much of the novel's essence. This means that filmmakers cannot always capture a novel's essence cinematically. The following examples of specific problems of adapting a novel into film should help to illustrate the point.

8. George Bluestone, *Novels Into Film*. Berkeley and Los Angeles: University of California Press, 1957, pp. 47–48.

First-Person Point of View

The first-person point of view also has no true cinematic equivalent. The completely consistent use of the subjective point of view (with the camera recording everything from the point of view of a participant in the action) does not really work effectively in film. Even if it did, it would not really be equivalent to the fictional first-person viewpoint. With the subjective camera, we feel that we are involved in the action, seeing it through a participant's eyes. But a fictional first person does not equate reader with participant; rather, the narrator and the reader are two separate entities. The reader "listens" while the first-person narrator "tells" the story.

In novels with a first-person point of view, such as *Huckleberry Finn* or *The Catcher in the Rye,* the reader has an intimate relationship with the narrator, who tells the story as a participant in the action. The writer "speaks" directly to the reader and forms emotional ties with him or her. The reader feels that he or she knows the narrator, that they are intimate friends. This bond between narrator and reader is much closer than any tie a remote, unseen director—who shows the story through pictures—might strive to create with a viewer. The intimacy of the warm, comfortable relationship between a first-person narrator and the reader can rarely be achieved in film, even with the help of voice-over narration.

Furthermore, the unique personality of the narrator is often extremely important in the first-person novel, and much of this personality may be impossible to show in action or dialogue, for it is the aspect of his or her personality revealed by the way he or she tells a story, not the way he or she looks, acts, or speaks in dialogue, that comes across in the novel. This quality, which would certainly be missing from the film, might be called the narrator's essence, a quality of personality that gives a certain flair or flavor to the narrative style and that, although essential to the tone of the book, cannot really be translated into film. Consider, for example, the verbal flow of Holden Caulfield's first-person narration from *The Catcher in the Rye:*

> Where I want to start telling is the day I left Pencey Prep. Pencey Prep is this school that's in Agerstown, Pennsylvania. You probably heard of it. You've probably seen the ads, anyway. They advertise in about a thousand magazines, always showing some hotshot guy on a horse jumping over a fence. Like as if all you ever did at Pencey was play polo all the time. I never once saw a horse anywhere near the place. And underneath the guy on the

> horse's picture, it always says: "Since 1888 we have been molding boys into splendid, clear-thinking young men." Strictly for the birds. They don't do any damn more molding at Pencey than they do at any other school. And I didn't know anybody there that was splendid and clear thinking at all. Maybe two guys. If that many. And they probably came to Pencey that way.[9]

Because of the unique personality of the narrator, the first-person point of view affects the tenor of the novel not as a way of seeing but as a way of telling, a verbal essence that sets the tone and style for the whole novel. Thus it is virtually impossible to imagine a film version of *The Catcher in the Rye* without a great deal of voice-over narration running throughout the film. Although such approaches have been tried in film (one example is Henry Miller's *Tropic of Cancer,* which also has a distinctly flavorful first-person narrative style), for the most part such extensive use of voice-over is not very effective in films.

One fairly successful attempt in which the flavor of the first-person narrator was suggested by the voice-over narration was *To Kill a Mockingbird.* The voice-over, however, was used with restraint, so that the feeling of unnaturalness that often results when someone tells us a story while we are watching it unfold was avoided. And the personality of the narrator here was not as unique as Holden Caulfield's in *The Catcher in the Rye* or that of Miller's narrator in *Tropic of Cancer,* so the burden of style and tone did not rest so much on the narrator's verbal essence.

The Problem of Length and Depth

Because of the rather severe limitations imposed upon the length of a film and the amount of material it can successfully treat, a film is forced to suggest pictorially a great many things that a novel could explore in more depth. In many ways, the film adaptation of a novel is like Ernest Hemingway's image of the iceberg:

> If a writer of prose knows enough about what he is writing about he may omit things that he knows and the reader, if the writer is writing truly enough, will have a feeling of those as strongly as though the author had stated them. The dignity of movement of an iceberg is due to only one-eighth of it being above water.[10]

9. J. D. Salinger, *The Catcher in the Rye*. New York: Bantam Books, Inc., 1951, p. 2.

10. Ernest Hemingway, *Death in the Afternoon*. New York: Charles Scribner's Sons, 1932, p. 192.

At best, the film version can capture one-eighth of the novel's depth. It is doubtful that it can ever capture the seven-eighths that lie beneath the surface. The filmmaker, nevertheless, must attempt to suggest the hidden material. The filmmaker's task will, of course, be much easier if he or she can assume that we have read the novel. But we still must accept the fact that there are dimensions to the novel that are inaccessible to film.

The long novel creates an interesting dilemma: Should the filmmaker be satisfied with doing only a part of the novel by dramatizing a single action that can be thoroughly treated within cinematic limits, or should he or she attempt to capture a sense of the whole novel by hitting the high points and leaving the gaps unfilled? If the latter is attempted, complex time and character relationships may wind up being implied rather than clearly stated. Usually the filmmaker must limit not only the depth to which a character can be explored, but also the actual number of characters treated. This may result in a necessity to create composite characters, who combine the plot functions of two or even more characters from the novel into one. Furthermore, in adapting the long novel to film, complex and important subplots might have to be completely eliminated.

Generally, then, the shorter the novel, the better the chances for effective adaptation to the screen. In length perhaps the short story is really better suited than most novels, for many short stories have been translated into film with little or no expansion.

Philosophical Reflections

Often, the most striking passages in a novel are those in which we sense an inner movement of the author's mind toward some truth of life, and are aware that our own mind is being stretched by his or her contemplation and reflection. Such passages do not stress external action, but rather lead to an internal questioning on the meaning and significance of events, taking the reader on a kind of cerebral excursion into a gray world where the camera cannot go. The following passage from *All the King's Men*, for example, could not really be effectively treated in film:

> Two hours later, I was in my car and Bruden's Landing was behind me, and the bay, and windshield wipers were making their busy little gasp and click like something inside you which had better not stop. For it was raining again. The drops swung and swayed down out of the dark into my headlights

> like a bead portiere of bright metal beads which the car kept shouldering through.
>
> There is nothing more alone than being in a car at night in the rain. I was in the car. And I was glad of it. Between one point on the map and another point on the map, there was the being alone in the car in the rain. They say you are not you except in terms of relation to other people. If there weren't any other people there wouldn't be any you, and not being you or anything, you can really lie back and get some rest. It is a vacation from being you. There is only the flow of the motor under your foot spinning that frail thread of sound out of its metal gut like a spider, that filament, that nexus, which isn't really there, between the you which you have just left in one place and the you which you will be when you get to the other place.
>
> You ought to invite those two you's to the same party some time. Or you might have a family reunion for all the you's with barbecue under the trees. It would be amusing to know what they would say to each other.
>
> But meanwhile, there isn't either one of them, and I am in the car in the rain at night.[11]

Because *All the King's Men* is full of such passages, this one could not be singled out for treatment in voice-over narration. It is also highly improbable that the dramatic scene described here (the narrator, Jack Burden, driving alone in the rain at night) could suggest his thoughts even to a viewer who had read the novel.

When a visual image in the novel is more closely related to the philosophical passage, and serves as a trigger to the reflection, there is greater probability that the filmmaker would be able to suggest the significance of the image to those who have read the novel, but even this is by no means certain. In the two passages quoted below (both from *All the King's Men*), the first gives us a rather clear visual image and could be effectively treated on film. The second passage is primarily the narrator's reflection on the significance of the visual image, and could at best be only suggested in a film:

> In a settlement named Don Jon, New Mexico, I talked to a man propped against the shady side of the filling station, enjoying the only patch of shade in a hundred miles due east. He was an old fellow, seventy-five if a day, with a face like sun-brittled leather and pale-blue eyes under the brim of a felt hat which had once been black. The only thing remarkable about him was the fact that while you looked into the sun-brittled leather of the face, which seemed as stiff and devitalized as the hide on a mummy's jaw, you would suddenly see a twitch in the left cheek, up toward the pale-blue eye. You

11. Excerpted from *All the King's Men*, copyright 1946, 1974 by Robert Penn Warren. Reprinted by permission of Harcourt Brace Jovanovich, Inc. Excerpt appears on pp. 128–129 of the Bantam Books (1974) edition.

would think he was going to wink, but he wasn't going to wink. The twitch was simply an independent phenomenon, unrelated to the face or to what was behind the face or to anything in the whole tissue of phenomena which is the world we are lost in. It was remarkable, in that face, the twitch which lived that little life all its own. I squatted by his side, where he sat on a bundle of rags from which the handle of a tin skillet protruded, and listened to him talk. But the words were not alive. What was alive was the twitch, of which he was no longer aware. . . .

We rode across Texas to Shreveport, Louisiana, where he left me to try for north Arkansas. I did not ask him if he had learned the truth in California. His face had learned it anyway, and wore the final wisdom under the left eye. The face knew that the twitch was the live thing. Was all. But, having left that otherwise unremarkable man, it occurred to me, as I reflected upon the thing which made him remarkable, that if the twitch was all, what was it that could know that twitch was all? Did the leg of the dead frog in the laboratory know that the twitch was all when you put the electic current through it? Did the man's face know about the twitch, and how it was all? Ah, I decided, that is the mystery. That is the secret knowledge. That is what you have to go to California to have a mystic vision to find out. That the twitch can know that the twitch is all. Then, having found that out, in the mystic vision, you feel clean and free. You are at one with the Great Twitch.[12]

Summarizing a Character's Past

In the novel, when a character first appears, the novelist often provides us with a quick thumbnail sketch of his or her past, as illustrated by the summary of the origins and past history of Billy, the deaf mute boy from Larry McMurtry's novel, *The Last Picture Show:*

While the boys worked Sam stood by the stove and warmed his aching feet. He wished Sonny weren't so reckless economically, but there was nothing he could do about it. Billy was less of a problem partly because he was so dumb. Billy's real father was an old railroad man who had worked in Thalia for a short time just before the war: his mother was a deaf and dumb girl who had no people except an aunt. The old man cornered the girl in the balcony of the picture show one night and begat Billy. The sheriff saw to it that the old man married the girl, but she died when Billy was born and he was raised by the family of Mexicans who helped the old man keep the railroad track repaired. After the war the hauling petered out and the track was taken up. The old man left and got a job bumping cars on a stockyards track in Oklahoma, leaving Billy with the Mexicans. They hung around for

12. Excerpted from *All the King's Men,* copyright 1946, 1974 by Robert Penn Warren. Reprinted by permission of Harcourt Brace Jovanovich, Inc. Excerpt appears on pp. 313–314 of the Bantam Books (1974) edition.

several more years, piling prickly pear and grubbing mesquite, but then a man from Plainview talked them into moving out there to pick cotton. They snuck off one morning and left Billy sitting on the curb in front of the picture show.

From then on, Sam the Lion took care of him. Billy learned to sweep, and he kept all three of Sam's places swept out: in return he got his keep and also, every single night, he got to watch the picture show. He always sat in the balcony, his broom at his side: for years he saw every show that came to Thalia and so far as anyone knew, he liked them all. He was never known to leave while the screen was lit.[13]

| 10.3 | Character Without a Past: Sam Bottoms as Billy, the deaf-mute boy in *The Last Picture Show* (Culver Pictures).

Here McMurtry summarizes a character's whole background in two brief paragraphs. In the film version, no background on Billy is provided whatsoever (Fig. 10.3). Such information could not be worked into the film's dialogue without bringing in an outsider, some character who didn't know Billy, to ask about his past. But having characters spend a great deal of time talking about the backgrounds of other characters does not make for good cinema—it becomes too static, too talky. The only alternative is to dramatize such paragraphs visually. But this type of material not only lacks the importance to justify such treatment, it would also have to be forced into the main plot structure in a very unnatural manner. Thus, the kind of background information in the passages above is simply not suited to a natural cinematic style, and the background of many film characters therefore remains a mystery. Because novels can and do provide this kind of information, they possess a dimension of depth in characterization that films usually don't have.

Cinematic Compression of Time Versus Novelistic Summary

Cinematic techniques are capable of giving us the impression that time is passing; even relatively long periods of time can be suggested by a well-made transition or even a montage. But film is severely limited by its inability to summarize what happens in that span of time. This kind of summary is not a cinematic art, for it does not always lend itself to images and dialogue. In *All the King's Men,* Robert Penn Warren summarizes seventeen years of a woman's life as follows:

13. Excerpted from *The Last Picture Show* by Larry McMurtry. New York: Dell Publishing Co., Inc., 1966, pp. 8–9.

As for the way Anne Stanton went meanwhile, the story is short. After two years at the refined female college in Virginia, she came home. Adam by this time was in medical school up East. Anne spent a year going to parties in the city, and got engaged. But nothing came of it. After awhile there was another engagement, but something happened again. By this time Governor Stanton was nearly an invalid, and Adam was studying abroad. Anne quit going to parties, except for an occasional party at the Landing in the summer. She stayed at home with her father, giving him his medicine, patting his pillow, assisting the nurse, reading to him hour by hour, holding his hand in the summer twilights or in the winter evenings when the house shook to the blasts off the sea. It took him seven years to die. After the governor had died in the big tester bed with a lot of expensive medical talent leaning over him, Anne Stanton lived in the house fronting the sea, with only the company of Aunt Sophonisba, a feeble, grumbling, garrulous, and incompetent old colored woman, who combined benevolence and vengeful tyranny in the ambiguous way known only to old colored women who have spent their lives in affectionate service, in prying, in wheedling, and chicanery, in short-lived rebelliousness and long irony, and in second-hand clothes. Then Aunt Sophonisba died, too, and Adam came back from abroad, loaded with academic distinctions and fanatically devoted to his work. Shortly after his return, Anne moved to the city to be near him. By this time she was pushing thirty.

She lived alone in a small apartment in the city. Occasionally she had lunch with some woman who had been a friend of her girlhood but who now inhabited another world. Occasionally she went to a party, at the house of one of the women or at the country club. She became engaged for a third time, this time to a man seventeen or eighteen years older than she, a widower with several children, a substantial lawyer, a pillar of society. He was a good man. He was still vigorous and rather handsome. He even had a sense of humor. But she did not marry him. More and more, as the years passed, she devoted herself to sporadic reading—biography (Daniel Boone or Marie Antoinette), what is called "good fiction," books on social betterment—and to work without pay for a settlement house and an orphanage. She kept her looks very well and continued, in a rather severe way, to pay attention to her dress. There were moments now when her laugh sounded a little hollow and brittle, the laughter of nerves, not of mirth or good spirits. Occasionally in a conversation she seemed to lose track and fall into self-absorption, to start up overwhelmed by embarrassment and unspoken remorse. Occasionally, too, she practiced the gesture of lifting her hands to her brow, one on each side, the fingers just touching the skin or lifting back the hair, the gesture of a delicate distraction. She was pushing thirty-five. But she could still be good company.[14]

14. Excerpted from *All the King's Men,* copyright 1946, 1974 by Robert Penn Warren. Reprinted by permission of Harcourt Brace Jovanovich, Inc. Excerpt appears on pp. 308–309 of the Bantam Books (1974) edition.

The scene above, comprising only 2 pages of a 602-page novel, could make an entire film by itself if treated in detail. Some of what happens to Anne Stanton could be *suggested* by a transitional montage, but no form of cinematic shorthand is capable of really filling in or summarizing a seventeen-year period the way the novelist can. Thus, film is capable of making clear transitions from one time period to another and suggesting the passage of time, but is not so effective at filling in the events that take place between the two periods.

Novelistic Past Tense Versus Cinematic Present Tense

Regardless of the point of view, most novels are written in the past tense, giving the reader a very definite sense that the events happened in the past, and are now being remembered and recounted. In the novel, there is a distinct advantage to using the past tense. It gives us a clear impression that the novelist has had time to think over the events, to measure their importance, reflect on their meaning, and understand their relationship to each other.

On the other hand, even though it may be set in a framework of the past or take us into the past by way of flashback, a film unfolds before our eyes, creating a strong sense of present tense, of a "here and now" experience. The events in a film are not things that once happened and are now being remembered and recalled—they are happening right now as we watch. Various techniques have been employed to overcome this limitation. Special filters have been used to create a sense of a past time, as with the Rembrandt effect in *The Taming of the Shrew,* the hazy and rather faded "memory" images from the *Summer of '42,* or the sepia-toned snapshot stills in *Butch Cassidy and the Sundance Kid.* In *To Kill a Mockingbird,* voice-over narration was used to capture the past tense, the sense of experience remembered.This was accomplished by a narrator's voice, obviously that of an adult, recalling childhood experiences (Fig. 10.4).

Another important distinction is the time spent in experiencing a novel versus that spent in watching a film. If the novel is long, readers may linger in its world for days or even weeks. They can control the pace and stretch the experience out as much as they like; they can even reread passages that interest them. And readers can take time out from the reading process, stopping or freezing

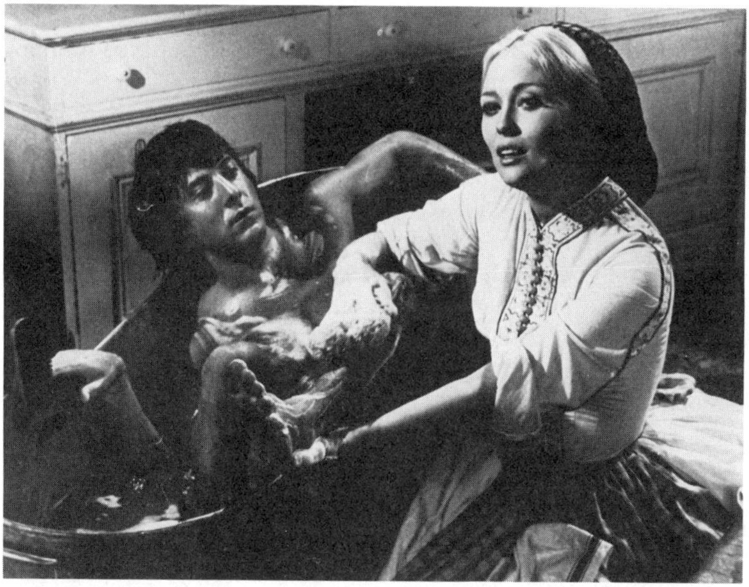

| 10.4 | Cinematic Past Tense: In *Little Big Man,* Dustin Hoffman was made up to look 121 years old to portray Jack Crabb, the sole survivor of Custer's last stand. The old man is being interviewed by a historian as the film begins, and as Crabb recounts his adventures, the film flashes back to scenes from his youth like the one above, with Faye Dunaway bathing the young Crabb.

the novel's flow to reflect on the writer's ideas at a certain point. In film, however, the pace is predetermined. The visual flow, the sparkling stream of images moves on. Beautiful images, significant truths, strong lines of dialogue cannot be replayed. Thus the very quickness with which a film sweeps by—its quality of cinematic restlessness—distinguishes it from the novel.

Other Factors Influencing Adaptations of Novels

Commercial considerations also play an extremely important role in determining whether or not a novel will be made into a film. A unique commercial interrelationship exists between film and novel. A best-selling novel may virtually assure a profit for the producer making a film version, whether the novel in question has real cinematic potential or not, because of the public's familiarity with the novel. In turn, a screen version that is a box-office success will further increase sales of the novel. A first-class film adaptation of an unknown novel may even make such a novel a best-seller.

In recent years, there has been a steadily increasing trend toward the *spin-off novel,* a novel written *after* the screenplay. Such novels as *2001: A Space Odyssey, Last Tango in Paris,* and

Love Story were written after the screenplays were completed. Spin-off novels not only sell well because they are based on popular films, but if released while the films are still playing, they help to promote box-office success as well. One of the best of these novels, Herman Raucher's *Summer of '42,* was released before the film and became a best-seller.

The popularity of a novel may also influence the filmmaker in the adaptation. If filmmakers know that a large percentage of their audience will be familiar with the novel, they can make creative decisions based on this assumption. Ideally, film adaptations of such novels should be fairly true to the novel: Creative tampering with the basic plot should be kept to a minimum, and the most important characters should be left unchanged and carefully cast. Most importantly perhaps, the director should attempt to capture the overall emotional spirit or tone of the novel. If creative and selective choices are carefully made in terms of a true understanding and appreciation of the novel, the filmmaker can remind viewers who have read the novel of the rich emotional and philosophical material beneath the surface and make them feel its presence.

Occasionally an outstanding film, such as *The World According to Garp,* may even be able to communicate or at least suggest the meaning that lies beneath the surface to those who haven't read the novel.

Some filmmakers seem to make the opposite assumption: that very few filmgoers will know the novel. These filmmakers totally disregard the basic spirit or essence of the novel in adapting it to film, thus destroying the film completely for those familiar with the novel. In such cases, the film must be judged as a completely distinct work of art. This type of film, a very loose adaptation, may actually be better suited to the medium than the close adaptation, and may seem a better film to those not familiar with the novel. Thus, a viewer who read the novel before seeing a film may have a distinct advantage when the film depends on the viewer's knowledge of the novel. But when the filmmaker so deviates from the essence of the novel as to create an entirely different work, reading the novel before seeing the film is a real disadvantage. By not knowing the novel, the filmgoer will be able to judge the film without preconceived notions—simply as a film.

It is often advantageous to see the film before reading the novel, for the film may provide a great aid to our visual imagination, and we may then read the novel with relatively clear-cut ideas of how the characters look and sound.

QUESTIONS

On Adaptations of Novels

After reading the novel, but before seeing the film, consider the following questions concerning the novel.

1. How well is the novel suited for adaptation to the screen? What natural cinematic possibilities does it have?
2. Judged as a whole, does the novel come closer to stressing a sensuous and emotional rendering of experience (as in the Hemingway excerpts), or an intellectual analysis of experience (as in the James excerpt)?
3. How essential is the author's verbal style to the spirit or essence of the novel? Could this verbal style be effectively translated into a pictorial style?
4. What is the novel's point of view? What will necessarily be lost by translating the story into film?
5. If the novel is written in the first-person point of view (as told by a participant in the action), how much of the spirit of the novel is expressed through the narrator's unique narrative style—that is, the particular flair or flavor built into his *way of telling* the story rather than the story itself? Could this verbal style be suggested through a minimum of voice-over narration of the soundtrack, so that the device would not seem unnatural? Is the feeling of a warm, intimate relationship between reader and narrator established by the novel, as though the story is being told by a very close friend? How could this feeling be captured by the film?
6. Is the novel's length suited to a close adaptation, or must it be drastically cut to fit the usual film format? Which choice would seem most logical for the filmmaker in adapting the novel:
   a. Should he or she try to capture a sense of the novel's wholeness by hitting the high points without trying to fill in all the gaps? What high points do you think must be dramatized?
   b. Should the filmmaker limit himself or herself to a thorough dramatization of just a part of the novel? What part of the novel could be thoroughly dramatized to make a complete film? What part of the story or what subplots should be left out of the film version?
7. How much of the novel's essence depends on the rendition of mental states: memories, dreams, or philosophical reflections? How effectively can the film version be expected to express or at least suggest these things?

8. How much detail does the author provide on the origins and past history of the characters? How much of this material can be conveyed cinematically?
9. What is the total time period covered by the novel? Can the time period covered be adequately compressed into a normal-length film?

   After seeing the film version, reconsider your answers to the questions above, and also answer those following.

10. Is the film version a close or a loose adaptation of the novel? If it is a loose adaptation, is the departure from the novel due to the problems caused by changing from one medium to another, or by the change in creative personnel?
11. Does the film version successfully capture the spirit or essence of the novel? If not, why does it fail?
12. What are the major differences between the novel and the film, and how can you explain the reasons for these differences?
13. Does the film version successfully suggest meanings that lie beneath the surface and remind you of their presence in the novel? In which scenes is this accomplished?
14. Did having read the novel enhance the experience of seeing the film, or did it take away from it? Why?
15. How well do the actors in the film fit your preconceived notions of the characters in the novel? Which actors exactly fit your mental image of the characters? How do the actors who don't seem properly cast vary from your mental image? Can you justify, from the director's point of view, the casting of these actors who don't seem to fit the characters in the novel?

ADAPTATIONS OF PLAYS

We can, of course, expect more similarity in a film adaptation of a play than a novel. To begin with, the problems of length and point of view are minimized. The actual running time for a play (not including time between acts or scenes) is seldom longer than three hours. Although some cutting in length generally occurs, and some selectivity and change may be apparent, these changes are usually not drastic.

The difference in point of view is primarily that theatergoers are bound to a single point of view because they must stay in their seats while the film version can use any one of the four cinematic viewpoints, spiriting the viewers back and forth, around and about, so that they see the action from a variety of viewpoints. Through the use of close-ups, the filmmaker can give us a sense of physical and emotional closeness, and of being involved in the action. This kind of closeness can sometimes be achieved in the small or intimate theater, but the point of view and the physical distance between theatergoer and actors remain essentially the same throughout the play.

In both mediums the director is able to comment on or interpret the action for the audience, but the film director probably has more options and techniques available for expressing subjective-interpretive views. Stage directors must rely primarily on lighting for these effects, while screen directors have at their command such additional techniques as fast motion, slow motion, distorting lenses, changes from sharp to soft focus, music and so on. Some carry-over exists between the two media, however, for some stage productions have begun simulating certain cinematic effects. For example, a flashing strobe light on actors in motion gives the effect of the fast, jerky motion of the early silent comedies, and such devices are used by stage directors for this effect.

Structural Divisions

Films and plays differ, however, in the fact that plays have clear-cut structural divisions called acts or scenes, which influence the positioning of peaks of dramatic power and intensity. The end of an act, for example, may build to a roaring emotional peak, setting up a strong dramatic echo to carry over into the next act. Although film has *sequences*, which roughly correspond to acts in plays, the flow in one continuous sequence flows smoothly into the next. Sometimes there are similarities even here, however, for the *freeze frame* gives a sequence a sense of ending in much the same way the end of an act might. The cinematic device also approximates the old effect of the *tableau*, where the actors froze themselves in dramatic postures for a few seconds before the curtain in order to etch the scene deeply in the audience's memory.

Such structural divisions may in some cases work well in both mediums, but sometimes an end of a stage act builds up too high a pitch for a cinema sequence, where its power would seem unnatural or out of place. A perceptive critic such as Renata Adler can spot such problems, as she does in her review of *The Lion in*

| 10.5 | Film as a Restless Medium: Goldie Hawn takes the blind Edward Albert on a brief shopping trip to get away from the apartment. The apartment provided the only setting for the stage play version of *Butterflies Are Free.*

Winter: "The film is far too faithful to the play. It divides neatly into acts, has a long sag in the middle, is weakest in its climaxes."[15]

Sense of Space

The change most certain to occur in a film adaptation of a play is the breaking out of the tight confining physical bonds and limitations imposed by the stage setting. Some kind of movement in space is almost essential to film, and to keep the image moving, the filmmaker will usually expand the concepts of visual space involved (Fig. 10.5). He or she may find some excuse to get the action moved outdoors for a while at least, or will introduce as much camera movement and editorial cuts between different viewpoints as possible to keep the image alive. In the film version of *Who's Afraid of Virginia Woolf?* for example, Mike Nichols moved the camera about constantly, dollying it down hallways and around corners for cinematic effect. He also extended space by adding the scene in the roadhouse, which required a wild car ride for getting there and back, whereas in the play, this scene was

15. Renata Adler, *A Year in the Dark.* New York: Berkley Medallion Books, 1971, p. 302.

confined to the living room set. The film of *Long Day's Journey into Night* did not go to such extremes, but it employed camera movement and editing effectively to keep the image alive in what was essentially a very confining set.

Such changes may alter a play's total effect significantly. The fact that the movement in a play is narrowly confined and restricted may serve a powerful end. By keeping the physical action and movement static, by narrowing the physical boundaries in which the characters operate and bottling up the dramatic scene, the director is often able to intensify the conflict. The dramatic tension among characters in psychological conflict seems more explosive when it is physically confined. For example, in the stage version of *Virginia Woolf* the guests, Nick and Honey, are virtually prisoners in the home of George and Martha. The narrow confines of the set stress the feeling. While the trip to the roadhouse in the film version adds a cinematic quality, it also relaxes this tension of confinement to some degree. Thus, dramatic tension created by psychological conflicts and developed through verbal means is often more potentially explosive when its physical setting is narrow and confined (Fig. 10.6).

Film is simply better and more naturally suited to action and movement, the kind provided by physical conflicts on an epic scale. The restless need for motion built into the film medium

| 10.6 | Four Characters on a Powder Keg: The tightly confined set of *Who's Afraid of Virginia Woolf?* makes the psychological conflicts even more explosive.

makes it difficult to cope with static, confined dramatic tension. Film builds its tension best through rhythmic physical action and especially by physical movement toward resolution. A typical example of cinematic tension and its emphasis on movement occurs in *Shane*. The tension is established through violent conflict in a prolonged fistfight between Shane (Alan Ladd) and Joe Starret (Van Heflin) to see who will ride into town for the big showdown. The movement and rhythm of Shane's ride to town further add to the building tension cinematically. Film is also better equipped to portray physical conflict than the stage. Camera angles, sound effects, and the ability to draw the viewer into close emotional involvement make a fistfight much more real than it could ever appear on stage.

Film Language Versus Stage Language

The special qualities that make film a unique medium call for an approach to dialogue that is also unique. Thus we can expect film dialogue to differ from stage dialogue. Generally, film dialogue is simpler than that used on the stage. Because the visual image carries so much more weight in film than on the stage, much that might require dialogue on the stage is stated pictorially in film. Filmmakers generally prefer to advance by showing what happens rather than by having someone—a character or narrator—tell what happens. Because of the additional burden carried by the visual element, film dialogue may be simpler, more casual, and even less poetic. Poetic dialogue is much better suited to the stage than to the film.

To some degree, differences in dialogue may be related to other differences in the medium. For example, the more physical space is expanded, the more dominant action and movement become, and the less natural poetic dialogue becomes. Consider what Renata Adler said of Zefferelli's *Romeo and Juliet:* "The prose suffers a bit, sounding more like *West Side Story* than perhaps it ought to. In the classic speeches, one begins to worry about diction and wish the modern world would recede and let Shakespeare play through."[16] But Ms. Adler has failed to take into account the basic difference between film language and stage language. Stage language—ornate, complex, refined, and poetic—carries the major burden of communication in a Shakespeare play. But in Zeffer-

16. Ibid., p. 287.

| 10.7 | Cinematic Shakespeare: Olivia Hussey as Juliet and Leonard Whiting as Romeo in a scene from Franco Zeffirelli's version of *Romeo and Juliet.*

elli's *Romeo and Juliet* (and *Taming of the Shrew*), we see a new Shakespeare, a more cinematic Shakespeare than had ever been produced before, created by a director who understands his medium well enough to recognize its limitations and utilize its strengths without holding the usual worshipful attitude toward the language of another medium. Zefferelli's *Romeo and Juliet* is a visual, cinematic experience rather than a verbal and "dramatic" one; the director captures the spirit and essence of Shakespeare's play without using the entire text. The result is what Zefferelli intended: good cinema, not pure Shakespeare (Fig. 10.7).

Thus language that is too refined, too elaborate, and too poetic is generally out of place and unnatural in film. If film is to speak poetically, it must do so not with words but with its primary element—the image.

Stage Conventions Versus Cinema Conventions

Certain conventions that are perfectly acceptable on the stage cannot always be reproduced cinematically. Among these is the Shakespearean soliloquy. In Sir Laurence Olivier's adaptation of *Hamlet,* for example, the "Frailty, Thy Name Is Woman" soliloquy is filmed in the following manner: Through some parts of the

| 10.8 | Stage Convention into Film: Sir Laurence Olivier tried several variations on the Shakespearean convention in the "Frailty, thy name is woman. . ." soliloquy in his 1947 *Hamlet* but failed to create a natural cinematic equivalent (Culver Pictures).

speech, Hamlet's face is pictured in tight close-up without lip movement, while Olivier's voice speaks the lines on the soundtrack as an interior monologue. At times, however, Hamlet's lips move, perhaps to show the intensity of his thought. Whatever the intention, the Shakespearean soliloquy, with its ornate, poetic language and structure, does not translate effectively as a cinematic interior monologue, and it seems equally artificial if done as it would be on the stage (Fig. 10.8).

Another stage convention that cannot always be translated in cinematic or visual terms is retrospective narrative, the recounting of past events in stage dialogue. Under some conditions such material is ideally suited for the cinematic flashback, but not in all cases. In Universal's 1968 version of *Oedipus the King,* for example, the "official" story of the murder of King Laius, that he was killed by a band of robbers, is recounted and accompanied by a flashback showing the murder as described. The problem is that we know that Oedipus himself killed Laius and his escorts single-handedly. Our difficulty with the flashback is that it pictures an event that did not really happen. When we see the scene in flashback, therefore, we are confused. We have seen a false version of the event take place before our eyes, but it has a semblance of truth that the *telling* of an event does not necessarily have. For this reason, the cinematic flashback does not work well with past events that are not recounted accurately or truthfully in dialogue. The fact that a later flashback may show the event as it actually happened does little to overcome the fact that the untrue flashback is not natural to the cinema.

Surrealistic and expressionistic renderings of the stage set also cause difficulties in translation to the film. To some degree, they can be represented or suggested through the use of special camera techniques, such as unusual points of view and distorting lenses. But for the most part we expect the physical setting and background in film to be realistic; for example, today we would probably reject as noncinematic the kind of distorted set used in *The Cabinet of Dr. Caligari,* made in 1919. If *Caligari* were remade, it would probably achieve its strange effects solely through the use of special filters and distorting lenses (Fig. 10.9). Whereas the stage audience expects and accepts the stage set or some part of it to suggest or represent reality without being real, the film audience is conditioned to real settings, and will accept no substitute.

These and many other conventions of the stage do not carry over into cinematic form, or at least cannot be replaced with an exact cinematic equivalent.

|10.9| Expressionistic Distortion of the Set: Robert Wiene's *The Cabinet of Dr. Caligari,* 1919.

Other Changes

Several other types of changes can be expected in an adaptation from a play. Even if the actors were available, the screen version may not use the same cast as the stage play, either because some of the stage actors cannot be convincing in front of the camera, or because a big name is needed as a box-office attraction.

In the past, the big-city theater audience was assumed to be more sophisticated than the nationwide movie audience, and changes were made with this difference in mind. An effort was usually made to simplify the play in the film version, and harsh language was censored to some degree. Endings were even changed to conform to expectations of the mass audience. The stage version of *The Bad Seed* (1956), for example, ends chillingly with little Rhoda, the beautiful but evil child-murderess who has killed at least three people, alive and well, still charming her naive and unsuspecting father. In the ending of the film version, however, she is struck with lightning; thus, the demands of the mass audience for poetic justice were satisfied. Such changes, of course,

| 10.10 | Poetic Justice: Sweet little Rhoda (Patty McCormack), shown here charming her mother (Nancy Kelly) in a scene from the film version of *The Bad Seed,* died at the end of the film but survived in the play (Culver Pictures).

are less frequent since the Motion Picture Rating System went into effect in the late 1960s. A modern version, in fact, would probably keep her alive for a possible sequel (Fig. 10.10).

QUESTIONS

On Adaptations of Plays

1. How does the film version differ from the play in terms of its concept of physical space? How does this affect the overall spirit or tone of the film version?
2. How cinematic is the film version? How does it use special camera and editing techniques to keep the visual flow of images in motion and to avoid the static quality of a filmed stage play?
3. What events does the filmmaker "show" happening that are only described in dialogue during the play? How effective are these added scenes?
4. Are the play's structural divisions (into acts and scenes) still apparent in the film, or does the film successfully blend these divided parts into a unified cinematic whole?

5. What stage conventions employed in the play are not translatable into cinematic equivalents? What difficulties and changes does this bring about?
6. How does the acting style of the film differ from that of the play? What factors enter into these differences?
7. What basic differences can be observed in the nature of the dialogue in the two versions? Are individual speeches generally longer in the play or in the film? In which version is the poetic quality of the language more apparent?
8. What other important changes have been made in the film version? Can you justify these in terms of change in medium, change in creative personnel, or differences in moral attitudes and sophistication of the intended audience?

CHAPTER 11

GENRE, REMAKES, AND SEQUELS

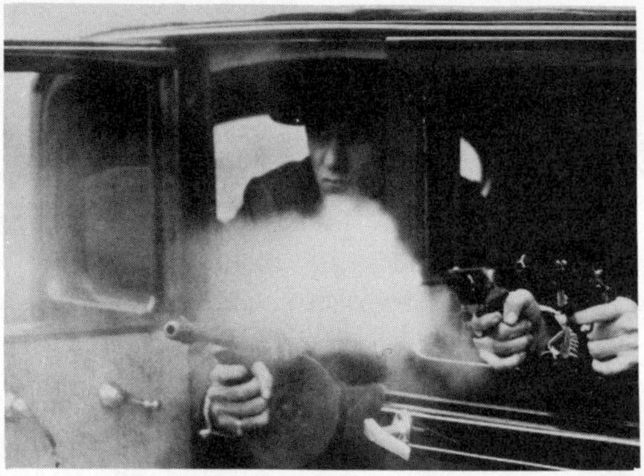

THE GENRE FILM

The term "genre film" refers to those film stories that have been repeated again and again in the same way, with slight variations. They follow the same basic pattern or formula, and include the same basic ingredients: setting, characters, plot (conflict and resolution), basic images, cinematic techniques, and conventions are practically interchangeable from one film to another in the same genre. (Much as the parts for Henry Ford's Model T were interchangeable from one car to another.)

It is important that we restrict our definition of the term genre to mean only the *formula* film. This problem arises because the term "genre" is often used broadly to refer to films dealing with a common subject matter. For example, Rex Reed said in his *Holiday* review of *Patton* and *M*A*S*H* that those films "raise the artistic level of the war-movie genre."[1] Since these are not formula films at all, they fail to fit our definition. Therefore, when we use the term "genre," we will be using it only as a synonym for "formula."

It is not really difficult to understand how these genre or formula films came into being, or why they have enjoyed such popular success. The repetition of the same basic formulas came about as a result of a unique interaction between the studio system and the mass popular audience. Because film production has always been an expensive undertaking, the studios were naturally interested in producing films that would draw a large audience, so they could realize a substantial profit. Thus the reaction of the mass audience, in flocking to westerns, gangster films, detective films, comedies, and musicals, let the studios know what the audience wanted (and expected), and the studios responded to the great popular success of these films by repeating the formulas.

Values

It must be remembered that the audience for which these assembly-line films were produced was in every sense of the word a "mass" audience, including all layers of society and, in the mid-to-late 1940s, numbering nearly ninety million viewers per week.

1. "Rex Reed at the Movies: From Blood and Guts to Guts and Blood." *Holiday Magazine*, vol. 47, no. 4, April 1970, p. 24. Permission to reprint granted by Travel Magazine, Inc., Floral Park, New York 11001.

Thus the true genre films constitute a fairly unsophisticated art form designed for a large number of unsophisticated people, and the popularity of these films was at least partly due to their ability to reinforce basic American beliefs, values, and myths.

All American films were encouraged to reflect and reinforce middle-class American institutions, values, and morality by the Motion Picture Production Code, which was enforced from the early 1930s until around 1960. (See Chapter 13.) But the sincerity of the genre films seems to indicate that, for the most part, the studio heads and directors probably shared those values.

The audience obviously took great pleasure in seeing their values threatened, and then triumph, for the triumph reinforced their belief in the strength and validity of these values and made them feel secure in "Truth, Justice, and the American Way." And these films completely fulfilled their expectations with easy, complete, and totally satisfying resolutions.

Variations and Refinements on the Formula

As the success of the genre films inspired continued repetition of the basic formulas, their popularity presented the studios and the directors assigned to direct them with an interesting challenge: So that the public would not become bored or "burned out," they were forced to introduce variations and refinements of the various genre conventions, while still keeping enough of the formula or pattern intact to insure success (much the same way that Volkswagen introduced variations and refinements every year or two into its popular Beetle, without significantly altering the essential values or familiar look of the beloved "basic Bug").

The Strengths of the Genre Film

For the director, there were certain advantages to working within a given genre. Because the characters, the plot formula, and the conventions were already established, they provided the director with a kind of cinematic shorthand that greatly simplified the task of storytelling. Since formula stories were easy for the audience to understand, they were also easier for the director to put on film.

But the good directors did not simply copy the conventions and string together a thoroughly predictable pattern of stock situations and images. Accepting the limitations and set formal patterns of the genre as a challenge, some of the better directors such as John Ford provided creative variations, refinements, and complexities that imprinted each film they directed with a rich and distinctive personal style.

The genre film also simplifies film watching. We don't, for example, have to "study" characters in a western. Because of the genre conventions of appearance, dress, social manners, and typecasting, the hero, sidekick, villain, female lead, and so on are prepackaged and prelabeled—we recognize them on sight, and know they will not violate our expectations of their conventional roles. And our familiarity with the genre not only makes watching easier, but in some ways more enjoyable. Since we know and are familiar with all the conventions of the genre, we gain pleasure from recognizing each character, each image, each stock situation. As they are revealed, our expectations are satisfied. The fact that the formula and conventions have been established and repeated also intensifies another kind of pleasure. Settled into a familiar, comfortable formula, with our basic expectations satisfied, we also become more keenly aware and responsive to the creative variations, refinements, and complexities that make the film seem fresh and original, and by exceeding our expectations each innovation becomes an exciting surprise.

The Formulas

While each genre has its own formula, it is perhaps easier to recognize a genre film than it is to delineate clearly all the elements of its formula. While the basic formula may seem simple when viewed from the distance of memory, observation reveals that the variations are almost infinite. The first task, therefore, is to compose a basic formula from memory, and test it against observation. The basic elements of a genre formula can be grouped under six distinct headings: characters, setting, conventions, conflict, resolution, and the values reaffirmed. The following examples are attempts to crystallize the formula elements of the western and gangster film.

THE WESTERN FORMULA

Setting The American west or southwest, west of the Mississippi River, usually at the edge of the frontier, where civilization encroaches upon the free, savage, untamed land beyond. Time span is usually between 1865 and 1900.

Western Hero The western hero is a rugged individualist, a "natural" man of the frontier, often a mysterious loner. Somewhat aloof, and very much his own man, he acts in accordance with his personal code, not according to community pressures or for personal gain. ("A man's got to do what a man's got to do.") His personal code emphasizes human dignity, courage, justice, fair play, equality (the rights of the underdog), and respect for women. Intelligent and resourceful, he is also kind, honest, firm, and consistent in his dealings with others, never devious, cruel, or petty. Even-tempered and peaceable by nature, he does not seek violent solutions, but responds with violent action *when the situation demands it.* Extraordinarily quick *and* accurate with pistol or rifle, he is also adept at horsemanship and barroom brawling, and is quietly confident of his own abilities. He can act as a capable leader or alone, as the situation requires. As a loner, he stands apart from the community, but believes in and fights to preserve its values. His lack of community ties (he usually has no job, no ranch or possessions, no wife or family) gives him the freedom and flexibility for full-time heroics. As a lawman or cavalry officer, however, his independence diminishes. Peace makes him restless. With order restored, he moves on to discover another troubled community (Fig. 11.1).

| 11.1 | The Western Hero: One of the most durable of American heroic types is the western or cowboy hero, who represented essentially the same code of values in hundreds of films over a span of four decades. Pictured is Bob Steele, a typical western hero of the '40s.

Heroine Four basic types seem to prevail. The first two are ranchers' daughters. (1) If the ranch is big and the father wealthy, she may be a southern lady of the *Gone with the Wind* school. (2) If the ranch is smaller and the father struggling, she may be the tomboy type, beautiful but tough and independent. (3) The schoolmarm is a product of eastern refinement, intelligent but helpless. (4) The dance-hall girl is worldly wise, with a tough exterior but a heart of gold.

Villain Two categories of villain seem to prevail. The first would include savages and outlaws (the uncivilized elements of the untamed frontier), who bully, threaten, and generally terrorize the respectable elements of the frontier community, trying to take what they want by force: rustling cattle, robbing banks or stages, or attacking stagecoaches, wagon trains, forts, or ranches. The other category works under the guise of respectability: crooked bankers, saloon owners, and sheriffs, or wealthy ranchers, all motivated by greed for wealth or lust for power. Slick, devious, and underhanded in their methods, they may hire or manipulate savages and outlaws to bring about their goals.

Real motives for Indian hostility are seldom developed. Indians are viewed not as individuals but en masse, innately savage and cruel, like a pack of mad dogs. Sometimes they are led by crazed chieftains seeking vengeance for past crimes against their tribe, or they are manipulated by renegade whites to facilitate their own evil purposes.

In some cases the villain, in addition to his present crimes, has harmed the hero in the past, leading to a more personal and intense desire for vengeance.

Other Important Characters The *sidekick* and the *initiate hero:* If the hero does not ride alone, he will often be accompanied by a single sidekick or initiate hero, or both. The *sidekick* is usually a comic character who provides a dramatic foil for the serious, rugged hero. While the sidekick is usually older than the hero, the *initiate hero* is younger. Clean-cut, handsome, and a bit naive, the initiate hero is a kind of son figure, anxious for maturity, but not quite there. Loyal and courageous, he tries to follow the hero's example and live up to his code.

Conflict Society (town, civilized ranches, wagon trains, stagecoaches, or forts) are threatened from within by corruption and greed or from uncivilized forces from outside (outlaws or savages).

Resolution Led by the hero, the "decent" citizens root out the corrupt villains within the community or succeed in fighting off the outlaws or savages attacking the society from without. The villains not killed in the gunfights are frightened off or imprisoned. With the society in decent, just, and capable hands, the hero is free to "move on."

Values Reaffirmed Justice has prevailed, civilization has conquered savagery, and good has triumphed over evil. Law and order are restored or established, and progress toward a better life on the frontier may resume.

Conventions The conventions of the western are so familiar that they need little description. To begin with, there is a clear and simple definition of character types by conventions of costume and grooming. The hero wears a white (or light-colored) hat, the villain a black hat. Heroes are clean-cut and clean-shaven. Mustaches are reserved for villains. Sidekicks and villains may have beards, but sidekick beards are gray and rustic, while villains' beards are black and impeccably groomed. To detail the differences in dress and appearance is unnecessary. We recognize the basic roles of the actors when we first see them.

While all other weapons are standard factory-produced guns, the hero's are unique, custom-made: pearl handles, filed sights, hair triggers, etc.

In addition to conventions of dress, appearance, and weapons, there are conventions of action. Most westerns, for example, will have one or more of the following: a climactic shoot-out between the hero and villain in the town's only street (Fig. 11.2) or among the rocks of a canyon, a prolonged chase scene on horseback (usually accompanied by shooting), a knock-down drag-out barroom brawl (with a scared bartender periodically ducking behind the bar), and a cavalry to the rescue scene.

While a love interest may develop between hero and heroine, and the attraction may be apparent, it never reaches fruition, and the hero moves on at the end. To create tension and direct more attention to the love interest, the heroine often misunderstands the hero's motives or his actions until the final climax, when he regains her trust and respect before goodbyes are said.

At least one convention is structural. Many westerns begin with the hero riding into view from the left side of the screen and end

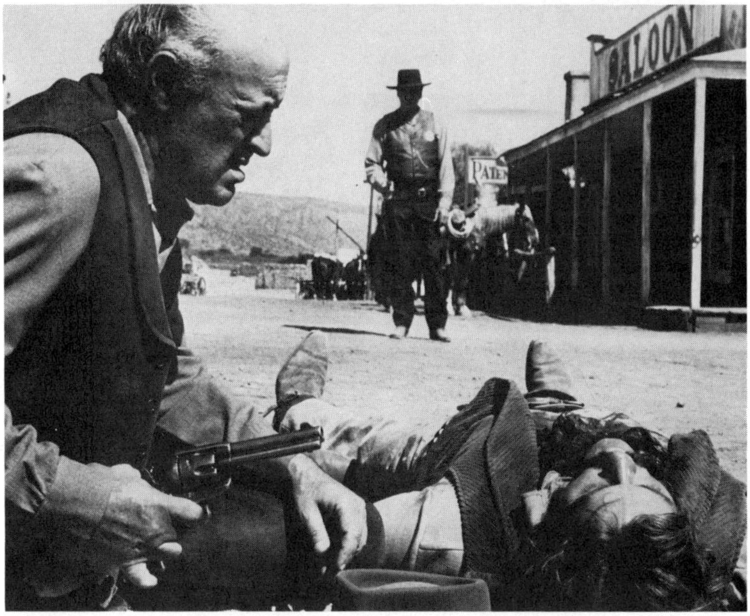

|11.2| Western Convention—The Main Street Shoot-Out: Scenes like this were part of almost every formula western, and the convention survived in more "adult" westerns like *Lawman* (1971).

with him riding off in the opposite direction, usually into a fading sunset.

THE GANGSTER FILM FORMULA

Setting The gangster film usually takes place in the "concrete jungle," among the endless streets and crowded buildings of an already decaying older part of the modern city. Much of the action occurs at night, and rain is often used to add atmosphere. The rural bandit gangster film, a variation on this, would set the action in a rural setting, with small depressed towns, roadhouses, and filling stations.

Gangster Hero The gangster hero is a brutal, aggressive, lone-wolf type. He is cocky and ambitious, the self-made man who fought his way up from nothing and graduated from the school of hard knocks (Fig. 11.3).

Henchmen The gangster's henchmen, who gain courage from their association with his power, are generally ignorant and nonverbal. Ususally there are at least three: a confession specialist ("I can make him talk, boss"), a henchman as blindly loyal as the family dog, and a henchman who is not only disloyal but too ambitious for his own good.

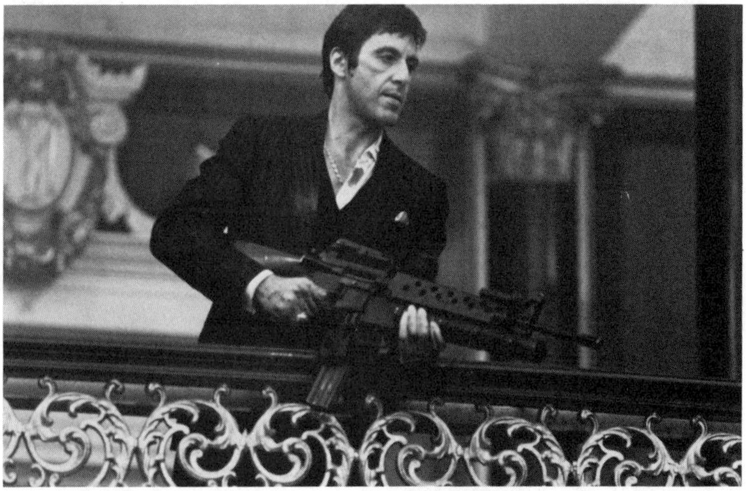

|11.3| The Gangster Hero: Al Pacino as "Scarface" Tony Montana in the 1983 remake of *Scarface* plays a character who fits practically every condition of the gangster hero formula.

Women Women are sexual ornaments, symbols of the hero's status. They are cheap, mindless, and greedy, totally fascinated by the hero's cruelty and power. Sometimes a decent, intelligent woman associates with the hero early in the film, but soon discovers his true nature and abandons him. The gangster's mother and sister are civilized and social women with traditional values; the mother is respected, the sister protected.

Gun Moll The gun moll is more intelligent and independent than the "sexual ornaments." Treated as a companion instead of a plaything, she's tough and cynical enough to function as the hero's partner in crime.

Conflict On the most abstract level, the basic conflict is the anarchy of the gangsters against the social order. Since the police represent the social order, the conflict also involves cops versus robbers. There is usually a conflict of robbers versus robbers, with the struggle involving leadership of the gang or a territorial-rights gang war against a rival mob. An internal conflict within the hero is also probable, with his latent good or social instincts struggling for expression against his essentially cruel and selfish nature.

Resolution The hero achieves success temporarily, but eventually meets his deserved end. Although he may be given a chance for reform and redemption, the criminal side of his nature is too strong to be denied. He often dies in the gutter, in a cowardly, weak manner. His dignity and strength are gone—everything we admired about him is destroyed. The other gang members are either killed or jailed, and the social order is restored.

Values Reaffirmed Justice prevails, good conquers evil, or evil destroys itself. Crime does not pay, and "the weeds of crime bear bitter fruit." Civilized values of human decency, honesty, and respect for law and order are reaffirmed.

Conventions Standard gangster dress is required. The hero is overdressed, usually in double-breasted, pin-striped suits, camel-hair coats, luxurious bathrobes, smoking jackets, etc. When engaged "in business," all gangsters wear overcoats and broad-brimmed hats, with hat brims turned down in front and coat collars up. Women wear gaudy jewelry, cheap-looking makeup, low-cut dresses, and expensive coats.

|11.4| Gangster Film Convention—Erasing the Competition: A typical gangland killing, with lots of blazing guns (including a submachine gun) as pictured in Sergio Leone's *Once Upon a Time in America.*

Machine guns, pistols, and bombs are standard weapons, and machine guns are often carried in violin cases.

At least one chase scene, with passengers in each car exchanging gunfire, is required (Fig. 11.4).

Whiskey and cigars are necessary props for every interior scene, and speakeasies or posh nightclubs are common sites for conducting business.

Montage sequences are frequently used for violent action, featuring fast editing, compression of time, and explosive sound effects (machine-gun fire or bombings).

Stretching and Breaking the Formulas

Such formulas were viable over a fairly long period of time, and offered directors working in such genre films enough flexibility to create a great many interesting innovations. But changes in social values, the advent of television, and a changing movie audience made some of the formula patterns much too limiting. Thus westerns like *Shane* and *High Noon* began to introduce complex new elements into the genre, and the western began to break away from the traditional formula.

Two elements in the formula are probably more important than any others to keeping it viable: the personal code of the hero and the values reaffirmed at the end of the film. When the hero's code is significantly altered, and the basic social values are no longer reaffirmed, the formula vanishes. The western and the gangster film formulas depend on good triumphing over evil, on law and order conquering chaos, on civilization overcoming savagery, and on justice prevailing. When these concepts are brought into question, when gray areas or shades of gray replace clear distinctions between black and white, when the complexities of reality replace the simplicity of myth (and the mythical values of the way things are supposed to be), the formula is destroyed. In like manner, if the western hero becomes an antihero, and is cruel, petty, and overly vengeful, the old formula is gone because our expectations for the hero will not be satisfied (Figs. 11.5, 11.6, and 11.7).

However, if these changes reflect changes within the society and its value system, and new heroic codes are established, a new formula may rise out of the ashes of the old, and this new formula will be repeated so long as those new values and "heroic" codes prevail. But it will be a very different kind of formula, a different

|11.5|

|11.6|

Genre-Based Satire: Most of the humor in recent parodies of film genres is based on our familiarity with their formula plots, characters, and conventions. Films like *Blazing Saddles* (western) [11.5], *Airplane!* (disaster) [11.6], and *Dead Men Don't Wear Plaid* (hard-boiled detective) [11.7], first build on our habitual expectations for their genre and then violate them. Because each of these films incorporates the plot, characters, and conventions of dozens of films, each can also be helpful in studying the genre that it satirizes.

|11.7|

genre. (Although the Volkswagen Beetle incorporated its refinements and variations over a long period of time without altering its basic look and characteristics, when progress finally demanded more significant changes, the "Beetle formula" gave way to the Rabbit, a very different kind of formula.)

QUESTIONS

On the Genre Film

1. Use the formulas for the western and gangster films above as a starting point for the study of a series of three or four films in either genre. How do the films being studied fit the formula? Is the formula valid, or do elements appear in each film that are not part of the formula? Do you find elements in the formula that do not occur in the films studied? Adjust the formula so that it fits all the films under study, then test your adjusted formula against two more films from the genre. As a part of your testing, try interchanging the parts from one film to another. What characters are interchangeable? What subtle differences exist between one character and another? Which corresponding characters could be exchanged without significantly altering the plot?
2. Using the formulas for the gangster film and the western above (or your adjusted versions) as models, study at least three films from any of the following genres and create your own formula for that genre: the hard-boiled detective film, the screwball comedy, the disaster film, the boy-meets-girl musical. Then test your formula against two or three more films. (Also test each film of your formula to see if parts are interchangeable.)
3. Study two or three films by the same director in one genre, along with at least two films by different directors. Are three different directorial styles apparent, or are the styles indistinguishable? Consider the three films by the same director in chronological order. Does he or she incorporate personal stylistic trademarks into each of the three films? What are those trademarks and what makes them stand out?
4. What innovations or refinements on the formula does the director provide? Does the director introduce innovations and further refinements as he or she moves from one film to another? Are the innovations and refinements the director introduces superficial and cosmetic, or are they significant enough to stretch the genre, creating a strain or tension against the outer boundaries of the formula? Does the director seem to learn something new with each film and build on that in the next? Do we see changes in the director's personal vision or world view from one film to another? How are those changes reflected? (For example, does the director seem to grow more serious, or less serious; more pessimistic or more optimistic?)
5. Compare and contrast the styles of two directors working within the same genre. Look at at least two films by each director, and decide how

their styles create important differences within the same genre. (For example, how is a Frank Capra screwball comedy different from a Preston Sturges screwball comedy?)

REMAKES AND SEQUELS

Remakes and sequels are not really new in the motion picture industry, as a picture caption in Kevin Brownlow's *Hollywood: The Pioneers* tells us:

> Violence was discouraged by the Hays Office, but this scene had strong precedents. Fannie Ward had been branded in *The Cheat* (1915), Pola Negri in the 1922 remake, Barbara Castleton in *The Branding Iron* (1920) and now Aileen Pringle in the remake of that, *Body and Soul.*[2]

Although remakes and sequels occur throughout film history, there are certain periods of peak production. The industry's most recent obsession with redoing the tried and true began sometime during the early 1970s and continues today. While it seems strange that Hollywood should be relying on remakes and sequels in a period when the number of feature films being released each year is declining drastically, there are several solid reasons behind this.

The first of these has to do with the tremendous increases in the costs of producing motion pictures. As movies become more expensive to make, the gamble becomes much greater. In a sense, running a movie studio is a lot like running an aircraft factory, but with significant differences. Consider how an aircraft manufacturer would operate if he continually had to build new models, with new configurations, untested control and power systems, and $10 to $20 million of investment in each plane. When finished, a plane would taxi to the runway, develop tremendous speed, and try to get off the ground. At this point, there would be no turning back. If it flew it flew, but if it crashed, most of the investment would be lost. Aircraft executives operating such a business would be very careful with the planes they designed, and there would be a great many remakes and sequels turned out.

2. Kevin Brownlow, *Hollywood: The Pioneers*. London: William Collins Sons and Co. Ltd., 1979, p. 129.

Of course the aircraft industry doesn't really operate this way. There are long periods of testing new models, with very little risk. Miniature models can be tested in a wind tunnel and then actually flown before the full-size prototype takes to the air. Some reliable constants also provide security: The laws of physics and aerodynamics do not change. They are constant and predictable. This is not true in the motion picture industry. There is really no way to test miniature versions in wind tunnels, and a film's success (its ability to fly) is not based on predictable constants like the laws of physics and aerodynamics, but on the unpredictable and whimsical laws of human likes and dislikes. Remakes and sequels at least have some degree of predictability in the marketplace.

Paul Schrader, director for the 1982 remake of *Cat People,* looks on most remakes with contempt:

> The whole remake trend is an indication of cowardice, obviously. Remakes, sequels, parodies are what I call "back born" movies. They come off something else. With the cost of movies being such, everybody's trying to protect their jobs. For an executive to redo *Animal House* or *Jaws* is clearly a much safer decision.[3]

Perhaps the sad thing about most remakes and sequels is that they are made of movies that, if they are not film classics, have proven by their continuing popularity that they really don't need to be remade at all, and usually don't really beg for a sequel. Therefore, in the kinds of films they choose to remake, the studios are guaranteeing themselves a strange combination of success and failure. The mass audience will go to see remakes of movies they know and love, just out of curiosity. It is almost an irresistible urge to want to make a critical judgment on the remake of any well-known film, probably one of the few laws of human behavior that the studios really can predict and trust. The better the original, and the more popular it is, the more people who can be counted on to see the remake or sequel; thus there is a kind of guarantee of financial return. It is also, however, a kind of guarantee of failure, for the better the original, the higher the expectations of the audience for the remake or sequel, which almost always fails to meet those expectations. (A natural human law governing audience response to remakes and sequels: The higher the expectations, the greater the disappointment.) Al-

3. Stephen Rebello, "Cat People: Paul Schrader Changes His Spots." *American Film,* April 1982, pp. 40–43.

though there are rare exceptions, remakes and sequels generally lack the freshness and creative dynamics of the original, so the disappointment is usually justified.

Taking for granted that the prime motivation for producing remakes and sequels is profit and the improved odds of betting on a proven winner, we should also admit that there are valid reasons for producing remakes and sequels, and there is a creative challenge involved. Directors of remakes have been clear on that point: They want to make creative changes in new versions—they never attempt to make a Xerox copy. These creative changes take different forms and are justified in different ways.

Remakes

Since a reasonably long period of time usually elapses between different versions of the same film, one of the most frequently used justifications for remaking a film is to "update" it. Filmmakers have their own ways of explaining what their goal is in updating a film: In their views, they are usually improving these works by giving them a "more contemporary quality" or providing a "new sensibility for modern audiences."

A movie actually can be updated in a variety of ways:

- **Important changes in style—updating to reflect social change, cinematic styles, lifestyles, or popular tastes:** *Heaven Can Wait* (1980)—a remake of 1941's *Here Comes Mr. Jordan; A Star Is Born* (1954/1976)—new music, new lifestyle, a whole new ambience for an old story (Figs. 11.8 and 11.9); *The Wizard of Oz* (1939)—*The Wiz* (1978)—modern music, black cast, filmed version of Broadway show.
- **Changes in film technology—updating to take advantage of new potential in the art form:** *Stagecoach* (1939/1966)—color, wide-screen, stereophonic sound; *Ben Hur* (1926/1959)—color, wide-screen, stereophonic sound (1926 version was silent); *King Kong* (1933/1976)—color, wide-screen, stereophonic sound, sophisticated animation techniques; *The Thing* (1951/1982)—color, wide-screen, stereophonic sound, special effects.
- **Changes in censorship:** *The Postman Always Rings Twice* (1946/1981)—explicit treatment of steamy passions; *The Blue Lagoon* (1949/1980)—emphasis placed on sexual awakening of young couple.

|11.8|

|11.9|

A Star Is Born Again . . . Again: The 1976 version of *A Star Is Born* [11.9] starring Kris Kristofferson and Barbra Streisand was actually the third retelling of that story. The 1954 edition [11.8], with James Mason and Judy Garland, was a musical remake of the 1937 non-musical drama starring Frederic March and Janet Gaynor.

- **New paranoias:** *Invasion of the Body Snatchers* (1956/1978)—from subconscious fears of communist takeover in the original to fears of Moonie takeover in the remake.
- **The musical version:** A type of remake that usually provides a greater challenge and greater creative freedom for the filmmaker is the "translation" of the film into a musical version, where words and music must be provided that are integrated into the dramatic framework of the original. Examples: *Oliver Twist* (1948) to *Oliver!* (1968); *A Star Is Born* (1937 drama to 1954 musical); *The Philadelphia Story* (1940) to *High Society* (1956); *Lost Horizon* (1937 drama to 1973 musical); *Anna and the King of Siam* (1945 drama) to *The King and I* (1956 musical); and *Pygmalion* (1938 drama) to *My Fair Lady* (1964 musical).
- **Change in format—the TV version:** Television movies have also gotten into the remake business, with the following contributions: *Of Mice and Men* (1939/1981), *The Diary of Anne Frank, All Quiet on the Western Front,* and *From Here to Eternity.*
- **Remakes of foreign films:** The creative challenge of transplanting a film from one culture to another has also produced some interesting results. *Seven Samurai* (Japan, 1954) became *The Magnificent Seven* (USA, 1960); *Smiles of a Summer Night* (Sweden, 1955) became first a Broadway show and later the film *A Little Night Music* (USA, 1978); and most recently, *Breathless*

(France, 1961 to USA, 1983). The 1983 *Breathless* changes the setting from Paris to Los Angeles and reverses the nationalities of the principal characters.

Sequels

The only example in history of a sequel being as good as the original is *Don Quixote,* and I should be crazy to attempt one on *The Razor's Edge.*
SOMERSET MAUGHAM, WHEN ASKED BY PRODUCER DARRYL F. ZANUCK TO WRITE A SEQUEL TO *THE RAZOR'S EDGE*

There is an important difference in the proper timing for remakes versus sequels. Whereas remakes generally allow the original to age for a while (sometimes long enough for a whole new generation or two to come along who may not know the original), sequels have the best chance of success when they follow quickly, so that they can follow in the wake of the original's success. The audience motivation for attending sequels is very similar to that for going to remakes. If they enjoyed the original, they go seeking more of the same, and they are curious as to how well the sequel will stand up to the original. The motivation for sequels is also similar to that for the remake—profit. But the thinking is a little different. In the remake it's a case of "Play it again, Sam. They liked it once, let's make it again." With the sequel, it's a matter of "We've got a good thing going, let's get all the mileage out of it we can" (Figs. 11.10, 11.11, and 11.12).

|11.10|

|11.11|

|11.12|

Maximum Mileage: The success of blockbuster hit *Butch Cassidy and the Sundance Kid* spawned a "prequel" and two sequels. The prequel, *Butch and Sundance: The Early Days* (1979) [11.10], featured William Katt and Tom Berenger (chosen because they looked like younger versions of Redford and Newman) [11.11]. The sequels were both TV movies: *Mrs. Sundance* (1974) starred Elizabeth Montgomery as survivor Etta Place; *Wanted: The Sundance Woman* (1976) [11.12] starred Katharine Ross (the original Etta), and was later retitled *Mrs. Sundance Rides Again.*

|11.13| Parody/Sequel: One of the most successful parodies in recent times is Mel Brooks' *Young Frankenstein.* Through striking black and white cinematography and attention to details of setting and atmosphere, the film captures the style so well that it pays homage to the originals.

|11.14| Continuity in the Sequel: Roy Scheider and Lorraine Gary (seen here in a scene from the original *Jaws*) provided some continuity by appearing in *Jaws II*, but changes in directing, editing, and writing produced a second-rate sequel. *Jaws III* was a dismal attempt to revive 3-D.

There are relatively few good reasons for making a sequel other than to realize the profit potential. There are, of course, some very natural sequels—sequels made simply because there is more story to tell—and these sequels can match the original in quality if this story is continued. First-class sequels, for example, have been made of *The Godfather (The Godfather, Part II)*, and of *The French Connection (The French Connection II)*. Most sequels, however, do not have the natural relationship to their original that these two do.

Because they don't try to tell the same story, but can build on characters already established in the original, sequels give the filmmakers much more room for creative freedom. So long as they pick up some characters from the original, maintain a certain degree of consistency in the treatment of those characters, and retain something of the style of the original, sequels can take off on almost any direction they want to go. A good example of flexibility in sequels can be seen in the sequels to James Whale's original *Frankenstein* (1931), which was followed by *Bride of Frankenstein* (1935), in which Whale introduced odd baroque elements and black humor, and a kind of combo-sequel, *Frankenstein Meets the Wolf Man* (1943). The parody-sequel *Young Frankenstein* (1974) combines elements of both the original Frankenstein films, and succeeds largely because it lovingly recaptures the style of the original (Fig. 11.13).

Much more important than the potential within the original story for a sequel is the interest the characters in the original generate within their audience. If it becomes clear that a large film audience is fascinated with the cast of the original, and would love to see them together again, we can be reasonably sure that a sequel will soon be in the making. On any film where the profit potential looks good enough to "inspire" a sequel, studio contracts with actors will obligate them to do the sequel as well. The continuity provided by keeping the actors of the original in the sequel is tremendously important to box-office appeal. Roy Scheider, Lorraine Gary, and Murray Hamilton, for example, served as important links between *Jaws* and *Jaws II*.

But *Jaws II* also provides an example of how important the behind-the-camera people are to making a successful sequel. When the writers, directors, and editors who participated in the original do not participate in the sequel(s), the film can suffer considerably, often losing the spirit, style, and impact of the original (Fig. 11.14). Therefore, the most successful sequels (or series of sequels) result when the whole "winning team" (actors, director, writers, editor, producers, etc.) stays pretty much intact throughout. The phenomenal success of the *Rocky* series is probably due to the continuing participation of most of the original *Rocky* team, but even that success probably won't last much longer. (Although the *Rocky* team has announced that *Rocky IV* is in the works, Superman seemed a tired, pale shadow of his former self in *Superman III* and hopefully will take a well-deserved rest.)

Similar in some ways to the *Rocky* and *Superman* sequels but very different in many regards from the ordinary "exploitation-of-a-smash-hit" sequel is the "character series." The character series can develop from a series of novels featuring the same character or characters (Tarzan, James Bond, and Sherlock Holmes) or the series may develop around a character or combination of characters appearing in a single film (Fig. 11.15).

If such a character or combination of characters has tremendous audience appeal, the result may be a series of films structured around the character or characters: Abbott and Costello, Crosby and Hope (the "Road" series), Peter Sellers as Inspector Clouseau (in the "Pink Panther" series), and Percy Kilbride and Marjorie Main as Ma and Pa Kettle (Fig. 11.16). *Raiders of the Lost Ark* and *Indiana Jones and the Temple of Doom* may be the start of a new character series.

|11.15| Long-Running Character Series: Chief Inspector Jacques Clouseau, the character played by Peter Sellers in *The Pink Panther* series, enjoyed a long and prosperous life, even after the great comic actor's death. When Sellers died after completing five *Pink Panther* films, director Blake Edwards put together a sixth, *The Trail of the Pink Panther,* made from outtakes (unused footage) from the earlier films woven into a new story featuring some of the series actors.

|11.16| Spin-Off Characters: The characters of Ma and Pa Kettle (played by Marjorie Main and Percy Kilbride, shown) were such a hit in the film version of Betty MacDonald's novel *The Egg and I* (1947) that they became the stars of a seven-film series between 1949 and 1953. These cheaply budgeted films extolling the virtues of small-town American life were the most profitable films produced by Universal Studios for several years running.

In the character series, continuation of the actors from one film to the next is essential, but so is good writing built around consistency of character. The overall style of the series should be consistent. In this way, audience expectations are satisfied, guaranteeing their return to the next film in the series. This audience need for the predictable, for seeing familiar faces in familiar kinds of story formats, has been almost completely satisfied by weekly situation comedies and dramatic series on television.

In rare cases, a series of films are designed as parts of a preconceived larger whole. Although each film can stand on its own as a unified work, each is linked by characters, setting, and events to a larger whole. George Lucas' *Star Wars* (1977), *The Empire Strikes Back* (1980), and *The Return of the Jedi* (1983) were designed as a trilogy. Their titles suggest that *Young Tom Edison* (1940) and *Edison, the Man* (1940) were designed to dovetail for a full Edison biography. Although the profit motive might also be involved in such plans, the writing and dramatic power should be superior to the "Hey! That one worked! Let's whip out a sequel!" kind of afterthought.

QUESTIONS

On Remakes and Sequels

1. Was the remake really necessary? Why is the older version outdated? Why do modern audiences need the story retold? What were the aspects of the original film that were inaccessible to modern audiences? Are these inaccessible aspects so important as to make the film incomprehensible to contemporary filmgoers, or are they relatively insignificant?
2. What important changes were made in the remake? Why were they made? Which changes would you consider improvements over the original, and which would you consider only changes?
3. Which is the better film? Does the remake have the freshness and the creative dynamic of the original? Were you disappointed in the remake? Why?
4. How is the remake like the original? Is an effort made through casting, cinematic style, etc., to capture the spirit and the flavor of the original? Do these efforts succeed?

5. If the remake is a musical version, how well is the spirit and story of the original captured in the words and music of the songs? What major changes in plot or setting had to be made in the musical version? How are the characters changed?
6. What advantages does the remake have over the original in terms of freedom from censorship and new technology in the medium? How does it make use of these advantages?
7. If the remake involves a foreign original, how does a change of setting, language, or cultural values affect the remake?
8. Does the sequel grow naturally out of the original? In other words, was there enough story left over from the original to make a natural sequel?
9. How many important members of the cast and of the behind-the-scenes team were involved in the sequel? If some characters had to be recast, how did that effect the quality of the sequel?
10. Does the sequel build on the original in such a way that it seems incomplete unless you've seen the original, or is it complete enough to stand on its own as a separate, unified work?
11. Does the sequel capture the flavor and spirit of the original in story and visual style? Is it equal in quality to the original in every aspect? Where does it surpass the original, and where is it weaker?
12. If the sequel becomes a character series, what are the qualities of the characters that make them wear well? Why do we want to see them again and again? Are the writers able to keep their characters consistent in film after film? How consistent are the other stylistic elements from one film to another?

CHAPTER 12

OTHER SPECIAL FILM EXPERIENCES

Most of us have grown up with movies, both in the theater and on television. We are so familiar with genre films, remakes, and sequels that we experience them as easily as drawing a breath . . . they are a part of our natural environment. But most of us are not as comfortable with foreign language and silent films. Products of other cultures, other life-styles, and other generations, their strangeness can pose formidable obstacles to appreciation and understanding. However, if we make a conscious effort to overcome these obstacles, we will be amply rewarded by the worlds of experience that await in these "special" films.

THE FOREIGN-LANGUAGE FILM

The most difficult problem in analyzing the foreign-language film, of course, is the language barrier itself. In spite of the fact that the image carries the major burden of communication in film, the spoken word still plays an important role. Therefore, some method must be used to help us understand the dialogue. There are two basic methods of translating dialogue in the foreign-language film: voice dubbing and the use of printed subtitles.

Voice Dubbing

In the case of a French film that also plays in America, the voice-dubbing process works as follows: The actor speaks the lines of dialogue in his native language (French), and this dialogue is recorded and becomes a part of the soundtrack for the French version. For the American market, however, the dialogue soundtrack in French is replaced by an English soundtrack, where voices in English are recorded to correspond to the mouth and lip movements of the French actors. To match image with soundtrack, the translator very carefully selects English words that phonetically approximate the French words being spoken, so that the image of the French actor and the spoken words in English seem synchronized. Perhaps the clearest advantage of voice dubbing is that it enables us to watch the film in the usual way, and, because the actors seem to be speaking English, the film does not seem so foreign.

But the disadvantages and limitations of the voice-dubbing process are numerous. Perhaps the primary flaw in dubbing is the effect that results from separating actors from their voices, often making the acting seem stiff and wooden. Renata Adler, a strong opponent of voice dubbing, states, "The process is hopeless, destroying any illusion of life, and leaving the actor somewhere between a mouthing fish and a blubbering grotesque."[1]

Another problem is that perfectly accurate lip synchronization is never really possible. For example, although the French phrase *mon amour* might closely approximate the lip movements of a translation such as *my dearest,* the French word *oui* does not come close to the lip movements of the English word *yes*. Even if perfect lip synchronization were possible, another very formidable obstacle would remain: Each language has its own emotional character, rhythmic patterns, and accompanying facial expressions and gestures, all of which seem unnatural when another language is dubbed in. French facial expressions, for example, simply do not correspond to English words. Schools of acting are certainly influenced by the nature of the language spoken, especially by its general emotional character. Consider for example, the difference between the Italian acting style, with its emphasis on elaboration and broad gestures, and the Swedish style, which is much more restrained. Thus, because of the impossibility of perfect synchronization and the differences in national emotional temperaments reflected in acting styles, dubbing can never really capture the illusion of reality. A certain artificial quality often permeates the entire film and becomes a gnawing irritation to the viewer.

Furthermore, the process of voice dubbing eliminates the natural power, character, and unique emotional quality of the original language, the very sound of which, understandable or not, may be essential to the spirit of the film. The sense of reality that is lost in the voice-dubbing process returns when the original language is spoken, for the foreign film in its own language has a resonance and an authenticity that is impossible to achieve through dubbing.

When the dubbed voices are not carefully chosen to fit the actors and the general tone of the film, the illusion of reality suffers even more. For example, in the Russian film *War and Peace,* the dubbing, according to Renata Adler, makes the inhabitants of Moscow sound as if they came from Texas. In such situations, a certain degree of authenticity might be saved by having the dubbed voices speak English with a Russian accent.

All too often the artificial quality of the dubbed foreign film is due not to the change of language or the casting of voices, but the

1. Renata Adler, *A Year in the Dark.* New York: Berkley Medallion Books, 1971, p. 167.

poor quality of the dubbing techniques. Sometimes there seems a general lack of concern with the dramatic performance of the dubbed voices. The dubbed lines usually have little dramatic emphasis; they possess no natural variations in pitch and stress, the rhythms are all wrong. The lines are often read in a lifeless monotone, providing little more than the basic "information" of the line without vocal subtleties.

Wifemistress (a 1979 Italian film directed by Marco Vicario, starring Marcello Mastroianni and Laura Antonelli) is a classic study in how a reasonably good film can be ruined by poor dubbing techniques. On the positive side, the actors are obviously mouthing English words, for the lip synchronization is extremely well matched. Here any sense of credibility ends. The dubbed dialogue is obviously "close-miked" in a studio, with the English-speaking actors very close to a microphone, so close that they have to speak softly to keep from distorting their voices as they are recorded. Thus, each speech gives the impression of being whispered in our ear.

There is no attempt to achieve any sense of depth: Each voice is recorded at the same volume level regardless of the actor's distance from the camera. And there is no ambient sound during conversations, even when the actors talking are in a room almost full of other people. In some cases, the music is overdone in an attempt to kill off some of this ghostly silence. While the dubbed voices are well-cast (Mastroianni speaks for himself), their acting sounds like reading; the dialogue is flat, listless, and completely lacking in dramatic punch.

In complete contrast to the problems of *Wifemistress* is the excellent dubbing job done on *Das Boot*. The natural rhythms, cadence, and pitch of human voices really talking to each other give the dialogue dynamic life even without completely accurate synchronization with lip movement, and three-dimensional ambient sound gives us enough exciting "information" to make us forget the film is even dubbed.

Subtitles

When voice dubbing is not employed, a foreign-language film makes use of printed subtitles. Here a concise English translation of the dialogue appears in printed form at the bottom of the screen while the dialogue is being spoken. By reading this translation, we have a fairly clear idea of what is being said by the actors as they speak in their native language.

The use of subtitles has several advantages over the use of voice dubbing. Perhaps most importantly, it does not interfere with the illusion of reality to the same degree as dubbing, even though the appearance of writing at the bottom of the screen is not completely natural to the film medium. Because the actors are not separated from their voices, their performances seem more real and human, as well as more powerful. Furthermore, by retaining the voices of the actors speaking in their native language, the subtitled film keeps the power, character, and unique emotional quality of the culture that produced it. The importance of this last point cannot be overestimated. To quote Renata Adler on the subject once more:

> One of the essential powers and beauties of the cinema is that it is truly international, that it makes language accessible in a highly special way. Only in movies can one hear foreign languages spoken and—by the written word in sub-titles—participate as closely as one ever will in a culture that is otherwise closed to one.[2]

Thus, subtitles interfere less with the viewer's overall aesthetic experience of the film, less with the film's cultural integrity, and therefore less with its essential reality. Since much of the film's reality comes through to us intuitively even in a language we cannot understand, it is more important that the voice–image link remain intact than that we clearly understand every word of dialogue.

This is not to say that the use of subtitles does not also have its disadvantages. One of the most obvious is that our attention is divided between watching the image and reading the subtitles. If we read slowly or if the editing is fast-paced, we may miss important parts of the visual image and lose a sense of the film's continuity. Furthermore, most subtitles are so concise that they are oversimplified and incomplete. They are designed to convey only the most basic level of meaning in the dialogue, and do not even attempt to capture the full flavor and quality of the dialogue in the original language.

Another problem often arises from the fact that subtitles are printed in white. The white letters appear on the bottom of the screen, and if the image behind the subtitles is white or light in color, the subtitles become completely illegible. This was the case

2. Ibid., pp. 158–159.

in *Tora, Tora, Tora!*, where the white subtitles often appeared against the white uniforms of the Japanese naval officers. Although it would seem to be a relatively easy matter to change the color of the subtitle letters so they stand out in contrast against the background, this is never done.

In spite of the disadvantages, the use of subtitles is still perhaps the best solution to the language barrier, especially in the slow-paced film that is edited in such a way that the dialogue can be read before the image changes. In a fast-paced film, where editorial cuts occurring at a very high frequency demand full attention to the image, voice dubbing may be the only answer.

Other Kinds of "Foreignness"

The language problem is not the only obstacle to understanding and appreciating foreign films. In addition to the language barrier, there are other important cultural differences that may limit or distract our response. A story told about a Russian attempt to use *The Grapes of Wrath* as a propaganda tool against the United States illustrates that cultural differences have a profound effect on how a film is received. Russian officials had "discovered" *The Grapes of Wrath* and saw in it an example of the horrible exploitation of migrant workers by the capitalistic big-ranch owners. The officials started showing the film to Russian peasants in order to demonstrate how terrible life in America was and to convince them of the evils of capitalism. The idea backfired when the peasants responded not with contempt for the capitalists but with envy for the Joads, who owned a truck and had the freedom to travel across the country.

When considering the difficulty of viewing films from another country, we might think of the problems a foreigner unfamiliar with the United States might have in understanding fine nuances in films like *Easy Rider* (hippie/drug culture of the '60s), *Bob, Carol, Ted, and Alice* (sexual revolution of the '60s), or *Serial* (ultra-with-it faddish life style of northern California's Marin County) (Figs. 12.1, 12.2, 12.3, and 12.4). Lina Wertmuller's *Swept Away*, for example, is an allegory on several different planes. On a very basic level, it is an allegory on the never-ending battle between the sexes. The principal actors, Giancarlo Giannini, as a deckhand, and Mariangela Melato, as a yacht owner's wife, are shipwrecked on an island. The couple are opposites in a variety of ways. He is dark-haired and dark-skinned; she is fair-skinned and blonde. He

|12.1|

|12.2|

|12.3|

|12.4|

Cultural Differences: An American audience might have difficulties understanding the symbolic importance of class distinctions in a French film like *Grand Illusion* [12.1]; European audiences might have an equally difficult time fully understanding American films like *Easy Rider* [12.2], *Bob, Carol, Ted, and Alice* [12.3], and *Serial* [12.4].

is a southern Italian and lower class; she is northern Italian and upper class. Politically, she is a capitalist; he is a social democrat. As the male/female battle is waged, a very "Italian" class and political struggle is also being waged, with levels of meaning beyond the understanding of the average American viewer. Although we can catch the broad outlines of these symbolic levels, the fine nuances and subtleties are lost to us. This is not to say that we cannot enjoy the film, but we must face the fact that we are not really seeing quite the same film a native Italian would see. The battle of the sexes, and the love story it evolves into, are universal and clearly understood. The north/south conflict, and the political/class struggle, are much less clear to an American, in the same way that an Italian would not be able to understand our basic myths of north/south differences, political parties, black/white social problems, our particular American concept of social status, or American democracy.

A great many other cultural differences might have important effects and cause us to misunderstand the movie because of its foreignness. If we fail to understand important customs, moral attitudes, or codes of behavior common to the culture producing the film, we will certainly lose something. Sometimes an understanding of politics or economics is essential to full understanding; sometimes a knowledge of the country's history may play a part. There may be subtle class distinctions or religious values that we must first understand.

We must, in addition, be very aware of cultural symbols that might be revealed in unusual clothes, hair style, or some other detail which makes a character seem different from the other characters. In *Wifemistress*, for example, a young woman stands out by sporting a very short haircut. She marries a naive young man who expects his wife to be a virgin, and kills himself when he discovers she isn't. Does the haircut identify her with a certain life-style, as a modern, sexually liberated woman? (The picture is set in the pre-automobile days in Italy, probably in the late 19th or early 20th century.) Many such clues to character may pass us by because we fail to understand the symbolic importance of such seemingly insignificant differences.

While a great many of these problems can be overcome with perceptive, attentive viewing, many will be beyond our understanding without an in-depth study of the culture.

Another factor that influences our responses is the editing rhythms of foreign films, which are paced differently than American films. Whether these filmic differences reflect the different pace of life in other countries would certainly make an interesting study. But, whatever the cause, there are differences. Italian films, for example, average about fifteen seconds per running shot, whereas American films average about five seconds per shot. This difference not only makes Italian films seem strange to American viewers, but there is danger that the viewer will be bored by the film without even recognizing the reason. The musical scores to many foreign films, especially the Italian and French, seem overdone, a kind of musical overkill, and the music often seems dated, like American music of an earlier era. Swedish and Danish films seem to use little or no music, which also takes some getting used to. In some cases, the music may be there to trigger responses that are particular to that culture, to which we simply have not been conditioned to respond.

Cultural Prejudice

"If you think this picture's no good, I'll put on a beard and say it was made in Germany. Then you'll call it art." So read a subtitle from Will Rogers's *The Ropin' Fool,* made in 1922. The statement reflects another problem in the analysis of the foreign-language film. Because of some long-standing American sense of cultural inferiority, we are much too prone to bow down before almost anything European. Thus, in the 1950s, many European films that were not above the standards of the American Grade B movies were lavishly praised by American critics and film buffs simply because they were made in France, Germany, or Italy. This is not to say that there were not some great films produced by these countries during that period, but a tendency existed to praise them all. At the same time, American filmgoers turned a somewhat jaundiced eye toward the films produced in their own country. Thus, any film made in Europe was automatically considered a highly serious and artistic statement, while the American film was generally ignored or dismissed as slick commercial trash.

The shoe also fits the other foot, for Europeans often appreciate certain aspects of American films that Americans cannot see or appreciate. For example, French critics were much more lavish in their praise of *Bonnie and Clyde* than were American critics. Jerry Lewis is also appreciated more by the French than by Americans. This phenomenon cannot easily be explained, but it is perhaps related to several factors. First, the language barrier may cause the audience to read things between the subtitles that are not there. At any rate, a more subjective and creative viewing is required when meanings are suggested rather than spelled out clearly. Also, a foreign director's cinematic style may have greater power and fascination because of its strangeness to viewers, who are not moved in the same way by the home-grown varieties they have become accustomed to.

Since a film gives us a reflection of the culture and society that produced it, the overly positive reaction to a foreign film may actually be caused by the same kind of desire that makes us want to travel. Often we simply want a change of scene, a brief escape from the ordinary and the familiar, or we are curious about other people in faraway places, about their similarities to us and their differences. And sometimes we are simply fascinated by the different flavor, essence, or spirit of another country, by its dominant lifestyle. All of these factors play a part in our reaction to the foreign-language film, and serve to make our analysis and evaluation more subjective.

QUESTIONS

On the Foreign-Language Film

1. Which method is used to translate the dialogue into English—subtitles or voice dubbing? Was this the best way to solve the language problem for this particular film? Why?
2. If subtitles are used, how well do they seem to capture the essence of what is being said by the actors? Are the subtitles ever difficult to read because of the light-colored backgrounds? Is the film's pace slow enough to allow for both reading the subtitles and following the image?
3. If voice dubbing is used, how closely do the English words spoken on the soundtrack correspond to the mouth and lip movements of the foreign actors? Do you get used to the fact that the voices are dubbed, or is it a constant irritation? How well suited are the voice qualities and accents on the soundtrack to the actors with which they are matched? Does the overall emotional quality of the English translation match the facial expressions and gestures of the foreign actors?
4. How good is the quality of the dubbing technique? Are the "voice-actors" obviously reading their lines close to a microphone in a studio so they seem to be whispering in your ear? Does the volume of spoken lines vary according to the distance of the actor from the camera? Is ambient sound present? Is music used as an unnatural filler?
5. How does the foreign director's style differ from American cinematic styles? What effect does this have on your response to the film?

6. How does the film reflect the culture of the country that produced it? How is this culture or life-style different from what we know in America? How is it similar? What different aspects of this foreign culture do you find most fascinating, and why?
7. In what ways does the film transcend its foreignness to communicate things that are universal? What aspects of film are so uniquely foreign that they are beyond your understanding?

THE SILENT FILM

The silent film also presents us with several problems with respect to film analysis. First of all, we seldom have the opportunity to see a silent film as it was intended to be shown; instead we see copies of these films that are dead, decayed, and corrupted, with much of their original brightness and impact lost forever.

Furthermore, most silent films are shown today without the musical accompaniment that normally was provided for the audiences of the silent era. Sometimes a complete score was distributed along with the film and played by a complete orchestra, as was the case with *Birth of a Nation*. Usually, a single piano or organ player simply improvised as the film was shown. Such music filled a definite vacuum, and the silent film without it has a ghostly kind of incompleteness. Thus, many of the silent film's best moments have lost their impact because their rhythmic qualities and emotional moods are not underscored as was intended.

Even more important is the fact that we are not "tuned in" to silent films as a unique means of expression. Used to the levels of communication conveyed by the sound film, and conditioned to "half-watch" everything by the ever-present television, we have lost our ability to concentrate on purely visual elements. If we are to fully appreciate the silent film, we must master a new set of watching skills, and become more sensitive and responsive to the language of the silent film, especially its most expressive vehicles: the human face and body.

In the last years of the silent film, the expressive qualities of the human face and body had developed into a complex and subtle art; the slightest bodily movement, gesture, or facial expression could express the deepest of passions or the tragedy of a human soul. The actors of the last silent films thus were able to speak clearly and distinctly to their audience, not through the voice, but through a pantomime of eyes, mouth, hands, and body movement. With this highly developed art of pantomime, the silent film possessed an expressive means that was self-sufficient and capable of conveying a narrative through purely pictorial means with a minimum of subtitles (Fig. 12.5).

The mass audience of the silent era learned the art of reading faces, gestures, and body movements by constant conditioning, but we must work a little harder at mastering this art. We are exposed to it in the modern film in "reaction" shots, but they are generally of short duration and often lack the subtlety of the best silent films. At its best, the language of the silent film could express some things that words cannot express, as Béla Balázs passionately points out:

> The gestures of visual man are not intended to convey concepts which can be expressed in words, but such inner experience, such non-rational emotions which would still remain unexpressed when everything that can be told has been told. Such emotions lie in the deepest levels of the soul and cannot be approached by words that are mere reflections of concepts: just as our musical experiences cannot be expressed in rationalized concepts, what appears on the face and in facial expression is a spiritual experience which is rendered immediately visible without the intermediary of words.[3]

If we are to respond properly to silent films, we must become aware of the subtlety and the power of the silent film language—a language capable of both silent soliloquy (a single face "speaking" the subtlest shades of meaning) and mute dialogue (where a conversation takes place between two human beings through facial expressions and gestures). The silent film language can, through the close-up, reveal not only what is visibly written on the face, but also something between the lines, and it is sometimes even capable of capturing contradictory expressions simultaneously on the same face.

The language of the silent film is not restricted to the face, however, for the hands, the arms, the legs, and the torso of the actor also become powerful instruments of expression. The language of the expressive face and body is perhaps more individual and personal than the language of words. As each actor in the sound film has distinct voice qualities that are unique to his or her means of verbal expression, each actor in the silent film had a personal style of facial and physical expression of emotion.

3. Edith Bone, trans., *Theory of the Film: Character and Growth of a New Art.* New York: Dover Publications, Inc., 1970, p. 40.

| 12.5 | The Price of Perfection without Words: In this scene from *City Lights* (1931), a blind flower girl believes the tramp to be a tycoon, sells him a flower for his last quarter, and keeps the change. Director/actor Chaplin had a problem figuring out how the blind girl would assume the tramp to be a rich man and finally solved it by having the tramp wander through heavy traffic and then walk on through the back doors of a limousine parked at the curb. The blind girl, hearing the heavy door close, assumed that the "tycoon" was getting out of an expensive car. To solve this problem and to achieve the exact effect he wanted, Chaplin shot a total of 342 different takes.

One of the most powerful means of expression involving the whole body is the actor's walk. In the silent film, because it is usually a natural and unconscious expression of emotion, the walk became an important aspect of each actor's own unique screen personality or style. When used consciously for expression, it could be changed to express such varying emotions as dignity, strong resolution, self-consciousness, modesty, or shame.

We should also recognize that the silent film is a product of another age and must be judged, at least to some extent, as a reflection of the society and culture of that day. Although these films express the mentality of their own age adequately, anything old-fashioned usually strikes us as comic at first, until we become accustomed to the older fashion or style. Then the strangeness recedes into the background, allowing us to see the more universal elements.

Full appreciation of the *earlier* silent film is often made difficult by the broad and exaggerated gesturing and grimacing of the actors, who were still using the melodramatic techniques of the stage acting of that day. These unnatural and forced gestures and expressions seem ridiculous when seen in microscopic close-up. As the art of film acting evolved, actors realized the necessity for restraint in gesture and subtlety of expression, but a great many otherwise memorable films remain seriously handicapped by the older acting style (Fig. 12.6).

Anyone who thinks the silent film was a primitive and crude art form compared to the modern sound film needs only to study two of the great masterpieces of the late silent era: *Sunrise*, the hauntingly beautiful melodrama directed by F. W. Murnau, and *Napoleon*, French director Abel Gance's great epic (recently restored and shown in four hour and five hour, 13 minute versions). Both films were made in 1927, but seem modern in every respect. Both

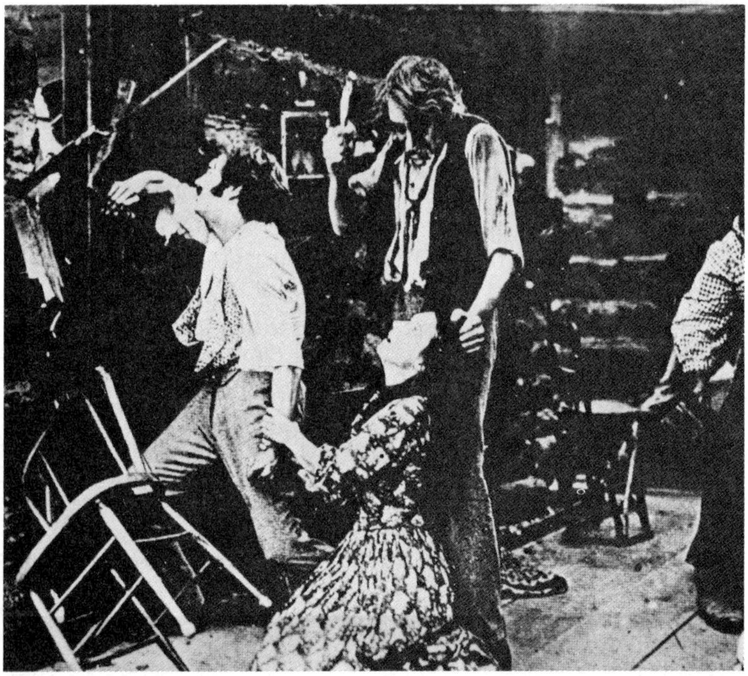

| 12.6 | Exaggerated Gestures and Expressions: In this scene from D. W. Griffith's classic *Birth of a Nation* (1915), the melodramatic and overblown stage acting style of the day is still much in evidence.

have dynamic, polished visual styles, capable of communicating nuances of meaning without titles. Both are extremely sophisticated in acting styles, editing, composition, lighting, use of montages, creating the illusion of three dimensionality, camera movement, superimposed images, and special effects. In fact, watching silent films of this caliber almost makes one wonder if the movies should ever have learned to talk.

All things considered, the silent film has much to offer us if we are willing to learn its special language and understand its own unique sophistication. We can observe a different kind of acting skill, and see its evolution from overblown exaggeration to the restraint and subtlety of a polished art. We can learn to appreciate the effectiveness of narrative told clearly and quickly through purely pictorial means or with a minimum of subtitles. The absence of dialogue can make us more sensitive to the film's visual rhythmic qualities. And, finally, we can learn to appreciate an art form that rose above the formidable barriers of language differences, for the silent film's greatest power is that it speaks a universal language.

QUESTIONS

On the Silent Film

1. Is the acting style melodramatic, with broad and exaggerated gestures and facial expressions, or is it subtle, refined, even understated?
2. What is unique about the acting styles of each of the major actors? Which actors depend most on facial expression, and which ones depend on gestures and bodily movements?
3. How many different emotions are expressed by actors through their walks? Which actors in the film have unique walks that become a part of their acting style and the total personality they project?
4. How effective is the film in telling its story without words? How much does the film need to rely on subtitles to make the action absolutely clear?
5. How sophisticated are the visual techniques used in the film compared to modern techniques? If the film were being made today (still silent), what modern visual techniques could be used to improve it? In what ways is the visual style old-fashioned? How much of this old-fashioned quality is due to technical limitations of the time?

THE HISTORICALLY IMPORTANT FILM

Another serious problem facing the modern viewer is the analysis and evaluation of the historically important film. This type of film, which proves to be significant in the years following its release because of the innovations in cinematic technique or style it introduces, must not be approached with the same expectations we have of the modern film. In many cases, the historically important film is neither effective aesthetically, nor as an immediate sensual experience. Such a film must be viewed and evaluated in a very specialized way, in terms of its historical context.

To place such a film in the proper perspective, we should consider it from at least two different viewpoints. First, we should be familiar with the films produced prior to the film being viewed, so that we can see it in relationship to what has been done before. In this way we will be able to appreciate the innovations in style or cinematic technique that the film introduced, and understand the significance of the film's contribution to the development of the medium. Next, we should examine it in terms of the modern film, to determine which of these innovations in style or technique have been assimilated by contemporary filmmakers.

It is in comparison to the modern film that the historically important film suffers most, for it is likely to seem time-worn and full of cinematic clichés. Ironically, often the more time-worn and out of date a film of this type seems, the more significant it is historically, for such an effect generally means that the film's innovations had such a strong effect on later directors that they have become standard practice. The difficulty in appreciating such films lies in the fact that the power, freshness, and originality of the innovations are often lost between the time they are introduced and the time we see the film, not because the innovations are not effective, but because they have become commonplace.

Some historically important films, even those that are most frequently imitated, somehow retain their original power and freshness. When such films prove themselves to be great in their own right, and appeal equally to viewers in any time period, they are known not only as historical groundbreakers or milestones, but as classics, the power of which no amount of imitation can really destroy.

Sometimes, however, we may encounter a film that might be called a "false classic," which retains its appeal over a fairly long period of time and then suddenly loses it because other works in the medium suddenly surpass it. According to Dwight Macdonald, this is what happened to Cocteau's *Blood of a Poet:* "It suddenly showed its age, looking mannered rather than stylized, more affected than affecting, terribly thin in content and slow in movement."[4]

A very different type of historical significance may be seen in films that are so unique that the innovations they introduce are never really imitated or assimilated generally into the medium. Such a film is *The Cabinet of Dr. Caligari,* which Dwight Macdonald calls "a unique anti-movie that came close to perfection by breaking all the rules."[5] Such a film may be interesting to study because of its one-of-a-kindness or because of the rebellious spirit that produced it, but its value as a part of any evolutionary study of the medium is very limited, for it is really a stepping stone to nowhere.

QUESTIONS

On the Historically Important Film

1. Based on your knowledge of the films produced prior to this film, what innovations in cinematic style or technique did this film introduce? Which of these innovations are still being used in the modern film?
2. Does the film seem crude, time-worn, or full of clichés when compared to the modern film, or is it still fresh and powerful? What specific elements or qualities in the film lead you to your answer?
3. What is the film's contribution to the overall development of the motion picture? What would the modern film be like if the innovations introduced by this film had never been? How have the innovations introduced by this film been polished and refined in the modern film?

4. Dwight Macdonald, *On Movies.* New York: Berkley Medallion Books, 1971, p. 18. Reprinted by permission of Dwight Macdonald. Copyright © 1969 by Dwight Macdonald.
5. Ibid., p. 20.

THE SOCIAL PROBLEM FILM

The social problem film is perhaps even more difficult to evaluate than the film of historical importance. The problem presented by both, however, is essentially the same—that of becoming outdated or time-worn. But with the social problem film, the aging process can occur very rapidly; the film can become not only dated, but completely irrelevant in just a few short years. This happens any time the social problem being attacked by the film is eliminated or corrected. Thus, in a sense the social problem film can enjoy a long and happy life only by failing in its purpose, for its impact is generally lost as soon as the problem portrayed no longer exists. This is especially true for the film that treats a narrow, topical, and very contemporary problem. On the other hand, the more universal the problem, the more widespread its effects, and the more resistant it is to reform, the longer the life span of the social problem film directed against it. So long as the social problem exists, the film will still have relevance.

Once in a while, if a social problem film is artistically done it becomes more than a mere vehicle to encourage social reform, and may also outlive the problem it attacks. Strong, memorable characters and a good story will give the social problem film durability even after the specific problem dealt with no longer has relevance.

QUESTIONS

On the Social Problem Film

1. Does the social problem being attacked by the film have a universal and timeless quality, affecting all people in all time periods, or is it restricted to a relatively narrow time and place?
2. Is the film powerful enough in terms of a strong story line, enduring characters, good acting, artistic cinematography, and so on, to outlive the social problem it is attacking? In other words, how much of the film's impact is caused by its relevance to a current problem and its timing in attacking the problem?
3. If the immediate social problems on which the film focuses were permanently corrected tomorrow, what relevance would the film have to the average viewer twenty years from now?

CHAPTER 13

CENSORSHIP AND OTHER FORCES THAT SHAPE THE AMERICAN FILM

DOES FILM SHAPE OR REFLECT AMERICAN VALUES?

Since 1922, the American film has never been free from some form of censorship or control. Therefore, a complete understanding of many American films requires an analysis of the complex social and economic pressures that have affected the final products as we see them on the screen.

No art form exists in a vacuum. The more popular an art is, and the wider its appeal to all segments of the population, the more closely it is tied to the social values, mores, and institutions of its audience. As both an extremely popular medium and an industry involving great financial risk and profit potential, the American film naturally must be responsive to social and economic pressures.

So film is not an independent entity, but an integrated part of the social fabric, for its very survival depends on maintaining and continuing its popularity. To achieve real popularity, a movie must, first, be believable. Its credibility must be built, at least in part, on some kind of real environment in which its action takes place, and on certain common "truths" of the society that produces it. This is not to say that a film must only reflect "reality" as the way things actually are within the society. The "truth" it projects may mirror the "dreamscape": the hopes, the dreams, the fears, the inner needs of the people. When reality within the society does not fulfill these needs, the people are primed to respond sympathetically to an artistic expression of them in cinematic form. In other words, film does not create *new* truths for society. It cannot reshape a society that is not ready for change.

But the fact that film does not create new currents of thought does not mean that it is not a powerful instrument of social change. The motion picture's power as a social force comes from its ability to pick up, amplify, and spread currents which already exist in segments of the population to the society as a whole. Film also serves to accelerate popular acceptance of social change. The dramatically powerful presentation of new ways of thinking and behaving on screens twenty-feet-high in thousands of movie theaters across the country gives those "new ways" a significant seal of approval.

It is because of film's potential for legitimizing new standards of behavior—and for inspiring imitation of that behavior, especially in the younger members of its audience—that most systems of censorship or control have originated. In fact, the way systems of censorship develop usually follows a pattern that goes something like this. Some traumatic event occurs that disrupts the stability of the social structure (some past examples: World War I, the Depression, World War II, the Viet Nam War, the Pill, the Women's Movement, the Sexual Revolution, the Drug Revolution, the Generation Gap of the '60s, the Civil Rights Movement). This event causes a significant shift in moral values and codes of behavior within certain segments of the population. Such changes create pressure for more freedom in entertainment media to reflect the "truth" of these more liberal attitudes and standards of behavior. But a conservative element within the society vigorously resists these changes, and demands that films be controlled or censored to prevent the spread of the "shocking" behavior, or so that the movies will reflect the truths of society as the conservative element believes they *should be*. Most censorship within the film industry consists of a kind of uneasy compromise between these two conflicting forces (Fig. 13.1).

| 13.1 | The Changing Face of Censorship: Producer/director Howard Hughes filmed *The Outlaw* in 1941 and released it in 1943. The Motion Picture Association of America withdrew its seal of approval in 1946 because Hughes had made use of unacceptable advertising copy, and local community pressures caused many theaters to cancel its showing. Although the Doc Holliday/Billy the Kid story featured full-figured starlet Jane Russell (shown) displaying more cleavage and passion than the Code allowed, the film would receive a ho-hum PG rating if released today.

THE HAYS OFFICE: 1922–1934

In the aftermath of World War I, Hollywood films began reflecting a change in moral standards: sex, seduction, divorce, drinking, and drug use—new symbols of the "sophisticated" life—all became standard film fare. In 1919, two agencies attempted to provide guidelines for censorship. The National Board of Review of Motion Pictures and the National Association of the Motion Pictures Industry (the film industry's trade association) established the "Thirteen Points," a list describing the kinds of scenes or topics that should be banned. But both agencies lacked the necessary financial and moral support from the industry and, as a consequence, their resolutions had little effect. Public outrage against the permissiveness and the decadence of Hollywood reached a peak in 1922, after a series of shocking scandals involving movie people rocked the film capital.

Believing that some form of self-control and regulation was preferable to the national censorship that seemed certain to be forthcoming, a frightened film industry organized the Motion Picture Producers and Distributors of America, Inc. The agency's first move was to hire Postmaster General (and Presbyterian elder) Will H. Hays to front the organization, calculating that the prominence and moral reputation of this "pillar of the community" would serve as a buffer against outraged citizens groups.

The Hays Office (as it came to be known) worked hard to convince civic groups that movies had indeed become cleaner and more moral. State and local censorship boards, however, were not always convinced—they cut offending sequences from many films, and banned a few entirely.

Hays and his staff reacted to state and local censorship by codifying the most frequent objections to film content and advising member companies on what to avoid. This codification, published in 1927 as the "Purity Code" but soon after facetiously termed the "Don't and Be Carefuls," listed eleven topics to be avoided completely, and twenty-six to be treated with special care. Not surprisingly, the list was very similar to the "Thirteen Points" of 1919.

Like the "Thirteen Points," the "Don't and Be Carefuls" did little to diminish growing public criticism. After a brief period of following the advice of the Hays Office, movie producers grew bold again as the protests faded. But they did try to guard against further objections by following the principle of "compensating moral values." By loosely interpreting the principle, a film's producers could show as much sin and debauchery as they liked, so long as virtue triumphed in the end, and all sinners paid for their sins. Thus the morality imposed on the motion picture by the Hays Office was not only superficial, but hypocritical as well. Another wave of stormy reactions was not long in coming.

THE MOTION PICTURE PRODUCTION CODE: 1930–1960

In 1930, the "Don't and Be Carefuls" was replaced by the Motion Picture Production Code. The Code itself was written by Father Daniel A. Lord, a Jesuit priest who had been a technical advisor on *The King of Kings*. Father Lord was encouraged and advised in this project by Martin Quigley, a prominent Catholic editor, who described the authorship of the Code in his own publication, *Exhibitor's Herald World:*

> The Code was formulated after intensive study by members of the industry and according to Will H. Hays, by church leaders, leaders in the field of child education, representatives of women's clubs, educators, psycholo-

> gists, dramatists and other students of our moral, social and family problems.[1]

Although he may have been trying to suppress the Catholic authorship of the Code, there was truth in Quigley's statement, for the Code incorporated the "Thirteen Points" of 1919 and all the "Don't and Be Carefuls" of 1927. Both of these lists had been based on cuts made by state censor boards and objections raised by various civil and religious groups.

But the 1930 Code differed from the two previous lists in two important ways. First, it was a complete document, not just a list, and it provided a philosophical and/or moral basis for each point presented. Secondly, it cured the vagueness of the earlier lists by drawing clear and specific boundary lines between the acceptable and the objectionable. The 1930 code, though, shared one fatal flaw with its predecessors: It was not rigorously enforced.

As a result, public outcry continued to mount. By the end of 1932, about forty national educational and religious groups had adopted resolutions calling for federal regulation of the industry, and during 1933 the White House received nine thousand letters protesting the "vulgarity and coarseness" of motion pictures.

The most important protests came from Catholic leaders, who were keenly disappointed in the failure of the Production Code to improve the films being released. They put real teeth into their protest in November of 1933, by creating the Legion of Decency, a group formed to foment economic boycott against films that violated the Code. Between seven and nine million Catholics took a pledge to remain away from offensive films, and fifty-four other religious organizations supported the plan.

This consumer's boycott hit the film industry in hard financial times, and attacked its most vulnerable spot—the box office. The strategy proved much more effective than the threat of governmental regulation, and also proved to be an efficient method of enforcing the Code. Joseph I. Breen, a young Catholic newspaperman, was put in charge of the administration of the Code, and the Hollywood staff of the Hays Office wrested control from the producers. Member companies agreed not to release or distribute a film without a certificate of approval. In addition, they were required to submit copies of all scripts under production, and each completed film had to be submitted for viewing by the board before it was sent to the laboratory for printing. A $25,000 penalty

1. Quoted by Ruth A. Inglis in *Freedom of the Movies*. Chicago: University of Chicago Press, 1947, p. 127.

for producing, distributing, or exhibiting any film without the seal encouraged member companies to fully comply with the agreement. Thus, through "voluntary" compliance, this industry-imposed regulation served to control the moral standards of the American film for the next three decades.

UNDERSTANDING THE CODE

Although the Code had strong ties with the Catholic church, its practical rules did not reflect any single theology. Translated into simplest terms, the Code and its rules were designed to require the motion pictures to reflect, respect, and promote the institutions and moral values of the American middle class (see Exhibit 1).

Evident throughout the document was a belief in the powerful influence that movies can exert on the moral standards of its audience. But, whereas most of the Code dealt with the dangers of film as a corrupting influence, film was also shown as having tremendous potential for good:

> If motion pictures consistently *hold up for admiration high types of characters* and present stories that will affect lives for the better, they can become the most powerful natural forces for the improvement of mankind.

The assumption was that if the motion picture's creative energies were correctly channeled (through conformity to the Code), it would become a Supermedium—"fighting for Truth, Justice, and the American Way."

The fact that film was a mass medium available to children as well as adults was a primary concern in the thinking behind the Code. In fact, the document can best be understood by relating it to the industry's concern with the "twelve year old mind." It was this young, highly impressionable age group, in the process of forming its values, its moral sense, and picking its role models that the Code was determined to protect.

The ways in which the document was interpreted and enforced is also extremely important in understanding its influence on the American films produced from 1934 to 1960. To put it simply, the Code was interpreted literally by administrator Joseph I. Breen, and its moral framework was strictly enforced. The principle of compensating values, applied hypocritically during the 1920s, was enforced with great sincerity by Breen, as illustrated by the

(Text continues on p. 373.)

EXHIBIT 1 EXCERPTS FROM THE MOTION PICTURE PRODUCTION CODE

REASONS SUPPORTING
PREAMBLE OF CODE

1. Theatrical motion pictures . . . are primarily to be regarded as ENTERTAINMENT. . . .
   The MORAL IMPORTANCE of entertainment is something which has been universally recognized. It enters intimately into the lives of men and women and affects them closely; it occupies their minds and affections during leisure hours; and ultimately touches the whole of their lives. A man may be judged by his standard of entertainment as easily as by the standard of his work. . . .
   Correct entertainment raises the whole standard of a nation.
   Wrong entertainment lowers the whole living conditions and moral ideals of a race.
   Note, for example, the healthy reactions to healthful sports, like baseball, golf; the unhealthy reactions to sports like cockfighting, bullfighting, bear baiting, etc.
   Note, too, the effect on ancient nations of gladiatorial combats, the obscene plays of Roman times, etc.
2. Motion pictures are very important as ART.
   Though a new art, possibly a combination art, it has the same object as the other arts, the presentation of human thought, emotion, and experience, in terms of an appeal to the soul through the senses.
   Here, as in entertainment,
   Art *enters intimately* into the lives of human beings.
   Art can be *morally good,* lifting men to higher levels. This has been done through good music, great painting, authentic fiction, poetry, drama. . . .
   It has often been argued that art in itself is unmoral, neither good nor bad. This is perhaps true of the THING which is music, painting, poetry, etc. But the thing is the PRODUCT of some person's mind, and the intention of that mind was either good or bad . . . Besides, the thing has its EFFECT upon those who come into contact with it . . . In the case of the motion pictures, this effect may be particularly emphasized because no art has so quick and so widespread an appeal to the masses. . . .
3. The motion picture . . . has special MORAL OBLIGATIONS:
   A. Most arts appeal to the mature. This art appeals at once *to every class*. . . .
   B. By reason of the mobility of a film and the ease of picture distribution . . . this art *reaches places* unpenetrated by other forms of art.
   C. Because of these two facts, it is difficult to produce films intended for only certain classes of people . . . Films, unlike books and music, can with difficulty be confined to certain selected groups.
   D. The latitude given to film material cannot . . . be as wide as the latitude given to *book material*. . . .
      a) A book describes; a film vividly presents. One presents on a cold page; the other by apparently living people.
      b) A book reaches the mind through words merely; a film reaches the eyes and ears through the reproduction of actual events.
      c) The reaction of a reader to a book depends largely on the keenness of the reader's imagination; the reaction to a film depends on the vividness of presentation. . . .
   E. Everything possible in a *play* is not possible in a film:
      a) Because of the *larger audience of the film,* and its consequential mixed character. Psychologically, the larger the audience, the lower the moral mass resistance to suggestion.
      b) Because through light, enlargement of character, presentation, scenic emphasis, etc., the screen story is *brought closer* to the audience. . . .

(*continued*)

c) The enthusiasm for . . . *actors* and *actresses,* developed beyond anything of the sort in history, makes the audience largely sympathetic toward the characters they portray and the stories in which they figure. Hence the audience is more ready to confuse actor and actress and the characters they portray. . . .

PARTICULAR APPLICATIONS:
CRIMES AGAINST THE LAW

The technique of murder must be presented in a way that will not inspire imitation. . . .
Revenge in modern times shall not be justified. . . .
Methods of crime should not be explicitly presented. . . .
The illegal drug traffic must not be portrayed in such a way as to stimulate curiosity concerning the use of, or traffic in, such drugs; nor shall scenes be approved which show the use of illegal drugs, or their effects. . . .
The use of liquor . . . when not required by the plot . . . will not be shown. . . .
There must be no display, at any time, of machine guns, submachine guns, or other weapons generally classified as illegal weapons in the hands of gangsters . . . and there are to be no off-stage sounds of the repercussions of these guns. There must be no new, unique or trick methods shown for concealing guns. . . .
Pictures dealing with criminal activities, in which minors participate, or to which minors are related, shall not be approved if they incite demoralizing imitation. . . .

PARTICULAR APPLICATIONS:
SEX, COSTUME, AND DANCE

SEX

The sanctity of the institution of marriage and the home shall be upheld. Pictures shall not infer that low forms of sex relationship are the accepted or common thing . . . Out of regard for the sanctity of marriage and the home, the *triangle,* that is, the love of a third party for one already married, needs careful handling. The treatment should not throw sympathy against marriage as an institution. . . .
Excessive and lustful kissing, lustful embraces, suggestive postures and gestures are not to be shown . . . passion should be treated in such a manner as not to stimulate the lower and baser emotions . . . Many scenes cannot be presented without arousing dangerous emotions on the part of the immature, the young or the *criminal classes.* . . .

COSTUME

The fact that the nude or semi-nude body may be *beautiful* does not make its use in the films moral. For, in addition to its beauty, the effect of the nude or semi-nude body on the normal individual must be taken into consideration.
Nudity or semi-nudity used simply to put a "*punch*" into a picture comes under the head of immoral actions . . . Nudity can never be permitted as being *necessary for the plot.* . . .
Transparent or *translucent materials* and silhouette are frequently more suggestive than actual exposure. . . .

DANCES

Dancing in general is recognized as an *art* and as a *beautiful* form of expressing human emotions . . . But dances which suggest or represent sexual actions, whether performed solo or with two or more; dances intended to excite the emotional reaction of an audience; dances with movement of the breasts, excessive body movement while the feet are stationary, violate decency and are wrong.

PARTICULAR APPLICATIONS . . . PROFANITY

No approval by the Production Code Administration shall be given to the use of words and phrases . . . including, but not limited to, the following:

Alley cat (applied to a woman); bat (applied to a woman); broad (applied to a woman); Bronx cheer (the sound); chippie; cocotte; God, Lord, Jesus, Christ (unless used reverently); cripes; fanny; fairy (in a vulgar sense); finger (the); fire, cries of; Gawd; goose (in a vulgar sense); "hold your hat" or "hats"; hot (applied to a woman); "in your hat"; louse, lousy; Madam (relating to prostitution); nance; nerts; nuts (except when meaning crazy); pansy; razzberry (the sound); slut (applied to a woman); S.O.B.; son-of-a; tart; toilet gags; tom cat (applied to a man); traveling salesman and farmer's daughter jokes; whore; damn, hell (excepting when the use of said last two words shall be essential and required for portrayal, in proper historical context, of any scene or dialogue based upon historical fact or folklore, or for the presentation in proper literary context of a Biblical, or other religious quotation, or a quotation from a literary work provided that no such use shall be permitted which is intrinsically objectionable or offends good taste). . . .

PARTICULAR APPLICATIONS: MISCELLANEOUS

RELIGION

No film or episode may throw *ridicule* on any religious faith. . . .

LOCATIONS

The treatment of bedrooms must be governed by good taste. . . .

NATIONAL FEELINGS

The use of the flag shall be consistently respectful. . . .

Editor's Note: To simplify the reader's task, some parts of the Code have been rearranged so that all materials relating to a given topic appear together. As originally presented, the Code consisted of two parts. The first part began with the section "Preamble," which was followed, in sequence, by the sections "General Principles" and "Particular Applications." The second part consisted of "Reasons Supporting" or "Reasons Underlying" each of the "Particular Applications." Here, the sections have been rearranged so that the supports or reasons appear beneath the particular application to which each pertains.

---

following excerpt from his letter to a member producer regarding a novel submitted as the basis for a film:

> The male lead, J_____, commits adultery in flagrant fashion. The Code says that adultery as a subject should be avoided. When adultery is absolutely necessary for the plot, there must be ample compensating moral values, in the nature of a strong voice for decency, of pointed suffering, of actual punishment of the guilty. We fail to find these in the story we have read.

The rigidity of Breen's approach to enforcement can be further seen in his explanation of what he called a "cardinal principle of the Code" (but which was not a part of the Code as published):

> *Wrong must always be characterized as wrong and not as something else.* Sin is not a mistake, but a shameful transgression. Crime is not an error of

> frailty but the breaking of the law. Wrong is not pleasant but painful, not heroic but cowardly, not profitable but detrimental, not plausible but deserving of condemnation.[2]

Breen's emphasis was clear: to pass muster with his Production Code Administration (PCA), a motion picture had to make clear distinctions between right and wrong; gray areas of ambiguity could not exist.

The PCA's insistence on black and white morality, and its insistence on a literal interpretation of the Code, forced some producers and directors into drastic compromises. A clear example of the Code's deleterious effect can be seen in Robert Rossen's film version of Robert Penn Warren's *All the King's Men.* Warren's demogogue, the richly complex and morally ambiguous Willy Stark, was twisted into a sinister, power-mad villain, and the novel's complex Machiavellian theory of the moral neutrality of history was reduced to Lord Acton's simple thesis "Power tends to corrupt, and absolute power corrupts absolutely." An anecdote told by Warren about the ending of the film version of his novel summarizes the effect of Code censorship. While the film was being edited, Rossen asked Warren to view four or five different endings which had been shot for the film, and to pick the ending he liked best. As Warren tells it:

> When I told him which one I liked, Bob just laughed, and said, "We made that one as a joke. The one you picked is an ironic ending, and we don't have ironic endings in movies . . . In the movies it's all cops and robbers.[3]

While it may be difficult for the modern film student to take the Code seriously, the in-depth study of any complex realistic or naturalistic novel of the period and the film based on that novel will illustrate the effect the Code had on such adaptations. The profound influence of the Code on the American film product can be seen by studying a relatively small number of American films produced between 1934 and 1966. The Code Administration's power to control the medium diminished slowly from 1952, when Otto Preminger released *The Moon Is Blue* without a seal of approval (but *with* box-office success) until 1966, when Jack Valenti was named president of the Code administration's parent agency, the Motion Picture Association of America (MPAA). At that time,

2. Ibid., pp. 158–62.
3. Conversation with Robert Penn Warren, Bowling Green, Kentucky, 25 February 1975.

machinery for developing a new method of control was set into motion, resulting in the Rating System of 1968.

CENSORSHIP IN TRANSITION: 1948–1968

The Production Code Administration continued to control the American film product with an iron hand until 1948, when an important Supreme Court antitrust decision (*U.S. v. Paramount Pictures*) ruled that the major producing companies could no longer own large theater chains. With thousands of theaters across the country no longer obligated to show any film, regardless of quality, just because the parent company produced it, the major studios lost control of a large captive audience. It also opened the door for independently produced movies to be distributed without a Code seal.

In the *Paramount* decision, Justice William O. Douglas also questioned the legality of film censorship. Whereas a 1915 ruling had regarded the movies as a "business pure and simple," Douglas suggested that "motion pictures, like newspapers and radio, are included in the press whose freedom is guaranteed by the First Amendment." This opinion was supported by the landmark *Burstyn v. Wilson* case in 1952, which overruled the New York State censors' banning of an Italian film, *The Miracle,* as sacrilegious. This decision, for all practical purposes, destroyed the power of state and local boards of censorship, and the PCA, relieved of the pressure of guarding against censorship action by such boards, relaxed some of its controls over film content.

As early as 1949, Samuel Goldwyn recognized that the industry would have a monumental fight on its hands "to keep people patronizing our theaters in preference to sitting at home and watching a program of entertainment" on television.[4] By 1954, movie attendance had dropped to half of what it had been in 1946. When this decline in attendance continued in spite of the industry's technical innovations such as Cinemascope, Cinerama, 3-D, and stereophonic sound, filmmakers recognized that they would also have to handle more mature subjects than were being treated on television if they hoped to lure their audience back into the theaters.

4. Charles Champlin, *The Movies Grow Up, 1940–1980.* Chicago: Swallow Press, p. 46.

Changes were made in the Code to allow more flexibility: In 1956, the Code was amended to allow themes of miscegenation, prostitution, and narcotics, and in 1961 discreet treatments of homosexuality and other sexual deviations were permitted.

These changes in the Code were possibly brought about as much by a spirit of rebellion within the industry as anything else. In 1953, United Artists had financed the Otto Preminger film *The Moon Is Blue,* and after being denied a seal of approval, released the film and resigned from the MPAA. The film's solid success at the box office made theater owners seriously question the necessity of Code approval. After Preminger successfully challenged the Code again in 1956 with *The Man With the Golden Arm* (at that time, a shocking story of drug addiction), the Code seal was awarded to Elia Kazan's controversial *Baby Doll* in the same year.

The release of *Baby Doll,* with its focus on sweaty sexual tension, raised an immediate protest from the Catholic quarter. Francis Cardinal Spellman called the film "an occasion of sin," and Catholics were forbidden to see it. The boycott and the great publicity generated by it failed to prevent (and perhaps even helped) the film's success, and it became clear to the industry that the moral climate of America in the mid-'50s had undergone significant changes.

In the 1950s and early 1960s, a number of powerful foreign films being shown in the larger cities were also having an important influence on American audiences. Seeing strong, provocative films like *Hiroshima, Mon Amour, The Seventh Seal, The Virgin Spring, The Lovers,* and *La Dolce Vita* made the Code-approved American products seem bland, antiseptic, and even dull by comparison, and American filmmakers were inspired to take some chances and push for more artistic freedom (Figs. 13.2 and 13.3).

This freedom was achieved primarily through independent productions or productions financed and distributed through subsidiary companies set up by the MPAA companies to avoid breaking their pledge not to release a film without a seal. Between 1963 and 1966, thirty-nine unapproved films were distributed by MPAA subsidiaries.

By the mid-'60s the industry had clearly begun to accept the idea that perhaps not all movies should be made for one mass audience. *Lolita* (1962) was given a seal despite its theme of a middle-aged man's obsessive love for an adolescent; *The Pawnbroker* (1965) was approved in spite of two nude scenes (Fig. 13.4); *Who's Afraid of Virginia Woolf?* (1966) won a seal despite clear violations in theme and language; and *Alfie* (1966) was cleared in

|13.2| **|13.3|**
Provocative Foreign Films: The Code-bound American film products of the '50s and early '60s seemed bland and antiseptic when compared to powerful imports like *Hiroshima, Mon Amour* [13.2] (France, 1960) and *La Dolce Vita* [13.3] (Italy, 1961).

|13.4| American Breakthrough: Rod Steiger gave a touching performance as a middle-aged man haunted by memories of his experiences in a Nazi concentration camp in *The Pawnbroker* (1965). The film was granted an MPAA seal of approval in spite of two nude scenes, both crucial to understanding the story.

spite of its frank treatment of sex. With the approval of the latter two films, the PCA made a significant move toward the present rating system: Warner Brothers agreed to restrict attendance to *Who's Afraid of Virginia Woolf?* to adults eighteen and over, and Paramount agreed to advertise *Alfie* as "recommended for mature audiences."

In 1966, the Code was greatly simplified, and the Code Administration divided approved films into two categories: The first category simply included those films that presented no problems for the mass audience; the second category had to be labeled "Suggested for Mature Audiences." The label was advisory only, and there were no enforced restrictions.

Two important court decisions in April of 1968 forced the industry to provide a clearer system of classification. The *Ginsburg v. New York* decision ruled that material protected by the constitution for adults could still be considered obscene for minors. The *Interstate v. Dallas* decision invalidated a city classification ordinance because its standards of classification were vague, but indicated that more tightly drawn standards of classification could be judged as being within constitutional rights. To prevent state and local classification boards from springing up in response to this ruling, the film industry hurriedly tightened up its own classification system and announced the MPAA Movie Rating System to the public six months after the *Dallas* decision. That Rating System, with slight modifications, remains in effect today.

THE MPAA RATING SYSTEM

The new rating system was announced to the public on October 7, 1968, and went into effect on November 1. Like the Motion Picture Production Code, which it was designed to replace, the Movie Rating System is a form of self-regulation, put into operation to guard against government, state, and local control. It was clear by 1966 that American society had outgrown the moral standards that governed the 1930 Code, and honest, realistic films could no longer be produced in conformance with its prohibition. Therefore, the new system was conceived as a system of classification rather than as censorship, and each film rated by the board was (and still is) classified in terms of its suitability for children.

The Rating System board does not prohibit or ban the production or distribution of any motion picture. Its responsibility is, therefore, limited to the classification of films, to labeling each film clearly so that theater managers can control the audience for each picture in accordance with its classification.

A brochure published when the rating system was announced still refers to it as a "Code" and describes it as follows:

> This Code is designed to keep in close harmony with the mores, culture, the moral sense, and change in our society.

The objectives of the Code are:

1. To encourage artistic expression by expanding creative freedom.
2. To assure that the freedom which encourages the artist remains responsible and sensitive to the standards of the larger society.

The brochure goes on to describe censorship as an "odious enterprise" that is alien to "the American tradition of freedom," especially freedom of choice. Perhaps the most important protection built into the new system is that it clearly places the responsibility for children's viewing habits on their parents.

> In our society parents are the arbiters of family conduct. Parents have the primary responsibility to guide their children in the kind of lives they lead, the character they build, the books they read, and the movies and other entertainment to which they are exposed.
>
> The creators of motion pictures undertake a responsibility to make available pertinent information about their pictures which will assist parents to fulfill their responsibilities.

The brochure goes on to state that a prime objective is a "sensitive concern for children."

From November 1968, practically every motion picture exhibited in the United States has carried a rating. Slight modifications have been made in the wording and symbols to clarify misunderstood points, but the rating system in use today is essentially the same one introduced in 1968. As it now stands, the MPPA Ratings System classifies films in the manner illustrated in Exhibit 2.

UNDERSTANDING THE RATING SYSTEM

Perhaps the simplest explanation of the Rating System (and a fairly accurate one) is found in a recent joke that explained the rating according to hat colors: "In a G- or PG-rated movie, the guy in the white hat gets the girl. In an R-rated movie, the guy in the black hat gets the girl. In an X-rated movie, everybody gets the girl."

Although the brochure published when the Rating System was introduced in 1968 included a list of eleven "Standards for Production," that list provides no help whatsoever in determining how films are actually classified.

Language is certainly a factor in many rating decisions. But unlike those of the Production Code of 1930, the current guidelines are very vague. Even the kind of detailed knowledge of the

EXHIBIT 2 THE MOVIE RATING SYSTEM

WHAT THE RATINGS MEAN

Essentially the ratings mean the following:

G: "General Audiences—All ages admitted."

This is a film which contains nothing in theme, language, nudity and sex, or violence which would, in the view of the Rating Board, be offensive to parents whose younger children view the film. The G Rating is *not* a "certificate of approval," nor does it signify a children's film. Some profoundly significant films are rated G (for example, *A Man for All Seasons*) [Fig. 13.5].

Some snippets of language may go beyond polite conversation but they are common everyday expressions. No words with sexual connotations are present in G-rated films. The violence is at a minimum. Nudity and sex scenes are not present.

13.5 A "Profoundly Significant" G: One of the prevalent misconceptions about the MPAA Ratings System is that G signifies a children's film. While this is often the case, an occasional "profoundly significant" film like *A Man for All Seasons* (starring Paul Scofield as Sir Thomas More with Orson Welles as Cardinal Wolsey) fits the "General Audiences" classification.

PG: "Parental Guidance Suggested; some material may not be suitable for children."

This is a film which clearly needs to be examined or inquired about by parents before they let their younger children attend. The label PG plainly states that parents *may* consider some material unsuitable for their children, but the parent must make this decision.

Parents are warned against sending their children, unseen without inquiry, to PG-rated movies.

There may be profanity in these films, but harsher sexually derived words will vault a PG rating into an R category. There may be violence but it is not deemed so strong that everyone under 17 need be restricted unless accompanied by a parent. Nor is there cumulative horror or violence that may take a film into the R category.

There is no explicit sex on the screen, although there may be some indication of sensuality. Brief nudity may appear in PG-rated films, but anything beyond that puts the film into R.

The PG rating, suggesting parental guidance, is thus a strong alert for special examination of a film by parents before deciding on its viewing by their children.

Obviously the line is difficult to draw and the PG-rated film is the category most susceptible to criticism. In our plural society it is not easy to make subjective judgments without incurring some disagreement. So long as parents know they must exercise parental responsibility, the PG rating serves as a meaningful guide and as a warning.

R: "Restricted, under 17s require accompanying parent or guardian."

This is an adult film in some of its aspects and treatment so far as language, violence, or nudity, sexuality or other content is concerned. The parent is advised in advance the film contains adult material and takes his children with this advisory clearly in mind.

The language may be rough, the violence may be hard, and while explicit sex is not to be found in R-rated films, nudity and lovemaking may be involved.

Therefore, the R rating is strong in its advance advisory to parents as to the adult content of the film.

X: "No one under 17 admitted."

This is patently an adult film and no children are allowed to attend. It should be noted, however, that X does *not* necessarily mean obscene or pornographic in terms of sex or violence. Serious films by lauded and skilled filmmakers may be rated X. The Rating Board does not attempt to mark films as obscene or pornographic; that is for the courts to decide legally. The reason for not admitting children to X-rated films can relate to the accumulation of brutal or sexually connected language, or of explicit sex or excessive and sadistic violence.

APPRAISAL

In any appraisal what is "too much" becomes a controversial issue. How much is too much violence? Are classic war-type films too violent; marines storming the beaches of Iwo Jima killing and wounding the enemy, is that too much? Is the dirt-street duel between the cattle rustler and the sheriff too violent, or does it require the spilling of blood to draw a more severe rating? How does one handle a fistfight on the screen, where is the dividing line between "all right" and "too much" for a particular classification?

The same vexing doubts occur in sex scenes or those where language rises on the Richter scale. The result is controversy, inevitable, inexorable, and that is what the rating system has to endure.

The raters try to estimate what most American parents think about the appropriateness of film content so that parents at the very least are cautioned to think seriously about what films they may wish their children to see.

Source: "The Movie Rating System." Official statement by Jack Valenti, president of the Motion Picture Association of America, 7 May 1982.

inner workings of the board provided by former member Stephen Farber in *The Movie Rating Game*[5] is little help as board members change over the years and, with those changes in personnel, come charges in interpretation. Therefore, the only real way to determine what the ratings mean is to study a series of films produced within a given year, representing all the ratings, and by using whatever general guidelines exist, try to second-guess the board on the reasons governing their decision.

The recent Rating System has not been accepted as a final solution by some segments of society. In May of 1971, the Film Commission of the National Council of Churches and the Catholic Office for Motion Pictures officially withdrew their support of the

5. Stephen Farber, *The Movie Rating Game*. Washington, D.C.: Public Affairs Press, 1972.

new system because they found the ratings "unreliable." The two groups issued a joint statement summarizing their objections:

> We can no longer commend this plan to the public. In fact, it is our judgment that the public's confidence in the plan has already been seriously eroded, and that its confidence will not be restored until the ratings become more reliable, more local theaters seriously enforce the ratings, and advertising reflects more concern with informing the public and less with exploiting sex and violence.

But the motion picture industry was obviously trying desperately to hang on to what had become a relatively small audience. In the late 1940s movies were a family affair, and over ninety million people went to them every week. By 1971, movie attendance had declined by 75 percent, with a weekly audience of around fifteen million. And the makeup of that audience had changed drastically. The movies were no longer a family habit. In the early 1970s, approximately fifty percent of moviegoers were between the ages of sixteen and twenty-four, and at least two-thirds of them were under thirty. This younger audience seems to have no problems with the present Rating System.

The biggest problem was the confusion it caused parents of children sixteen or under, and most of the confusion existed in the PG category, those films that anybody could see with "parental guidance suggested." (Although television has certainly made the modern child a more sophisticated viewer than his pre-television counterpart, there is a great deal of difference between the maturity of an eight year old and that of a sixteen year old.) And many parents were confused about what could really be expected in a PG movie, and whether their eight year old or twelve year old should be allowed to go alone on a Saturday afternoon.

An attempt to solve this problem was first made in 1972, when the industry added this caution to its PG rating: *Some material may not be suitable for pre-teenagers*. Although some pressure was applied to encourage the MPAA to follow the example of the European systems, which distinguish between children (up to twelve) and teenagers (thirteen to sixteen), there was no move to do so until the summer of 1984.

When *Indiana Jones and the Temple of Doom* and *Gremlins* came out in June of 1984, there was an immediate negative reaction from critics and parents alike over the amount and intensity of violence portrayed in both films. A new cautionary rating called PG-13 (to cover the gray area between the PG and the R ratings)

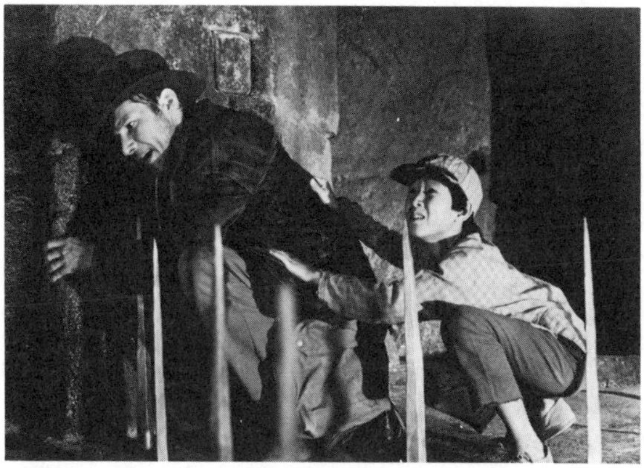

|13.6|

|13.7|

Too Intense for Young Children: Steven Spielberg's *Indiana Jones and the Temple of Doom* [13.6] and Joe Dante's *Gremlins* [13.7] drew so much criticism for their intensity of violence that the industry instituted a new PG-13 rating for such films.

was instituted on July 1, 1984, designed to warn parents to use extra caution in allowing young children to attend such films (Figs. 13.6 and 13.7).

Because theater owners do not want to enforce a second restrictive rating, a PG-13 puts the burden of control squarely on parents, a philosophy very much in tune with the MPAA's stated policies since 1968. Even with the confusion over the PG rating, nationwide surveys prior to 1980 indicated that the public was reasonably well satisfied with the rating system, with three out of five parents approving the present system. Only time will tell if the new PG-13 rating will solve the "gray area" problem.

Behind the scenes, the power that the board exercises over the film industry still comprises a form of censorship, for they continue to interfere with the creative process. The assigning of classification holds tremendous power over a film's potential for commercial success: An X rating reduces the potential audience for a film by 50 percent, and an R rating automatically eliminates 20 percent. To guard against such "automatic" elimination of potential audience, studio contracts with producers and directors have established a common practice of specifying that an X rating be avoided or that the film be granted a G or PG rating before it shall "be deemed to have been delivered."[6] Under such contracts, the producer is obligated to make whatever changes are necessary to obtain a desirable rating. If the producer cannot secure an

6. Ibid., p. 117.

acceptable rating, the studio has two options: It can refuse to accept delivery of the picture (and presumably refuse to pay the producer or director for his or her efforts), or it may accept the film with the right to make "such changes, alterations, or deletions . . . as may be necessary or desirable"[7] for achieving an acceptable rating. Thus the producer and/or director lose creative control over these changes if they do not secure the specified rating *before* the film is delivered to the studio.

To prevent the loss of creative control at this late stage of production, producers and directors often submit scripts to the board for approval ahead of time—so that rating problems can be solved before the expensive process of shooting begins. Thus the Code and Rating Administration, in advising what changes have to be made, enters into the filmmaking process itself, by editing both scripts and "finished" films. Although the pressures bringing about this censorship are economic rather than social, they are nevertheless very real and constitute a form of censorship not totally unlike that of the 1930 Code.

A filmmaker who has not secured a satisfactory rating does have the option of appealing the board's decision. The Code and Rating Appeals Board meets in New York, and is separate from the Code and Rating Administration. When a film's rating is appealed, the Appeals Board screens the film, then hears arguments from both the company challenging the rating and the Code and Rating Administration before voting. Ratings are rarely reversed. During the first three years of the rating system, only ten of thirty-one appeals were successful. Between 1974 and 1980, around 2,500 films were rated, with only seven successful appeals.

Perhaps the most successful appeal yet heard by the board involved *Ryan's Daughter,* an MGM film. When the film received an R rating, the studio threatened to pull out of the MPAA, and claimed that an R rating would so limit the audience for this expensive ($10 million) film that the studio's very life was at stake. Under this considerable pressure from a great and historic motion picture institution, the board changed its rating of *Ryan's Daughter* to a PG so they would not have the demise of a major studio on their conscience. Paramount was in serious financial trouble also when it made a similar appeal for *Paint Your Wagon,* but the board twice refused its appeal for a G rating.

Other important films have been re-rated. *Midnight Cowboy,* rated X when it came out in 1969, was re-rated to an R without change to the film. *A Clockwork Orange,* originally rated X, be-

7. Ibid.

came an R after a few seconds of violence were cut out. *Saturday Night Fever,* originally shown as an R, was cut and redistributed as a PG to take advantage of its appeal to the "under seventeen" crowd, and for showing on network television. *Last Tango in Paris,* released in theaters as an X, has been cut and re-released for television cable as an R, but without the impact of the original.

More recently, Steven Spielberg's appeal to change the R rating on *Poltergeist* to a PG was granted, and *Lone Wolf McQuade,* which received an R rating for violence, received a PG from the board after actor Chuck Norris appealed that the violence in *McQuade* "was of a stylized nature similar to that in John Wayne westerns" (Fig. 13.8). Brian De Palma fought long and hard and cut some violent scenes to prevent his *Scarface* from getting an X rating.

In its effort to adjust to changing parental attitudes in our society, the Rating Board has in recent years become "harder" on violence and "softer" on nudity and sensuality. In the words of Richard D. Heffner, Chairman of the Classification and Rating Administration since 1974:

> A moment of nudity that automatically drew an R years back may be PG-rated today, while violence is often rated R now that was not restricted before. It's a result of what we perceive to be changing parental attitudes toward these subjects.[8]

As long as the rating board remains responsive to such shifts in parental attitudes, it will continue to function as the effective instrument of industry control it was designed to be.

|13.8| Rating Appeals: The Classification and Ratings Administration has recently approved appeals for new ratings on *Poltergeist, Scarface,* and *Lone Wolf McQuade* [13.8]. *McQuade*'s star, Chuck Norris, successfully argued that the film's violence was of a stylized nature comparable to John Wayne westerns.

CHANGING FORMULAS FOR THE TREATMENT OF SEX, VIOLENCE, AND LANGUAGE

Contrary to popular belief, the motion picture did not invent violence, sex, or even rough language. Other art forms, such as fiction and drama, also make use of such materials. And each art form, even without a formal code of censorship, has its own standards of what's acceptable and what's not in any given time period. And it is not a simple matter of what a given art form can get away with, but with what might be called "the fashion of the day." The result is what we might call "formulas for realism." These formulas are determined much the way the proper length

8. "What G, PG, R, and X Really Mean." *TV Guide,* 4 October 1980, p. 44.

for hemlines is determined—by what everyone else is doing. Thus, at least to some degree, the prevalence of violence, sex, and rough language on the screen today is more than just the exploitation of shocking material. It is the fashion. If it were not, we would be offended by what we see and stop going to movies altogether.

Changes do occur in these formulas, and we should have some awareness of how these changes come about. Changes in formulas usually follow shortly after social changes. In film, changes in fashion are usually tied to popular success, and films would not have such popular success unless they struck responsive chords in large segments of the population. Thus, when a "breakthrough" film becomes a popular success, it sets new fashions, for imitators begin to treat it as a standard.

Consider, for example, how the formula for realism has evolved in the treatment of death by gunshot, what we might call the "dance of death." In *Birth of a Nation,* men shot during the Civil War battles typically threw their arms skyward and fell sidewise to the ground. By the 1940s, a cowboy shot in a grade B western simply clutched one hand to his chest (usually where cowboys were wounded) and crumpled forward. The fashion for the dance of death in the '50s was set by *Shane,* where the impact of the bullet from villain Jack Palance's gun knocked his victim ten feet straight backwards into a mud puddle. In the '60s, *Bonnie and Clyde* introduced a new vogue, the slow-motion dance of death, with bullets exploding holes through clothing. When a sensational new effect is introduced in a milestone film like *Bonnie and Clyde,* audiences feel cheated if the same sense of heightened reality is not achieved in the films they see after it. Similar patterns can be traced in the way sexual intimacy is suggested, from *Tarzan of the Apes* (1932) to *Last Tango in Paris* (1971); and in the way rough language is treated, from *Gone With the Wind* (1939) to *Scarface* (1983).

QUESTIONS

On Censorship

1. Study three or more films with censorable subject matter made under the Motion Picture Production Code (prior to 1950), and answer the following questions:
   a. Where in these films do you find obvious examples of Code-caused suppression and restraint?

b. How would these films be different if they were being made today? Which film (or films) could be significantly improved by being made today with a PG or R rating? How or why would they be improved?

c. Do the films studied seem too mild-mannered to have much impact, or do they effectively suggest such things as violence and sexuality in ways acceptable to the Code?

d. Do these films seem to go out of their way to promote traditional American values? Are American values or institutions questioned in any of these films? If so, how and where are such questions dramatized, and how are such problems resolved?

2. Examine three or more films with censorable subject matter made during the transitional period (1950–1967) and consider questions a–d above. What evidence do you find of the Code's being stretched or disregarded? How do the films of the transitional period differ from those before 1950?

3. Examine a film made under the Motion Picture Production Code and compare it with its remake produced under the MPAA Ratings System (examples would be *Scarface,* 1932/1983; *The Postman Always Rings Twice,* 1946/1981; and *Here Comes Mr. Jordan,* 1941, remade as *Heaven Can Wait,* 1978). To what degree are these films different because of the difference in censorship restrictions? Where are those differences most obvious and how is the overall effect of the film changed by these differences? Which of the two is the better film? Why?

4. Examine three current films presently playing at your local theatre: a G, a PG, and an R. What are the dividing lines between the different classifications based on these films? In other words, what separates a G from a PG, and what separates a PG from an R?

5. Make an attempt to examine the evolution of the Rating System's classification decisions by checking what makes the difference between a PG and an R rating at four-year intervals, using films released in 1972, 1976, 1980, and 1984. Can you discern any patterns of change in where the dividing line is drawn? If so, what do these patterns indicate?

6. Examine several films from each decade from the 1930s to the present, and try to describe the fashion of the age in terms of each decade's formulas for sexual intimacy, the dance of death, and rough language. What other changing patterns or fashions are apparent in the films you viewed?

FILM: AN INDUSTRY AND AN ART FORM

As we have seen, film is a sophisticated art form as well as a multimillion-dollar business. As we have also seen, this commercial element, the pressure for films to make money, often determines the kind of films that are produced.

The initial investment required to produce a motion picture today is tremendous. In an effort to ensure these large sums of money, to make the safest possible investment, the film industry tends to repeat past successes rather than risk new and unproven products, hence the extensive use of sequels, remakes, adaptations, and genre films. This practice can, of course, be at odds with a filmmaker's artistic vision—though that is not always the case.

Nevertheless, this commercial influence is a strong force in shaping films. Even "small" films today represent multimillion-dollar investments. Individual film budgets can range from $6 million for a relatively small release like 1980's zany *Airplane!* to in excess of $30 million for a special-effects-laden film like *Return of the Jedi.* Additionally, there is the promotional budget; with films now opening at once in literally thousands of theaters nationwide, such advertising budgets can be considerable. Approximately $10 million went into advertising 1981's *Reds* (Fig. 13.9).

Because these expenses determine the kinds of movies that are made, a film's commercial viability is often considered more important than its relative artistic merit, as evidenced by the rash of low-quality, high-profit "hack 'n slash" horror movies of the late 1970s. Commercial success is a difficult thing to predict, however, and few films are really safe. Genres wear out, sequels are often disappointing, remakes fail to match the unique appeal of their predecessors—and they do not make money.

Even a track record of hits from a successful director or star does not guarantee a future hit, though the industry will often justify a sizable investment by citing the track record. Warren Beatty had a series of successful films to his name (*Bonnie and Clyde,* as producer and star; *Heaven Can Wait,* as producer, director, and star) before he could raise funding for *Reds,* a critically acclaimed but expensive period film that foundered at the box office; major hits like *Jaws* and *Close Encounters of the Third Kind* failed to guarantee Steven Spielberg's over-budget, out-of-control comedy *1941*—though Spielberg has since maintained strict control of his budgets and produced a number of blockbuster films; and Michael Cimino's successful *The Deer Hunter* won financing from

| 13.9 | Big-Budget Advertising: A major factor in the high cost of modern films is the expense of advertising. In spite of an advertising budget of approximately $10 million, *Reds* was a disappointment at the box office.

United Artists for *Heaven's Gate,* an incredible $50 million misjudgment on that studio's part (Fig. 13.10).

Successful filmmakers must meet the demands of both industry and art form if they are to flourish. An interesting parallel can be drawn between filmmakers George Lucas and Francis Ford Coppola, both of whom separated from the mainstream of industry to form their own production companies (Lucasfilm and Zoetrope, respectively). Lucas has continued to meet the demands of filmmaking as an industry, crafting such commercial successes as *Raiders of the Lost Ark* and the *Star Wars* series; Coppola has bankrolled his own personal fortune on the self-indulgent *Apocalypse Now* and the financially disastrous *One from the Heart*—which cost over $26 million to produce and returned only $1.2 million at the box office in 1982.

Yet an artistic film is not automatically a failure, even considering the commercial responsibilities incumbent on it. For example, films no longer have to cater to a mass audience; more and more, films are being designed for specific markets. This target audience is usually the twelve to twenty-five year old age group; while only approximately 20 percent of the total population, this audience now buys 80 percent of the tickets for American movies. More significantly, this age group is the repeat audience, who see popular films three, six, a dozen times and create such mega-hits as *Star Wars.* As long as these films produce such enormous profits, studios can afford to invest in "adult" films, more mature and complex films that allow filmmakers to flex their artistic muscles.

| 13.10 | Epic Disaster: After the great success of Michael Cimino's *The Deer Hunter*, United Artists gambled over $50 million on his next film, the epic western *Heaven's Gate*, which failed miserably at the box office.

These films generally require a relatively modest investment, and can occasionally prove tremendously successful at the box office; *Kramer vs. Kramer, Ordinary People,* and *On Golden Pond* are recent examples (Fig. 13.11). There is still room for the "nice little film" as well, which costs far less to make and generally appeals to a limited audience, though even these small films can become major hits on occasion, as was the case with 1979's *Breaking Away.*

No longer must the industry rely on the theaters as their only source of income, either. Today, quite a number of new markets for motion pictures are available, where an unsuccessful film can recoup its investment and a major blockbuster can become an industry unto itself. These markets, called "windows," follow a fairly standard sequence: (1) first-run release of a motion picture in major metropolitan theaters; (2) second-run several months later in smaller, less expensive theaters; (3) release of the film in the various videocassette and videodisc formats, rental-only for the first few months in some cases; (4) a subsequent run on cable television; (5) a possible re-release of the film to theaters for a limited run (particularly if the film was extremely successful on first run); (6) sale of the film to network (commercial) television for a specific number of showings over a specific period of time; and finally (7) syndicated sale of the film to affiliate stations for repeated showings on afternoon and late-night local movie slots.

This formula varies widely with specific properties; films like *Gone With the Wind* and *Jaws* alternate between cable, network,

| 13.11 | Box Office Success: While the major audience market consists of the twelve to twenty-five year old age group, studios are also having some success with films that appeal to those over twenty-five, such as *Kramer vs. Kramer,* starring Dustin Hoffman as a single parent and Justin Henry as his young son.

and periodic re-release to theaters for long periods of time; unsuccessful films may appear on cable literally within weeks of their first-run release; and companies like Lucasfilm and Disney are reluctant to release such films as the *Star Wars* series and the Disney animated classics to the videocassette and videodisc markets, preferring instead to perpetually re-release such films in the theaters to new generations of audiences.

Finally, in addition to the windows for the film itself, there are markets for licensed merchandise; film-related books, games, toys and apparel, as well as traditional related merchandise such as soundtrack albums, became a potentially huge marketplace after *Star Wars* (Fig. 13.12).

This diversity of marketplaces, all fairly recent developments, has taken a measure of the risk out of the film industry. Nonetheless, the motion picture remains as much a child of the commercial industry that funds it as the artist who crafts it.

| 13.12 | The Mega-Hit: The profit potential for a film like *Star Wars* is doubled or tripled by a large repeat audience who also buy books, posters, records, and toys associated with or inspired by the film. Toy versions of the robots See-Threepio and Artoo-Detoo have been especially popular.

QUESTIONS

On Film: An Industry and an Art Form

1. What market was the film aimed for? Was it aimed primarily at the twelve to twenty-five year old age group, or at a more mature audience? Could it appeal equally to both groups? Why or why not?

2. Why do you think the studio backed the production of this film? Identify the factors that made this particular film a good gamble. How is it similar to other films that have made money? Does it have a name director or popular stars that might help its success? Does it seem to be part of a trend in current films? If so, how does it fit into the overall pattern of recent films?

3. Imagine that your film class is a group of potential film investors. Each of you has inherited a million dollars from a wealthy relative, but there are strings attached to the inheritance: You must invest all of the money in the production of a major motion picture. If the movie makes money, you get your million dollars back plus a share of the film's profits. If it loses money, your entire inheritance is forfeited. The money required to make the film exactly equals (in millions) the number of people in your class so each person must agree with the decisions reached by the "investment group." With the rules of the game thus established, make the following basic decisions: (1) the kind of screenplay to be bought or commissioned, (2) the director, and (3) the principal actors in the cast (male and female leads). Once unanimous agreement on these choices is reached, consider the following questions:
   a. What were the primary factors involved in making each basic choice?
   b. Did your investment group emphasize artistic quality or profit potential in its final choices?
   c. How close were the final choices to your personal preferences when the discussion began?

CHAPTER 14

THE ART OF WATCHING MOVIES ON TV

Can we ever hope to fully experience a theatrical film shown on TV? Consider the simple factor of size. An image approximately 20 feet high on the average movie screen is reduced to a maximum height of $1\frac{1}{2}$ feet on television. That's an important difference so far as your personal involvement in the movie goes. At television size, you must give the movie maximum concentration just to follow the story. It is practically impossible to become physically involved in the action in the same way you would in a theater. For example, a viewer who is susceptible to car sickness can get a little queasy during the car chase in *Bullitt* or the rollercoaster ride through the underground tunnel in *Indiana Jones and the Temple of Doom*. But the same visceral sensation—that we are actually behind the wheel of a speeding automobile or careening out of control in a mining car—is practically impossible while we're watching that little box across the room. The events occurring on the television set are pretty much remote from us, locked in the safety of a 19-inch screen, unable to truly threaten us, to pull us to the edge of our easy chairs. In the theater, the image is larger than life; on television, the same image is life-size or smaller. The reduction naturally reduces the intensity of our experience and the degree of our involvement.

In addition to reducing the intensity of the experience, some clarity may be sacrificed as well. For example, in a typical long shot, a lone human figure projected life-size may take up a relatively small space on the theater screen. When this image is reduced to the size of the average television image, the actor may not even be recognizable.

In addition to this size reduction, in many cases the basic shape of the composition is altered—for example, when a film in a wide-screen format is "squeezed" onto the TV screen. So that essential information will not be lost in translating wide-screen formats to television, a special editing process is used: A scanning device determines when the most significant information in each frame is so far to the left or right of center as to be outside the perimeter of the narrower television picture. TV producers can thereby adjust accordingly. Of course, the cinematographer's art suffers from this process, since the visual composition is compromised when part of the image is sliced off. Combined with the reduced size of the image, this scanning process can sometimes interfere with clear communication of the story, especially in situations where we must keep a clear picture of the actor's relationship to the setting, and often we simply lose our bearings because the setting in which the action is occurring is not properly revealed in the reduced and narrowed image. Even with the narrowest screen format, the standard size that the television's screen shape approximates, information is always cropped around the borders. This cropping around the edges also adds to the difficulty of reading the subtitles of foreign films on television. Reading white letters on light backgrounds can be difficult even in the theater. But on television, in addition, letters or words are cut off at the bottom or at the sides of the screen. And the reduced sharpness of the television image compounds the problem, making reading subtitles next to impossible. For these reasons, voice dubbing is often the best means for presenting the foreign language film on television.

SOUND

Television compromises a film's sound even more than its image. A modern movie theater equipped with multiple speakers can surround viewers with sound, immerse them in an encompassing aural environment. In *Das Boot,* the rumble of a destroyer passing back and forth over a submerged U-boat moves all over the theater as the sound increases and decreases in volume and shifts from speaker to speaker. Most television sets, even the largest ones, have a single small speaker (5″ maximum) and some don't even have a tone control. Although at present television manufacturers are improving their sound quality and some cable networks (MTV) even broadcast in stereo, movies are presently broadcast only in monaural sound. Television sound is broadcast in FM, so the quality of sound broadcast by TV stations *could* equal that of the best FM radio stations. But even if television stations did broadcast better quality sound, the tinny speaker of the average TV set would be incapable of picking it up.

THE TV VIEWING ENVIRONMENT

The TV watching environment in the normal household also reduces the quality of the viewing experience. A movie theater is dimmed to a level designed to focus the viewer's attention on the screen. Even the soft lights of the exit signs are situated far enough from the screen so as to not distract the viewer. In the home, apartment, or dorm room, however, it's "lights up" while the movie is running. Our attention is drawn to the screen only because it contrasts with its surroundings: The screen is brighter, more colorful, and of course the moving image has a life of its own. But there are many clearly visible distractions throughout the room, and our attention is not *focused* on the television set in the same way it is on the movie screen. In the movie theater there is simply nowhere else to look.

In addition to the visual distractions, there are a multitude of aural distractions. Few households control (or mute) external sounds, so we are constantly distracted by the sounds of daily living: horns, sirens, automobile engines, lawn mowers, barking dogs, ringing telephones, airplanes, heating systems, cooling systems, a roommate practicing the tuba. Thanks to insulation, the modern movie theater muffles or completely eliminates extraneous sounds. Of course, it's possible to concentrate enough on the TV sound to "hear through" such distractions, but the effort does diminish the movie's magic. In a theater, sound and image wash over you, immerse you, massage you. You needn't direct your attention. Seeing a movie in a theater is like diving into a heavy surf with the tide coming in; seeing a movie on television is like taking a sponge bath out of a gallon pail. There's a vast difference in the experience.

CONVENTIONS AND HABITS OF WATCHING TELEVISION MOVIES

Even more detrimental to the art of watching movies on TV are the habits of TV watching we have established over the years. Because of its constant presence in our lives, we have a distinct tendency to watch television too much (time wise). But we often give it only half of our attention; we have it on as background to whatever else we're doing, a kind of visual Muzak. In a sense, watching movies on television has become too convenient, something we take for granted. We frequently watch movies on TV because we are there in the same room with a television set, and we use it for company, because we are used to having it on, not because we are really interested in watching what is on. It's warm, it's alive, it's comfortable—pretty much like the family dog. And we pay it about the same kind of attention.

COMMERCIAL BREAKS

One basic reason that we "half watch" television—especially feature movies on network television—is the distraction of commercial breaks. There is absolutely no way to enjoy a "theatrical" movie on television as it was intended to be seen. To begin with, the film was designed to be shown without interruption, structured as a continuous flow, with the whole having a kind of organic rhythm of its own: a gradual building of tension in some spots, relief from tension in others. There is a pace to the editing, to the dialogue, to the way the story unfolds, to the revelations about the characters, and to the building surges of conflict. All these rhythms interact in a way that contributes significantly to the overall feel of the film. The director, editor, and composer weave the film's rhythm, shapes, and contours into a single unified and flowing fabric. But when the film is cut into eight or more fragments with commercial breaks, its sense of rising and falling tensions, its surging life pulse, its distinctive wholeness are irretrievably lost.

This is not to say that we cannot follow the plot (for we can), and we can remember the characters as we left them before the break. But it is difficult after a long commercial break to settle back into the rhythm, into the feel or spirit of the film. Let's remember that we're seeing the film in segments that average around fifteen minutes long. While the first segment shown usually runs longer than this (so as to hook the audience), *most* of the segments are shorter. After a commercial break, there's barely enough time to readjust our rhythms back to the film before four to six more commercials interrupt.

Since they've not really given us a chance to get fully involved with the movie anyway, there's no reason for the TV producers to give us time to resonate at the end. In the split second before the ending credits would have started to roll in a theater presentation, we're taken instead to a commercial (or two, or three), and the credits, which would have given us a little time to reflect, are finally run (if they are run at all) under the network promo for next week's movie in the same time slot.

Some movies suffer less than others from this kind of treatment. But none gain by it, and some are practically destroyed. To fully understand the effect of commercial breaks on the viewer's concentration, consider the task of trying to watch *Airport '77* as recently shown on "The ABC Sunday Night Movie":

> 8:00 network promo for featured movie: *Airport '77* * * * {Brim Coffee, Pepperidge Farms, Sears: *3 minutes*} * * * MOVIE: *25 minutes* * * * {One-a-Day Vitamins, Alka Seltzer, Avis, network promo—"Benson," "ABC movie will continue . . ." network promo—"That's Incredible," local promo—"Donahue": *3 minutes*} * * * MOVIE: *13 minutes* * * * {Sears, Mrs. Paul's, Canon, Minute Maid: *2 minutes*} * * * MOVIE: *10 minutes* * * * {Ford, AT&T, "ABC movie will continue . . ." "Sports Update"—tennis, Michelob, "Sports Update"—football, network promo, Coca-Cola, local promo—"M*A*S*H": *5 minutes*} * * * MOVIE: *15 minutes* * * * {Gillette, Bare Elegance, Intellivision, Kentucky Fried Chicken, network promo—"Love Boat": *3 minutes*} * * * MOVIE: *10 minutes* * * * {Corduroy, Centrum, "ABC movie will continue . . ." network promo—"ABC Evening News," Chevron, local promo: *2–3 minutes*} * * * MOVIE: *12 minutes* * * * {Ford, Ragu, Anbesol Gel, Anacin-3, network promo: *2–3 minutes*} * * * MOVIE: *15 minutes* * * * {Denny's, Irish Spring, "ABC movie will continue . . ." "News Brief," Cover Girl, "News Brief," network promo, Pepsi Free, Nature Valley Granola Bars, local station identification: *3–4 minutes*} * * * MOVIE: *9 minutes* * * * {Oil of Olay, Betty Crocker, Clorox, Breath Savers: *2 minutes*} * * * MOVIE: *7 minutes* * * * {AT&T, Sears, Atari, Inglenook, "ABC movie will continue . . ." promo, local update, Country Boy Waterbeds: *4 minutes*} * * * MOVIE: *8 minutes* * * * {Sure and Natural, Flintstones Vitamins, Thunderbird, Kodak: *3 minutes*} * * * MOVIE: *15 minutes* * * * {McDonald's, Arrid, Sears: *2 minutes*} * * * MOVIE (final segment): *3 minutes* * * * {network promo for David Hartman on "Good Morning America" on voice-over just as ending credits start to role . . . credits continue to roll without interruption to end}.

Made-for-TV movies will be interrupted by commercials in much the same manner, but they have one distinct advantage over theatrical films. Made-for-TV movies are scripted with network broadcast in mind, and the networks provide script writers with suggested times for commercial breaks, so that they can structure their script accordingly. By knowing that a commercial break must come within a relatively narrow time span, the writers can make slight adjustments to accommodate those breaks, usually by structuring a *natural* break close to the suggested times and by rewriting the last few lines of dialogue before a break to help end a scene.

Even network theatrical features have improved recently, for a real effort is being made to insert commercials at natural break points in such movies as *Oh, God!*

| 14.1 | Cutting Beyond the Bone: A last-minute scheduling conflict with a Bob Hope Special led NBC to cut the running length of *This Man Stands Alone*, starring Lou Gossett, Jr., as a courageous sheriff, from two hours to ninety minutes, including commercials. The plot was incoherent in the abbreviated debut.

MISSING SEGMENTS

Of equal importance is the problem of fitting the feature film into a time period shorter than the original length of the film. When the film is too long for the time allotted by the television station or network, segments are simply cut out to make it fit the scheduled period. Since the original creators of the film, the director and the editor, have no control over what is cut, the cutting is seldom done with much concern about its effect on the artistic structure of the film as a whole. Thus, what the viewer sees on television may be a badly butchered shell of the film the director intended (Fig. 14.1). Directors such as Otto Preminger have complained about the distortion of their art caused by such butchering, and some have even threatened legal action against the networks, but no real solution has yet been worked out.

NETWORK VERSUS LOCAL STATIONS

The editing of commercial scheduling in network films should perhaps be expected to be better than that done by local stations. In many cases, however, the best films on television are the late-night movies aired by local stations. There are fewer commercial breaks in the late time slot and no definite time period is set for ending, so the film can be shown in its entirety. Even network films now often run over the rigid two-hour time slot, so that there is probably less butchering of films on television than in the past.

Other methods are used for showing an entire film on television. Sometimes, for example, longer films are broken in half and shown on successive nights or a week apart in the same time slot. This is certainly not the best way to get a feeling for the whole, but it may be preferable to mindless butchering.

While there does seem to be an increased sensitivity on the networks about the scheduling of commercial breaks, local station sensitivity swings from one extreme to the other. Some

| 14.2 | From G to Network—A Few Choice Words: In *True Grit*, just before taking the reins in his teeth for his headlong charge toward Crazy Ned Pepper (Robert Duvall) and his gang, Rooster Cogburn (John Wayne) yells a challenge containing an unkind reference to the villainous Pepper's mother. As is common practice on network television, the epithet was bleeped out, but the spirit of the scene was unaffected.

stations seem to have no concern for the movie's structure, and will even interrupt a crucial line of dialogue; others have been known to simply let the projector roll during some shorter commercial breaks so that segments of the films are lost. On the other hand, some local stations show great sensitivity to the film's natural break points and schedule their commercials accordingly.

CENSORSHIP

Censorship has caused problems for many feature films shown on television. In the standard feature film, objectionable segments were simply cut out so they would not be seen by the television audience. Some experiments have been made with shooting two versions of the same film: one for the theater market, which can restrict its audience through the movie rating code, and a precensored version for the television market, which cannot restrict its audience. The television versions of such films may differ radically from the theater version in such aspects as treatment of sexual material, nudity, coarseness of language, and violence. Plot changes may be so extensive that the two versions really have little in common, as was the case with one of these experiments, *Secret Ceremony*.

The trend today does not involve such extreme changes, but when a feature film with definite network potential is in production, "cover shots" are often filmed to substitute for sexually explicit or strong language shots. In this way, a milder version of the film can be created for network TV showing. The original R-rated version of *Saturday Night Fever*, for example, was re-edited in 1979, given a PG rating, and rerun in theaters and on TV.

Special audience warnings are provided concerning "language" or "mature subject matter" when the networks feel that special care should be exercised in allowing young children to watch certain films, but as a general rule of thumb, nothing appears on network television until it is edited to at least a PG level (Fig. 14.2).

The real problem occurs when network greed overcomes good sense, and an R-rated movie is scheduled that simply does not lend itself to PG editing. By the time *Serpico* had been edited for coarse language, the raw thrust of the movie was gone and the plot was almost incoherent (Fig. 14.3). The ribald *Animal House* was totally fragmented by the necessary butchering, which left eleven minutes of its running time on the cutting room floor (Fig. 14.4).

|14.3| From R to Network—A Great Many Choice Words: The script of *Serpico,* starring Al Pacino as an honest policeman in a corrupt system, was so loaded with four-letter words that the necessary cutting for network television completely destroyed the grim, realistic power of the original.

|14.4| Censoring Sex and Ribald Humor: The eleven minutes cut from *Animal House* for its network showing practically destroyed its ribald humor and left its plot almost incoherent.

THE MADE-FOR-TELEVISION FILM

A partial solution to several of the problems that affect the feature film on television is provided with the increasingly respected made-for-television film. As the term implies, these films are designed for showing on television instead of theaters, and are usually financed and produced at least in part by one of the major networks. In watching such films, we should be able to detect at least four areas of improvement over the regular theater feature on television.

1. The film should be structured with some regard for the timing of interruptions, so that the film breaks for commercials at dramatically appropriate times. Networks provide script writers with suggested times for commercial breaks, and although scripts are not structured to make each unbroken portion of film equivalent to an act or a scene in a stage play, writers do tailor their scripts so that "little endings" occur at each scheduled commercial break.
2. Since it is designed and written for a specified time slot (average: two hours), the made-for-television film should exist as an integrated and complete whole, exactly as the director intended it.
3. The problems caused by the small size of the television screen should be solved by the fact that the film is usually conceived, composed, and shot with the size and shape of the television screen in mind. Since television is essentially a "close-up" medium, the made-for-television movie will emphasize the intimate, personalized "information" best suited to the small screen. The visual emphasis will be on the actors' faces, usually in interior shots, shots in automobiles, and telephone conversations. Since a "small" personal drama works better on the small screen than the sweep and grandeur of an epic, character will be emphasized over action, and conflicts will be more psychological than physical.
4. Censorship should provide no real problem for the made-for-television film, since it is designed with the mass unrestricted audience in mind. With network supervision all the way, the result is usually a G- or PG-level product. There is little vulgarity or nudity allowed, and the political bite is mild. The networks obviously want enough controversy to be interesting,

but not enough to be offensive. In spite of the networks' basically middle-of-the-road posture, some made-for-television films have courageously treated some sensitive social problems such as rape, teenage suicide, homosexuality, Viet Nam, drugs, alcoholism, breast cancer, mental retardation, and prostitution (Fig. 14.5).

|14.5| Testing New Waters: Network television has grown bolder in recent years, as evidenced by made-for-TV movies like *Flesh and Blood* [14.5], with an incestuous relationship in a subplot (Suzanne Pleshette as boxer Tom Berenger's mother, shown), Ann-Margret as Blanche Dubois in a remake of *A Streetcar Named Desire,* and a hard-hitting attack on incest, *Something About Amelia.*

In comparing the quality of made-for-TV movies to theater features, we should take into account that made-for-TV movies are made with much lower budgets. In 1979, when at least six theater features cost more than $20 million to produce, the average budget for TV movies was around $1.5 million. Lower budgets mean faster shooting schedules and lower production quality.

There is also a certain snobbery among dedicated film buffs against the TV movie. Some is justified; some is not. In the early days most of these movies were run-of-the-mill exploitation films or star vehicles, and many were pilots for television series. Barry Diller, formerly in charge of ABC's prime-time programming, admits they made "a lot of junky movies" then.[1] Now, however, he points with pride to some landmark films, well-written, hard-biting social-problem films like *Friendly Fire.* And some made-for-TV products are so well made that they stand up equally well on the large screen, as witnessed by the success of Steven Spielberg's *Duel.*

One great advantage of the made-for-TV movie is the great flexibility it provides. It can be designed to fit a variety of different length time slots. Stories can be filmed with a variety of approaches: as a "movie-of-the-week," as a "novel-for-television," as a docudrama, or as a miniseries. And the length can range from ninety minutes to twenty-five hours, broadcast over a period of weeks. (While the miniseries format solves many of the problems of adapting a long, complex novel into a film, it also requires a *major* commitment of time from the viewer.)

This flexibility of format, some well-written scripts, the general seriousness of the subject matter treated, and the overall improvement in quality of the made-for-TV product have combined with the decreasing number of theater features produced each year to lure some top movie names to television: Henry Fonda, Joanne Woodward, Marlon Brando, Robert Mitchum, and Jane Fonda have all worked in TV movies in recent years.

1. Quoted by Patrick McGilligan in "Movies Are Better Than Ever—On Television." *American Film,* March 1980, p. 52.

A new hybrid, the made-for-cable movie, has recently been introduced by Home Box Office with two big name vehicles, *Mr. Halpern and Mr. Johnson,* starring Laurence Olivier and Jackie Gleason, and *Between Friends* with Elizabeth Taylor and Carol Burnett. If these two samples are any indication, the style and quality of the made-for-cable movie will fall somewhere between the lower budgeted made-for-TV movie and the higher cost theatrical film.

CHANGING TV WATCHING HABITS

We really need to accept the fact that we are conditioned animals, and most of us simply haven't adjusted to the fact that we need to make important changes in our habits if we're going to really learn to watch movies on the pay cable channels. If we have one or more of the pay movie channels, or one of the new videodisc players or a VCR, we have what every real movie lover has always dreamed of: complete, uncensored, uninterrupted viewing of recent and classic movies at home. Yet most of us have watched TV movies for so many years on the major commercial networks or on local station programming that we have literally "programmed" ourselves for the rhythms of the commercial breaks. We have depended on the interruptions for so long that we are not really prepared to sit down and watch a movie from beginning to end. We leave the set to visit the kitchen, or the bathroom, or we answer the telephone or even make calls and talk while we watch. We think nothing of conversing with family members, roommates, etc., as they come and go. The movie-watching habits described in the following confession by Roger Director in *The Movies* magazine are unfortunately more the rule than the exception:

> I don't watch movies at home so I can pretend I'm at the Bijou. I rarely watch a movie all the way through on my TV. I watch it in stitched-together stops and starts depending on what is in the refrigerator, who is on the phone, and my maniacal penchant for speeding breathlessly around the dial. I may watch one scene in a movie repeated on cable a dozen times, another scene once. A one-hour-fifty-minute movie I may spend six hours and forty-three minutes watching, spread out over two months. If I have seen *Raggedy Man* eighteen times, I have seen it once—almost.
>
> Sometimes when watching TV I even find time to read. Lately, in bizarre concordance with my multiple viewings of John Carpenter's *The Thing,* I

have been reading Rousseau's *Confessions.* It's a good book. Better than *The Thing.*[2]

It's fortunate that filmmakers don't have to watch people watching their movies on television, for much of the subtlety of their work is totally lost, along with many things that are not even subtle. In all fairness, a great many of the movies shown on television actually deserve the kind of casual viewing described above. But a good movie, a really first-class movie, deserves all of our attention, and we can give it the attention it really deserves by following a few simple rules.

Making Choices

Since we are going to operate under the assumption "that any movie that's worth watching is worth watching well," the first step clearly involves choosing a movie that we know will be "worth watching." It may be a movie you've already seen once in a theater and want to see again, or it may be something you wanted to see in its theater run, but missed seeing, or it may simply be a movie you've heard good things about. It may even be a movie you've heard bad things about; it may be that it's worth watching to see for yourself if it's as bad as you've heard it is. If we're really interested in movies, we can often learn a great deal from watching a bad movie, by understanding what makes it bad.

Making a Commitment

Once you've decided to watch a movie, then watch the movie. Set aside the time to watch it, clear your schedule, and prepare yourself and your TV environment for two hours (more or less) of uninterrupted viewing. Pretend that you're at the theater. Visit the snack bar (kitchen) and the rest room (bathroom) before the movie starts. Prepare your environment for minimum distraction; dim or turn off all room lights, put out dogs, cats, uninterested roommates, relatives, or friends. Take the phone off the hook, lock all doors (with a DO NOT DISTURB sign on each). Remember also, that once you've created your own little temporary TV

2. "Video Confidential: Cable Days and Sleepless Nights." *The Movies,* September 1983, p. 16.

theater, you also have the right to the best seat in the house, so move your favorite chair to what you consider the best viewing distance. Then settle in and watch yourself a movie.

Anticipating the Event

TV movie watching can also be enhanced by making each movie you choose to watch an event, something that is achieved by separating or isolating the movie to be watched from the constant and continuous flow that constitutes The Entertainment Glut. Most modern television sets come equipped with something called an "on/off switch." If your set is functioning properly, this switch, whether a button or knob, can actually be used to make the video screen go completely dark, and at the same time make the speaker go completely dead. While most TV repairmen will tell you that overusing this switch may be harmful to your set's health, the danger has been greatly overstated. Some people with perfectly healthy, bright, and functioning sets even admit that they use this switch several times a day without apparent ill effects. To make a movie into a real event, the on/off switch should be placed in the "off" position and left there for a period of time between an hour and a week. During the time that the switch is in the off position, you should be actively working at anticipating the event. A mental countdown might even be helpful, something like "six days until movie time and counting." The switch should be returned to the "on" position no more than seven minutes prior to movie time, and the volume should be turned low. This assures that the picture tube has sufficient warmup to reach full brilliance, and should give you a sense of watching a preview. The important thing here is active anticipation of a movie event, a procedure designed to make the movie a special experience. The volume should, of course, be turned to the proper level a few seconds before the movie starts.

Locking in the Experience

We must also recognize that we have experienced an event by properly respecting the movie when it is over. Any movie worth making into an event is worth some time for resonation at its conclusion. When the movie ends, immediately return the on/off switch to the off position, settle back into the comfort of your best seat in the house, and resonate silently on what you have seen, giving the emotional system and the mind a chance to digest the event. This is extremely important to the entire art of watching films, whether it be on television or in the theater. It is particularly important in powerful movies with strong, provocative or emotional endings. *Ordinary People, The Elephant Man, Reds, The World According to Garp, Bonnie and Clyde, Coming Home, The Deer Hunter, Shoot the Moon,* and *On the Waterfront* absolutely demand some time for resonation. It's almost as though such movies take form, make sense, and lock themselves into our memories only with a proper period of quiet "echo" time. Their impact on our emotions, their messages, and our full appreciation of their art become bright, sharp, and clear in the same way that a Polaroid image appears several seconds after the picture has been taken. In this area alone, the TV movie watching experience has an edge on the theater experience. Theater managers are so anxious to clear the theater for the next showing that they often pull the scrim curtains over the screen before the ending credits are over, or they blur out the credits by bringing up the house lights before the audience has had a chance to resonate. Many moviegoers do not understand the resonation process, and leave the theater as soon as the musical score goes into a few bars of "ending music."

Different Kinds of Events

Although you don't want to complicate your movie event if you don't have to, there are certain situations where having several friends over to share the event can really make it more enjoyable. This would be an advantage especially if your event film is a classic comedy, because the herd instinct, the response to humor of a number of people laughing together, can add a special quality to the whole experience. A small number of powerful "black" comedies seem to be two different movies: one when viewed in a room or a theater full of people, another when viewed alone. *Dr. Strangelove, A Clockwork Orange,* and *Catch-22* seem to literally cry out for people to help warm the room. Viewed alone, the horror underlying the humor is almost too much to endure.

STATE-OF-THE-ART VIDEO EQUIPMENT

The revolution is not just coming, it is here. Most of the significant problems with television watching of movies have been solved. But the major problem still remains in that most people are not in a financial position to upgrade their present home television and sound setups to handle the new technology that is available. The basic problem is that setting up a movie theater in the home with the most recent state-of-the-art video equipment would cost a minimum of $5,000.

Size of Image

Over the past ten years gradual improvement has been made almost yearly in the overall picture quality of the large-screen projection systems. In the beginning the images were "soft," dim, and somewhat blurred. With normal lighting in the room, this already soft and dim image practically faded from view. An additional problem was seen in the curved screen required for the front projection systems. The screens, which were curved inwardly (concave) to catch all the projected light, required that the viewer sit right in front of the screen to avoid distortions caused by the curved surface. The screens were plenty large enough, but the image simply did not have the clarity, brightness, and sharpness to create a very impressive image. In other words, the increase in size of image was not enough of an advantage to offset the decrease in sharpness, brightness, and clarity. That problem has now been solved with the new rear-projection systems now in operation. The Mitsubishi 45-inch rear projection system captures the clarity and brightness required to make the large screen not only acceptable but almost movie-screen bright and clear, and seems comparable to watching a movie on a small screen.

There is obviously some ideal screen size (assuming the image is sharp and bright) at which viewers become completely immersed in the film experience and can simply let the film wash over them in the same way it does in a good theater experience, so that they can become involved, manipulated, and overwhelmed by the film experience. It seems that the 45-inch size of the flat (not curved) rear projection image can meet that requirement if the distance between viewers and screen is not too great.

Another system receiving rave notices these days is a roll-about component front projection system, from Kloss Video and Panasonic; housed in a cabinet a little larger than a piano bench, it can easily be positioned to throw a giant television picture on either a flat, white wall, a standard movie screen, or its own special separate screen, capable of picking up the projected image while rejecting ambient light (daylight or room light reflected on the screen). One model, presently listing for $3,300, produces a 6½-foot (diagonal) image with "more than five times the brightness of commercial movie theaters." Other models, designed for use in darkened rooms, project images measuring 10 feet and 5 feet, 4 inches (both diagonal measurements).

Shape and Quality of Image

There are also new and revolutionary changes in the shape of the tube in many standard-sized sets. They are flatter and squarer, offering a greater viewing area (with less cropping of border information), almost no distortion, and far less reflected ambient light.

Picture-tube resolution will drastically improve on sets soon to be introduced with medium- and high-resolution picture tubes capable of displaying the fine detail available from videodisc players. Just over the horizon is another important innovation: the true digital circuit television receiver, equipped with built-in computers capable of taking a standard, 525-line broadcast television picture and processing it into a 1,000-line image as clear as that available from motion picture film.

Sound

Sound quality, the long neglected element of broadcast television, is finally coming into its own. Broadcast stereo is scheduled to be introduced this year, offering not just two but three separate channels of sound (with the extra channel used to provide the original foreign language track for a dubbed foreign language film). Component systems are already on the market to handle such stereo broadcast, but most TV sets are not yet ready to handle it. Since 40 percent of the viewing audience is now cable-connected, TV set manufacturers want to be sure that cable TV operators will be required to feed stereo sound to subscribers' homes before they commit themselves completely to the manufacture of stereo-ready sets.

The makers of Beta format and VHS video cassette recorders are just coming out with recorders capable of stereo sound. And furthermore, it's extraordinarily high-quality stereo sound, offering full-frequency record and playback performance exceeded only by the latest in digital audio equipment. Stereo sound has been possible for some time with the videodisc and laserdisc players, and many of the discs manufactured for these players have stereo soundtracks. Pre-recorded video cassettes, in both Beta and VHS formats, are now being made available in Dolby Stereo for VCRs, especially for movies where music is featured (*Flashdance*) or where the separation of sound effects is crucial to a film's overall effect (*Das Boot*).

VCRs, Videodiscs, and Laserdiscs

With the recent innovations of video cassette recorders (VCRs), laserdiscs, and videodiscs, the art of watching films becomes an incredibly easy, enjoyable, and rewarding practice. For a little more than the price of a top stereo sound system, we can purchase one of these modern miracles that enable us to enjoy current and classic films at our own leisure. We can build our own library of favorite films, purchasing almost any film we would want from the large assortment of pre-recorded discs and tapes available. We can cut the cost of purchasing by exchanging tapes and discs with friends with the same types of players or by renting tapes and discs at a nominal fee. An extra bonus of the VCRs is that we can record movies from network or cablecasts, and most VCRs are equipped with special programming circuits that allow us to record films being received by our television systems even when we're not home, so that we may view them later, when it suits us. If we don't choose to keep such recorded films permanently, we can use the tape again to record another movie.

The important thing about these new innovations is that their potential for the study of film is incredible. Whether we own the movie, rent it, or borrow it, for the time it is in our possession it is ours to study like a book. We can watch it as many times as we like, and study it sequence by sequence, shot by shot, and sometimes frame by frame. We can locate the portions of the movie we want to study, play the segment, then back it up and play it again—all without doing any damage to the movie whatsoever.

This ability to stop a VCR or disc player, back it up, and watch a single scene over and over can provide a much deeper understanding of the elements of the film than we can acquire just watching the movies shown from beginning to end in a theater or classroom.

Because of its use of the instant replay on television, professional football is perhaps the best understood art form in America today. In watching a pass play, for example, we will see the receiver go downfield and watch the quarterback fade back and throw the ball. As the play develops, we focus on several questions: (1) Will the quarterback be able to get the ball away before he is tackled by the defensive lineman? (2) Will the ball be thrown accurately enough for the receiver to catch it? (3) Will the receiver catch the ball, drop the ball, or will it be intercepted by a defensive back? (4) What will happen after the reception or interception?

Note that all the questions we are concerned with above are "what will happen" questions, the kind of questions we would identify with plot in a movie. Then, of course, comes the instant replay. Now we are freed from concentrating our attention on *what* will happen and we can study the replay to understand *how* it happened, understanding the art of the play. Let's say, for example, we want to study the art of the receiver. During the replay, the analysts will tell us what to look for. They may use slow motion or freeze frame techniques to point out important aspects of the play. And during the instant replay, we see many wonderful things we didn't notice during the line action. We may see, for example, how the receiver used a subtle head fake, jerking his head almost imperceptibly to the left, to cause the defensive back to think he was going to turn and thereby throwing him offstride. Or we may see another receiver come into the general area where the ball was to be thrown to decoy another defender away from the real receiver.

We can use the VCR or the disc player in the same fashion, first by viewing the movie in its entirety, trying to follow its plot, recognize its themes, and respond with sensitivity to its emotional and sensual "messages." Then, if the movie is good enough to earn our respect, we can study the parts we consider most powerful through the instant replay technique. Whereas the football analysts isolated the receiver for their detailed analysis during the replay, we can run a brief sequence as many times as we like, isolating or focusing our attention on a different element each time we run it. We can take a brief segment of a classic film like

The Graduate, for example, and study the first five minutes or the first fifteen minutes. Knowing *The Graduate,* we should think during each replay about the contribution the element being studied is making both in the segment being studied and the film as a whole. We might focus our attention better on the cinematography (composition, framing, camera movement, camera positioning, camera angles, lighting, etc.), set designs, and costuming by turning off the sound. By doing so we will also sense what an important contribution the dialogue, sound effects, and music make. To fully appreciate the complexity of the soundtrack, we could face away from the picture and just listen to the sound. To understand the contribution color makes, we might adjust the color out of the TV tube and watch this segment in black and white. With a remote control switch, we might want to stop the movie every time there is an edit, to gain an appreciation of how many different shots are required to make a brief segment of film, how each shot relates to the shot following it, and how the editing affects the rhythm, pace, and feel of a scene.

The potential value of these new video toys in helping us understand and appreciate the motion picture art is tremendous. If we have the opportunity to practice these movie watching skills and habits on television, we can quickly sharpen our perceptions and become masters of the art of watching films.

QUESTIONS

On Watching Movies On TV

1. To what degree is the film's continuity destroyed by commercial breaks? Which of these breaks occur at appropriate times in terms of the film's dramatic structure, and which breaks weaken the dramatic tension appreciably?
2. If you saw the film in a theater, can you remember portions that were cut out of the television showing? How important were these segments to the spirit or plot of the film? Can you justify these deletions in terms of the new medium or its mass audience? Were these segments cut out because of time limitations or censorship?
3. If the film is a made-for-television film, how successful is it in solving the problems of the theater film on television?
4. How well is the film suited to viewing on the small screen with minimal sound quality? In what scenes do you feel you lack the intensity of in-

volvement needed to enjoy the film? In which scenes does the small-screen format work?

5. Was the movie originally made in a wide-screen format? In what scenes is important information cut off? Are you ever unsure of the character's spatial relationship to his or her environment? How is the aesthetic quality of the composition affected?

COMPREHENSIVE LIST OF QUESTIONS FOR ANALYSIS

Each subsection of questions is given a letter identification so that the instructor may simply assign questions by letter and number. The page numbers beside the lettered heads locate text information that may be helpful in answering the questions.

A THEME AND FOCUS 12–26

1. What is the film's primary concern or focus: plot, emotional effect, character, style or texture, or idea? On the basis of your decision, answer one of the questions below.

  a. If the film's primary concern is plot, summarize the action abstractly in a single sentence or a short paragraph.

  b. If the film is structured around a mood or emotional effect, what is the mood or feeling it attempts to convey?

  c. If the film focuses on a single unique character, describe the unusual aspects of his or her personality.

  d. If the film seems to be structured around a unique style or texture, describe the qualities that contribute to the special look or feel of the film.

  e. If the film's primary focus is an idea, answer the following questions:

    (1) What is the true subject of the film? What is it really about in abstract terms? Identify the abstract subject in a single word or phrase.

    (2) What comment or statement does the film make about the subject? If possible, formulate a sentence that accurately summarizes the idea dramatized by the film.

2. Although a filmmaker can attempt to do several things with a film, one goal usually stands out as more important than the others. Decide which of the following was the filmmaker's *primary* aim and give reasons for your choice.

a. Providing pure entertainment, that is, temporary escape from the real world.
b. Developing a pervasive mood or creating a single, specialized emotional effect.
c. Providing a character sketch of a unique, fascinating personality.
d. Creating a consistent, unique feel or texture by weaving all of the complex elements of film together in a one-of-a-kind film experience.
e. Criticizing humankind and human institutions, and increasing the viewer's awareness of a social problem and the necessity for reforms.
f. Providing insights into human nature (demonstrating that human beings *in general* are like that).
g. Creating a moral or philosophical riddle for the viewer to ponder.
h. Making a moral statement to influence the viewer's values and/or behavior.
i. Dramatizing the struggle for human dignity against tremendous odds.
j. Exploring the complex problems and pleasures of human relationships.
k. Providing insight into a "growing" experience, the special kinds of situations or conflicts that cause important changes in the character or characters involved.

3. Which of the above seem important enough to qualify as secondary aims?

4. Is the film's basic appeal to the intellect, to the funnybone, to the moral sense, or to the aesthetic sense? Is it aimed primarily at the groin (the erotic sense), the viscera (blood and guts), the heart, the yellow streak down the back, or simply the eyeballs? Support your choice with specific examples from the film.

5. How well does your statement of the film's theme and purpose stand up after you have thoroughly analyzed all the film elements?

6. To what degree is the film's theme universal? Is the theme relevant to your own experience? How?

7. If you think the film makes a significant statement, why is it significant?

8. Decide whether the film's theme is intellectually or philosophically interesting, or self-evident and boring, and defend your decision.

9. Does the film have the potential to become a classic? Will people still be watching it twenty years in the future? Why?

FICTIONAL AND DRAMATIC ELEMENTS

B STORY ELEMENTS 31–39

How does the film stack up against the five characteristics of a good story?

1. How well is it unified in plot or story line?

2. What makes the story believable? Pick out specific scenes to illustrate what kinds of truth are stressed by film: (a) objective truth, which follows the observable laws of probability and necessity, (b) subjective, irrational, and emotional inner truths of human nature, or (c) the semblance of truth created by the filmmaker?

3. What makes the film interesting? Where are its high points, its dead spots? What causes you to be bored by the film as a whole or by certain parts?

4. Is the film a proper blend of simplicity and complexity?

a. How well is the story suited in length to the limits of the medium?

b. Is the film a simple "formula" that allows you to predict the outcome at the halfway point, or does it effectively maintain suspense until the very end? If the ending is shocking or surprising, how does it carry out the tendencies of the earlier parts of the story?

c. Where in the film are implication and suggestion effectively employed? Where is the film simple and direct?

d. Is the view of life reflected by the story simple or complex? What factors influenced your answer?

5. How honest and sincere is the film in its handling of emotional material? Where are the emotional effects overdone? Where is understatement used?

C DRAMATIC STRUCTURE 40–43

1. Does the film use the expository (chronological) or the *in medias res* beginning? If it begins with expository material, does it capture your interest quickly enough, or would a beginning "in the midst of the action" be better? At what point in the story could an *in medias res* beginning start?

2. If flashbacks are used, what is their purpose and how effective are they?

D SYMBOLISM 44–53

1. What symbols appear in the film and what do they represent?

2. What universal or natural symbols are employed? How effective are they?
3. Which symbols derive their meaning solely from their context in the film? How are they charged with symbolic value? (In other words, how do you know they are symbols, and how do you arrive at their meaning?)
4. How are the special capabilities of film (the image, the soundtrack, and the musical score) employed to charge symbols with their meaning?
5. Which symbols fit into a larger pattern or progression with other symbols in the film?
6. How are the major symbols related to the theme?
7. Is the story structured around its symbolic meanings to the extent that it can be called an allegory?
8. Which of the symbols' meanings are clear and simple? Which symbols are complex and ambiguous? What gives them this quality?
9. Are visual similes employed effectively? Are they primarily extrinsic (imposed artificially in the scene by editing) or intrinsic (a natural part of the setting)?
10. How fresh and original are the film's symbols and similes? If they seem clichéd or time-worn, where have you encountered them before?

E CHARACTERIZATION 54–65

1. Identify the central (most important) character or characters. Which characters are static and which ones are developing? Which characters are flat and which are round?
2. What methods of characterization are employed, and how effective are they?
3. Which of the characters are realistic, and which ones are exaggerated for effect?
4. What about each character's motivation? Which actions grow naturally out of the characters themselves, and where does the filmmaker seem to be manipulating the characters to fit the film's purpose?
5. What facets of the central character's personality are revealed by what he or she chooses or rejects?
6. Which minor characters function to bring out personality traits of the major characters, and what do these minor characters reveal?

7. Pick out bits of dialogue, images, or scenes that you consider especially effective in revealing character, and tell why they are effective.
8. Which characters function as stock characters and stereotypes, and how can the presence of each be justified in the film?

F CONFLICT 66–69

1. Identify the major conflict.
2. Is the conflict internal (man against himself), external, or a combination of both? Is it primarily a physical or a psychological conflict?
3. Express the major conflict in general or abstract terms (for example, brains versus brawn, man against nature).
4. How is the major conflict related to the theme?

G SETTING 70–75

1. Which of the four environmental factors (temporal factors, geographical factors, social structures and economic factors, and customs, moral attitudes, and codes of behavior) play significant roles in the film? Could the same story take place in any environment?
2. Which environmental factors are most important, and what effect do these factors have on the plot or the characters?
3. Why did the filmmaker choose this particular location for filming this story?
4. How does the film's setting contribute to the overall emotional atmosphere?
5. What kind of important interrelationships exist between setting and the characters, or between setting and plot?
6. Is the setting symbolic in any way? Does it function as a microcosm?

H SIGNIFICANCE OF TITLE 76–77

1. Why is the title appropriate? What does it mean in terms of the whole film?
2. How many different levels of meaning can you find in the title? How does each level apply to the film as a whole?
3. If the title is ironic, what opposite meanings or contrasts does it suggest?
4. If you recognize the title as being an allusion, why is the work or passage alluded to an appropriate one?

5. If the title calls your attention to a key scene, why is that scene important?
6. How is the title related to the theme?

I IRONY 77–82

1. What examples of irony can be found in the film?
2. Is irony employed to such a significant degree that the whole film takes on an ironic tone? Is an ironic world view implied?
3. Do any particular examples of irony achieve comic and tragic effects at the same time?
4. Where in the film is suspense or humor achieved through dramatic irony?
5. How do the ironies contribute to the theme?

VISUAL ELEMENTS

J CINEMATIC QUALITIES 84–104

1. To what degree is the film cinematic? Cite specific examples from the film to prove that the director succeeds or fails in (a) keeping the image constantly alive and in motion, (b) setting up clear, crisp visual and aural rhythms, (c) creating the illusion of depth, and (d) using the other special properties of the medium.
2. Does the cinematography create clear, powerful, and effective images in a natural way, or does it self-consciously show off the skills and techniques of the cinematographer?
3. Which methods does the director use to draw our attention to the object of greatest significance?
4. Does the director succeed in keeping the screen alive by avoiding large areas of dead screen?
5. What are the primary or most memorable techniques used to create the illusion of a three-dimensional image?

K PRODUCTION DESIGN/ART DIRECTION 106–109

1. How important is the set and/or location to the overall look of the film? Is it essentially a realistic or authentic set, or is it stylized to suggest a heightened reality?

2. Was the movie filmed primarily on location or in the studio? What effect does this have on the style or look of the film?
3. How do the settings serve as personalized environments to enhance or reinforce the actors' performances? To what degree do the settings underscore or enhance the mood or quality of each scene?
4. Is the setting so powerful and dominant that it upstages the actors?
5. If the film is a period piece, a fantasy, or a science fiction story taking place in a future time or on a strange planet, is the set convincing enough to make us believe (during the film) that we are really in another time and place? If so, what factors or details present in the set contribute to its convincing effect? If the set is not completely convincing, why does it fail?

L EDITING 110–122

1. How does the editing effectively guide your thoughts, associations, and emotional responses from one image to another so that smooth continuity and coherence are achieved?
2. Is the editing smooth, natural, and unobtrusive, or is it tricky and self-conscious? How much does the editor communicate through creative juxtapositions, such as ironic transitions, montages, and the like, and how effective is this communication?
3. What is the overall effect of editorial intercutting and transitions on the pace of the film as a whole?
4. How does the cutting speed (which determines the average duration of each shot) correspond to the emotional tone of the scene involved?
5. What segments of the film seem overlong or boring? Which parts of these segments could be cut without altering the total effect? Where are additional shots necessary to make the film completely coherent?
6. In the "stolen base" editing sequence on pages 124–126, only minimal information has been provided. Analyze the sequence carefully, considering the following questions for each shot:
   a. What information does the shot convey, and what is its particular function in the editing sequence at this point?
   b. Why have the director and editor chosen to show us the action from this particular position? Does it represent the viewpoint of a player? Would another position or angle be equally good or better? Why?
   c. Which player do you identify with most strongly? Why?
   d. How does each shot relate to the shots before and after it in the sequence? Are other shots necessary to make the chain of events

coherent? Is each shot made more meaningful by the shot that comes before it?

e. Count out the number of beats (at two beats per second) that you would hold each shot on the screen. What is your total running time for the sequence? Which shots would be the longest and which the shortest? Why?

f. Which shots could be relocated in the sequence? Which could be eliminated? Which could be repeated more than once? What effect would repeating them have?

M CINEMATIC VIEWPOINT AND VISUAL EFFECTS 127–144

1. Although the director will probably employ all four cinematic viewpoints in making the film, one point of view may predominate to such a degree that it leaves the impression of a single point of view. With this in mind, answer the following questions:

a. In terms of your reaction to the film as a whole, do you feel that you were primarily an objective, impersonal observer of the action, or did you have the sense of being a participant in the action? What specific scenes can you remember that used the objective point of view? In what scenes did you feel like a participant in the action? How were you made to feel like a participant?

b. In what scenes were you aware that the director was employing visual techniques to comment on or interpret the action, forcing you to see the action in a special way? What were the techniques used to achieve this, and how effective were they?

2. Although a thorough analysis of each visual element is impossible, make a mental note of those pictorial effects that struck you as especially effective, ineffective, or unique, and consider them in light of the following questions:

a. What was the director's aim in creating these images, and what camera tools or techniques were employed in the filming of them?

b. What made these memorable visual images effective, ineffective, or unique?

c. Justify each of these impressive visual effects aesthetically in terms of its relationship to the whole film.

N LIGHTING 145–150

1. How would you characterize the lighting of the film as a whole: (a) direct, harsh, and hard, (b) medium and balanced, or (c) soft and diffused? Does high-key or low-key lighting predominate?

2. Does the lighting throughout the film seem artificial, coming from places where there would be no light sources, or does it seem to emanate naturally from sources visible or suggested on screen?
3. Are special lighting effects used for brief moments in the film? If so, what are the effects intended and how successful are they?
4. Does the lighting seem to create an effect designed to make the film have the look of a painting? How effective is this technique, and how well does the "painterly" style fit the subject matter of the film?
5. How does the lighting contribute to the overall emotional attitude or tone of the film?
6. In what individual scenes is the lighting especially effective, and what makes it effective?

O COLOR, BLACK AND WHITE, AND SCREEN SIZE 150–155

1. Was the filmmaker's choice of black and white or color film correct for this story? What factors do you think influenced this decision? Try to imagine the film as it would appear in the other film type. What would the important differences in total effect be?
2. Are any special color effects attempted? If so, what was the director or cinematographer trying to achieve with the unusual effect? How successful is the overall effect achieved?
3. Is the film designed for standard or wide-screen projection? What factors do you think influenced this decision?

P SPECIAL EFFECTS 159–164

1. How effective are the special effects employed in the film? Do they dominate the film to the point that the film is just a showcase for the effects, or are they an integrated part of the film as a whole?
2. Identify the types of special effects used in the film as "credible" effects, "incredible" effects, and "amazing" effects. Which kind of effects are used most often?
3. To what degree does the credibility of the entire film depend on the audience believing in its special effects? Do special effects overshadow the major characters so much that they seem secondary to the effects?

Q SOUND EFFECTS AND DIALOGUE 166–187

1. Where in the film are off-screen or invisible sounds effectively employed to enlarge the boundaries of the visual frame, or to create mood and atmosphere?
2. What sound effects in particular contribute to a sense of reality and a feeling of being there?
3. Does the film attempt to provide a sense of three dimensionality or depth in sound? If a stereophonic soundtrack is used, what does it contribute to the overall effect of the film?
4. Where is sound employed to represent subjective states of mind, and how effective is it?
5. Where is unusual emphasis placed on sound in the film and what is the purpose of such emphasis?
6. Is sound used to provide important transitions in the film? Why is sound needed to provide these transitions?
7. If voice-over soundtracks are used for narration or internal monologues (thoughts of a character spoken aloud), can you justify their use, or could the same information have been conveyed through purely dramatic means?
8. Is dialogue used unnecessarily, repeating information already adequately communicated by the image? Where?
9. Where in the film is silence employed as a sound effect to intensify suspense, to increase the impact of sounds which follow, or to create other special dramatic effects?
10. Where in the film is sound used for other specialized purposes, and how effective is each use?
11. How do the pace of the dialogue and the rhythmic qualities of the sound effects influence the pace of the film as a whole?

MUSICAL SCORE

R GENERAL FUNCTIONS 190–193

1. Where in the film is music used to match exactly the natural rhythms of the moving objects on the screen? At what points in the film does the music simply try to capture a scene's overall emotional mood?

2. Where does the film employ rhythmic and emotive variations on a single musical theme or motif?
3. Does the musical score remain inconspicuous in the background, or does it occasionally break through to assert itself?
4. If the music does demand your conscious attention, does it still perform a subordinate function in the film as a whole? How?
5. Where in the film is the main purpose of the music to match structural or visual rhythms? Where is it used to create more generalized emotional patterns?
6. How would the total effect of the film differ if the musical score were removed from the soundtrack?

S SPECIAL FUNCTIONS 194–203

1. Which of the following functions of film music are used in the film, and where are they used?
   a. To cover weaknesses and defects.
   b. To heighten the dramatic effect of dialogue.
   c. To tell an "inner story" by expressing a state of mind.
   d. To provide a sense of time or place.
   e. To evoke remembered experiences or emotions.
   f. To foreshadow events or build dramatic tension.
   g. To add levels of meaning to the image.
   h. To aid characterization.
   i. To trigger conditioned responses.
   j. To characterize rapid movement (traveling music).
2. Does the music accompanying the titles serve basically to underscore the rhythmic qualities of the title information, or to establish the general mood of the film? If lyrics are sung at this point, how do these lyrics relate to the film as a whole?
3. Where are sound effects or natural noises employed for a kind of rhythmic or musical effect?
4. If lyrics sung within the film provide a kind of interior monologue, what feeling or attitude do they convey?
5. If music is used as a base for choreographed action, how appropriate is the piece selected? How appropriate are its rhythms to the mood and the visual content? How effectively is the choreographed sequence integrated into the film as a whole?
6. Does the score use a full orchestra throughout, a smaller number of well-chosen instruments, or a synthesizer? How well suited is the instrumentation chosen to the film as a whole? If it is not well chosen,

what kind of instrumentation should have been used? How would your choice of instrumentation change the quality of the film, and why would it be an improvement?

7. Does the amount of music used fit the requirements of the film, or is the musical score overdone or used too economically?
8. How effectively does the score perform its various functions?

T ACTING 206–236

1. Which actors did you feel were correctly cast in their parts? Which actors were not cast wisely? Why?
2. How well were the physical characteristics, facial features, and voice qualities of the actors suited to the characters they were attempting to portray?
3. If a performance was unconvincing, was it because the actor was miscast in the role to begin with, or did he simply deliver an incompetent performance?
   a. If faulty casting seems to be the problem, what actor would you choose for the part if you were directing the film?
   b. If the actor proved incompetent in the part, what were the primary reasons for his failure?
4. What kind of acting is required of the actors in the starring roles—action acting or dramatic acting? Are the actors well-suited to the type of acting demanded by the roles they play? If not, why not? Where are their weaknesses or limitations most evident? If they are well-suited, in what scenes is their special type of acting skill most apparent?
5. Based on your knowledge of their past performances, classify the actors in the major roles as "impersonators," "commentors and interpreters," or "personalities."
6. Try to determine whether the following actors and actresses are impersonators, interpreter/commentors, or personalities: George C. Scott, Cary Grant, Laurence Olivier, Steve McQueen, Robert Duvall, John Wayne, Marlon Brando, Sophia Loren, Elizabeth Taylor, Faye Dunaway, Dustin Hoffman, Anne Bancroft, Shirley MacLaine, Clint Eastwood, Gene Hackman, James Stewart, Raquel Welch, Glenda Jackson, Peter O'Toole, Woody Allen, Diane Keaton, Humphrey Bogart, Peter Sellers, Harrison Ford, William Hurt, Debra Winger, Jack Lemmon, Jane Fonda, Jack Nicholson, Henry Fonda, Doris Day, Joan

Crawford, Gary Cooper, Sean Connery, Al Pacino, Mia Farrow, etc. Justify your decision in categorizing each actor by describing the degree of similarities or differences in his or her roles in at least three movies. Which of the actors are most difficult to categorize and why?

7. Consider the following questions with respect to each of the starring actors:
   a. Does the actor seem to depend more on the charm of his or her own personality, or does he or she attempt to "become" the character?
   b. Is the actor consistently believable in the portrayal of the character, or does he or she occasionally fall out of character?
   c. If the actor seems unnatural in the part, is it because he or she tends to be overdramatic, or wooden and mechanical? Is this unnaturalness more apparent in the way he or she delivers the lines, or in his or her physical actions?

8. In which specific scenes is the acting especially effective or ineffective? Why?

9. In which scenes are the actors' facial expressions used in reaction shots? What reaction shots are particularly effective?

10. How strong is the cast of supporting actors, and what does each contribute to the film? How does each help bring out different aspects of the star's personality? Do the supporting players create memorable moments or "steal the show" in spots? If so, where in the film do such moments occur?

11. What contributions do the small parts and extras make to the film? Are the faces and bodies well-chosen to fit our preconceived notions of what they should look like? Are their "working tasks," if any, performed with confidence and naturalness?

12. Taking as your model Lily Tomlin's description of what Warren Beatty projects (see the caption to Fig. 7.35), describe the qualities projected by the following: Marilyn Monroe, James Stewart, Henry Fonda, Debra Winger, Richard Gere, Humphrey Bogart, Bette Davis, Goldie Hawn, Burt Reynolds, Robin Williams, Sophia Loren, Jill Clayburgh, Katherine Hepburn, Spencer Tracy, Sidney Poitier, Marlon Brando, James Dean.

U THE DIRECTOR'S STYLE 240–251

1. After viewing several films by a single director, what kinds of general observations can you make about his or her style? Which of the adjectives listed below describe his or her style?

a. Intellectual and rational *or* emotional and sensual.
b. Calm and quiet *or* fast-paced and exciting.
c. Calm and quiet *or* rough and crude-cut.
d. Cool and objective *or* warm and subjective.
e. Ordinary and trite *or* fresh and original.
f. Tightly structured, direct, and concise *or* loosely structured and rambling.
g. Truthful and realistic *or* romantic and idealized.
h. Simple and straightforward *or* complex and indirect.
i. Grave, serious, tragic, and heavy *or* light, comical, and humorous.
j. Restrained and understated *or* exaggerated.
k. Optimistic and hopeful *or* bitter and cynical.
l. Logical and orderly *or* irrational and chaotic.

2. What common thematic threads are reflected in the director's choice of subject matter? How is this thematic similarity revealed in the nature of the conflicts he or she deals with?

3. In the films you have seen, what consistencies do you find in the director's treatment of space and time?

4. Is a consistent philosophical view of the nature of man and the universe found in all the films studied? If so, describe the director's world view.

5. How is the director's style revealed by the following visual elements: composition and lighting, philosophy of camera, the nature of the camera movement, and methods of achieving three dimensionality?

6. How does the director use special visual techniques (unusual camera angles, fast motion, slow motion, distorting lenses, and so on) to interpret or comment on the action, and how do these techniques reflect overall style?

7. How is the director's style reflected in the different aspects of the editing in the films, such as the rhythm and pacing of editorial cuts, the nature of transitions, montages, and other creative juxtapositions? How does the style of editing relate to other elements of the director's visual style, such as the philosophy of camera or how the point of view is emphasized?

8. How consistent is the director in using and emphasizing setting? What kind of details of the natural setting does the director emphasize, and how do these details relate to his or her overall style? Is there any similarity in the director's approach to entirely different kinds of settings? How do the sets constructed especially for the film reflect the director's taste?

9. In what ways are the director's use of sound effects, dialogue, and music unique? How are these elements of style related to the image?
10. What consistencies can be seen in the director's choice of actors and in the performances they give under his or her direction? How does the choice of actors and acting styles fit in with the style in other areas?
11. What consistencies do you find in the director's narrative structure?
12. If the director seems to be constantly evolving instead of settling into a fixed style, what directions or tendencies do you see in that evolution? What stylistic elements can you find in all his or her films?

The pictures on pages 254–261 represent films by four different directors. Although it is difficult, if not impossible, to capture a director's visual style in a limited number of still pictures, most of the pictures here contain strong stylistic elements. Study the pictures listed below as representative of each director's style, and try to answer the questions that follow about each director.

Ingmar Bergman: Figs. 8.1a, b, c, and d

Woody Allen: Figs. 8.2a, b, c, and d

Federico Fellini: Figs. 8.3a, b, c, and d

Alfred Hitchcock: Figs. 8.4a, b, c, and d

13. What does each set of pictures reveal about the director's visual style, as reflected by such elements as composition and lighting, "philosophy of camera" or point of view, use of setting, methods of achieving three dimensionality, and choice of actors?
14. The pictures represent four films by each director. Study the pictures *from each film* and see what you can deduce about the nature of the film.
    a. What do the pictures reveal about the general subject matter of the film or the kind of cinematic theme being treated?
    b. Characterize as clearly as possible the mood or emotional quality suggested by the stills from each film.
    c. If you are familiar with other films by the same director, how do these thematic concerns and emotional qualities relate to his other films?
15. Considering all the stills from each director, characterize each director as to how he fits the following descriptive sets:
    a. Intellectual and rational *or* emotional and sensual.
    b. Naturalistic and realistic *or* romantic, idealized, and surreal.
    c. Simple, obvious, and straightforward *or* complex, subtle, and indirect.

d. Heavy, serious, and tragic *or* light, comical and humorous.

16. Which directors represent *extremes* of each of the descriptive sets above?

17. Which director seems most formal and structured in composition? Which director seems most informal and natural in composition?

18. Which director seems to be trying to involve us emotionally in the action or dramatic situation portrayed in the stills? How does he attempt to achieve this effect? Which director's viewpoint seems most objective and detached, and why do the pictures have that effect?

19. Which director relies most on lighting for special effects, and what effects does he achieve?

20. Which director places the most emphasis on setting to create special effects or moods?

21. Compare the visual styles of the foreign directors (Bergman and Fellini) with the styles of the American directors (Allen and Hitchcock). Can you see any basic differences between the foreign and American directors' styles? If so, what is the nature of those differences?

22. Based on your answers to all the preceding questions, what general observations can you make about each director's style?

23. For additional pictures representing the style of these four directors, see the following figures: 3.12, 4.15, and 4.69 (Allen); 2.28, 4.28, and 4.29 (Bergman); 7.27 (Hitchcock); and 13.3 (Fellini).

ANALYSIS OF THE WHOLE FILM

V VIEWER-CENTERED PROBLEMS 264–270

1. Do you have any strong prejudices against this particular type of film? If so, how did these prejudices affect your responses to the film? Does this film have any special qualities that set it apart from other films of the same genre?

2. How much do your personal and highly subjective responses to the following aspects of the film affect your judgment: actors and actresses in the film, treatment of sexual material, and scenes involving violence? Can you justify the sex and violence in the film aesthetically, or are these scenes included strictly for the box-office appeal?

3. What were your expectations before seeing the film? How did these expectations influence your reaction to the film?

4. Do you have some specialized knowledge about any subject dealt with by the film? If so, how does it affect your reaction to the film as a whole?
5. Was your mood, mental attitude, or physical condition while seeing the movie less than ideal? If so, how was your reaction to the film affected?
6. If the physical environment in which you watched the film was less than ideal, how did this influence your judgment?

W ANALYSIS OF THE WHOLE FILM 271–279

1. What is the director's purpose or primary aim in making the film?
2. What is the true subject of the film, and what kind of statement, if any, does the film make about that subject?
3. How do all the separate elements of the film relate to and contribute to the theme, central purpose, or total effect?
4. What is the film's level of ambition?
5. In terms of the director's intentions and the film's level of ambition, how well does the film succeed in what it tries to do? Why does it succeed or fail?
6. What elements or parts make the strongest contribution to the theme and why? What elements or parts fail to function effectively in carrying out the director's intentions? Why do they fail?
7. What were your *personal* reactions to the film; what are your *personal* reasons for liking or disliking it?

X DEVELOPING PERSONAL CRITERIA FOR FILM EVALUATION 280–291

1. Try to construct a set of five or ten questions that *you* think should be answered in judging the merits of a film, *or* list the five to ten qualities *you* think are essential to a good movie.
2. If you fall short on the question asked for above, or lack confidence in the validity of the qualities you're listed as essential, try another approach: List ten all-time favorite films.
3. Now answer the following questions about your list, and see what your answers reveal about your personal criteria for film evaluation:
   a. Consider each film on the list carefully, and decide what three or four things you liked best about the film.Then decide which of these played the most important role in making you like or respect the film.
   b. How many of the films on your list share the qualities that most

appeal to you? Which films seem to be most similar in the characteristics you like best?

c. Do the qualities you pick show an emphasis on any single critical approach, or are you eclectic in your tastes? To decide this, answer the following:
   (1) How many of the films listed do you respect primarily for their technique?
   (2) Do several of the films you chose feature the same actor?
   (3) How many of your favorite films are done by the same director?
   (4) Which of the films listed make a significant statement of some kind?
   (5) Which of the films have a powerful, intense, and very real emotional or sensual effect?
   (6) Which of the films listed could be classified as genre or formula films, and how many of them belong to the same genre?

d. What do your answers to questions (1) through (6) above reveal about your personal preferences? Do your tastes seem restricted?

e. How does your list of favorite films measure up against your first attempt at establishing a personal criteria for evaluation? How can your standards be changed, perhaps added to, in order to better match your list of film favorites?

ADAPTATIONS

Y ADAPTATIONS OF NOVELS 294–312

After reading the novel, but before seeing the film, consider the following questions concerning the novel.

1. How well is the novel suited for adaptation to the screen? What natural cinematic possibilities does it have?
2. Judged as a whole, does the novel come closer to stressing a sensuous and emotional rendering of experience (as in the Hemingway excerpts), or an intellectual analysis of experience (as in the James excerpt)?
3. How essential is the author's verbal style to the spirit or essence of the novel? Could this verbal style be effectively translated into a pictorial style?
4. What is the novel's point of view? What will necessarily be lost by translating the story into film?

5. If the novel is written in the first-person point of view (as told by a participant in the action), how much of the spirit of the novel is expressed through the narrator's unique narrative style—that is, the particular flair or flavor built into his *way of telling* the story rather than the story itself? Could this verbal style be suggested through a minimum of voice-over narration of the soundtrack, so that the device would not seem unnatural? Is the feeling of a warm, intimate relationship between reader and narrator established by the novel, as though the story is being told by a very close friend? How could this feeling be captured by the film?
6. Is the novel's length suited to a close adaptation, or must it be drastically cut to fit the usual film format? Which choice would seem most logical for the filmmaker in adapting the novel:
   a. Should he or she try to capture a sense of the novel's wholeness by hitting the high points without trying to fill in all the gaps? What high points do you think must be dramatized?
   b. Should the filmmaker limit himself or herself to a thorough dramatization of just a part of the novel? What part of the novel could be thoroughly dramatized to make a complete film? What part of the story or what subplots should be left out of the film version?
7. How much of the novel's essence depends on the rendition of mental states: memories, dreams, or philosophical reflections? How effectively can the film version be expected to express or at least suggest these things?
8. How much detail does the author provide on the origins and past history of the characters? How much of this material can be conveyed cinematically?
9. What is the total time period covered by the novel? Can the time period covered be adequately compressed into a normal-length film?

   After seeing the film version, reconsider your answers to the questions above, and also answer those following.

10. Is the film version a close or a loose adaptation of the novel? If it is a loose adaptation, is the departure from the novel due to the problems caused by changing from one medium to another, or by the change in creative personnel?
11. Does the film version successfully capture the spirit or essence of the novel? If not, why does it fail?
12. What are the major differences between the novel and the film, and how can you explain the reasons for these differences?

13. Does the film version successfully suggest meanings that lie beneath the surface and remind you of their presence in the novel? In which scenes is this accomplished?
14. Did having read the novel enhance the experience of seeing the film, or did it take away from it? Why?
15. How well do the actors in the film fit your preconceived notions of the characters in the novel? Which actors exactly fit your mental image of the characters? How do the actors who don't seem properly cast vary from your mental image? Can you justify, from the director's point of view, the casting of these actors who don't seem to fit the characters in the novel?

Z ADAPTATIONS OF PLAYS 314–322

1. How does the film version differ from the play in terms of its concept of physical space? How does this affect the overall spirit or tone of the film version?
2. How cinematic is the film version? How does it use special camera and editing techniques to keep the visual flow of images in motion and to avoid the static quality of a filmed stage play?
3. What events does the filmmaker "show" happening that are only described in dialogue during the play? How effective are these added scenes?
4. Are the play's structural divisions (into acts and scenes) still apparent in the film, or does the film successfully blend these divided parts into a unified cinematic whole?
5. What stage conventions employed in the play are not translatable into cinematic equivalents? What difficulties and changes does this bring about?
6. How does the acting style of the film differ from that of the play? What factors enter into these differences?
7. What basic differences can be observed in the nature of the dialogue in the two versions? Are individual speeches generally longer in the play or in the film? In which version is the poetic quality of the language more apparent?
8. What other important changes have been made in the film version? Can you justify these in terms of change in medium, change in creative personnel, or differences in moral attitudes and sophistication of the intended audience?

GENRE, REMAKES, AND SEQUELS

AA THE GENRE FILM 326–335

1. Use the formulas for the western and gangster films above as a starting point for the study of a series of three or four films in either genre. How do the films being studied fit the formula? Is the formula valid, or do elements appear in each film that are not part of the formula? Do you find elements in the formula that do not occur in the films studied? Adjust the formula so that it fits all the films under study, then test your adjusted formula against two more films from the genre. As a part of your testing, try interchanging the parts from one film to another. What characters are interchangeable? What subtle differences exist between one character and another? Which corresponding characters could be exchanged without significantly altering the plot?
2. Using the formulas for the gangster film and the western above (or your adjusted versions) as models, study at least three films from any of the following genres and create your own formula for that genre: the hard-boiled detective film, the screwball comedy, the disaster film, the boy-meets-girl musical. Then test your formula against two or three more films. (Also test each film of your formula to see if parts are interchangeable.)
3. Study two or three films by the same director in one genre, along with at least two films by different directors. Are three different directorial styles apparent, or are the styles indistinguishable? Consider the three films by the same director in chronological order. Does he or she incorporate personal stylistic trademarks into each of the three films? What are those trademarks and what makes them stand out?
4. What innovations or refinements on the formula does the director provide? Does the director introduce innovations and further refinements as he or she moves from one film to another? Are the innovations and refinements the director introduces superficial and cosmetic, or are they significant enough to stretch the genre, creating a strain or tension against the outer boundaries of the formula? Does the director seem to learn something new with each film and build on that in the next? Do we see changes in the director's personal vision or world view from one film to another? How are those changes reflected? (For example, does the director seem to grow more serious, or less serious; more pessimistic or more optimistic?)
5. Compare and contrast the styles of two directors working within the same genre. Look at at least two films by each director, and decide how

their styles create important differences within the same genre. (For example, how is a Frank Capra screwball comedy different from a Preston Sturges screwball comedy?)

BB REMAKES AND SEQUELS 337–344

1. Was the remake really necessary? Why is the older version outdated? Why do modern audiences need the story retold? What were the aspects of the original film that were inaccessible to modern audiences? Are these inaccessible aspects so important as to make the film incomprehensible to contemporary filmgoers, or are they relatively insignificant?
2. What important changes were made in the remake? Why were they made? Which changes would you consider improvements over the original, and which would you consider only changes?
3. Which is the better film? Does the remake have the freshness and the creative dynamic of the original? Were you disappointed in the remake? Why?
4. How is the remake like the original? Is an effort made through casting, cinematic style, etc., to capture the spirit and the flavor of the original? Do these efforts succeed?
5. If the remake is a musical version, how well is the spirit and story of the original captured in the words and music of the songs? What major changes in plot or setting had to be made in the musical version? How are the characters changed?
6. What advantages does the remake have over the original in terms of freedom from censorship and new technology in the medium? How does it make use of these advantages?
7. If the remake involves a foreign original, how does a change of setting, language, or cultural values affect the remake?
8. Does the sequel grow naturally out of the original? In other words, was there enough story left over from the original to make a natural sequel?
9. How many important members of the cast and of the behind-the-scenes team were involved in the sequel? If some characters had to be recast, how did that effect the quality of the sequel?
10. Does the sequel build on the original in such a way that it seems incomplete unless you've seen the original, or is it complete enough to stand on its own as a separate, unified work?
11. Does the sequel capture the flavor and spirit of the original in story and

visual style? Is it equal in quality to the original in every aspect? Where does it surpass the original, and where is it weaker?

12. If the sequel becomes a character series, what are the qualities of the characters that make them wear well? Why do we want to see them again and again? Are the writers able to keep their characters consistent in film after film? How consistent are the other stylistic elements from one film to another?

OTHER SPECIAL FILM EXPERIENCES

CC THE FOREIGN-LANGUAGE FILM 348–356

1. Which method is used to translate the dialogue into English—subtitles or voice dubbing? Was this the best way to solve the language problem for this particular film? Why?

2. If subtitles are used, how well do they seem to capture the essence of what is being said by the actors? Are the subtitles ever difficult to read because of the light-colored backgrounds? Is the film's pace slow enough to allow for both reading the subtitles and following the image?

3. If voice dubbing is used, how closely do the English words spoken on the soundtrack correspond to the mouth and lip movements of the foreign actors? Do you get used to the fact that the voices are dubbed, or is it a constant irritation? How well suited are the voice qualities and accents on the soundtrack to the actors with which they are matched? Does the overall emotional quality of the English translation match the facial expressions and gestures of the foreign actors?

4. How good is the quality of the dubbing technique? Are the "voice-actors" obviously reading their lines close to a microphone in a studio so they seem to be whispering in your ear? Does the volume of spoken lines vary according to the distance of the actor from the camera? Is ambient sound present? Is music used as an unnatural filler?

5. How does the foreign director's style differ from American cinematic styles? What effect does this have on your response to the film?

6. How does the film reflect the culture of the country that produced it? How is this culture or life-style different from what we know in America? How is it similar? What different aspects of this foreign culture do you find most fascinating, and why?

7. In what ways does the film transcend its foreignness to communicate things that are universal? What aspects of film are so uniquely foreign that they are beyond your understanding?

DD THE SILENT FILM 357–361

1. Is the acting style melodramatic, with broad and exaggerated gestures and facial expressions, or is it subtle, refined, even understated?
2. What is unique about the acting styles of each of the major actors? Which actors depend most on facial expression, and which ones depend on gestures and bodily movements?
3. How many different emotions are expressed by actors through their walks? Which actors in the film have unique walks that become a part of their acting style and the total personality they project?
4. How effective is the film in telling its story without words? How much does the film need to rely on subtitles to make the action absolutely clear?
5. How sophisticated are the visual techniques used in the film compared to modern techniques? If the film were being made today (still silent), what modern visual techniques could be used to improve it? In what ways is the visual style old-fashioned? How much of this old-fashioned quality is due to technical limitations of the time?

EE THE HISTORICALLY IMPORTANT FILM 362–363

1. Based on your knowledge of the films produced prior to this film, what innovations in cinematic style or technique did this film introduce? Which of these innovations are still being used in the modern film?
2. Does the film seem crude, time-worn, or full of clichés when compared to the modern film, or is it still fresh and powerful? What specific elements or qualities in the film lead you to your answer?
3. What is the film's contribution to the overall development of the motion picture? What would the modern film be like if the innovations introduced by this film had never been? How have the innovations introduced by this film been polished and refined in the modern film?

FF THE SOCIAL PROBLEM FILM 364

1. Does the social problem being attacked by the film have a universal and timeless quality, affecting all people in all time periods, or is it restricted to a relatively narrow time and place?
2. Is the film powerful enough in terms of a strong story line, enduring char-

acters, good acting, artistic cinematography, and so on, to outlive the social problem it is attacking? In other words, how much of the film's impact is caused by its relevance to a current problem and its timing in attacking the problem?

3. If the immediate social problems on which the film focuses were permanently corrected tomorrow, what relevance would the film have to the average viewer twenty years from now?

CENSORSHIP AND OTHER FORCES THAT SHAPE THE AMERICAN FILM

GG CENSORSHIP 366–386

1. Study three or more films with censorable subject matter made under the Motion Picture Production Code (prior to 1950), and answer the following questions:

a. Where in these films do you find obvious examples of Code-caused suppression and restraint?

b. How would these films be different if they were being made today? Which film (or films) could be significantly improved by being made today with a PG or R rating? How or why would they be improved?

c. Do the films studied seem too mild-mannered to have much impact, or do they effectively suggest such things as violence and sexuality in ways acceptable to the Code?

d. Do these films seem to go out of their way to promote traditional American values? Are American values or institutions questioned in any of these films? If so, how and where are such questions dramatized, and how are such problems resolved?

2. Examine three or more films with censorable subject matter made during the transitional period (1950–1967) and consider questions a–d above. What evidence do you find of the Code's being stretched or disregarded? How do the films of the transitional period differ from those before 1950?

3. Examine a film made under the Motion Picture Production Code and compare it with its remake produced under the MPAA Ratings System (examples would be *Scarface,* 1932/1983; *The Postman Always Rings Twice,* 1946/1981; and *Here Comes Mr. Jordan,* 1941, remade as *Heaven Can Wait,* 1978). To what degree are these films different because of the difference in censorship restrictions? Where are those differences most obvious and how is the overall effect of the film changed by these differences? Which of the two is the better film? Why?

4. Examine three current films presently playing at your local theatre: a G, a PG, and an R. What are the dividing lines between the different classifications based on these films? In other words, what separates a G from a PG, and what separates a PG from an R?

5. Make an attempt to examine the evolution of the Rating System's classification decisions by checking what makes the difference between a PG and an R rating at four-year intervals, using films released in 1972, 1976, 1980, and 1984. Can you discern any patterns of change in where the dividing line is drawn? If so, what do these patterns indicate?

6. Examine several films from each decade from the 1930s to the present, and try to describe the fashion of the age in terms of each decade's formulas for sexual intimacy, the dance of death, and rough language. What other changing patterns or fashions are apparent in the films you viewed?

HH FILM: AN INDUSTRY AND AN ART FORM 388–391

1. What market was the film aimed for? Was it aimed primarily at the twelve to twenty-five year old age group, or at a more mature audience? Could it appeal equally to both groups? Why or why not?

2. Why do you think the studio backed the production of this film? Identify the factors that made this particular film a good gamble. How is it similar to other films that have made money? Does it have a name director or popular stars that might help its success? Does it seem to be part of a trend in current films? If so, how does it fit into the overall pattern of recent films?

3. Imagine that your film class is a group of potential film investors. Each of you has inherited a million dollars from a wealthy relative, but there are strings attached to the inheritance: You must invest all of the money in the production of a major motion picture. If the movie makes money, you get your million dollars back plus a share of the film's profits. If it loses money, your entire inheritance is forfeited. The money required to make the film exactly equals (in millions) the number of people in your class so each person must agree with the decisions reached by the "investment group." With the rules of the game thus established, make the following basic decisions: (1) the kind of screenplay to be bought or commissioned, (2) the director, and (3) the principal actors in the cast (male and female leads). Once unanimous agreement on these choices is reached, consider the following questions:

a. What were the primary factors involved in making each basic choice?
b. Did your investment group emphasize artistic quality or profit potential in its final choices?
c. How close were the final choices to your personal preferences when the discussion began?

II THE ART OF WATCHING MOVIES ON TV

394–412

1. To what degree is the film's continuity destroyed by commercial breaks? Which of these breaks occur at appropriate times in terms of the film's dramatic structure, and which breaks weaken the dramatic tension appreciably?
2. If you saw the film in a theater, can you remember portions that were cut out of the television showing? How important were these segments to the spirit or plot of the film? Can you justify these deletions in terms of the new medium or its mass audience? Were these segments cut out because of time limitations or censorship?
3. If the film is a made-for-television film, how successful is it in solving the problems of the theater film on television?
4. How well is the film suited to viewing on the small screen with minimal sound quality? In what scenes do you feel you lack the intensity of involvement needed to enjoy the film? In which scenes does the small-screen format work?
5. Was the movie originally made in a wide-screen format? In what scenes is important information cut off? Are you ever unsure of the character's spatial relationship to his or her environment? How is the aesthetic quality of the composition affected?

GLOSSARY

Allegory A story whose every object, event, and person have a corresponding symbolic meaning.
Auteur Literally, the "author" of the film. An auteur may conceive of the idea for the story, write the script, and then supervise every step in the filmmaking process.

Caricature The exaggeration or distortion of one or more personality traits, a technique common in cartooning.
Climax The point at which the complication reaches its point of maximum tension, and the forces in opposition confront each other at a peak of physical or emotional action.
Close-up A close shot of a person or object; a close-up of a person generally focuses on the face only.
Commentors *See Interpreters.*
Complication The section of a story in which a conflict begins and grows in clarity, intensity, and importance.

Dead screen A frame in which there is little or no dramatically or aesthetically interesting visual information. *See also Live screen.*
Dead track The complete absence of sound on the soundtrack.
Deep focus The use of special lenses that allow the camera to focus simultaneously on objects anywhere from two feet to several hundred feet away—all with equal clarity.
Dénouement A brief period of calm following the resolution of the conflict, in which a state of relative equilibrium returns.
Developing characters Characters who are deeply affected by the action of the plot and who undergo some important change in personality, attitude, or outlook on life as a result of the action of the film.
Director's interpretive point of view *See under Point of view, cinematic.*
Dissolve The gradual merging of the end of one shot with the beginning of the next, produced by superimposing a fade-out onto a fade-in of equal length, or by imposing one scene over another.
Dolby-Surround Sound A multitrack stereophonic system for theaters that employs an encoding process to achieve a 360-degree sound field—thus creating the effect of more speakers than are actually present.
Dolly shot A shot taken from a mobile platform.
Dramatic point of view *See under Point of view, literary.*

Editing patterns Two different editing patterns have become standard in making transitions in time and space:

Inside/out A dynamic editing pattern, in which the editor takes us suddenly from a line of action that we understand to a close-up of a detail in a new setting. Since this detail is not shown in the context of a setting, we don't know where we are or what is happening. Then, in a series of related shots, the editor backs us off from the close-up to reveal the detail in relationship to its surroundings.

Outside/in The traditional editing pattern, whereby the editor begins with an establishing shot of the new setting—to help the audience get its bearings—and then follows with shots that gradually takes us farther into the setting. Only after we are completely familiar with our surroundings does the editor focus our attention on details.

Ensemble acting A type of acting that involves a number of leading roles with none of the roles standing out or dominating the others in "starring" positions.
Establishing shot A beginning shot of a new scene in which the director and/or editor shows us an overall view of the new setting and the relative position of the actors in that setting.
Expository beginning An opening to a story characterized by an *exposition,* which introduces the characters, shows some of their interrelationships, and places them within a believable time and place. Sometimes called *chronological beginning. See also In medias res.*
Extrinsic simile *See under Simile, visual.*
Eye-line shot A shot that shows us what a character is seeing.

Fade-out/fade-in A transitional device in which the last image of one scene fades to black as the first image of the next scene is gradually illuminated.
Fast motion The frantic, herky-jerky movement that results when a scene is filmed at less than normal speed (twenty-four frames per second) and then projected at normal speed.
Final cut A film in its finished form. A guarantee of final cut assures the filmmaker or producer that the film will not be tampered with after he or she approves it.
First person point of view *See under Point of view, literary.*
Fish-eye lens A special type of extreme wide-angle lens that bends both horizontal and vertical planes and distorts depth relationships.

Flashback A filmed sequence that goes back in time to provide expository material—either when it is most dramatically appropriate and powerful or when it will most effectively illuminate the theme. *See also Flashforward.*
Flash-cutting Fragmented "machine-gun" bursts of images used to compress action.
Flashforward The opposite of a flashback—the visual scene jumps from the present into the future.
Flat characters Two-dimensional, predictable characters who lack the complexity and unique qualities associated with psychological depth.
Flip frame A transitional device in which the entire frame seems to flip over to reveal a new scene—an effect very similar to turning a page.
Foils Contrasting characters whose behavior, attitudes, opinions, life-style, physical appearance, and so on are opposite to those of the main character and thus serve to clearly define the personality of the main character.
Form cut A transition accomplished by framing objects or images of similar contour in two successive shots, so that the first image flows smoothly into the second.
Freeze frame An effect, achieved in the laboratory after the film is shot, whereby the same frame is reprinted so many times on the film strip that the motion seems to stop as though frozen. *See also Thawed frame.*

Generalized score A musical score that attempts to capture the overall emotional atmosphere of a sequence and the film as a whole, usually by using rhythmic and emotive variations on only a few recurring motifs or themes. Also called *implicit score.*
Genre film A film based on a formula, such as a western, that plays on the expectations of the audience regarding formulaic plot structures, characters, settings, and so on.
Glancing rhythms The built-in sense of excitement or boredom created by fast or slow editing. Slow editing simulates the glancing rhythms of a tranquil observer; quick cutting simulates the glancing rhythms of a highly excited observer.

Hand-held camera Jerky, uneven movement of the camera that heightens our sense of reality by simulating the subjective viewpoint of a character in motion.
High-angle shot A shot taken with the camera placed above eye level that dwarfs the subject and thereby diminishes its importance. *See also Low-angle shot.*
High-key lighting Lighting that has more light areas than shadows; subjects are seen in middle grays and highlights, with little contrast. *See also Low-key lighting.*

Impersonators Actors who have the talent to completely leave their real identity and personality behind and assume the personality and characteristics of a character with whom they may have little in common.
Implicit score *See Generalized score.*
In medias res A Latin phrase meaning "in the middle of things" that refers to a method of beginning a story with an exciting incident that, chronologically, occurs after the complication has developed. *See also Expository beginning.*
Interpreters Actors who play characters that closely resemble themselves in personality and physical appearance, and who interpret these parts dramatically without wholly losing their own identity. Also called *commentors.*
Intrinsic simile *See under Simile, visual.*
Invisible sound Sound emanating from a source *not* on the screen. *See also Visible sound.*
Irony A literary, dramatic, and cinematic technique involving the juxtaposition or linking of opposites.

Jump cut The technique of cutting out a strip of insignificant or unnecessary action from a continuous shot.

Leitmotif The repetition of a single phrase or idea by a character until it becomes almost a trademark or theme song for that character.
Live screen A frame packed with dramatically or aesthetically interesting visual information, usually with some form of motion incorporated into the composition. *See also Dead screen.*
Long shot A shot, taken from some distance, that usually shows the subject as well as its surroundings.
Look of outward regard An objective shot that shows a character looking off screen and thereby cues us to wonder what he or she is looking at.
Low-angle shot A shot taken with the camera placed below eye level, thereby exaggerating the size and importance of the subject. *See also High-angle shot.*
Low-key lighting Lighting where most of the set is in shadow and just a few highlights define the subject. *See also High-key lighting.*

Mickey Mousing The exact, calculated dovetailing of music and action that precisely matches the rhythm of the music with the natural rhythms of the objects moving on the screen.
Microcosm ("the world in little") A special type of isolated, self-contained setting in which the human activity is actually representative of human behavior or the human condition in the world as a whole.
Montage An especially effective series of images and sounds that derive their meaning from complex internal relationships to form a kind of visual poem in miniature.
Motifs Images, patterns, or ideas that repeat throughout the film.

Name typing The use of names possessing appropriate qualities of sound, meaning, or connotation to help describe the character.

Objective point of view *See under Point of view, cinematic.*

Omniscient narrator point of view *See under Point of view, literary.*

Opticals Effects created in the process of printing the film where the primary image is superimposed on another image and the two are composited onto one strip of film by an optical printer. Today, most optics are guided by computers, affording precise matching of a tremendous number of different images.

Panning Moving the camera's "line of sight" in a horizontal plane to the right or left.

Parallel cutting The quick alternating back and forth between two actions taking place at separate locations, creating the impression that the two actions are occurring simultaneously and will possibly converge at the same point.

Personality actors Actors whose primary "talent" is to be themselves. Although personality actors generally possess some dynamic and magnetic mass appeal, they are incapable of assuming any variety in the roles they play, for they cannot project sincerity and naturalness when they attempt to move outside their own basic personality.

Peter-and-the-Wolfing To aid in characterization, the use of certain musical instruments or motifs to represent and signal the presence of certain characters.

Point of view, cinematic Essentially, there are four points of view that may be employed in a film:

Director's interpretive Using the special techniques of the medium, the director manipulates us so that we see the action or the character in the way the director interprets them.

Indirect-subjective A viewpoint that brings us close to the action and increases our involvement. It provides us with the feeling and sense of immediacy of participating in the action without showing the action through a participant's eyes.

Objective The viewpoint of a sideline observer, which suggests a relatively great emotional distance between camera and subject, with the camera simply recording, as straightforwardly as possible, the characters and the actions of the story.

Subjective The viewpoint of a character participating in the action.

See also Point of view, literary.

Point of view, literary There are five viewpoints employed in literature:

Dramatic A viewpoint wherein we are not conscious of a narrator, for the author does not comment on the action but simply describes the scene, telling us what happens and what the characters say, so we get a feeling of being there, observing the scene as we would in a play.

First person An eyewitness gives us a first-hand account of what happened as well as his or her response to it.

Omniscient narrator An all-seeing, all-knowing narrator, capable of reading the thoughts of all the characters and capable of being in several places at once if need be, tells us the story.

Third person limited The narrator is omniscient except for the fact that his or her powers of mind reading are limited to or at least focused on a single character, who becomes the central figure through which we view the action.

Stream of consciousness or interior monologue A kind of first person narrative, except the participant in the action is not consciously narrating the story. What we get instead is a unique inner view, as though a microphone and movie camera were in the character's mind—recording every thought, image, and impression that passes through, without the conscious acts of organization, selectivity, or narration.

See also Point of view, cinematic.

Rack focus Changing the focus setting on the camera during a continuous shot so that audience attention is directed deeper and deeper into the frame as it follows the plane of clearest focus. The technique can also be reversed so that the plane of clearest focus moves closer and closer to the camera.

Reaction shot A shot that shows a character "reacting" rather than acting. The reaction shot is usually a close-up of the emotional reaction registered on the face of the person most affected by the dialogue or the action.

Rembrandt effect The use of a subtle, light-diffusing filter to soften focus slightly and subdue the colors so that the whole film has the quality of a Rembrandt painting.

Rough cut A "first draft" of the film prepared by the editor from the best take of each shot.

Rough-grain film stock A film stock that produces a rough, grainy-textured image with harsh contrasts between blacks and whites, and almost no subtle differences in contrast. *See also Smooth film stock.*

Round characters Unique, individualistic characters who have some degree of complexity and ambiguity and who cannot easily be categorized. Also called *three-dimensional characters.*

Scene A series of shots joined so that they communicate a unified action taking place at one time and place.

Sequence A series of scenes joined in such a way that they constitute a significant part of a film's dramatic structure, like an act in a play.

Shot A strip of film produced by a single continuous run of the camera.

Simile, visual A brief comparison that helps us understand or perceive one image better because of its similarity to another, usually achieved through the editorial juxtaposition of two images in two successive shots. Two types of visual similes are commonly used in films:

Extrinsic A simile that has no place within the context of the scene itself but is imposed artificially into the scene by the director.

Intrinsic A simile found within the natural context of the scene itself.

Skycam A small, computerized, remote-controlled camera that "flies" on wires at speeds of up to twenty miles per hour and can go practically anywhere cables can be strung.

Smooth film stock Film stock capable of reproducing an image that is extremely smooth or "slick," registering a wide range of subtle differences between light and dark, and creating fine tones, artistic shadows, and contrasts. *See also Rough-grain film stock.*

Soft focus A slight blurring of focus for effect.

Sound link A bridge between scenes or sequences created through the use of similar or identical sounds in both.

Standard screen A screen whose width is 1.33 times its height.

Static characters Characters who remain essentially the same throughout the film, either because the action does not have an important effect on their lives or simply because they are insensitive to the meaning of the action.

Steadicam A portable, one-person camera with a built-in gyroscope that prevents any sudden jerkiness and provides a smooth, rock-steady image.

Stereotypes Characters who fit into preconceived patterns of behavior common to or representative of a large number of people (at least a large number of fictional people), allowing the director to economize greatly in treating them.

Stills The use of still photographs in a film, with movement imparted to the image by the camera zooming in or out or simply moving over their surface.

Stock characters Minor characters whose actions are completely predictable or typical of their job or profession.

Stream of consciousness *See under Point of view, literary.*

Subjective point of view *See under Point of view, cinematic.*

Symbol Something that stands for something else and communicates that "something else" by triggering, stimulating, or arousing previously associated ideas in the mind of the person perceiving the symbol.

Tableau A technique used in melodrama, where the actors froze themselves in dramatic postures for a few seconds before the curtain in order to etch the scene deeply in the audience's memory.

Take Variations of the same shot. In the cutting room, the editor will assemble the film from the best take of each shot.

Telephoto lens A lens that, like a telescope, draws objects closer but also diminishes the illusion of depth.

Thawed frame An effect opposite to that of a freeze frame—the scene begins with a frozen image that suddenly "thaws" and comes to life.

Theme The central concern around which a film is structured, the focus that unifies a film. In film, this central concern can be broken down into five categories: plot, emotion, character, style or texture, and idea.

Third person limited point of view *See under Point of view, literary.*

Three-dimensional characters *See Round characters.*

Tilting Moving the camera's "line of sight" in a vertical plane so it "looks" up or down.

Time-lapse photography An extreme form of fast motion, where a single frame is exposed at regularly spaced intervals (from a second to an hour or even longer) and then projected at normal speed (twenty-four frames per second), thus compressing an action that usually takes hours or weeks into a few seconds on the screen.

Visible sound Sound that would naturally and realistically emanate from the images on the screen. *See also Invisible sound.*

Voice dubbing A process whereby the dialogue soundtrack in a foreign language is replaced by an English soundtrack, where voices in English are recorded to correspond to the mouth and lip movements of the foreign actors.

Voice-over A voice off screen conveys necessary background information or fills in gaps for continuity.

Wide-angle lens A lens that takes in a broad area and increases the illusion of depth but sometimes distorts the edges of the image.

Wide screen Known by a variety of trade names, such as Cinemascope, Panavision, and Vistavision. The width varies from 1.85 to 2.55 times the height of the screen.

Windows A term used to refer to the different markets for motion pictures.

Wipe A transitional device in which a new image is separated from the previous one by a horizontal, vertical, or diagonal line that moves across the screen to "push" the old image off.

Zoom lens A complex series of lenses that keep the image constantly in focus and, by magnifying the subject, give the camera the apparent power to vary movement toward or away from the subject without requiring any movement of the camera.

INDEX

A

Abbott, Bud, 343
Academy of Motion Picture Arts and Sciences, 267
Acting, action, 215
 as element of style, 247
 assisted by editing, 213–214
 dramatic, 215
 film and stage compared, 208–215
 Italian style of, 349
 style in silent film, 357–361
 Swedish style of, 349
Action, external, 35–36, 56–57
 internal, 36, 57–59
 types of, 35–36
Actors, critical responses to, 235–236
 personality, 217
 qualities projected by, 236
 supporting, 227–229, 230
 types of, 215–217
Adaptation, close, 312
Adaptation, loose, 312
 of novels, 298–312
 problems of, 294–298
Adaptations of novels, problems with, 302–312
Adaptations of plays, problems with, 314–322
Additive architecture, 108
Adler, Renata, 277, 315–316, 318, 349, 351
Aimée, Anouk, 174
Airplane!, 335, 388
Airport '77, 114, 398
Alambrista!, 133
Albee, Edward, 296
Albert, Edward, 316
Alda, Alan, 60
Alemendros, Nestor, 148, 151
Alexander, Jane, 227, 228
Alfie, 376–377
Alien, 13, 160
Allegory, 51, 352–353
Allen, Woody, 36, 68–69, 80, 98, 110, 219, 220, 250, 256–257
All Quiet on the Western Front, 340
All That Jazz, 47, 176, 224
All the King's Men, 76, 305–309, 374
Allyson, June, 220, 222
Altered States, 3, 162
Altman, Robert, 181, 249
Amarcord, 258
American Gigolo, 203
American Graffiti, 22, 196
American Werewolf in London, An, 14, 162
Analysis, defined, 7–8
 arguments against, 6–7
 film (compared to literary analysis), 30
 literary, 30
 of whole film, 275–280
 process of, 30–31
Analytical approach, function and purpose of, 7–9
"Andy Griffith Show, The," 59
Animal House, 338, 400–401
Anna and the King of Siam, 340
Annie Hall, 68, 110–111, 152, 250
Ann-Margret, 403
Antonelli, Laura, 350
Apocalypse Now, 52, 184–185
Arsenal, 289
Art director, 106
Arthur, 13, 61
Arthur, Jean, 47, 137
Art of Fiction, The, 56
Ashby, Hal, 234–235
Astaire, Fred, 61
Audience, film, 382, 389
Auteur, 240, 281–282

B

Baby Doll, 376
Bad News Bears, The, 201
Bad Seed, The, 321–322
Bananas, 250
Bancroft, Anne, 66
Bang the Drum Slowly, 140–141, 225
Barrie, Barbara, 230
Bartkowaik, Andrezej, 150
Bates, Alan, 89
Battle for the Planet of the Apes, 34
"Battler, The," 297
Beatty, Warren, 179, 181, 223, 236, 272–273, 388–389
Becky Sharp, 153
Beginning, chronological or expository, 40–43
 in medias res, 40–43
Belázs, Béla, 210, 358
Ben Hur, 339
Benson, Lucille, 229
Berenger, Tom, 341
Bergman, Ingmar, 47, 67, 252–255
Bernstein, Leonard, 166
Berridge, Elizabeth, 91
Best Friends, 220, 222
Bethurum, Dorothy, 296
Between Friends, 404
Big Chill, The, 196, 220
Bill, 213
Billy Budd, 60
Billy Jack, 25
"Bionic Woman, The," 140
Birth of a Nation, The, 243, 357, 360, 386
Bitzer, Billy, 243
Black Hole, The, 163
Black Stallion, The, 33, 229
Blade Runner, 108–109, 162–163, 203
Blazing Saddles, 264, 335
"Bliss," 300
Blood of a Poet, 363
"Blue Danube, The," 192
Blue Lagoon, The, 339
Blue Thunder, 36
Bluestone, George, 302
Bob, Carol, Ted, and Alice, 352–353
Body and Soul, 337
Body Heat, 61
Body Language, 210

Body language, in acting, 210, 214–215
Bogart, Humphrey, 69, 164, 212, 236
Bonnie and Clyde, 180, 187, 199, 229, 230, 264, 267, 272–274, 355, 386, 388, 407
Boorman, John, 137, 153
Boy on a Dolphin, 219
Branding Iron, The, 337
Brando, Marlon, 20, 53, 175, 185, 223, 403
Brave New World, 4
Breaking Away, 199, 229, 248, 390
Breathless, 340–341
Breen, Joseph I., 369–370, 373–374
Bride of Frankenstein, 342
Broadway Danny Rose, 257
Broken Blossoms, 289
Brooks, Mel, 342
Brownlow, Kevin, 96, 337
Bullitt, 63, 394
Buñuel, Luis, 278
Burghoff, Gary, 61
Burlinson, Tom, 73
Burnett, Carol, 404
Burstyn v. Wilson, 375
Burton, Richard, 215
Busey, Gary, 226
Butch and Sundance: The Early Days, 341
Butch Cassidy and the Sundance Kid, 142–144, 202, 229, 310, 341
Butterflies Are Free, 316
Bwana Devil, 104

C

Cabinet of Dr. Caligari, The, 289, 320–321, 363
Caine Mutiny, The, 212
Caine, Michael, 23
"Call of the Faraway Hills, The," 195
Camera angles, function of, 134–136
Camera, mobile, 96
Canby, Vincent, 285
Cannery Row, 106, 184, 248
Cannes Film Festival, 267
Capra, Frank, 167, 218
Caravaggio, 149–150
Caricature, 60–62
Carmen, 201
Carpenter, John, 404
Carrie, 37
Carson, Shawn, 91
Casablanca, 26, 236
Casting, 218–233
  as element of style, 246–247
  extras, 229–233
  problems with, 219, 223–224
Castleton, Barbara, 337
Cat Ballou, 200
Cat People, 161–162, 203, 211, 338
Catch-22, 152, 407
Catcher in the Rye, The, 303–304
Catholic Office for Motion Pictures, 381
Censorship, 366–386
  of feature films on TV, 400–401
Chamberlain, Richard, 295
Chaney, Lon, Jr., 161–162
Changing Places, 269
Chaplin, Charlie, 359
Characterization, methods of, 54–62
Characters, developing, 63–64
  flat, 64
  round, 64
  static, 63–64
  types of, 62–65
Character series, 343–344
Chariots of Fire, 139–141, 143, 203
Cheat, The, 337
Children of Paradise, 289
China Syndrome, The, 19
Christie, Julie, 89, 148, 158
Christopher, Dennis, 199
Cimino, Michael, 388–390
Cinemascope, 154, 156–157, 375
Cinematic composition, elements of, 86–104
Cinematic film, defined, 85–86
Cinematic potential, of literary work, 296–298
Cinematography, as element of style, 243–244
Cinerama, 4, 375
Citizen Kane, 64, 144, 167, 168, 179–180, 183, 243, 247, 280
City Lights, 359
Clayburgh, Jill, 21, 35, 220
Clift, Montgomery, 223
Climax, 40–41
Clockwork Orange, A, 141, 200–201, 202, 384–385, 407
Close Encounters of the Third Kind, 160, 388
Close-up, extreme, 89
Coal Miner's Daughter, 225
Code and Rating Administration (CARA), 384–385
Code and Rating Appeals Board, 384–385
Cocteau, Jean, 363
Collector, The, 206
Color
  experimentation with, 152–154
  versus black and white, 151–152
Come Back to the Five and Dime, Jimmy Dean, Jimmy Dean, 249
Coming Home, 196, 234–235, 407
Comingore, Dorothy, 179
Complication, 40–41
Conan the Barbarian, 160–161
Conflict, 66–69
  internal, 68–69
  symbolic or abstract values in, 69
  types of major, 67–69
Connelly, Jennifer, 231
Contrast, use of, 90–91
Cool Hand Luke, 229
Cooper, Gary, 218
Coppola, Francis Ford, 389
Cort, Bud, 61
Costello, Lou, 343
Coyote, Peter, 91
Criteria, developing personal, 288–291
Crosby, Bing, 343
Crothers, Scatman, 229
Crowther, Bosley, 274
Curtis, Ken, 61

D

Danson, Ted, 61
Darby, Kim, 56
Dark Passage, 164
Dark Star, 139
Darwell, Jane, 148–149

Das Boot, 169–170, 350, 395, 410
David Copperfield, 62
Davies, John Howard, 300
Davis, Brad, 224
Davis, Viveka, 231
Day, Doris, 266
Day the Earth Stood Still, The, 33
Days of Heaven, 12, 16, 107–108, 148, 185–186
Dead Men Don't Wear Plaid, 164, 335
Dead screen, 97–98
Dean, James, 223
Death in the Afternoon, 304
Deep focus, 99–101, 168
Deer Hunter, The, 85, 225, 388–389, 407
De la Tour, 148–149
Deliverance, 18, 153
DeMille, Cecil B., 149
DeNiro, Robert, 140, 179, 225–226, 231
Dennis, Sandy, 219–220
Denouement, 40–41
DePalma, Brian, 37, 385
Derek, Bo, 65
DeWilde, Brandon, 59
Dialogue
  machine gun, 167
  overlapping, 167
  poetic, 318
Diary of Anne Frank, The, 340
Dickens, Charles, 61
Diller, Barry, 403
Diner, 36, 220
Director, intentions of, 276
Director, Roger, 404
Dissolve, 113
Doctor Zhivago, 73, 148, 158, 267
Dolby Stereo, 169, 410
Dolby-Surround Sound, 169
Don Quixote, 341
"Don't and Be Carefuls," 368–369
Dooley, Paul, 62, 229
Double viewing, 276
  techniques of, 5
Douglas, William O., 375
Downs, Lenthiel H., 216
Dracula, 160
Dragonslayer, 160–161
Dramatic foils, 59–61
Dramatic structure, types of, 40–43
Dressed to Kill, 37
Dreyfuss, Richard, 224
Dr. Strangelove, 81, 152, 192, 197, 229, 407
Duel, 403
Dunaway, Faye, 272–273, 311
Duvall, Robert, 39, 61, 227–228, 400

E

Earthquake, 160, 168–169
East of Eden, 223
Eastwood, Clint, 215, 218
Easy Rider, 43, 352–353
Edison, The Man, 344
Editing
  contribution of, 110–111
  in foreign films, pace of, 354–355
  inside/out, 114–115, 119
  outside/in, 114–118
  patterns, 114–119
  to compress time, 120–121
  to expand time, 120
  transitions, 112–115
Editor, responsibilities of, 111–123
Educating Rita, 23
Egg and I, The, 343
8½, 258
Eisenstein, Sergei, 52, 113, 121
Elephant Man, The, 151, 160, 407
Eliot, T. S., 57
Empire Strikes Back, The, 160–161, 344
Erasmus, 80
E.T., the Extra-Terrestrial, 33, 91, 160, 163, 229
"Everybody's Talkin' at Me," 200
"Everything Is Beautiful," 80
Excalibur, 137, 160
Exhibitor's Herald World, 368
Exposition, 40–41

F

Fade out/fade in, 113
"Fall of the House of Usher, The," 72
Fanny and Alexander, 107
Fantastic Voyage, 162
Farber, Stephen, 381
Farmer Takes a Wife, The, 209
Fast, Julian, 210
Fast (or speeded) motion, 141
Faulkner, William, 299, 301
Fellini, Federico, 67, 258–259, 276
Field, Sally, 220
Film
  as conventionalized form, 284
  as emotional or sensual experience, 283
  as industry and art form, 2, 388, 391
  as moral, philosophical, or social statement, 282–283
  as showcase for actor, 281
  as social force, 366–367
  as technical achievement, 280
  as work of auteur director, 281–282
  classic, 25–26
  compared to literary forms, 30
  compared to other art forms, 2
  eclectic approach to, 285–286
  evolution towards realism, 4
  experimental or underground, 8
  level of ambition of, 277–278
  made-for-television, 402–404
  objective evaluation of, 278–279
  scope of subject matter and approach, 2–3
  structured, 8
  subjective evaluation of, 279
  unstructured, 8
Film: A Montage of Theories, 7
Film Commission of the National Council of Churches, 381
Film stock
  rough grain, 155, 158
  smooth grain, 155, 158
Filter, light diffusing, 137
Finney, Albert, 21, 185
Firefox, 159
First Monday in October, 35
Fischer, Gunnar, 243
Fisk, Jack, 107–108
F.I.S.T., 154, 232
Fitzcarraldo, 223
Flashback, 41, 43, 320
Flash cutting, 120

Flashdance, 33, 410
Flash-forward, 43
Flatt and Scruggs, 199
Fleming, Victor, 209
Flesh and Blood, 403
"Flight," 42, 46, 53
Flim Flam Man, The, 230
Focus
sharp, 87
soft or blurred, 88, 136–137
"Foggy Mountain Breakdown," 199
Fonda, Henry, 64, 148, 209, 218, 221–222, 403
Fonda, Jane, 51, 235, 403
Ford, Harrison, 79, 108–109
Ford, John, 122, 127, 129, 177, 218
Foreign language film, difficulties of, 348–356
Form cut, 113–114
Formula
for gangster genre film, 332–335
for western genre film, 328–332
variations and refinements in genre film, 327–328
For Whom the Bell Tolls, 156
Fosse, Bob, 47, 176, 224, 232
Four Friends, 220
Foxes, 203
Framing, foreground, 89–91, 100–102
Frankenstein, 342
Frankenstein Meets the Wolf Man, 342
Freeze frame, 143, 315
French Connection, The, 342
French Connection II, The, 342
Frenzy, 285
Freud, 151
Friday the 13th, Part III, 104
Friendly Fire, 403
From Here to Eternity, 340
Front Page, The, 233
Funhouse, The, 91

G

Gance, Abel, 96, 360–361
Gandhi, 91
Gardner, Ava, 195
Garland, Judy, 229, 340
Gary, Lorraine, 342
Geer, Will, 61
Genre film, 326–336
defined, 326
strengths of, 327
Giannini, Giancarlo, 90, 352
Gibson, Mel, 69, 232–233
Gielgud, John, 61
Gilliatt, Penelope, 274
"Gilligan's Island," 75
Ginsburg v. New York, 378
Glancing rhythms, 115
Glass Menagerie, The, 183
Go-Between, The, 89
Godfather, The, 64, 342
Godfather, Part II, The, 342
Godzilla, 160
Gold Diggers of 1933, 272
Gold, Tracy, 231
Goldwyn, Samuel, 375
Gone with the Wind, 160, 229, 267, 329, 386
Gordon, Ruth, 61
Gossett, Lou, Jr., 399
Graduate, The, 69, 137, 225–226, 234, 412
Grand Illusion, 353
Grant, Cary, 62
Grapes of Wrath, The, 25–26, 64, 103, 122, 148–149, 177, 179, 352
Great Santini, The, 15, 61
Greed, 153
Gremlins, 382
Greystoke: The Legend of Tarzan, 41
Griffith, Andy, 59
Griffith, D. W., 37, 360
"Gunsmoke," 61

H

Hackman, Gene, 223–224, 227–229
Hamilton, Murray, 342
Hamlet, 151, 295, 319–320
Hand-held camera, 133–134
Hardcore, 103–104
Harlan County, U.S.A., 158
Harlow, Jean, 220
Harold and Maude, 61
Hauser, Arnold, 7
Hawn, Goldie, 220, 222, 230, 316
Hayden, Sterling, 229
Hays Office, 337, 368–369
Hays, Will H., 367–368
Heaven Can Wait, 339
Heaven's Gate, 389–390
Heffner, Richard N., 385
Heflin, Van, 180, 318
Hemingway, Ernest, 296–297, 300–301, 304
Henry V, 151
Henry, Justin, 391
Hepburn, Audrey, 223, 225
Hepburn, Katherine, 48, 220, 222
Here Comes Mr. Jordan, 339
Herzog, Werner, 223
High-angle shot, 134–136
High Noon, 32, 75, 200, 334
High Society, 340
Hill, Walter, 178
Hiroshima, Mon Amour, 376–377
Historically important film, 362–363
Hitchcock, Alfred, 13, 110, 129, 206, 233, 242, 251, 260–261, 285
Hoffman, Dustin, 69, 137, 207, 225–226, 233–234, 311, 391
Holden, William, 223
Hollywood, The Pioneers, 337
Homer, 78
Hope, Bob, 343
Hopscotch, 201
Howling, The, 162–163
Huckleberry Finn, 303
Hud, 59, 64, 152
Huffman, David, 232
Hughes, Howard, 367
Hummell, Jody, 230–231
Hurt, William, 3
Hussey, Olivia, 319
Huston, John, 151, 153, 184
Huxley, Aldous, 4

I

Iliad, The, 41
Image, importance of, 84–85
Impersonators, 216
Indiana Jones and the Temple of Doom, 79, 343, 382–383, 394

Informer, The, 296
Interiors, 111, 251, 256
Interpreters/commentors, 216
Interstate v. Dallas, 378
Intolerance, 37, 289
Invitation to the Theatre, 206
Irony
  cosmic, 81–82
  dramatic, 78
  of setting, 80
  of situation, 79
  of tone, 80–81
  types of, 77–82
Irving, John, 295
Ivan the Terrible, 289

J

Jacobs, Rusty, 231
Jagger, Mick, 223
James, Henry, 56, 296–297
Jaws, 338, 342
Jaws II, 342
Jaws 3-D, 104, 342
Jean Hersholt Award, 285
Johnson, Ben, 229
Jump cut, 120

K

Kael, Pauline, 274, 287
Kane, Carol, 176–177
Katt, William, 341
Kazan, Elia, 175, 376
Keaton, Diane, 21, 98, 220, 231
Kelly, Nancy, 322
Kernodle, George R., 206
Kerr, Deborah, 220
Kidder, Margot, 160
Kilbride, Percy, 343
Killers, The, 300–301
King and I, The, 340
King Kong, 33, 160–161, 339
King of Kings, The, 368
Kingsley, Ben, 91
Kinski, Klaus, 223
Knotts, Don, 59–60
Kovaks, Laszlo, 154
Kramer vs. Kramer, 148, 390–391
Kristofferson, Kris, 340
Kubrick, Stanley, 141, 192, 250
Kuleshov, Lev, 213

L

Ladd, Alan, 47, 180, 219, 318
La Dolce Vita, 259, 376–377
Lady in the Lake, 129
Lamarr, Hedy, 220
Lancaster, Burt, 219
Lange, Jessica, 47
Language
  film and stage compared, 318–319
  of silent films, 358
"Lara's Theme," 267
Laserdiscs, 410–412
La Strada, 259
Last Picture Show, The, 72, 196, 229, 307–308
Last Tango in Paris, 311, 385
Last Year at Marienbad, 43, 289
Laughton, Charles, 103
Lawman, 331
Lawrence, D. H., 299–300
Lawrence of Arabia, 73
Lean, David, 73
Legion of Decency, 369
Leigh, Janet, 135
Leitmotif, 60–62
  in music, 198
Lelouch, Claude, 174
Lemmon, Jack, 114
Lens
  fish-eye, 139
  telephoto, 137–138
  wide-angle, 137–138
  zoom, 95, 99
Leone, Sergio, 334
Light
  character of, 146–147
  direction of, 146–147
Lighting
  high-key, 145–146
  low-key, 145–146
  painterly effects with, 149–150
  special effects with, 148–149
Lion in Winter, The, 315–316
Little Big Man, 183, 199, 311
Little Fauss and Big Halsey, 55
Little Night Music, A, 340
Live screen, 97
Lolita, 376
"Lone Ranger, The" (radio), 192
Lone Wolf McQuade, 385
Long Day's Journey into Night, 317
Longest Day, The, 265
Long Riders, The, 178
Lord, Father Daniel A., 368
Lord of the Flies, 18, 51, 64, 75, 134
Loren, Sophia, 219
Lorre, Peter, 172, 227
Lost Horizon, 340
Lovers, The, 376
Lovesick, 219
"Love Song of J. Alfred Prufrock, The," 58
Love Story, 14, 39, 312
Low-angle shot, 134–136
Lucas, George, 344, 389
Lumet, Sidney, 150
Lynn, Vera, 197

M

M, 172
*M*A*S*H,* 166, 249, 265, 326
"M*A*S*H" (TV), 60–61
MacDonald, Betty, 343
Macdonald, Dwight, 276, 289–290, 363
MacLaine, Shirley, 21, 66, 211
Magic Flute, The, 254
Magnificent Seven, The, 340
Main, Marjorie, 343
Malden, Karl, 175
Malick, Terrence, 107
Maltese Falcon, The, 227
Mamoulian, Rouben, 153
Man and a Woman, A, 13, 136, 152, 174
Man for All Seasons, A, 380
Man from Snowy River, The, 73
Manhattan, 36–37, 68, 98, 111, 151–152, 250, 257
Mansfield, Katherine, 300
Man with the Golden Arm, The, 376
Manz, Linda, 185
March, Frederic, 340
Market "windows," 390–391

Martin, Steve, 163, 221
Martin, Strother, 229–230
Mary Poppins, 33
Mason, James, 340
Mastroianni, Marcello, 350
Matthau, Walter, 35, 201
Maugham, Somerset, 341
Mazursky, Paul, 233
McCabe and Mrs. Miller, 72, 137, 181, 249
McCann, Richard Dyer, 7
McCarten, John, 273
McCormack, Patty, 322
McDowell, Malcolm, 141, 211
McDowell, Roddy, 266
McGovern, Elizabeth, 219, 231
McMurtry, Larry, 307–308
McQueen, Butterfly, 229
McQueen, Steve, 63, 223
Medavoy, Mike, 235
Melville, Herman, 60
Mickey Mousing, 193
Microcosm, 75
Midnight Cowboy, 21, 200, 207, 225, 247, 384
Midnight Express, 17, 135, 203, 224
Midsummer Night's Sex Comedy, A, 250, 256
Midway, 168–169
Miller, Henry, 304
Miracle, Irene, 224
Miracle, The, 375
Mister Roberts, 48
Mitchell, Thomas, 229
Mitchum, Robert, 103, 134, 198, 403
Mitty, Walter, 57, 68
"Modest Proposal, A," 80
Monroe, Marilyn, 198
Montage, 121–122
  transitional, 310
Montgomery, Elizabeth, 341
Montreal Film Festival, 272
Moon Is Blue, The, 374, 376
Moonraker, 12
Moore, Dudley, 61, 219
Moore, Mary Tyler, 219, 221
Moral implication, 17
Moroder, Giorgio, 203
Mosjukhin, 213–214
Motifs, 23
Motion Picture Association of America (MPAA), 367, 375–383
Motion Picture Producers and Distributors of America, 367
Motion Picture Production Code, 327, 367–378
Moulin Rouge, 153
Movie Rating Game, The, 381
MPAA Movie Rating System, 322, 373, 378–385
Mr. Deeds Goes to Town, 167
Mr. Halpern and Mr. Johnson, 404
Mr. Smith Goes to Washington, 68, 122, 137, 167, 229, 236
Mrs. Sundance, 341
Mrs. Sundance Rides Again, 341
MTV, 395
Murder on the Orient Express, 97
Murnau, F. W., 360
Music
  affinity to film, 190–191
  generalized or implicit, 193
  special functions of, 194–203
Musical score
  as element of style, 245–246
  general functions of, 192–193
  importance of, 191–192
My Bodyguard, 22
My Fair Lady, 340

N

Name-typing, 62–63
Napoleon, 96, 360–361
Narrative structure, as element of style, 247
Nashville, 249
National Association of the Motion Picture Industry, 367
National Board of Review of Motion Pictures, 367
Negri, Pola, 337
Newman, Paul, 59, 64, 143, 220, 223, 341
New York Film Critics' Awards, 267
Nichols, Mike, 233, 316
Nicholson, Jack, 20, 211, 223
Night of the Hunter, The, 103, 134
Norris, Chuck, 385
North by Northwest, 260
Nosferatu the Vampire, 34
Novels into Film, 302

O

Oates, Warren, 223
October, 289
Odd Couple, The, 61
Odyssey, The, 41, 78
Oedipus Rex, 78–79
Oedipus the King, 320
Of Human Bondage, 198
Of Mice and Men, 340
O'Herlihy, Dan, 101
O. Henry, 79
Oh, God!, 399
Oliver!, 340
Oliver Twist, 340
Olivier, Laurence, 151, 223, 295, 319–320, 404
Olympia, 289
On Approval, 289
Once Upon a Time in America, 229, 231, 334
One Flew Over the Cuckoo's Nest, 20, 229
One From the Heart, 389
On Golden Pond, 221–222, 390
On Movies, 289
On the Beach, 195
On the Waterfront, 20, 25, 61, 166, 171, 175, 223, 407
Operation Secret, 101
Ordinary People, 42, 221, 224, 390, 407
Orpheus, 289
Outlaw, The, 367

P

Pacino, Al, 64, 332, 401
Paint Your Wagon, 384
Palance, Jack, 55, 59, 214
Panning, 92–94
Papillon, 225–226
Parallel cutting, 120–121
Parker, Alan, 201, 224

Parsons, Estelle, 180, 229
Past tense, creating in film, 310–311
Patton, 26, 122, 264, 265, 326
Paull, Lawrence G., 108–109
Pawnbroker, The, 376
Peck, Gregory, 195
Penn, Arthur, 180, 272
Pennies from Heaven, 113, 221
Perkins, Tony, 74, 89
Persona, 24
Peter-and-the-Wolfing, 198
PG-13, 382–383
Philadelphia Story, The, 340
Pickens, Slim, 229
Pink Floyd: The Wall, 12, 201
Play It Again, Sam, 68
Pleshette, Suzanne, 403
Plot, unity of, 31–32
Poetic justice, 321–322
Poetic license, in adaptations, 295–296
Point of view
 director's interpretive, 132–133
 dramatic, 300–302
 first person, 299, 302–304
 indirect-subjective, 131–132
 objective, 127–128
 omniscient, 299, 302
 stream of consciousness, 301–302
 subjective, 129–131
 third-person limited, 300, 302
Points of view, cinematic, 127–133
Pollack, Sydney, 234
Pollard, Michael J., 55, 229–230
Poltergeist, 34, 162, 229, 385
Popeye, 62, 229, 249
Postman Always Rings Twice, The, 339
Potemkin, 113, 289
Potts, Daniel, 41
Powers, Mala, 198
Preminger, Otto, 374, 376, 399
Presley, Elvis, 278
Primer for Playgoers, A, 216
Pringle, Aileen, 337
Private Benjamin, 230
Production Code Administration (PCA), 374–378
Production design, 106–109
 as element of style, 245
Production designer, 106
Psycho, 74
Psycho II, 74, 89
Pudovkin, V. I., 110, 213
Purity Code, 368
Pygmalion, 340

Q

Quigly, Martin, 368
Quinn, Anthony, 20

R

Rack focus, 99–100
Raft, George, 227
Raggedy Man, 404
Raging Bull, 15, 169, 179, 225
Raiders of the Lost Ark, 12, 108–109, 169–170, 343, 389
"Raindrops Keep Fallin' on My Head," 202
"Ransom of Red Chief, The," 79
Rating appeals, 385
Raucher, Herman, 312
Razor's Edge, The, 341
Reaction shot, 211, 213
Realism in film, formulas for, 385–386
Rear Window, 230, 261
Redford, Robert, 55, 143, 220, 223, 341
Reds, 12, 179, 267, 388, 407
Reed, Rex, 265, 326
Reeve, Christopher, 160
Reflections in a Golden Eye, 153
Remakes, reasons for, 337–341
Rembrandt, 148–149, 154, 310
Rembrandt effect, 137
Requiem for a Heavyweight, 20
Resnais, Alain, 43
Resolution, 40–41
Return of the Jedi, 160, 344, 388
Reviewers, evaluating, 287–288
Reviews
 reading, 271–272
 rereading, 286
Reynolds, Burt, 21, 220, 222
Right Stuff, The, 101, 220
Ringwald, Molly, 105
Ritter, Thelma, 229–230
River, The, 108, 230, 232–233
Road Warrior, The, 12, 36, 55, 69, 73, 160
Robards, Jason, 223
Robe, The, 215
Rockinghorse Winner, The, 299–300
Rocky, 20, 122, 343
Rocky III, 33
Rogers, Will, 355
Romeo and Juliet, 318–319
Rooney, Mickey, 229
Ropin' Fool, The, 355
Rosemary's Baby, 33
Rosen, Chuck, 108
Rosenblum, Ralph, 110
Ross, Katharine, 137, 341
Rossen, Robert, 374
Russell, Jane, 367
Ryan, Robert, 60
Ryan's Daughter, 72–73, 384
Rydell, Mark, 206–207

S

Saint, Eva Marie, 175
Sarandon, Susan, 233
Sarrazin, Michael, 51
Satire, genre-based, 335
Saturday Night Fever, 385, 400
Scarface, 65, 332, 385
Scene, 111
Scheider, Roy, 176, 186, 235, 342
Schickel, Richard, 235
Schrader, Paul, 104, 338
Schutzman, Scott, 231
Scofield, Paul, 380
Scorsese, Martin, 179
Scott, George C., 103–104, 109, 230, 278
Scott, Ridley, 108
Screen formats, 154–157
Screenplays, difficulty of studying, 30
Secret Ceremony, 400
Sellers, Peter, 219, 343
Sensurround, 168

Sentimentality, 38–39
Sequels, 341–345
Sequence, 111, 315
Sergeant York, 15
Serial, 352–353
Set, distortion of, 320–321
Setting
as determiner of character, 71
as microcosm, 75
as reflection of character, 71–72
as symbol, 74–75
for verisimilitude, 72
for visual impact, 73
functions of, 70–76
to create mood or atmosphere, 74
Settings
as personalized environments, 106–107
composite, 109
Serpico, 400–401
Seven Beauties, 90
Seven Samurai, 340
Seventh Seal, The, 47, 51, 243, 254, 376
Shakespeare, William, 121, 318–320
Shane, 47, 55, 59, 73, 152, 180–181, 195, 214, 273–274, 318, 334, 386
Sharif, Omar, 148, 158
Shaw, Robert, 209
Sheen, Martin, 53, 184–185
Shining, The, 229
Shoot the Moon, 21, 229, 231, 407
Shot, 111
Silence, as "sound effect," 186–187
Silent film, 357–361
Silkwood, 32, 235
Silver Streak, 14, 229
Similes, 52–53
extrinsic, 52–53
intrinsic, 52–53
Single frame animation, 160–161
"Six Million Dollar Man, The," 140
Six Weeks, 219
Skycam, 96
Slaughterhouse-Five, 229, 247
Slow motion, uses of, 139–141
Smiles of a Summer Night, 340
Smokey and the Bandit, 12
Smokey and the Bandit II, 38
Social problem film, 364
Soliloquy
in silent film, 358
Shakespearean, 319–320
Somebody Up There Likes Me, 223
Something About Amelia, 403
Somewhere in Time, 14
Sonnet #73, 121
Sophie's Choice, 153
Sorcerer, 203
Sound
as element of style, 245–246
as transitional element, 182–183
for texture, use of, 181–182
invisible, 170–172
monaural, 168
off-screen, 172
point of view in, 172–174
slow motion, 178–179
special effects in, 172–174
stereophonic, 168–170
three dimensionality in, 168–170
visible, 170–171
Sound track, complexity of, 166
Sound and the Fury, The, 301
Sound of Music, The, 206
"Sounds of Silence, The," 200
Spacehunter, The, 104–105
Spacek, Sissy, 225
Special effects, 159–164
Spellman, Francis Cardinal, 376
Spence, Bruce, 55
Spielberg, Steven, 388, 403
Spin-off novel, 311–312
Spoils of Poynton, The, 297
Stagecoach, 229, 339
Stahl, Andy, 232–233
Stallone, Sylvester, 20, 232
Stalmaster, Lynn, 232
Standard screen, 154–157
Standards of Production, 379
Star Is Born, A, 339–340
Star system, 217–218
Star Trek: The Motion Picture, 163
Star Trek: The Wrath of Khan, 162–163
Star Trek III: The Search for Spock, 160, 163
Stardust Memories, 151, 250
Starting Over, 21
Star Wars, 36, 160, 344, 391
Steadicam, 96
Steele, Bob, 329
Steenburgen, Mary, 227–228
Steiger, Rod, 377
Stereotypes, 62–63
Stevens, George, 273
Stewart, James, 68, 137, 156, 218, 220, 222, 230, 236
Stewart, Randall, 296
Stiers, Charles Ogden, 61
Still of the Night, 186, 235
Stills, 145
Stock characters, 62–63
Story
complexity in, 36–38
elements of good, 31–39
emotional restraint in, 38–39
simplicity in, 36–38
Strauss, Peter, 105
Streep, Meryl, 186, 235
Streetcar Named Desire, A, 403
Streisand, Barbra, 340
Strike, 52–53
Stunt Man, The, 38
Style
director's, 240–242
qualities which reflect, 241
Styles, evolving, 249–250
Subject matter, as element of style, 241
Subthemes, 23
Subtitles, 350–352
Sudden Impact, 215
Suddenly Last Summer, 48–49, 75, 98, 298
Summer of '42, 22, 137, 144, 183, 310, 312
Sunrise, 360–361
Sunset Boulevard, 223
Superman, 78, 140, 160, 162, 343
Surround-sound, 169
Suspense, 34
Sutherland, Donald, 265
Swept Away, 51, 352–354
Swift, Jonathan, 80
Symbol
defined, 45
natural, 45–46
universal, 45

Symbolic meanings, methods of creating, 46–51
Symbolic patterns and progressions, 49–51
Symbolism, 44–53
Symbols, complex or ambiguous, 52
Synthesizers, in film scoring, 202–203

T

Tableau, 315
Take the Money and Run, 250
Taming of the Shrew, 137, 149, 154, 233, 310
Tarzan of the Apes, 386
Taylor, Dub, 229–230
Taylor, Elizabeth, 50, 98, 149, 404
Tempest, The, 233
Temple, Shirley, 229
10, 65
Terms of Endearment, 21, 211
Terror, The, 157
Tesich, Steve, 295
Thawed frame, 143–144
Theme
  as moral or philosophical riddle, 22
  as social comment, 19
  basic types of, 12–17
  character as, 14–15
  coming of age/loss of innocence/growing awareness, 22
  complexity of human relationships as, 20–21
  determination of, 12–23
  emotional effect or mood as, 13
  function of, 12
  human nature as, 18
  moral statement as, 17
  relationship of elements to, 276–277
  plot as, 13
  struggle for human dignity as, 19–20
  style or texture as, 16
  comedy/horror, 14
  definition of, 12–13
  evaluation of, 24–26
  idea as, 16
  limited appeal, 25
  universal, 25–26
They Shoot Horses, Don't They?, 43, 51
Thief, 203
Thing, The (1951), 339
Thing, The (1982), 162–163, 339, 404–405
Thirteen Points, The, 367, 369
This Is Cinerama, 4, 168
This Man Stands Alone, 399
Thomas, Henry, 91
Thornton, Sigrid, 73
3-D, 375
  problems of, 104
Three dimensionality, methods of creating, 98–104
Three Women, 16, 249
Through a Glass Darkly, 255
Thunderball, 206
"Thus Spake Zarathustra," 192
Tilting, 92–94
Time After Time, 162
Time Bandits, 160
Time-lapse photography, 141
Tiomkin, Dimitri, 190, 198
Title, significance of, 76–77
To Kill a Mockingbird, 39, 183–184, 304, 310
Toland, Gregg, 168, 243
Tom Jones, 206
Tomlin, Lily, 104, 236
Tootsie, 225–226, 234
Tora! Tora! Tora!, 160, 352
Touch of Evil, 135
Toulouse-Lautrec, 153
Tracy, Spencer, 184, 220, 222
Trail of the Pink Panther, The, 343
Tron, 163
Tropic of Cancer, 304
True Grit, 56, 73, 229, 400
Truth, in film stories, types of, 32–33
"Try a Little Tenderness," 197
Turner, Lana, 220
Turning Point, The, 66
29 Clues, 91
TV watching habits, 404–405
  changing, 405–407
TV, problems of watching films on, 394–401
Two for the Road, 185
2001: A Space Odyssey, 24, 113, 192, 280, 311
Type-casting trap, 224–227

U

Understatement, 39
Urban Cowboy, 32
U.S. v. Paramount Pictures, 375

V

Valenti, Jack, 374, 381
Vangelis, 203
Vaughn, Robert, 63
Verdict, The, 150
Vermeer, 148–149
Vicario, Marco, 350
Video cassette recorders (VCRs), 5, 410–412
Videodisc players, 5
Videodiscs, 410–412
Video equipment, state-of-the-art, 408–412
Viewer-centered problems, 264–270
Viewpoints, fictional, 299–304
Virgin Spring, The, 376
Vistavision, 154
Visual arts, elements of, 2
Voice dubbing, 348–350
Voice-over narration, 183–186
Voight, Jon, 234
von Stroheim, Eric, 153

W

Wagner, Robert, 213
Wallace, Dee, 91
Walters, Julie, 23
"Waltons, The," 61
"Waltzing Matilda," 195

Wanted: The Sundance Woman, 341
War and Peace, 349
Ward, Fannie, 337
War Lover, The, 213
Warren, Robert Penn, 66, 374
Wayne, John, 56, 62, 80, 198, 218, 277, 385, 400
Wedding, A, 249
"We Don't Want No Education," 201
Welles, Orson, 64, 135, 167–168, 179, 183, 380
"We'll Meet Again Some Sunny Day," 197
Wertmuller, Lina, 90, 352
West Side Story, 318
Whale, James, 342
When a Stranger Calls, 176–177
"When I Heard the Learned Astronomer," 6
"When Johnny Comes Marching Home," 192
Whiting, Leonard, 319
Whitman, Walt, 6
Who's Afraid of Virginia Woolf?, 219–220
Wide screen, 154–157
Wiene, Robert, 321
Wifemistress, 350, 354
Wilde, Cornell, 101
Wilder, Billy, 221, 223, 233
Wilder, Gene, 229
Wild in the Streets, 25
Wild Strawberries, 255
"William Tell Overture," 141, 192
Williams, Robin, 221
Williams, Tennessee, 48, 75, 297
Williamson, Nicol, 295
Winger, Debra, 21
Wipe, 113
Wiz, The, 339
Wizard of Oz, The, 33, 152, 339
Woman in the Dunes, 51, 64
Woods, James, 231
Woodward, Joanne, 403
Wordsworth, William, 7
World According to Garp, The, 64, 143, 221, 247, 267, 295, 312, 407
Wright, Edward A., 216

Y

Yothers, Tina, 231
Young, Robert, 133
Young Frankenstein, 342
Young Tom Edison, 344

Z

Zanuck, Darryl F., 341
Zavattini, Cesare, 35
Zeffirelli, Franco, 136–137, 149, 154, 233, 318–319
Zelig, 164, 250
Zsigmond, Vilmos, 85, 147, 149, 153